"The Damnedest Set of Fellows"

A History of Georgia's Cherokee Artillery

MERCER UNIVERSITY

MERCER UNIVERSITY PRESS

Endowed by

TOM WATSON BROWN

and

THE WATSON-BROWN FOUNDATION, INC.

"The Damnedest Set of Fellows"

A HISTORY OF GEORGIA'S CHEROKEE ARTILLERY

Zack C. Waters and Garry D. Fisher

MERCER UNIVERSITY PRESS
Macon, Georgia
2020

MUP/ H983

Published by Mercer University Press
1501 Mercer University Drive
Macon, Georgia 31207

9 8 7 6 5 4 3 2 1

Books published by Mercer University Press are printed on acid-free paper that meets the requirements of the American National Standard for Information Sciences—Permanence of Paper for Printed Library Materials.

Printed and bound in the United States.

This book is set in Adobe Garamond Pro (text) and Georgia (display)

Cover/jacket design by Burt&Burt

ISBN 978-0-88146-739-0
Cataloging-in-Publication Data is available from the Library of Congress

Contents

For our families:
Vonda, Luke, Amy, Maddie, Lauren, and Dallas;
and Zela, Andrea, and Christopher.

Without your patience, tolerance, and support we could have never lost ourselves in the search for these gallant men nor heard the roar of their long-silent guns.

Maps

Illustrations

Preface

This book had its roots both in the desire to more deeply explore personal family history and in the realization that relatively little historical research has focused on telling the story of individual units of the artillery of the Confederate Army of Tennessee. Like the Army of Tennessee itself, its "long arm" has mostly lived in the shadow cast by the Confederacy's more famous and more successful Army of Northern Virginia. Thus, despite their fame and reputation among the soldiers of the Army of Tennessee, the men of the Cherokee Artillery, otherwise known as Van Den Corput's Battery or simply Corput's Battery, have waited far too long for someone to tell the world their story.

From the beginning, our intent in writing this book has been to craft a thoroughly researched, yet highly readable account of the events surrounding America's greatest conflict, as viewed through the eyes of the men of the Cherokee Artillery. As a result, we have studiously avoided any attempt to interpret or render any sort of moral judgment on the motivations, opinions or actions of the men themselves or on the broader society in which they lived and for which they went to war. Instead, to the greatest extent possible we have labored to present them here exactly as they saw themselves, with all their strengths, flaws, and foibles. Sometimes slovenly, other times war-weary and tattered, always opinionated and ready for a scrap, the soldiers of the Cherokee Artillery embodied that uniquely American spirit found on both sides of the Mason-Dixon line.

Zack Waters and Garry Fisher
September, 2019

Chapter 1

"March to the Defense of Georgia"

Organization (1860–1861)

In 1840, only two years after the United States Army finished the brutal, forced relocation of Georgia's Cherokee Indians west along the infamous "Trail of Tears," Floyd County, Georgia, had a population of just 4,441 people. The next twenty years witnessed rapid growth in the area. According to the 1860 census, the number of residents grew to 15,135, comprising 9,209 whites, 5,913 black slaves, and 13 free Negroes. Most Caucasians earned their livelihood as farmers or laborers, but Rome, the county seat, also boasted a fair collection of businessmen, professionals, ministers of the Gospel, and teachers. The nationality of most white Floyd County residents was English, Scots-Irish, or Scottish but also included a few Irish, Jews, and a tiny enclave of Belgians who had arrived in northwestern Georgia in 1848.[1]

Situated approximately sixty miles south of the Tennessee border and adjacent to Alabama to the west, Floyd County is home to 514 square miles of natural resources and arable farmland, which drew many new inhabitants to the area. Rome and the surrounding countryside, nestled in the gently rolling foothills of the Appalachian Mountains, elicited a favorable reaction from newcomers. The mountainous counties just north and east of Floyd contained large tracts of poor, rocky soil, but the fertile land surrounding Rome made it ideal for growing cotton and food grains.[2]

---

[1] Gassman, "A History of Rome and Floyd County," 1–4; Aycock, *All Roads to Rome*, 62–67.

[2] Gassman, "A History of Rome and Floyd County," 1–4; Aycock, *All Roads to Rome*, 62–67.

In downtown Rome, the Etowah and Oostanaula rivers come together to form the Coosa and created a natural transportation system for moving the area's crops and merchandise to market. Early planters used these natural avenues to transport their cotton and other goods. Flat-bottomed steamboats plied the Coosa from Rome as far south as central Alabama, and smaller vessels brought crops and merchandise up and down the Oostanaula River from the region's mountain counties.[3]

The Rome Railroad, which began operation in the 1840s, connected the city to the state-owned Western & Atlantic line at Kingston. This greatly stimulated trade and growth in the area and allowed the prosperous planters and merchants in Rome and the Coosa Valley to engage in lively trading with such business centers as Atlanta, Savannah, and Charleston. The arrival of the Noble Brothers Foundry in 1855 represented the beginning of a new type of commerce—local manufacturing—that not only aided Rome's economy, but also that of adjoining Cherokee County, Alabama. Iron ore from mines near Cedar Bluff and Rock Run, Alabama supplied the Noble Brothers with the raw materials they needed to create metal goods for local use and export. In early 1860, the *Rome Weekly Courier* could truthfully boast that the City of Seven Hills was "no mean city" and had begun "making rapid strides to the position of influence and importance to which the hand of nature points."[4]

Cave Spring, located fourteen miles southwest of Rome and four miles east of the Alabama state line, was the second-largest town in Floyd County. The early pioneers built their village among the rolling, fertile hills of Vann's Valley on the former home site of a Cherokee leader named Chief Vann. They constructed their homes first, followed by churches and educational academies. The Georgia School for

---

[3] Gassman, "A History of Rome and Floyd County," 1–4; Aycock, *All Roads to Rome*; Reynolds, *Coosa Valley*, 109–12.

[4] Battey, *A History of Rome and Floyd County*, 94–95; R. S. Davis, "Cannon Makers for the Confederacy," 1–4; *Rome Weekly Courier* (hereafter cited as *RC*), May 9, 1860.

the Deaf, for example, opened in 1846 and continues its operation today. Little Cedar Creek, which meandered through the center of town and the grotto that gave the village its name, provided the region with a supply of clean water. The population of Cave Spring, which likely numbered 300–400 people in 1860, comprised settlers from central Georgia and Virginia. As an early local historian noted, the settlers were overwhelmingly Protestant, mostly Baptist or Methodist.[5]

Floyd County seemed to have a bright future ahead of it, and in 1856, the Boston journal *Ballou's Pictorial* ran a cover story touting the area as an ideal place for Northern manufacturers to relocate or invest their money. However, politics, sectional pride, and the threat of war would soon change everything: men from Floyd County began putting aside their economic concerns and enlisting to fight for their homes and the new Confederacy. Soon, they were enlisting in such numbers that Rome and its outlying districts became the center of Confederate recruiting in Northwest Georgia.[6]

During the mid-1850s, many people in the slaveholding states became increasingly alarmed by the national political situation. More and more white Southerners concluded they could no longer rely on the Federal government to protect their rights—chief among them the "right" to own slaves. The rising tide of abolitionism and the 1860 election of Abraham Lincoln, the antislavery Republican Party's presidential candidate, led many voters in the Deep South to conclude that secession represented the only viable way to protect their way of life and its "peculiar institution." Fire-eating politicians and editors fanned the flames with their rhetoric, and in December 1860 South Carolina voted to leave the Union.[7]

---

[5] Harris, *Cave Spring and Vann's Valley*, 9–10.

[6] *Ballou's Pictorial*, (Boston, MA) November 1, 1856, 1.

[7] Glatthaar, *General Lee's Army*, 14; *RC*, January 26, 1860, quoting a denunciation of the book *Impending Crisis in the South*, by Rome resident John H. W. Underwood, on the floor of the U.S. House of Representatives. See generally, Battey, *A History of Rome and Floyd County*, 113–34.

On the morning of December 4, 1860, Romans awoke to a headline in the *Tri-Weekly Courier* that read, "Georgia's Only Hope for Safety Is Secession." Editor Melvin Dwinell, a Vermont native who had moved to Floyd County in the 1850s to teach school, had earlier advocated less-radical tactics such as a "non-intercourse resolution wherein Southerners would voluntarily refrain from buying Northern-made goods." Dwinell had, however, recently decided that Georgians needed to adopt a more forceful course of action. Disunion, even if it led to war, seemed the only reasonable recourse to the editor and many of the inhabitants of Floyd County. Summarizing the South's complaints, Dwinell's list of demands included the repeal of all personal liberty bills freeing slaves. He also advocated that the many abolitionist groups providing sanctuary to escaped slaves be compelled to surrender the escapees to their owners. Additional stipulations included releasing Southerners arrested for attempting to recover their runaway slaves, granting slave owners the right to settle anywhere in the nation (including Free States) without freeing their slaves, and annulling laws giving freed blacks the right to vote in congressional and presidential elections. The Rome journalist's enumerated conditions proved to be a pipe dream. The time for reasonable debate had passed, and the season for war rapidly approached.[8]

Many ordinary Southerners, recognizing the impending danger long before the politicians and editors, had already begun taking more practical measures. Harking back to a tradition first brought to the New World by the early English settlers, they began forming volunteer military companies charged with protecting their communities should the North invade. Such militia companies historically had spotty records during wartime, but the companies recruited in 1860 and 1861

[8] *Rome Tri-Weekly Courier* (hereafter cited as *TWC*), September 4, 1860, 1; Aycock, *All Roads to Rome*, 66–67. Dwinell fought for the Confederacy in the 8th Georgia Infantry during the Civil War and remained an Unreconstructed Rebel throughout the rest of his life.

would form the backbone of the Confederate armies during the early years of the War Between the States.[9]

In 1860, Floyd County citizens had formed three home guard companies—one infantry, one cavalry, and one of artillery. The Rome Guards, soon renamed the Rome Light Guards, began organizing in January 1860. With Capt. John Frederick Cooper as its commander, this infantry unit would serve the Confederacy from First Manassas to Appomattox as Company A of the 8th Georgia Regiment. The Floyd Cavalry, organized in April 1860, reportedly tendered their services to Gov. Joseph E. Brown before any other militia unit in the state. Brown, however, failed to accept the company until 1863. Angry at the delay, Capt. John R. Towers and two lieutenants resigned in disgust and immediately joined the "Miller Rifles," which already had orders to move to the front in Virginia. Despite the frustration of some members, the Floyd Cavalry maintained its organization, eventually becoming Company E of the Floyd Legion (Georgia State Troops). Capt. Wade S. Cothran commanded the horse troops after Towers's departure.[10]

The third company created during the presecession era was the Cherokee Artillery. The *Rome Weekly Courier* announced its formation on August 14, 1860. Under the headline "Artillery Company," the journal reported,

> This corps was organized on Saturday night by the election of the following officers: J. G. Yeiser, Captain; M. A. Stovall, 1st Lieutenant; J. H. Lawrence, 2nd Lieutenant; T. W. Hooper, 3rd. The name adopted by the company is "Cherokee Artillery." Forty-two members have been enlisted and there is a prospect of procuring cannon

---

[9] For the strengths and weaknesses of the volunteer militias, see Mahon, *The American Militia: Decade of Decision, 1789–1800* (Gainesville: University of Florida Press, 1960); Marcus Cunliffe, *Soldiers and Civilians: Martial Spirit in America, 1775–1865* (New York: Little, Brown, 1968). In the New World, Spanish Florida had organized citizen soldiers long before the English arrived.

[10] Gassman, "A History of Rome and Floyd County," 24–26; Battey, *History of Rome and Floyd County*, 137–38; Mull, "Answering the Call," 1–12. Towers became colonel of the 8th Georgia.

at an early day. There is every reason to believe the enterprise will be successful.[11]

Three of the four original officers would go on to achieve the rank of colonel, with Stovall ultimately becoming a brigadier general. Yeiser, Stovall, and Hooper would all effectively lead troops in battle, but J. H. Lawrence appears to have peaked as captain of a Floyd County Home Guard unit. Thomas W. Hooper, a twenty-year-old native of Rome who had resigned from the U.S. Navy as sectional tensions reached the boiling point, served only briefly with the Cherokee Artillery. Like many young fire-eaters, Hooper switched to a company he thought would most quickly get him to Virginia. By 1864, Hooper had risen to the rank of colonel in the 21st Georgia Infantry. He ended the war in a Union prison.[12]

James Garrard Yeiser, a native of Danville, Kentucky, had, by 1860, crammed a lot of living into his thirty-four years of life. Yeiser had attended Centre College and had briefly fought in the Mexican War. He had also worked as a druggist in various Southern cities including Danville, New Orleans, and Savannah before moving to Rome in 1858. With his thick, luxurious beard, education, and stories of the Mexican War, Yeiser quickly established himself as a community leader and a dashing "man about town." More than just a humble druggist, he also supplied the local medical community with pharmaceutical supplies.[13]

Marcellus A. Stovall, born in Sparta, Georgia, in 1818, felt called to a career in the military from his earliest youth. Both of his grandfathers had been officers during the American Revolution, and tales of their bravery fired Marcellus's imagination. The son of a wealthy Augusta, Georgia, merchant, Stovall had attended a private academy in Massachusetts before seeing his first combat as the youngest member of the Richmond Blues, an elite militia company from Augusta. After

---

[11] *TWC*, August 14, 1860, 1.

[12] Krick, *Lee's Colonels*, 198.

[13] "Col. J. G. Yeiser: Firm-hearted Old Veteran Summoned by the Long Roll," *Hustler of Rome* (GA), March 4, 1895; Anderson, "James Garrard Yeiser," http://www.tmason1.com/pafn83.htm.

serving a tour of duty with the unit in Florida during the Second Seminole War, he returned home to enter the United States Military Academy in 1836 but dropped out the following year. According to some sources, bouts of rheumatism caused the Academy to invalid him out of the corps of cadets; other sources suggest that he left because he did not like the discipline. Whatever the reason, after a brief trip to Europe, Stovall moved his wife and growing family to Rome, Georgia. Located north of town on the Summerville Road, his beautiful plantation home (called Greenwood) consisted of 350 acres and thirty slaves plus an overseer, tutors, and visiting kin and friends. In addition to cotton—the cash crop—Stovall practiced diversified farming, raising wheat, corn, sweet and Irish potatoes, and cattle. As a result, his property doubled in value between 1850 and 1860.[14]

Stovall and Yeiser began as allies in the formation of the Cherokee Artillery, but their relationship soon became strained. Both men were strong-willed, stubborn, and opinionated. In the October election for captain of the unit, there were thirty-three votes for Stovall, seven for Yeiser, and one for C. M. Pennington. Stovall had lived in the county far longer than the druggist, and that may have swayed the vote in Stovall's favor.[15]

Stovall immediately began pressuring Gov. Brown to supply the Cherokee Artillery with cannon, which would allow the unit to hone their skills. The volunteers who enlisted in infantry companies could easily obtain rifles, and cavalry troopers, almost without exception, had access to horses. But none of the men who joined Stovall's Company had a spare field piece in the barn. The old, smoothbore cannon rusting on the town square was likely the only artillery piece most of the recruits had ever even seen. The newly elected captain wrote to Brown,

> Our Corps numbers in its membership some of our [county's] best citizens. We have already uniformed 45 men and hope soon to have

[14] Snellgrove, "Marcellus Augustus Stovall," 12–13; Bragg, *Distinction in Every Service*, 35–45.

[15] Snellgrove, "Marcellus Augustus Stovall," 12–13; Bragg, *Distinction in Every Service*, 35–45; Stovall to Gov. J. E. Brown, November 13, 1860, Brown letters, LOC.

> 60. Three of our commissioned officers have received military education and altogether we are in a flourishing condition. We all highly approve of Your Special Message and only ask you to commission our Officer's request for suitable arms, and we will then be ready to march to the defense of Georgia, should it become necessary.[16]

When he did not hear from Brown within two weeks, Stovall continued his campaign to obtain the guns Brown had purchased for the state, writing to the governor's secretary for help. Pleading his case, the captain noted that the Cherokee Artillery members had uniforms "nearly the same as the Chatham Artillery of Savannah," none too subtly comparing his unit to one of Georgia's oldest and most elite militia organizations. "I think," Stovall asserted, "that if the state will furnish us a battery of 6 six pounders, side arms, and musketoons or Carbines we will have a company that will compare favorably with any in the South."[17]

Politics, and the power it brought, represented the driving force in Brown's life. Raised poor in the North Georgia mountains, he obtained an education by hard work and opened a law office in Cherokee County. However, it wasn't long before he found his true calling after voters elected him to the Georgia House of Representatives in 1849. Brown may have lacked charisma—he had earned a reputation for giving dull speeches—but his real power was in his superior organizational skills and his uncanny ability to identify and leverage issues important to his constituents. One recent historian suggested that Brown "had spoken of principles and acted without them." Another writer boldly concluded, "Joseph E. Brown...obstructed, hindered, delayed, and defeated the bold schemes of the Southern Revolution, and...in no small measure contributed to the downfall of the Confederacy." Georgia's chief executive's desire to appeal to the largest percentage of the voters

---

[16] Stovall to Gov. Brown, November 13, 1860, Brown letters, LOC.

[17] Marcellus Stovall to J. B. Campbell, Esq., November 30, 1860, personal collection of Zack Waters, Rome, GA.

would doom the Cherokee Artillery's initial attempts to obtain weapons.[18]

Stovall practiced a little politicking himself, convincing Col. William Phillips to endorse the Floyd County company's plea for artillery. Phillips, one of Brown's fellow jurists in the Blue Ridge Circuit, served as a Brown ally during the early days, even advocating Brown as a compromise candidate in his first gubernatorial contest. Later he served as an adviser to the raw, young politician, so his opinion should have carried considerable weight with the chief executive. "I hope you will turn over the pieces [guns] to Capt. Stovall...," Phillips wrote. "Capt. Stovall is a most excellent officer; one who will do credit to his state & [the] South. He will be the commander of the artillery battalion & one which every Georgian will be proud of. He ought to have a battery."[19]

What happened next confused and outraged the Floyd County unit. In mid-December 1860, Brown pushed through the legislature a bill titled "An Act to Encourage Volunteer Artillery," and the bill specifically named the Cherokee Artillery as the first unit to meet the law's requirements. In a letter to an unidentified newspaper, a member of the company also asserted that Brown had assured them that he would send the Cherokee Artillery the first available guns. The politician, however, immediately broke his promise. In February 1861 the *Atlanta Gate-City Guardian* reported, "[We] learn His Excellency Gov. Brown ordered three beautiful heavy brass cannon, which have arrived in this city, intended for the Atlanta Grays, to be shipped immediately to Savannah, as there is the probability that they will be needed for immediate use." If Brown broke his word to the Cherokee Artillery, he probably justified his duplicity by his fear that Savannah might come under Federal attack right after Georgia seceded. (The fact that both Atlanta and Savannah had more voters than Rome likely served as the primary impetus for the politician's decision.) The governor suffered additional

---

18 Murphree, "Rebel Sovereigns," 16; Escott, "Georgia," 82; Niven, "Joseph E. Brown, Confederate Obstructionist," 233.

19 Wm. Phillips to "Dear Gov." [no date], Phillips letter; Allardice, "William Phillips," in *More Generals in Gray*, 184–85.

embarrassment the following month when the Atlanta Grays switched from artillery to infantry and joined the 8th Georgia Infantry Regiment. Though the political hypocrisy disappointed them, the Cherokee Artillery continued to train and recruit.[20]

The Georgia Secession Convention assembled on January 19, 1861, at Milledgeville, then the state capitol, and voted to leave the Union by a vote of 208 to 89. Strong Unionist sentiment existed in mountainous North Georgia and the hardscrabble Wiregrass region (in the southwestern section of the state), but the vote was a mere formality. Two weeks earlier Gov. Brown had ordered the Georgia Militia to occupy Ft. Pulaski on Tybee Island near Savannah. As soon as the vote became official, the governor sent state troops to occupy the Federal Arsenal and Powder Works at Augusta and the U.S. Mint at Dahlonega. Then, in a move guaranteed to enrage the government of the fledgling Confederacy, Brown approved legislation preventing the Georgia Militia from serving beyond the state's borders.[21]

The secession crisis dominated the thoughts and conversation of Floyd County citizens. The local newspapers and even sermons from the pulpits of local churches inflamed the citizens with a martial spirit. The people eagerly perused any newspaper they could find, wondering where the spark would come to ignite the powder keg of war. Many thought that events in West Florida might provoke the desired fireworks. Volunteers from Florida, Georgia, Alabama, Mississippi, and Louisiana rushed to Pensacola, where Federal troops occupied Fort Pickens, on nearby Santa Rosa Island. President James Buchanan and Florida senator Stephen Mallory, however, arranged the so-called Fort Pickens Truce, and the area soon settled into an uneasy stalemate. Meanwhile, Floyd County citizens rejoiced at news of Texas's secession

---

[20] Candler, *Confederate Records of the State of Georgia*, 739; *Atlanta Gate-City Guardian*, February 20, 1861, 3; *Atlanta Southern Confederacy*, April 27, 1861, 2.

[21] Scaife and Bragg, *Joe Brown's Pets*, 2.

and wondered when Tennessee, Virginia, Arkansas, North Carolina, Kentucky, and Missouri would follow suit.[22]

Describing the period between secession and the firing on Fort Sumter, a Georgia historian noted, "The war spirit boomed like a storm. The rivalry to enlist was universal and unquenchable." New companies seemingly sprang up overnight, and the local companies used Broad Street as a drill and parade ground. The Cherokee Artillery certainly experienced a surge in enlistments, almost doubling their pre-war numbers, with a few of the newcomers even hailing from adjoining Cherokee County, Alabama."[23]

Swept up in the euphoria surrounding the birth of the new nation, Stovall's unit drilled as often as the winter weather permitted, awaiting the arrival of the promised field pieces. The Cherokee Artillery marched down Broad Street on Saturday, March 19, 1861, as the city raised the new flag of the Confederacy and fired a salute to the banner. While the *Tri-Weekly Courier* editor, Melvin Dwinell, praised the company's enthusiasm and devotion to Dixie, he indignantly protested their poor armament, writing, "The only guns they have are Law muskets....We are never reminded of this fact without thinking that it is a great outrage that this company is not provided with cannon." Despite Dwinell's consternation, it would still be months before the company received their weapons.[24]

As spring approached, the city of Kingston, an important railhead in Cass (now Bartow) County, announced a day of parades and military festivities for April 6, 1861, inviting every volunteer unit in Northwest Georgia to attend. Unfortunately, the weather failed to cooperate, and a cold rain dampened the martial splendor of the event. Only five of the invited units showed up, and the crowd was far smaller than had

---

[22] Battey, *A History of Rome and Floyd County*, 137; Tucker, *Civil War Naval Encyclopedia*, 231. For events near Pensacola, see Waters, "The Wildest Disorder Reigned," 46–47.

[23] Battey, *A History of Rome and Floyd County*, 137; see appendix, Cherokee Artillery roster.

[24] Aycock, *All Roads to Rome*, 77.

been expected. The *Tri-Weekly Courier* blamed the turnout on the superintendent of the Western & Atlantic Railroad, who charged the volunteers full fare to and from Kingston. Three of the units that participated in the exhibition hailed from Rome because the Rome Railroad offered free passage to the Floyd County troops.[25]

Despite those difficulties, the five companies—the Floyd County Cavalry, the Rome Light Guards, the Cherokee Artillery, the McDonough Guards, and the Etowah Cavalry—dazzled the crowd with a display of marching, maneuvering, and drills that belied the units' lack of experience. The grand finale was a mock battle between the Rome Light Guards and the Cherokee Artillery, in which the artillerymen, used their rifles in lieu of cannon.[26]

Following a feast, former U.S. congressman and minister to Austria, W. H. Stiles, made, in the words of the *Tri-Weekly Courier*, "a most interesting speech, in which he showed the entire ability of the Confederate States to successfully carry on a war with the United States." Finally, after a rousing, patriotic speech by William Phillips, now a general of Georgia State Troops, the men and women from Rome boarded the cars for the hour-long trip home.[27]

After the firing on Fort Sumter, Georgia's preparations for war took a more serious tone. On the morning of April 23, the commissioned officers and sergeants of the Cherokee Artillery and Rome Light Guards, as part of Gen. Phillips's militia brigade, received orders to report to Camp Smyrna at Marietta. There they would learn the basics of military tactics. Maj. Frances W. Capers, superintendent of the Georgia Military Institute and adjutant to Phillips, served as drill officer for the volunteer officers. Capers, the son of a distinguished Huguenot family from South Carolina, had previously taught at the Citadel before moving to Georgia, and he provided an invaluable service to these officers and the South.[28]

---

[25] *TWC*, April 9, 1861, 1.

[26] Ibid.

[27] Ibid.

[28] *TWC*, April 23, 1861; Allardice, "Frances Withers Capers," in *More Generals in Gray*, 49–50.

An unnamed member of the Rome contingent, in a letter to a Rome newspaper, broke the news that the name of the encampment had been changed to Camp Brown, in honor of the governor. He described their temporary home, noting,

> Camp Brown is five miles below Marietta, and has hitherto been known as the Smyrna Camp Meeting Ground. It is [in] a beautiful grove, now neatly cleared off, and, in all respects, is a really delightful place. There are fourteen of the old camp meeting tents still standing and in tolerable condition. These are occupied—two by the commissary department—(one for provisions for the men, the other for forage for the horses), and the other twelve make very comfortable quarters for the men—the five members of one company to a tent. Besides those there are twelve canvas tents—each affording pleasant quarters for one company.

The tracks of the Western & Atlantic ran along the south side of the tenting grounds, making transporting men, materials, and animals to Camp Brown much easier.[29]

The men received plenty of food, but they rankled at guard duty, described by one soldier as nothing more than "pacing back and forth…in the hot sun." Gen. Phillips encouraged his nascent officers by reminding them that Gov. Brown had ordered them there to learn the skills they would need as officers of the brigade. He emphasized that, far from being a Home Guard unit, their brigade was destined for Confederate States Army service wherever it might be needed. After this speech they dispersed to escort Capt. R. Blair Mayes's Toombs Volunteers, from Gordon County, to the train for the trip to "the seat of the war." Likely envious of their North Georgia comrades, the officers returned to camp, where the Rome Light Guards also found orders to prepare for the trip to Virginia.[30]

Instruction in tactics continued at Camp Brown, and on April 29 the Georgia chief executive arrived to visit the men and thank them for

---

[29] *TWC*, April 30, 1861.

[30] Ibid. Mayes's unit became Co. F of the 4th Georgia Infantry in the Doles-Cook Brigade.

renaming the camp for him. It seemed a perfect chance for the neophyte soldiers to show off their skills. The cavalry corps escorted Brown to the parade grounds where he reviewed the troops and made a few congratulatory remarks.[31]

After supper, the officers called for the governor to deliver an oration. Rather than praising the men for putting aside their private affairs for the public good, Brown delivered what one officer described as "a most ill-timed and inappropriate speech." According to the correspondent,

> He said the 4th Brigade was organized for the defense of Georgia. He said the state might be invaded—he feared [it] would be—and this corps was to be "Home Guards."… [Furthermore] it was his intention to keep this brigade at home until it was well disciplined, or until there should be no reasonable apprehension of the invasion of the State. He said he did not [intend] to send off all the best companies of the State, so as to leave it in a comparatively defenseless condition.

This first step in Brown's scheme to create a "Georgia Army," allowed him to dictate policy to Pres. Jefferson Davis and essentially hold the Confederacy hostage to his whims and directives.[32]

The men, all of whom had devoted weeks to preparing for a chance to fight the hated "Black Lincolnites," stood upon the drill field in stunned silence. Had not Gen. Phillips just assured them that they would not be a militia unit? Some of their friends had already been dispatched to Virginia, and they wanted nothing more than to join them. According to the *Courier* reporter, "There was great disaffection throughout the encampment on account of this speech, and no little murmuring.… A petition was drawn up and signed by all officers who had an opportunity, and presented to him [Brown], praying that he should change his policy and send to earliest service all of the oldest and best disciplined companies." Representatives immediately went to the governor's quarters and presented the petition. Brown appeared the

---

[31] *TWC*, May 4, 1861.

[32] Ibid.; Niven, "Joseph E. Brown, Confederate Obstructionist," 233.

next morning and somewhat modified his previous message, declaring "that all would get service as soon as they could reasonably desire it, in Georgia, or elsewhere in the Confederate states." He reiterated, however, "that some might be called upon to exercise the cardinal virtue of patience."[33]

The damage had been done, and the repercussions spread through the camp like ripples across a farm pond. One company disbanded immediately and about 500 men left camp and headed home. Gen. Phillips informed the state's chief executive that unless the brigade was taken into Confederate service, it would be impossible to hold it together. Brown, however, expressed no remorse for his divisive oration. The soldiers who remained went back to training, likely unaware that they had witnessed the flashpoint for a political battle between Joe Brown and Jefferson Davis that would last longer than the Confederate nation.[34]

Despite the discouragement spawned by Brown's political posturing, Gen. Phillips persisted in his efforts to build a solid fighting force. By May 7, he had sorted the various units into infantry, cavalry, and artillery battalions. Phillips designated Col. W. T. Wofford's battalion as infantry, Maj. W. W. Rich's battalion as cavalry, and Capt. M. A. Stovall's as artillery. Stovall strove diligently to improve the artillery battalion despite having almost no weapons, caissons, limbers, or horses. Stovall's Battalion had four companies: Company 1, the Cherokee Artillery, from Floyd County, Capt. J. G. Yeiser commanding; Company 2, the Spring Place Volunteers, from Murray County, under the leadership of Capt. N. A. Meger; Company 3, the Dixie Guards,

---

[33] *TWC*, May 4, 1861; Niven, "Joseph E. Brown: Confederate Obstructionist," 233; Petitions, Putnam County, Worth County, 0001-01-005, Petition 4th Brigade, in Brown collection, GDAH; Coffman and Graham, *To Honor These Men*, 12–27.

[34] *TWC*, May 4, 1861; Niven, "Joseph E. Brown: Confederate Obstructionist," 233; Petitions, Putnam County, Worth County, 0001-01-005, Petition 4th Brigade, in Brown collection, GDAH; Coffman and Graham, *To Honor These Men*, 12–27.

from Early County, Capt. Lyman Griswold commanding; and Company 4, the Whitfield Brown Infantry, from Whitfield County, under the command of Capt. C. E. Broyles.[35]

Finally, on June 3, the enlisted men of the Cherokee Artillery received orders to join their officers at Marietta. Stovall stated very clearly that military rules would be followed and not to expect a frolic. Stovall required each recruit to bring "a uniform coat, two pair trousers, 1 forage cap, 2 shirts, 2 pair draw[er]s, 3 pair socks, 1 pair of shoes, 2 colored pocket handkerchiefs, 1 black necktie, 1 comb, 1 tin cup, 1 iron spoon, 1 knife, 1 fork, [and] 1 blanket." The captain ended his directive with a warning about their attitudes. "Each man who comes to the Camp," he wrote, "will come prepared to yield a willing obedience to its discipline, and to meet the hardships and privations of a soldier's life."[36]

While the officers trained at Camp Brown, the enlisted men at Rome had been quite busy. Col. Cunningham J. Pennington, an early Rome pioneer, civil engineer, and agent for wealthy entrepreneur Alfred Shorter, served as the unit's recruiting officer. Recruitment continued to be a major source of concern: With only about seventy men on the rolls, advertisements continued to run in the *Courier* seeking additional volunteers for the Cherokee Artillery. One such notice even resorted to enticing new recruits by offering free uniforms and equipment, along with free passage to Virginia.[37]

Pennington's most important contribution to the Cherokee Artillery has been largely forgotten. The Noble Brothers Foundry early on received a contract from the Confederacy to cast and build artillery pieces for the new nation. The brothers had a passing acquaintance with Pres. Jefferson Davis, and when these natives of England attempted to enlist in the Rebel army, the chief executive reportedly told them, "We have plenty of men who can fight, but few who can make cannon." Within weeks of secession, the Nobles began turning out

---

[35] *TWC,* May July 61; "Georgia Artillery Units," http://freepages.military.rootsweb.ancestry.com/~pudig/GAGuns.htm.

[36] *RC,* June 4, 1861, 2.

[37] *TWC,* August 23, 1861, 1; Battey, *History of Rome and Floyd County,* 93.

cannons using Round Mountain, Alabama, iron ore. A local historian related, "[T]he Cherokee Artillery…[received] two of the first cannons, supplied at Col. Pennington's expense." The two guns appear to have been a three-pound rifled cannon and a six-pound smoothbore. In addition to the gun barrels, the foundry also produced cannon carriages, limber wagons for carrying ammunition, and caissons.[38]

On June 12, the common soldiers of the Cherokee Artillery assembled to leave Floyd County. A local newspaper reported, "they left at 7½ o'clock on a special train for Camp near Big Shanty on the W & A Railroad." They fired a two-gun salute "with Col. Pennington's 'private battery'" before boarding the cars. With Stovall commanding the artillery battalion, J. G. Yeiser assumed leadership of the Cherokee Artillery. The *Courier* described the druggist-turned-warrior as "a most able and energetic officer, and deservedly popular." Max Van Den Corput, who would play a pivotal role in the unit's history, received the company's vote for 1st lieutenant; G. W. Bowen, as 2nd lieutenant; and C.O. Stillwell, as 3rd lieutenant. Van Den Corput had been born in Belgium but had been raised in Floyd County, and his selection to lead the company should anything happen to Yeiser reflected the men's high regard for him.[39]

Upon arrival at Camp Brown, the enlisted men spent the next two weeks busily learning the art of warfare with artillery. Firing a cannon involved a complicated procedure that had to become second nature to the neophyte cannoneers. A modern writer described the process of firing Civil War artillery:

> At the command "Commence firing," the gunner ordered "Load." [Soldier] Number 1 sponged the tube [barrel]. Number 2 took a round [shell] from Number 5 and placed it in the muzzle. Number 1 rammed the round home [drove it down the barrel], while Number 3 held his thumb on the vent [a small hole at the rear of the barrel]. The gunner sighted the cannon. When the gun was loaded, [Number] 3 moved to the trail [wooden brace behind the barrel that rested on the ground] and moved it left or right with the trail spike [wooden

---

38 R. S. Davis, "Noble Brothers," 1–2; Aycock, *All Roads to Rome*, 79–84.

39 *TWC*, May 31, 1861, and June 13, 1861.

> lever] as directed by the gunner. [While this was being done] Number 5 got another round from Number 6 or 7 [two men standing several feet behind the cannon] at the limber where [Number] 6 cut fuses (if needed) for [an artillery] shell and /or case [shot]. The gunner stepped clear to the side of the piece to observe the effect of fire, and gave the command "Ready." Number 1 or 2 stepped clear. Number 3 punctured the cartridge with the vent pick [an instrument similar to an ice pick with a wooden cross handle]. Number 4 attached the lanyard [a wooden handle with a cord and hook attached] to a friction primer [a tube containing powder used to ignite the charge] and inserted the primer in the vent. Number 3 covered the vent with his left hand while [Number] 4 moved to the rear. At the gunner's command "Fire," [Number] 3 stepped clear of the wheel. Number 4 [then] yanked the lanyard.

Then the unit repeated the process until ordered to cease firing. The men practiced this procedure over and over until it became second nature. They also learned what to do if one, or more, of the gun crew became casualties.[40]

Though it varied according to the number of men wounded or killed and other circumstances, a lieutenant usually commanded two guns, called a section. The section had two noncommissioned officers; each was in charge of one of the pieces in a section and often served as the gunner as well. Corporals and privates tended to the other functions in firing the cannon. In addition to the officers and enlisted men, other troopers cared for horses, drove the wagons, repaired the equipment, and filled in as replacements when members of the gun crew were disabled or killed.[41]

While at Camp Brown, the Cherokee Artillery participated in an event that occurred in virtually every Southern city during 1861—the presentation of the company flag. The banner served as a reminder for

---

[40] Thomas, *Cannons*, 5; Humphries, "Notes on Confederate Artillery Instruction and Service," 560–88, provides the training and experiences of a former CSA cannoneer.

[41] Thomas, *Cannons*, 5.

the men, in battle and on the march, of home and their reason for enduring privations and dangers. Usually the ladies of the community sewed the flag and ceremoniously tendered it to the unit right before they left home. Yeiser's troops, however, did not receive their company banner until after they had been at Big Shanty for almost a month.[42]

Miss Helen Lee and Miss Savannah E. Stillwell, the daughter of Rev. Charles H. Stillwell and sister to three members of the unit, tendered the flag to the Cherokee Artillery on July 4, 1861. The ladies of Floyd County had taken two large pieces of bright red silk, stitched them together, and attached gold fringe around the perimeter of the banner. A painting, likely by a professional artist, in an off-white oval in the middle of the flag represented a scene, set in the rolling hills of North Georgia, of a standing Native American maiden gazing at a fiery altar. Over the circular rendering, two floating blue ribbons bore the word "Cherokee" on one strip and "Artillery" on the other.[43]

Miss Stillwell began her oration, stating, "Permit me to present your company this banner in behalf of the Ladies of Rome, as a feeble expression of the heartfelt interest which they now have and will ever feel, in the cause to which you have devoted yourselves." She acknowledged that this July 4 would have been the eighty-fifth anniversary of the Declaration of Independence, but stated, "the United States [are] but a thing of the past." She closed, dramatically requesting,

> Take it [the flag] and when in the midst of warfare, with the din of battle sounding upon your ears, if you should catch the rustle of these silken folds, let it be to you but the echo of the prayers that will daily and hourly ascend to the God of Battles in your behalf. May it nerve your hearts in braver deeds of valor and give greater strength to your

---

[42] "Address," *RC*, July 11, 1861, 1.

[43] Ibid.; "Analysis Report by Textile Preservation Associates, Inc. [Cherokee Artillery flag], September 20, 1993, Zack C. Water's collection. The painting in the center of the flag has now faded away, but the description is based on a wartime photo of the banner in the Anderson collection, Rome, GA.

arm until the enemy is put to confusion and this, "Our own native land" be forever free.[44]

Sgt. John S. Panchen made the acceptance reply for the men, noting that "assembled before you are grouped a corps of volunteers banded together by the ties of dignified patriotism, our hearts cemented together in one desire, one purpose—the establishment of the independence of this glorious Confederacy." After other similar statements, he ended with the lines of a popular poem: "Then go forth and conquer—all heroes who fight—for home and for family—for freedom and right." Cheers erupted from the assembled throng, and for the first time, the flag of the Cherokee Artillery floated on the breeze above the Floyd County soldiers.[45]

The Cherokee Artillery, along with the rest of Stovall's 3rd Georgia Battalion, left Marietta, Georgia, on August 7, traveling north through the mountainous regions of Georgia and Tennessee to Bristol, Virginia, and then to Lynchburg. Moving the fewer than 300 men to the Old Dominion required a large train with two cars to carry the cannon and four cars to carry the battery's baggage. Due to several stops along the way, it took four days to make the 200-mile journey. The patriotism expressed by locals at each stop impressed the men. "The 'Stars and Bars' were flying on every hand," noted a member of the battalion, "and we were agreeably surprised by the demonstrations of loyalty displayed in East Tennessee. At Knoxville, not an avowed Unionist could be seen....Every evidence of enthusiasm and devotion to the Southern cause, were exhibited along the entire route."[46]

At the fairgrounds west of Lynchburg lay Camp Davis, a major training camp in Virginia. The Georgians were pleased with their encampment, which was located in a grove on a high ridge two miles outside of Lynchburg. From camp, the men had a fine view of the surrounding countryside. The local springs provided ample fresh water,

---

[44] *RC*, July 11, 1861, 1. The celebration of July 4 did not resume in the South until after World War I.

[45] Ibid. A reporter would later declare that unit veterans valued the old banner "more than gold."

[46] *RC*, August 30, 1861; Bragg, *Distinction in Every Service*, 45–47.

rations were plentiful, and the ladies of Lynchburg impressed the men with their hospitality. Less agreeable was the reaction of their non-Georgia comrades encamped nearby, who held a grudge against Stovall and Yeiser's men. The other Confederates referred to them as "Governor Brown's 'pet lambs' because of the perception that the governor had kept them overlong in Georgia when they had been needed in Virginia."[47]

While the men spent their days at Camp Davis repeatedly drilling to improve their efficiency, both Stovall and Yeiser sought to enlarge their units. Stovall telegraphed Gov. Brown, informing him that he had been asked by the senior officer at Camp Davis to bring his battalion to the size of a regiment. "Will you give me five companies armed?" Stovall requested. Joe Brown, of course, refused to aid the Davis Administration, and the Rebel secretary of war, Judah P. Benjamin, claimed he had no weapons with which to equip the new regiment.[48]

One of Stovall's men complained that they had become a lost battalion, all but abandoned by both the Confederacy and their native state. "We seem to have been entirely forgotten by the War Department," he groused, "for we are the only corps left to guard Lynchburg, with its mountains, valleys, dilapidated campgrounds.... Our Colonel has gone to Georgia, via Richmond, first to try and get us arms to turn the battalion into a regiment; next to try the Gov'nor to do us justice, and place good armed companies at the disposal of our commander."[49]

Capt. Yeiser had somewhat better luck. Despite Stovall's repeated requests to rejoin his battalion and transfer to the infantry, Yeiser had steadfastly refused. Yeiser based his refusal upon his orders from Gen. Samuel Cooper, the Confederate inspector general. Cooper's directive, dated September 17, read, "Capt. J. G. Yeiser's Light Battery Company

---

[47] *RC*, August 30, 1861; Bragg, *Distinction in Every Service*, 45–47; Smedlund, *Camp Fires*, 105–106.

[48] *RC*, September 13, 1861; Bragg, *Distinction in Every Service*, 47–48.

[49] Bragg, *Distinction in Every Service*, 47–48; "Our Special Correspondence from Colonel Stovall's Regiment," Stovall scrapbooks, vol. 1, n.p. This collection, apparently assembled by Stovall's wife, contains four scrapbooks of news articles about the general and his units between 1861 and 1865.

is to remain at Lynchburg until fully armed.... It is to be regarded as an independent Artillery Company, entirely Independent of regimental or battalion organization." Truth be told, Yeiser likely breathed a sigh of relief because he and Stovall could no longer work together without their egos clashing at every turn.[50]

At last, on October 12, Yeiser could announce that Gov. Brown had finally given the Cherokee Artillery the six-pound artillery pieces that had been gathering dust since the Atlanta Grays had switched from artillery to infantry. With the Floyd County unit now equipped with artillery, Stovall and Yeiser began bickering about side arms for the men. Cooper stepped in, suggesting that the men be outfitted with sixty-five muskets, but Yeiser opted, instead, for seventy-five Navy Colt revolvers. Stovall objected to returning the muskets because he could arm another company with them. Yeiser, refusing to let Stovall dictate policy for his unit, reiterated the newly won independent status of the Cherokee Artillery. The Confederate government, scrambling to find arms for all the companies entering the Southern armies, insisted that Yeiser send the long arms back to Richmond, an order with which he complied.[51]

As the North Georgia troops languished at Camp Davis, additions and subtractions occurred in the roster. W. O. Connor, who had been sick in Georgia, returned to the Cherokee Artillery, and the men "greet[ed] his smiling phiz with a hearty welcome." Sgt. John S. Panchen, who had accepted the flag a couple of months previously, left to become secretary for Col. Stovall. Although disease ravaged many of the Rebel regiments early in the war, especially those who hailed from extremely rural areas, Yeiser's unit had yet to experience a death. Yeiser wrote, "We have 22 on the sick list [in late October], all from measles, and all are doing well."[52]

The folks at home had not abandoned "their boys," and a constant stream of boxes containing clothes and baked goods arrived in camp

---

[50] *RC*, October 25, 1861.

[51] Ibid.

[52] *RC*, September 13, September 24, and October 24, 1861.

during the early months of the war. Yeiser's unit issued a heartfelt, public vote of thanks to the ladies of the Soldier's Aid Society of Cave Spring for their generosity. With understandable hyperbole, the declaration concluded by stating "the efforts of our Southern women in behalf of the soldiers has afforded an example of patriotic devotion unparalleled in the history of the world."[53]

During their last days at Lynchburg, the Cherokee Artillery participated in a social function that they long and fondly remembered. Maj. Gen. Edmund Kirby Smith, a Floridian and West Pointer now famous for saving the day with the timely arrival of his troops upon the field at First Manassas, had suffered a chest wound during the battle. While recuperating in nearby Lynchburg, Kirby Smith met and fell in love with one of the town's belles, Cassie Selden. At their marriage ceremony, conducted at the local Episcopal Church, the Cherokee Artillery turned out "and nine loud 'marriage peals' were [sent] belching forth in honor of the wedding [party]."[54]

Finally, on October 20, the order that the Georgians had been longing for finally arrived. The next morning, they boarded a thirteen-car train loaded with the battery's ordinance, horses, and baggage, and headed toward Richmond. Though the common soldiers thought they were destined for Maj. Gen. Joseph E. Johnston's Virginia Army, Stovall and Yeiser's men remained at nearby Camp Lee for only two days before heading south to the "Turpentine State," as the Georgians referred to North Carolina.[55]

Stovall's Battalion, now consisting of the Spring Place Volunteers, the Lewis and Phillips Guards, the Barnesville Blues, the Holloway Grays, the Jackson Avengers, the Baker Volunteers, as well as the "independent" Cherokee Artillery, arrived at Goldsboro, North Carolina, on October 26. Confederate authorities feared that a large Federal fleet now situated off the comparatively unprotected North Carolina coast would land troops at either Swainsboro's Inlet or Wilmington. From

---

[53] *TWC*, October 26, 1861, 2.

[54] *TWC*, November 1, 1861.

[55] Bragg, *Distinction in Every Service*, 49–50; *RC*, October 31, 1861.

there, they could move to seize the all-important railroads in that part of the state. Goldsboro, situated about forty miles inland from New Bern, Beaufort, and Wilmington, made it an ideal place to confront the Yankees away from the cover of the artillery on their gunboats, while still protecting the vital railroad.[56]

The stalls at the town's racetrack provided quarters for the Georgians at Goldsboro. The Confederate government had designated the barns as Camp Advance, and the Georgians used their spare time to explore their new surroundings. The town, they found, was a pleasant oasis amid the sand, turpentine distilleries, and stands of pine. In addition to the town's supply of pretty girls and oysters, the soldiers enjoyed the services at the various churches. Despite these agreeable distractions, the men resented the exorbitant prices the local merchants charged and complained bitterly about their heartlessness toward their Georgia protectors. Officials in Richmond even recognized that, due to state pride, Georgia and Tar Heel troops also exhibited a great deal of animosity toward one another.[57]

Yeiser's Battery failed to get their baptism of fire in North Carolina, but they did meet some Union troops. On the night of November 1, a gale raged through the area. The Georgians, in their tents, watched in horror as the storm blew away their canvas shelters and personal belongings. The men laughed at their comrades as they "perform[ed] excited antics in the too often fruitless endeavor to restore…[their] canvas domicile." But the storm that tore up the Rebel's camp struck the Federal fleet, sinking or damaging at least three vessels. A member of Stovall's unit reported, "We were in quite a bustle of excitement yesterday, having had temporary charge of 73 prisoners en route from Beaufort to Raleigh. They were attached to the steamer *Union*, which was wrecked during the late gale, upon Pogue Island, about fifteen miles from Fort Macon…. [T]hree other Federal vessels had been wrecked and a large quantity of stores, horses, & c. secured."[58]

---

[56] *RC*, November 8, 1861; *OR*, ser. 1, vol. 4, 692.

[57] *TWC*, November 8 and 12, 1861; Smedlund, *Camp Fires*, 47; *OR*, ser. 1, vol. 4, 693.

[58] *RC*, November 8, 1861; *TWC*, November 12, 1861.

With the danger of a naval attack alleviated, the nomadic Georgians received orders to return to Virginia. They expressed great disappointment that they had once again missed an opportunity to fight, but they knew that their time would come. "Captain Yeiser and the Cherokee Artillery," a Georgian wrote, "are eager for a fight, and will doubtless acquit themselves creditably when the opportunity presents itself."[59]

[59] *RC*, November 8, 1861; *TWC*, November 12, 1861.

Chapter 2

"Soldiering Is Sometimes a Hard Business"

Tennessee and Kentucky (1862)

The long trip by rail back to Richmond proved a slow and tedious ordeal for the men of the Cherokee Artillery and Stovall's Battalion. They left Goldsboro on Thursday evening, November 7, halting first for several hours at Weldon, Virginia, and then for an additional day and a half at Petersburg. Finally arriving back in Richmond around 10 P.M. on November 10, they received electrifying news. New orders directed the battery and the 3rd Georgia Battalion to proceed immediately to join Major General Joseph E. Johnston's Confederate forces at Manassas, Virginia—the heart of the war effort in the eastern Confederacy.[1]

Their exhilaration at the thought of helping to drive the Yankees out of the Old Dominion lasted less than a day, however. A few hours later, new orders arrived, countermanding the directive to proceed to Manassas. Instead of protecting Northern Virginia, they would now make their way westward to the town of Bristol, in the East Tennessee mountains. There, they would report to Col. Danville Leadbetter, whom Insp. Gen. Samuel Cooper had recently assigned the duty of protecting communications between Chattanooga and Bristol. As part of Leadbetter's reinforcements, the Cherokee Artillery and Stovall's 3rd Georgia Battalion would help suppress pro-Union irregulars and bushwhackers. Those guerillas had vowed to do everything in their power to damage Rebel interests in the region and had already burned an alarming number of vital railroad bridges.[2]

---

[1] *TWC*, November 11, 1861; Connor, *Confederate Diary of Wesley Olin Connor*, November 11, 1861 (hereafter cited as WOC).

[2] *OR*, ser. 1, vol. 4, 234; *OR*, ser. 1, vol. 52, part 2, 205.

Overestimating the importance of the Volunteer State to the young Southern nation would have been difficult. The second most populous state to join the Confederacy, its large manpower pool alone made it an indispensable resource. Tennessee, living up to its nickname, provided 115,000 soldiers who fought for the South. An additional 31,000, primarily from East Tennessee, battled for the Union. (An unknown number of African Americans also joined the Federal army, perhaps raising the total of Yankee combatants from the state to 50,000 men.) In total, Tennessee provided more soldiers than any other state, north or south of the Mason-Dixon Line.

Stretching from the Mississippi River to the Blue Ridge Mountains, Tennessee also served as both a natural barrier to the invasion of the Deep South states of Mississippi, Alabama, and Georgia, and a crucial hub for various types of transportation. Three of the South's most important railways—the Memphis & Charleston, the Western & Atlantic, and the Virginia & East Tennessee lines—crisscrossed the Volunteer State, providing a vital resource for moving troops and supplies. Hundreds of miles of spur lines, connected to the main lines, linked scores of smaller towns and villages to the outside world.[3]

Water transport may have had a greater importance than rail lines in nineteenth-century America, which increased the value of Tennessee to both the Yankees and the Rebels. The Mississippi, Tennessee, and Cumberland rivers provided natural avenues for trade and military operations from the Ohio Valley to the Gulf of Mexico. The Cumberland River afforded large steamships the ability to navigate southeastward all the way to Nashville, and smaller craft could go even farther inland. Future Confederate general P. D. Roddey provided an early example of the significance of the state's waterways. In early 1861, using his steam vessel, the *Julius H. Smith*, Roddey traversed the Mississippi, Tennessee, and Cumberland rivers to deliver a large shipment of rifles "procured" in St. Louis to Tennessee governor Isham Harris.

Besides its network of railroads and navigable rivers, Tennessee was also home to a wide variety of other important resources and

[3] Connelly, *Army of the Heartland*, 4–6; Atkins, *Parties, Politics*, 228–59; Lepa, *Civil War in Tennessee*, 3–4.

goods. The state's fertile soil produced vast amounts of cattle, swine, and food crops while Memphis served as a conduit for livestock and other commodities raised or created in the trans-Mississippi region. In East Tennessee, the Unaka Mountains contained the Confederacy's largest deposit of copper and large supplies of saltpeter, necessary for the production of gunpowder. Nashville and its environs were home to some of the largest powder mills in the Confederacy, while both Nashville and Memphis housed a large number of machine shops and foundries that produced weapons and other military supplies.[4]

The debate over leaving the Union created major divisions among the people of Tennessee. In February 1861, Tennesseans rejected outright a proposal to convene a conference on secession. While a majority of voters in West and Middle Tennessee supported joining the Confederacy, East Tennessee remained stubbornly pro-Union. Like the other states of the Upper South, Tennessee decided to leave the United States only after President Abraham Lincoln's mid-April call for 75,000 volunteers to forcibly return the seceded states to the Union.[5]

This time, the Tennessee State Assembly voted on May 6, 1861, to approve secession subject to voter ratification. Then, on June 8, the citizens of the state voted overwhelmingly in favor of seceding from the United States. Nevertheless, many East Tennesseans retained a strong devotion to the Union. Gov. Isham Harris initially took a tolerant stance toward the region's reactionary attitude, but he ordered a crackdown on the dissenters after winning re-election in August. The resulting arrests of pro-Union sympathizers and operatives infuriated the tough mountain folk. By October 1861, the situation in East Tennessee bordered on full-fledged rebellion that did not abate until Confederate forces under Gen. Albert Sidney Johnston arrived to restore control.[6]

---

[4] Connelly, *Army of the Heartland*, 4–6; Lepa, *Civil War in Tennessee*, 4–6. "The Camp at Cairo, Illinois," *Philadelphia (PA) Press*, May 31, 1861, 2, states that Roddey delivered "450 Colt rifles."

[5] Durham, "Tennessee Heritage," https://sos.tn.gov/products/tsla/tennessee-heritage-walter-durham; Atkins, *Parties, Politics*, 246–48. Prior to his death, Durham served as Tennessee state historian.

[6] Connelly, *Army of the Heartland*, 42–43; Atkins, *Parties, Politics*, 246–48.

On Monday morning, November 11, the men of the Cherokee Artillery and the 3rd Georgia Battalion cooked three days rations, boarded two different Danville Railroad trains, and prepared to depart on their journey to East Tennessee. A Floyd County Rebel wryly reported, "we soon shall be 'rattling on the railroad,' through old Virginia, not exactly in a direction toward either Manassas or the coast, but returning over a route familiar to us three months ago, in search of the enemy in a new quarter."[7]

At high noon, the trains carrying the two units left Richmond and began clattering toward Bristol, Tennessee. It proved to be a difficult and dangerous three-day journey. After detraining in Lynchburg, Virginia, for several hours and being held up for a full day in Abington, the two units had gone only a few miles when tragedy struck. Nearing Centerville around midnight on the evening of November 12, the train carrying Stovall's unit slammed into a bull that had wandered onto the tracks. The impact derailed six or seven of the rail cars, killing one member of the battalion and injuring fifteen others. Both Stovall's men and the Cherokee Artillery spent the rest of the night and part of the next day clearing the wreckage from the tracks.[8]

Continuing their pilgrimage the next day, the trains again had to halt—this time at the aptly named hamlet of Union, Tennessee. There, pro-Yankee raiders had burned a bridge over the Holston River. After sweating all day manhandling cannon, tents, and baggage across the river, the Cherokee Artillery set up camp near the burned-out span. With their tents and baggage unopened in anticipation of moving out early the next morning, the men bedded down wherever they could find refuge, including a courthouse, a church, and in the rail cars. Some cannoneers even camped out under the stars. One fortunate group, "Mess No. 3," managed to secure quarters in a nearby private residence. Wesley O. Connor, a corporal and gun commander in the Cherokee Artillery, wrote in his diary that the artillerymen happened

[7] *TWC*, November 11, 1861.

[8] *TWC*, November 21, 1861.

upon "twelve or fifteen barrels, and the men were not long in discovering their contents, which was government whiskey. Helped ourselves pretty freely." Assisted no doubt by the liquor, the gloom that had settled over the men after the accident at Centerville began to evaporate. In its place came a grim determination and eagerness to take the fight to the enemy.[9]

The next day, November 14, the battery and Stovall's unit once again boarded the trains. This time they moved only a few miles down the line to Carter's Depot. The units expected to spend the next couple of weeks in the village before marching into the mountains, presumably in the direction of Elizabethtown and a large camp of Unionists. However, the recent rains had made all the local fords impassable. Without them, any serious hope of conducting military operations in the area dissipated. The artillerymen had barely finished rolling their guns off the rail cars when a directive arrived to re-board the train and push on to Johnston's Station. After hefting the guns back onto their flat cars, the exhausted Rebels arrived at their destination an hour later, at about 7 P.M.[10]

This time, their luck held. Capt. Yeiser's company, Stovall's unit, a cavalry company, and two or three local militia groups spent the next week conducting a series of scouting expeditions into nearby settlements suspected of harboring Tory (pro-Union) raiders. Typical of such operations was one that began on the morning of November 16. Under the command of Col. Leadbetter, the entire force toiled ten miles through the nearby mountains, halting for the night about five miles from the enemy force. Their foe, supposedly numbering 300 to 500 men, had reportedly encamped at a place known locally as the Doe River Cave.

Pushing forward the next morning, the Confederates reached the Unionist's lair only to discover that the Tories had fled. Leadbetter sent his horse soldiers and a detachment of infantry to pursue the raiders, while the rest of the graycoats burned the Unionist's encampment. The

---

[9] *TWC*, November 21, 1861; WOC, November 13–14, 1861.

[10] *TWC*, November 20–21, 1861; WOC, November 13–14, 1861.

Confederate commander then ordered the Floyd County battery to fire "a dose of 'spherical case' [shot] up the side of the mountains for the benefit of stragglers, in particular, and admonitory to the Tories generally."[11]

All told, the expedition captured sixty-eight prisoners, along with assorted horses, mules, and wagons. The cannoneers of the Cherokee Artillery had conducted their first real foray against the enemy. The Floyd County soldiers facetiously dubbed the campaign the "Battle of Pig Run," on account of the dozen or so swine they managed to chase down. In addition, some of the boys engaged in a spirited chase against "Union geese," that resulted in Sgt. R. M. (Reps) Jones "being guilty of pressing one [bird] into Confederate Service." Perhaps Cpl. Connor best summed up the battery's first brush with the enemy, writing, "Upon the whole had a right gay time. Got some tremendous cursings from the women."[12]

On November 20, new orders arrived. A section of the Cherokee Artillery and their two six-pound howitzers, along with Col. Stovall's 3rd Georgia Battalion, received instructions to proceed to Greenville, Tennessee, where Col. Leadbetter had established his new headquarters. Stovall and his men arrived at Greenville by train later the next day. Yeiser's two-gun section, following their foray into the mountains, was not so fortunate. A shortage of rolling stock on the Virginia & East Tennessee rail line forced the luckless artillerymen to march the thirty miles to Greenville with their guns, wagons, and equipment. The rest of the Cherokee Artillery missed the trying ordeal. They and their comrades in the 3rd Georgia battalion left by train for Leadbetter's camp on the afternoon of November 22, arriving later that night.[13]

Their new post failed to impress the Floyd County gunners. The "Artillery Correspondence," which chronicled the unit's exploits for

---

[11] *TWC*, November 23, 1861.

[12] Ibid.; WOC, November 14, 1861.

[13] *TWC*, November 23, 1861; WOC, November 23, 1861; *OR*, ser. 1, vol. 7, 712.

the Rome papers, described the municipality in less than glowing terms: Greenville is an old fashioned, dingy looking town of one thousand inhabitants," [the correspondent wrote]. "It is the home of the notorious [Union sympathizer and future U.S. president] Andy Johnson who is supposed to be in Kentucky. We feel as if we had 'turned up' in a very queer place; we miss that cordial greeting and hospitality which has been extended toward us in more patriotic sections."[14]

But the Georgians had little time to spend getting acquainted with the locals. Shortly after their arrival, the Cherokee Artillery and the companies of Stovall's Battalion that had not been detached to guard key bridges began hunting down local pro-Union partisans. To aid their pursuit of the enemy across the rugged terrain, the authorities issued the cannoneers horses and they temporarily declared themselves a "cavalry" company.[15]

On Sunday, November 24, Stovall's boys and the mounted detachment of the Cherokee Artillery with two guns set out on another raid. The foray would prove typical of their military actions in and around Greenville. This time, their orders were to eliminate a Tory stronghold twenty-five miles from Greenville at a place known to the locals as Chimney Top Mountain. Along with two companies of Col. Samuel Powell's 29th Tennessee and half a company of Capt. John B. McLin's 2nd Tennessee Cavalry, they set out to oust the insurgents from their hideout. Once again, however, the Unionists received a warning of the approach of this formidable force and melted away into the forest.

Due to a worsening illness, Col. Leadbetter turned command of the Rebel column over to Col. Stovall. He directed the Georgian to pursue the Tory band, thought to be heading toward North Carolina. Stovall led the chase as far as the Chucky River, near Rheatown. Deeming the river impassable, Stovall decided to end the pursuit and return to Greenville.[16]

---

[14] *TWC*, November 23, 1861.

[15] *TWC*, December 7, 1861.

[16] *OR*, ser. 1, vol. 7, 712.

At this point in the expedition, a minor event occurred that hinted at the simmering rivalry between Stovall and Yeiser. Leadbetter seemingly tolerated the competition, as he noted without comment in his report: "Captain Yeiser, of the artillery, crossed, however, with his two pieces, and succeeded in mounting most of his two companies, also crossed the Chucky and joined the cavalry. This was on the 25th, and today he has sent in for reenforcements, which have gone to him—something over a hundred men, under Major [A. F.] Rudler."[17]

Yeiser and his men showed their courage and drive, but they reaped only a tiny prize for all their effort. The plucky artillerymen-turned-cavalry captured the grand total of two Lincolnites: a local schoolteacher, whom they arrested in front of his stunned students, and the captain of a local Tory band.[18]

Over the next two and a half months, the Cherokee Artillery and the other units under Leadbetter's command engaged in frequent cat-and-mouse games with the Unionists. More often than not, the bushwhackers simply disappeared into the surrounding countryside rather than risk a toe-to-toe battle with Confederate troops. They returned when the pressure decreased, burning unprotected bridges and attacking targets of opportunity. Despite the frustration of rarely coming to grips with the enemy, whom they viewed as "the most ignorant and illiterate people that can be found in any country," the Cherokee Artillery generally regarded these wild goose chases through the East Tennessee countryside as good fun.[19]

At the same time, the Georgians had few illusions regarding the local Tennessee units' dependability and willingness to fight. The commanders of these companies sent to help quash Unionist insurrection seemed to be men with political aspirations. They often appeared slow to act on reports of Unionist activity, apparently believing that the current problems would be short-lived and that they should act leniently toward those whose votes they would need in the future. More than

[17] Ibid.

[18] *TWC*, December 7, 1861.

[19] WOC, December 14, 1861.

once a detachment of Yeiser's Company found itself abandoned by their Tennessee "allies" during a confrontation with a force of Unionists.[20]

Occasionally, the scouting expeditions resulted in the capture of a wanted partisan. The Confederates treated most combatants as prisoners of war and shipped them off to a camp near Tuscaloosa, Alabama. Those who had engaged in burning bridges, however, immediately appeared before a drumhead court. If the court found them guilty, they were immediately hanged.[21]

Perhaps the greatest success in countering the Unionists was accomplished by the stroke of a pen, rather than by force of arms. In December 1861, Col. Leadbetter, acting on orders from Secretary of War Judah P. Benjamin, issued a proclamation stating that the Confederate authorities would pardon all Union partisans who voluntarily turned in their arms and took an oath of allegiance to the Confederacy. Almost immediately, hundreds of "repentant" Tories swarmed Leadbetter's headquarters, and for several days a constant stream of men stacked arms and pledged to obey the laws of the Confederate government.[22]

With the onset of the harsh Volunteer State winter came the necessity of locating suitable cold weather quarters for both men and horses. Capt. Yeiser managed to secure a large building once used as a college, which the Cherokee Artillery converted into horse stalls, cook houses, and rooms to store equipment. The men, meanwhile, found their own accommodations, with each "mess" taking up residence in an outbuilding or a room within the defunct school. While it may not have been home, Yeiser's men generally remained warm, comfortable, and in good health. Other units had a harder time. Four companies of the 3rd Georgia Battalion, for example, reported seventy men in the hospital as of December 21. And, thanks to the army paymaster, the cannoneers now had money in their pockets to spend where they

---

[20] *RC*, December 13, 1861.

[21] *OR*, ser. 1, vol. 7, 701; *TWC*, December 12, 1861.

[22] *OR*, ser. 1, vol. 7, 701; *TWC*, December 12, 1861.

could. Many simply gambled it away. Some whiled away the time reading in the old college library, singing, spinning yarns, or horsing around.[23]

Christmas and New Year's Day passed, but the joy of the season was tinged with grief for the Georgians. On Christmas Eve, their comrade, J. E. F. Avery, died of pneumonia. At least some of the soldiers now clearly realized how much their lives had changed. A year ago, they had been civilians, at home among family and friends, leading ordinary, workaday lives. Now they were soldiers far from home, among enemies, or at least strangers, and many pondered what the next year might bring.[24]

However, life wasn't all sadness and contemplation. Efforts to suppress the Unionist rebellion seemed to have been effective, and the local populace gradually warmed to the presence of the Georgia cannoneers and the other Confederate troops in their midst. Treats and delicacies began appearing on a regular basis for the inmates of the local Confederate soldiers' hospital, which the Rebels established in the home of Andrew Johnson. The ladies of Greenville began attending the local military dress parades and demonstrations in growing numbers, occasionally bestowing a smile or a wave of the hand on the Southern soldiers.[25]

As January 1862 progressed, sheer boredom became the men's biggest enemy. The disagreeable weather kept them indoors for long stretches. They tried to combat the boredom and dullness with activities such as reading, writing, or smoking "killikanick," a tobacco substitute made of dried leaves and bark. Weather permitting, the men whiled away the time by wandering around the artillery camp, even dropping in at Col. Stovall's headquarters to see the happenings there or visiting the commissary to chat with quartermaster B. F. Jones, or his assistant, a lieutenant from Augusta, Georgia. The hospital, which at one point had been the grateful recipient of two sorely needed boxes

[23] *TWC*, December 12, 14, and 21, 1861; *OR*, ser. 1, vol. 7, 842.

[24] WOC, December 24, 1861, and January 1, 1862.

[25] *TWC*, December 17, 1861.

of hospital stores from "Mrs. Dr. Kincaid and friends" back home in Rome, now stood nearly empty. The ill and injured had mostly gone home on furlough along with a few lucky, able-bodied men whom the authorities had granted permission to return to Floyd County.[26]

By mid-January, life in Greenville for the Floyd County cannoneers had become dull, comfortable, and predictable. Events in Kentucky—and the grand schemes of generals—would soon change that.

Early in the morning of January 19, 1862, near the town of Mill Spring, Kentucky, Confederate troops under Brig. Gen. George B. Crittenden launched an audacious but ill-considered assault on Union troops under the command of Gen. George H. Thomas. Crittenden, who had recently assumed command of all Rebel troops in Kentucky and most of East Tennessee, had a reputation as "a common drunk." His troops consisted of a small, poorly armed force charged with controlling the huge, generally hostile territory along the East Tennessee and Kentucky borderland. Brig. Gen. Felix Zollicoffer, a former journalist with no combat experience, had earlier crossed the Cumberland River with his equally untrained army and had become trapped with the rain-swollen waterway at their backs. Crittenden hurried north to support Zollicoffer.[27]

At first, the Confederate attack achieved a measure of success, and with Zollicoffer's Brigade in the lead, they pushed the Union 10th Indiana Regiment back in disorder. However, the Union 4th Kentucky, arriving as reinforcements, held the line without wavering. During the ensuing melee, the near-sighted Zollicoffer mistook the bluecoats for his own men and died in a hail of bullets as he rode toward them shouting orders.[28]

---

[26] *TWC*, January 23, 1862.

[27] Connelly, *Army of the Heartland*, 99; Horn, *Army of Tennessee*, 67–69. See generally, Kenneth Hafendorfer, *Mill Springs: The Campaign and Battle of Mill Springs, Kentucky* (Louisville: KH Press, 2001).

[28] Connelly, *Army of the Heartland*, 99; Horn, *Army of Tennessee*, 67–69.

After rallying Zollicoffer's disorganized troops, Crittenden launched a broad frontal counterattack to stem the advancing Yankee tide. The assault failed dismally. The Confederates, many of whom carried ancient flintlock muskets that would not fire in the pouring rain, retreated in disorder and confusion. Decisively beaten, Crittenden and his men hastily re-crossed the Cumberland River that night, losing a number of men in the ordeal. Abandoning all his artillery and large stores of equipment, the Rebel leader withdrew his bedraggled army toward Knoxville, Tennessee. That retreat left virtually the entire eastern section of Kentucky under Federal control.[29]

For the Cherokee Artillery and the other Confederate troops in Greenville, the uneventful life in winter quarters continued for several more days. They remained blissfully ignorant of the fight at Mill Springs and the series of events that followed. A number of officers had sent for their families to join them for the winter, boarding them at various residences in town. Meanwhile, the men in the ranks spent their time improving their quarters, reading letters from home, writing a few letters themselves, and generally whiling away the time as best they could until winter ended.[30]

Then, on the evening of January 23, an urgent telegram arrived for Stovall from Col. Leadbetter, now headquartered at Knoxville. Its contents shattered the winter calm like the peal of a sudden thunderbolt: The Federals had inflicted a decisive defeat on Crittenden's force at Mill Springs and Gen. Zollicoffer was among the dead. Leadbetter canceled all furloughs and directed Stovall's 3rd Georgia Battalion and Yeiser's Battery to proceed to Knoxville without delay.[31]

The news spread rapidly among the troops in and around Greenville. They worked quickly to pack baggage and equipment in anticipation of moving out the next morning. Railway workers prepared

---

[29] Connelly, *Army of the Heartland*, 99; Horn, *The Army of Tennessee*, 67–69. See generally, Hafendorfer, *Mill Springs: The Campaign and Battle of Mill Springs.*

[30] *TWC*, January 30, 1862.

[31] Ibid.

trains to move the troops while the commissary shipped stores needed to supply the men and animals. No sooner had they completed all the preparations to move than another telegram from Leadbetter arrived for Stovall. The situation with Crittenden's battered army turned out not to be as dire as originally believed. Leadbetter ordered Stovall's unit and the Cherokee Artillery to remain at Greenville until further notice.[32]

The routine of winter quarters resumed, but the men noted a decided change of attitude among some of the newly minted Rebel "patriots." The news of Crittenden's defeat, coupled with what appeared to be signs of the imminent departure of the local Rebel troops, had emboldened Greenville's Tories. In some places, Old Glory mysteriously appeared in place of the Stars and Bars. On another occasion, bushwhackers cut the telegraph lines between Greenville and Knoxville and vandalized the Greenville telegraph office. Local Confederate government officials also reported incidents in which Tories disrupted recruiting drives to raise local regiments for Confederate Army service. Pro-Union sympathy, it appeared, still had a very strong pulse in East Tennessee.[33]

Several more weeks of limbo ensued in which the Confederates in Greenville launched several expeditions to put down "Lincolnite" insurrections in the surrounding mountains. When not pursuing bushwhackers, the officers devised occasional events designed to keep the men occupied and let them practice their soldierly skills—and perhaps to remind the locals of the might of Confederate arms. One such event occurred on January 25. The Cherokee Artillery put on a demonstration in which two of their guns under the command of Daniel Millen and Felix Van Den Corput fired a total of thirteen rounds at a twelve-foot target at 1,200 yards. The guns, a smooth-bore six-pound howitzer and the rifled gun (probably the Noble Foundry three-inch rifle that Col. Pennington bought for the unit when it left Rome) struck their targets a total of seven times. Given their limited practice in recent weeks, and the gunners' need to estimate the distance to the targets, all

---

[32] *TWC*, February 1, 1862.

[33] *TWC*, January 30 and February 1, 1862.

agreed it had been "a fine display of marksmanship." Another event, this one completely impromptu, occurred when Gen. Pierre G. T. Beauregard passed through Greenville, on February 2, on his way to assume command of the Confederate forces at Columbus, Kentucky. The "Hero of [Fort] Sumter and Manassas" apparently impressed the troops and raised their hopes for ultimate victory in Kentucky.[34]

The Confederate troops at Greenville continued to bide their time, but the uproar created by Crittenden's defeat at Mill Spring resounded throughout Confederate Gen. Albert S. Johnston's Second Department and the government in Richmond. Not only had these events shattered the appearance of Southern invincibility in Tory East Tennessee, but, more importantly, Crittenden's defeat left Johnston's entire right flank up in the air. Johnston had a 300-mile line to guard, stretching from Knoxville to the Mississippi River. Scattered within the department were various detachments: Gen. Leonidas Polk, at Columbus, Kentucky, had 11,000 men; what remained of Zollicoffer's army, about 4,000 soldiers, huddled in Knoxville while Maj. General William J. Hardee had about 5,000 more in central Kentucky. Johnston did not have, nor could he get, sufficient arms, equipment, and ammunition for even this meager force. Col. James Rains, a young Nashville lawyer-turned-soldier stationed at Cumberland Gap, now directed the only sizable, organized body of Rebel troops in all of East Tennessee. The path appeared to be wide open for a Federal invasion of Tennessee between Bowling Green, Kentucky, and the Gap.[35]

No one had a deeper appreciation for this predicament than Rains himself. Writing to Adj. Gen. Samuel Cooper in Richmond on February 3 and again on February 14, Rains pointed out in no uncertain terms that his small force of fewer than 2,000 men could not hope to match the nearly 22,000 Yankee troops rumored to be heading for Cumberland Gap. While he and his men would put up a spirited defense, wrote Rains, the Rebels could not expect to defeat the enemy

---

[34] *TWC*, February 1 and 11, 1862; WOC, February 2, 1862.

[35] Connelly, *Army of the Heartland*, 99; Horn, *Army of Tennessee*, 67–69.

unless he received reinforcements of two or three regiments of infantry and a company of artillery.[36]

This request put Cooper and the Confederate War Department in a bind. On one hand, Rains's plea for additional troops certainly appeared well-founded. With the bluecoats pressing hard along the Mississippi River in West Tennessee and pushing in Middle Tennessee toward Nashville, the various small units scattered throughout East Tennessee constituted the only troops immediately available to support Johnston's army. Of course, Cooper recognized the need to keep enough troops in East Tennessee to prevent a resurgence of pro-Union activity. Col. Leadbetter had, in fact, reminded him of this concern in a letter requesting reinforcements. He had dispatched his entire cavalry force—400 men—to Crittenden in Knoxville after learning of the debacle in Kentucky. Finally, on February 16, Cooper made his decision. With several regiments from Tennessee, Georgia, Alabama, and Florida on their way to Knoxville to beef up Rebel troop strength in East Tennessee, he directed Leadbetter and Col. R. B. Vance to move immediately, with as many troops as possible, to reinforce Rains at Cumberland Gap.[37]

Almost simultaneously with the arrival of Cooper's directive came devastating news from the battlefront. Fort Donelson, a key Confederate bastion on the Cumberland River, had fallen. Federal troops under Maj. Gen. Don Carlos Buell now threatened Nashville, and the remaining Rebel outposts in Kentucky, at Columbus and Bowling Green, could not long survive a determined Federal assault.

The situation remained confusing and uncertain for the Rebel high command. On Monday, February 17, new orders arrived countermanding the earlier directive to reinforce Cumberland Gap. Government officials in Richmond had grown increasingly concerned about potential Federal assaults on Knoxville, Chattanooga, and against the East Tennessee & Virginia Railroad. Despite the uncertainty, it seemed abundantly clear that both the Cherokee Artillery and the 3rd Georgia Battalion would be going *somewhere* and *soon.*

---

[36] *OR*, ser. 1, vol. 52, part 2, 262; *OR*, ser. 1, vol. 7, 417.

[37] *OR*, ser. 1, vol. 7, 848, 862, 888.

The Army had commandeered the railroad to move troops to Tennessee, and already regiments from other commands had begun arriving to assume the responsibility for guarding the vital line of communication. Finally, the families of officers who had been staying the winter at Greenville left on February 18. All was now ready. They did not have long to wait. Late on the night of February 19, a dispatch arrived for the Cherokee Artillery and Stovall's Battalion to leave the following morning on a forced march to Cumberland Gap.[38]

Early on the morning of February 20, the battery set out. After nearly two months of being shut up in winter quarters, it took time for the unit to adjust to the rigors of marching all day in the cold Tennessee winter and to the misery of spending the frigid nights trying to sleep in their tents. By the evening of the next day, the Cherokee Artillery had trudged into Russellville. There, they met Leadbetter with the 3rd Georgia Battalion, which had had the good fortune to travel to that point by train.[39]

Leaving Russellville the following morning, the two units slogged onward. It had started to rain during the night, soaking everything from uniforms to food and blankets. For the next two days, the continual downpour turned roads into quagmires, which greatly increased the misery of men and animals alike. Soaked, cold, and miserable, the troops slogged through the East Tennessee mire, keenly aware of the sullen hostility of the locals they passed. After fording the Holston River, they crossed Clinch Mountain. By February 24, the Georgia units arrived at the Clinch River, only to discover that it had overflowed its banks and flooded the lowlands, making any crossing impossible.

The next two days offered a brief respite from the hardships of the march as the soggy and footsore Georgia troops waited for the river to recede enough to cross. The incessant rain had finally stopped, offering the men the chance to relax, dry out, and enjoy themselves. Some climbed to the top of Clinch Mountain, which offered spectacular

---

[38] *TWC*, February 25, 1862.

[39] *TWC*, March 1, 1862; WOC, February 20–21, 1862.

views of Tennessee, Virginia, Georgia, and even North Carolina. A few of the adventurous types visited Bean Station Springs to drink the white, red, and black sulfur water found there. Others read, wrote to family and friends back home, or just relaxed.[40]

They crossed the Clinch on February 26 and continued their march. The following evening, after eight grueling days and fifty rain-soaked miles, the Cherokee Artillery and the 3rd Georgia Battalion arrived at Cumberland Gap. Shortly thereafter Col. Leadbetter handed over the command of the two units to James Rains. The next morning, Rains assigned the battery to his tactical reserve. From their camp on one of the area's numerous mountains, the Cherokee Artillery could quickly move to the front to aid a Confederate attack, or to the rear to bolster the defenses and plug any breaks in the line should the Yankees achieve a breakthrough. Few considered that likely. Even with the impending loss of one regiment whose enlistments would soon expire, Rains now had four and a half infantry regiments defending the Gap. Additionally, six pieces of artillery—two howitzers from Capt. Henry B. Latrobe's Maryland battery and the four guns of Yeiser's Cherokee Artillery—added teeth to Rains's command. The troops were well-armed and well-supplied with ammunition and meat, even if the constant precipitation made the roads almost impassable for shipments of bread. In addition, the fortifications Rains and his men had constructed, though unfinished, appeared well-designed and made good use of the surrounding high ground to command the approaches to the Gap.[41]

After months of wintering in comfortable quarters, the rugged life at the battlefront came as a shock to Yeiser's men. They keenly felt the absence of the cooking utensils, tents, and other equipment they had left at Greenville. To make things even worse, the weather had once again turned bitterly cold. It drenched the troops with rain and coated the trees with sleet, making it nearly impossible to keep campfires burning for cooking and warming themselves.

---

[40] *TWC*, March 8, 1862; WOC, February 22–26, 1862.

[41] *TWC*, March 18, 1862; WOC, February 27–28, 1862; *OR*, ser. 1, vol. 52, part 2, 282.

Cold and sullen, the men waited for an attack by the Federals, now encamped just fourteen miles away. Brushes with Yankee cavalry pickets had become a frequent occurrence all along the Confederate line. Still, a major Union campaign failed to materialize. Instead, the two opposing forces continued their deadly game of cat-and-mouse for the next several weeks. Pickets from both sides regularly traded shots. Occasionally, the Federals launched small feints to probe the Confederate positions; the Rebels, in turn, would launch local counterassaults to drive them away.[42]

Capt. Yeiser's return on March 10 from a recruiting trip to Rome with thirty-one new volunteers provided a welcome, if momentary, respite from life at the front for the Floyd County artillerymen. Soon after Yeiser and the recruits arrived, the Floyd County cannoneers received instructions to move from their hillside position to one atop Cumberland Mountain, on the west side of the Gap. Technically, the Georgians now held a position just inside Kentucky.

From their new mountaintop encampment, the cannoneers had a commanding view of the valley and the main road to the Gap stretching out northward toward Cumberland Ford, and the main Union base of operations. At times, they could see Yankee troops moving in the distance during the day and the distant flickering of their campfires at night. All the signs indicated that the battery would occupy this new position for some time, so the men began busily cutting roads through the rugged terrain. They also used the newly- cut timber to construct permanent quarters for their stay at the "Gibraltar of East Tennessee."[43]

Unknown to the men of the Cherokee Artillery and the other Confederate soldiers at Cumberland Gap, the Rebels' hold on East Tennessee was growing more precarious every day. On March 8, Maj. Gen. Edmund Kirby Smith arrived in Knoxville to take command of the Department of East Tennessee. What he found upon his arrival deeply concerned him. To maintain control of thirty-two counties, of which

[42] *TWC*, March 18 and 20, 1862.

[43] *TWC*, March 20, 1862; WOC, March 12, 1862.

twenty-eight were deemed hostile to the Confederacy, he had only about 9,000 troops. Nearly half of them, under Col. Rains, protected Cumberland Gap. The remainder were scattered across the department guarding railroads, bridges, and key installations. To add to his woes, disease had ravaged all of his units except Lt. Col. Stovall's battalion, Yeiser's Battery, and two Alabama regiments. Almost all of the two Alabama units consisted of twelve-month volunteers, many nearing the expiration of their service. Smith had, not counting his men at the Gap and guarding the railroad, only 2,300 effectives with which to protect a line extending from Cumberland Gap to Chattanooga. Even the troops already promised, from Virginia and from Maj. General Braxton Bragg's department, also consisted primarily of twelve-month volunteers. Smith simply had to have more reliable men to avoid disaster.[44]

As if the Florida-born commander did not have enough troubles, the enemy pressure at Cumberland Gap continued to increase. In a letter to President Davis dated March 10, Smith estimated that five or six Federal regiments, totaling some 5,000 to 6,000 men, supported by twelve pieces of artillery, hovered between Cumberland Ford and Barboursville, Kentucky—within striking distance of the Gap. On March 16, word arrived that four Yankee regiments had marched through the Cumberland Mountains to Jacksborough, Tennessee, about forty miles southwest of Cumberland Gap. From there, they could cross the Clinch River, push into Powell's Valley, and either attack the Cumberland Gap defenses from the rear or strike at Knoxville.

Kirby Smith directed Col. Leadbetter, now leading the 1st Brigade, to move his troops to Clinton, Tennessee, to prevent the bluecoats from traversing the Clinch at that point. Concurrently, Smith would proceed to Cumberland Gap and take command of the soldiers there. He then planned to rendezvous with Leadbetter at Jacksborough to attack the enemy there or harass them if they began to retreat.[45]

---

[44] *OR*, ser. 1, vol. 10, part 2, 307–308, 355.
[45] Ibid., 332–33.

Arriving at the Gap on March 18, Smith inspected the Confederate defenses and met with his commanders. That evening, the Cherokee Artillery, the section of Latrobe's Battery, the 3rd Georgia Battalion, and three infantry regiments received orders to cook three days rations and be prepared to move out. The next morning, they set out toward Wheeler's Gap under the command of Kirby Smith. Spirits were high as the graycoats moved to meet up with Leadbetter's troops and cut off the Yankees' retreat. Capt. Yeiser's men felt confident they would finally get a crack at a real enemy instead of chasing phantoms through the hills. Once again, however, local Unionists warned the bluecoats of the Confederate's presence. After three days spent vainly attempting to bring the Federals to battle, Smith and his troops reluctantly returned to Cumberland Gap on March 21. The men of the Cherokee Artillery felt particularly disappointed that their elusive foe refused to stand and fight. It had begun to seem to some that they would never have a chance to be real soldiers and fight a real enemy.[46]

The Georgia cannoneers did not have long to wait for another chance to tangle with the Yankees. During the afternoon of March 20, local Federal sympathizers sent word to Brig. Gen. Samuel Carter, commanding the Union XXII Brigade, that Smith had departed Cumberland Gap, taking with him four Confederate regiments and six pieces of artillery. Carter assumed that the Confederates had significantly weakened their force at the Gap. He immediately ordered forward four infantry regiments, a cavalry battalion, and an artillery section with two Parrott rifles—2,300 men in all—to attack the weakened Confederate line. However, the next morning, as he approached Cumberland Gap, he received intelligence that Smith, after a forced march, had returned to the Gap's fortifications.

Carter, an East Tennessee native who had been detached by Pres. Lincoln from the U.S. Navy to lead several regiments of pro-Union Tennesseans, knew that his small command could not successfully assault the heavily defended Confederate position. He determined to take this opportunity, however, to thoroughly test and reconnoiter the

[46] *TWC*, March 29, 1862.

enemy's position. Sending his troops against the right of the Rebel lines, the bluecoats drove in the enemy pickets and made camp for the night.[47]

Meanwhile, inside the defenses at Cumberland Gap, the Southerners made ready to repulse the impending attack. Rains encouraged his mostly untested troops with a stirring speech, exhorting them to "perform their duty with cheerfulness, alacrity, and coolness, and to 'die in the trenches before surrendering to the enemy.'" Bolstered by Rains's eloquence and eager for a stand-up fight, the Confederates waited for daylight.[48]

Around 6 A.M. on Saturday, March 22, skirmishers from Col. John De Courcy's 16th Ohio opened the main assault, pushing the Rebel skirmishers out of the woods in front of the Gap and back into the breastworks. From a nearby ridge, his two long-range rifled Parrott guns began lobbing shells at the fortifications from a range of two thousand yards. Many of the Yankee shells proved defective and failed to explode. Rebel sharpshooters, ensconced in their rifle pits and entrenchments began regularly picking off the Yankee skirmishers while two twelve-pound howitzers within the Gap blasted the advancing blue line with canister.[49]

About the same time, the Cherokee Artillery received orders to engage in counter-battery fire against the two Federal howitzers. Their six-pounder guns proved useless against the two Parrott guns at that range. As a result, only the Noble Brothers three-inch rifle, ably served by Sgt. R. M. Jones, Cpl. Isaac Hume, and the rest of the gun crew, inflicted any damage on the Union artillery section.

For the rest of the Georgia cannoneers, their first real fight devolved into a mostly "look and listen" affair until late in the afternoon. Past noon the whole battery deployed to fire spherical case shot at Carter's reserves as they gathered in the valley below. Though well-protected behind the abatis and earth-filled gabions, they flinched at

---

[47] *OR*, ser. 1, vol. 10, part 1, 42.

[48] *RC*, April 11, 1862.

[49] *OR*, ser. 1, vol. 10, part 1, 42.

the "indescribable whiz" of the incoming artillery rounds and found themselves instinctively dodging the shots as they sailed "overhead and around us on their mission of death."[50]

Farther down the line on the Confederate left, Latrobe's Marylanders opened fire on the 49th Indiana as the Yankees unsuccessfully attempted to breach the Rebel defenses. Both sides kept up a brisk fire from their infantry and artillery that continued all day and well into the evening. Finally, after failing to entice the Confederates to leave their fortifications and attack in the open, Carter withdrew his men to their bivouac just outside of the range of the Rebel guns. Having completed his objective—feeling out the Cumberland Gap defenses—Carter's troops retreated to Cumberland Ford later that night.[51]

Nearly as quickly as it began, the fighting ceased. More an extended skirmish than a full-fledged battle, each side suffered only one killed and just a handful of wounded. Nevertheless, the March 22 fighting had two important effects. First, the Confederates now realized that they could successfully defend Cumberland Gap from a frontal assault in force. Second, the Federals confirmed that a direct attack, as many had suspected, could not breach the Gap's fortifications without incurring heavy casualties.[52]

The Cherokee Artillery had finally tasted combat against an organized Union force. Despite a few close calls—they discovered an enemy cannonball lodged in the gabion immediately in front of the three-inch rifle, and several shells landed close to the battery's ammunition magazines and caissons—the cannoneers from Georgia had "seen the elephant," and performed well.[53]

For the defenders of Cumberland Gap, life temporarily reverted back to the relative calm and boredom of camp routine. Reality now began to set in for the Cherokee Artillery, and the glamor and excitement

---

[50] *RC*, April 11, 1862; *TWC*, May 8, 1862.

[51] *OR*, ser. 1, vol. 10, part 1, 42.

[52] Ibid.; *RC*, April 11, 1862.

[53] *RC*, April 11, 1862.

they had envisioned when they enlisted began to fade. In its place came the daily grind of soldiering. Awaking at dawn to the blaring of a bugle sounding reveille, they would stand roll call, eat breakfast, and then spend the next several hours drilling new recruits and strengthening their already formidable fortifications. After that, they could spend their time however they wished. The Floyd County artillerymen often spent time exploring the local mountains and caves. In particular, they spent hours exploring a magnificent cavern discovered by Cpl. Sidney Blasingame, marveling at "the solemn grandeur of its halls and galleries." They named several chambers for various members of the company. One chamber became "Big Red's Room" while others they called "Yeiser's Parlor," "Connor's Alcove," and "Brown's Study." Word of this natural wonder apparently reached the top of the chain of command as Kirby Smith even honored the cave with a brief visit.[54]

Like soldiers throughout the Confederate Army, the Floyd County troops also began experiencing the hardships and shortages that would plague them, more or less, for the rest of the war. The ample supplies of things like fresh vegetables, real coffee, sugar, beef, and rice disappeared from the chow line. Meals, when available, now consisted of barely palatable army bacon, supplemented by whatever they could make from flour, lard, and salt. Gone also were niceties like razors, neckties, shined boots, and boiled shirts. Instead, their once-handsome uniforms now hung from their sinewy frames, tattered and worn by the rigors of army life.[55]

The cold and rain of March gave way to a sunny, pleasant April—excellent campaigning weather for armies in the field. That contributed, no doubt, to the rumors circulating of an impending Yankee attack on Cumberland Gap. The men of the Cherokee Artillery began the month with the selection of new lieutenants to replace George Bowen and Charles O. Stillwell, who had recently resigned their com-

---

[54] *TWC*, April 24, 1862.

[55] Ibid.

missions. Once they had tallied the votes, Meshack L. McWhorter became the unit's first lieutenant and William S. Hoge received the most votes for second lieutenant.[56]

McWhorter and Hoge were not the only new officers at Cumberland Gap that April. Brig. Gen. Carter L. Stevenson arrived mid-month under orders from the Confederate War Department to report to Kirby Smith in East Tennessee. A West Pointer from Virginia, Stevenson had served in the army during the Mexican War and fought Native peoples on the Plains and Mormon settlers in the "Mormon War" in Utah. As the new commander at Cumberland Gap, Stevenson began quickly instilling a rigorous military discipline in his new units. He canceled all leaves, medical and personal alike, until further notice; required stricter order and discipline; and directed the officers to read the articles of war nightly to each company after retreat. In a reorganization of the troops, the new commander assigned the Cherokee Artillery to the 2nd Brigade, along with [Capt. R. B.] Rhett's Tennessee Battery and the Eufaula Light Artillery from Alabama.[57]

Not all of the Cherokee Artillery's fighting occurred along the rocky slopes of the Gap. The unit's horse holders and drivers had spent the last several weeks at various posts along the Virginia Road, grazing the battery's horses. When word arrived that a marauding band of pro-Union guerrillas had moved into the area, Cpl. Isaac "Ike" Hume, commanding the detachment, distributed the contents of his cartridge box among the drivers. Joined by several members of a recently disbanded cavalry unit and a company of militia, they set out in pursuit. Using the expertise they had gained from their months of hunting bushwhackers around Greenville, the intrepid drivers separated their force into small groups and managed to outflank their prey. The Georgia "wranglers" captured seventeen of the partisans as the Tennessee Loyalists attempted to escape by way of nearby Mulberry Gap. Sidney Gattis and John Carr, finding themselves suddenly surrounded by a group of Unionists, drew their revolvers and ordered them to "stand and deliver," capturing ten more. Meanwhile, John Hammitt and

---

[56] *TWC*, April 24, 1862; *RC*, May 1, 1862.

[57] *RC*, May 1, 1862; *OR*, ser. 1, vol. 10, part 2, 573.

Henry Wilkerson captured five more of the enemy. One captive quickly confessed that they had left home heading for Kentucky, in hopes of avoiding conscription into the Confederate Army. Altogether, the artillerymen and their comrades captured forty-two of the fifty-three Federals without suffering a single casualty. After turning their prisoners over to Confederate authorities in nearby Sneedsville, Virginia, they "retired in good order to their original position."[58]

By late April 1862, the situation in East Tennessee had deteriorated even further for the Confederates. Responding to Gen. Beauregard's urgent plea for troops to shore up the Rebel defenses against an expected Federal attack on Corinth, Mississippi, and its vital railheads, Kirby Smith had reluctantly relinquished six infantry regiments. According to troop returns dated April 24, 1862, Smith had only 8,619 effective troops, including 1,143 cavalry of dubious value with which to defend several hundred square miles of mostly hostile territory against a rapidly growing enemy force. A large number of Union troops (some reports indicated as many as fourteen infantry regiments), their supporting artillery, and as many as 7,000 East Tennessee pro-Yankee irregulars had begun massing before the less than 2,500 Confederate troops at Cumberland Gap. Smith warned Richmond that if he did not soon receive significant reinforcements, he might lose his ability to maintain control over the mountainous region.[59]

The Federals had noticed the reduction in Confederate troop strength in East Tennessee. Maj. Gen. Don Carlos Buell, commanding the Union Army of the Ohio, decided the time had now come to seize Cumberland Gap and East Tennessee. While Kirby Smith fretted constantly about the growing number of troops arrayed against him, Buell likewise worried about not having sufficient soldiers to oust the Rebels from the "American Gibraltar." The Union commander realized he needed someone who could force the graycoats from the Gap using

[58] *RC*, May 1, 1862.

[59] *OR*, ser. 1, vol. 10, part 2, 409, 424, 453; *RC*, May 10, 1862.

only the single division available. On March 28, the Federal commander selected Brig. Gen. George W. Morgan, a crafty veteran of the Mexican War, and gave him the 7th Division, Army of the Ohio, to do the job.[60]

Morgan arrived with his new command at Cumberland Gap on April 11 and immediately conducted a personal reconnaissance of the Rebel positions. He described the mountain stronghold as "the strongest I have ever seen except Gibraltar." Morgan initially thought he had found a fatal flaw in the defenses. The Southerners had left their right flank relatively weakly defended, relying upon the strong natural barriers to frustrate any attempted assaults. If his men could occupy the undefended hill overlooking Forts Pitts and Mallory, Morgan reasoned, they could mount siege guns on the unguarded heights. The Confederates would then have no choice but to evacuate the Gap.[61]

A brief skirmish on April 29 between four of Morgan's brigades and Rebel troops defending Cumberland Gap's right flank resulted in the Rebels occupying the very hill Morgan had selected as his target. The Union leader, of course, changed his mind. From that point on, Morgan determined to avoid what he now believed would be a costly frontal attack. Instead, he decided to oust the enemy by confusing them as to his true intentions. The Union leader resolved to cross through one of the passes in the Cumberland Mountains below Cumberland Gap, and either assault the Rebel position from the rear or force them to retire through maneuver. Either way, the "American Gibraltar" would be his for the taking.[62]

For their part, the Confederate defenders at Cumberland Gap took advantage of the relative calm during May and early June to systematically improve their fortifications. During that time death once again visited the Cherokee Artillery, taking the lives of two of the unit's recent recruits. William Newton died in the army hospital in nearby Tazewell, and Daniel N. Cooper succumbed to a relapse of pneumonia at a farmhouse three miles from camp. Their comrades had liked both

---

[60] W. C. Davis, "Cumberland Gap, 1862," 25.

[61] *OR*, ser. 1, vol. 10, part 1, 57.

[62] Ibid.

men and their death from disease, rather than enemy action, made their loss even harder to bear. "Disease makes sad havoc in the ranks of our volunteers," noted the company's correspondent to the Rome newspapers. "It kills more than the bullet; the hospital is more dreaded than the battlefield."[63]

But the Georgians had scant time for grieving. On June 7, Federal Maj. Gen. Ormsby Mitchel, whose 7,000 troops had been threatening Chattanooga since late May, launched an attack on that key transportation and supply hub. Alarmed, Kirby Smith rushed as many men as he could spare to blunt Mitchel's assault.

With the Florida general's attention focused on protecting Chattanooga, Morgan launched the next phase of his operation to take Cumberland Gap. On June 7, he ordered the brigades of Brig. Gen. John De Courcy and Brig. Gen. Absalom Baird to move from their encampments in and around a small defile four miles below Cumberland Gap. According to Morgan's scheme, they would then proceed toward Rogers Gap, approximately twenty miles southwest of Cumberland Gap, and enter Powell's Valley. From there they would be in a position to threaten Knoxville, Clinton (Smith's primary supply depot), or the rear of Cumberland Gap. To further bewilder the Rebel leader, Morgan ordered Brig. Gen. James Spears's brigade to move through Big Creek Gap, approximately thirty-five miles southwest of the American Gibraltar. There, they would pose an additional threat to the Rebel lifeline at Clinton. Lastly, Samuel Carter's brigade would move from Cumberland Ford to rendezvous with De Courcy and Baird at Rogers's Gap.[64]

Kirby Smith, unable to clearly discern Morgan's intentions, was in a bind. Required to simultaneously protect Chattanooga and his supply depot at Clinton, as well as keep Cumberland Gap from being taken, the Confederate leader obliged Morgan by doing exactly what the Union commander had hoped—spreading his forces ever thinner. After wiring Beauregard for more troops, Smith directed Brig. Gen.

[63] *TWC*, June 10, 1862.

[64] *OR*, ser. 1, vol. 10, part 1, 57; W. C. Davis, "Cumberland Gap, 1862," 26; Morgan, "Cumberland Gap," 63.

Seth Barton's brigade and Col. A. W. Reynolds's brigade to rendezvous at Tazewell. From there, he hoped to be able to protect Clinton and prevent Morgan's bluecoats, currently marching into Powell's Valley, from moving up the canyon and attacking Cumberland Gap from the rear. By his maneuvers, Morgan had succeeded in forcing Smith to weaken the defenses of both Chattanooga and Cumberland Gap.[65]

After nearly a week of watching and waiting as the two armies maneuvered all around them, the Cherokee Artillery and the rest of the Cumberland Gap garrison began to grasp the precariousness of their situation. For the last few days, they had actually expected to be ordered northward as part of Kirby Smith's long-rumored invasion of Kentucky while Beauregard simultaneously moved to retake Nashville. Now, however, with Smith's removal of Rebel troops guarding the mountain passes on their left flank in order to protect Chattanooga and Clinton, they faced the very real prospect of being cut off and attacked from the rear.[66]

On June 11, rumors began circulating among the Rebel soldiers at the Gap regarding the large bodies of Yankee troops advancing on their position. Preparations began early that day that led the Cherokee Artillery to believe that they and their comrades would soon evacuate Cumberland Gap. By that evening, as they completed their arrangements to withdraw, new orders arrived. The enemy had been repulsed at Chattanooga, and Smith directed the defenders at Cumberland Gap to stand fast. Yeiser and his cannoneers, pleased with the decision to remain and fight, made camp for the night.[67]

No sooner had they bedded down, however, then new orders arrived to get ready to move. The rapid approach of the Yankees, 20,600 strong, meant that the sooner the garrison left, the better. Around them, the infantry regiments began forming into columns, preparing to move out. In the dark of night, many of the men passed the time gazing at the total eclipse of the moon, waiting expectantly for orders.

---

[65] *OR*, ser. 1, vol. 16, part 2, 679–81.

[66] *TWC*, June 18, 1862.

[67] WOC, June 11, 1862.

Instead, once more, a directive arrived ordering them to stand down and go back to bed.[68]

June 12 started quietly. The men of the Cherokee Artillery and the rest of the Cumberland Gap garrison arose and busied themselves in the quiet routine of camp duties. Their breathing spell did not last long. Gen. Carter Stevenson moved westward toward Wilson's Gap to help thwart the move of Morgan's troops into Powell's Valley. He took with him detachments from all the infantry units at the Gap and several pieces of artillery, including a two-gun section from Yeiser's Battery. A fight for Cumberland Gap again seemed imminent.[69]

In addition to the Yankees moving to the rear of Cumberland Gap, Smith now had a new concern. On June 14, Leadbetter had sent him an urgent telegram from Chattanooga. The Florida regiments ordered to that city to help bolster its defenses had not left Chattahoochee, Florida, and Ormsby Mitchel once more had his bluecoats moving toward the city in force. Smith could not defend both ends of his line with his small contingent, and he knew full well the importance of holding Chattanooga. Arriving at Bean's Station late on June 14, the Florida general made his decision—he would evacuate Cumberland Gap.

The next morning, Smith sent Carter Stevenson a directive to abandon the American Gibraltar. After briefly outlining the situation at Chattanooga, he ordered Stevenson to leave his position "promptly and quietly." The Rebel commander also directed Stevenson to retire to the southeast by way of Morristown toward Chattanooga and to send ahead of him as much ordinance, stores, and equipment as possible. From there, he would establish a defensive line anchored on Bean's Station and Clinch Mountain to protect the East Tennessee & Georgia Railroad line. Hopefully, this would prevent Federal units from advancing toward Knoxville or Chattanooga and keep Morgan's troops bottled up at Cumberland Gap. Seth Barton's Rebel brigade would

---

[68] WOC, June 12, 1862.

[69] *OR*, ser. 1, vol. 16, part 2, 681; WOC, June 15, 1862.

cover their withdrawal. They were to destroy anything they could not take with them.[70]

After a hard march lasting twenty-four hours, the exhausted men of the Cherokee Artillery crossed to the south side of the Clinch River on June 18. There they made camp for the night. Continuing their trek the next day, they once again traversed Clinch Mountain. Finally, they reached the south side of the Holston River during the night of June 19 and made camp. The Floyd County artillerymen expected to reach Morristown in two days' time. Instead, June 21 found Yeiser's men, along with the rest of the 2nd Brigade, marching back toward Clinch Mountain. There they spent the next several days awaiting orders while Kirby Smith and his generals adjusted their lines, shifting troops along the new defensive perimeter protecting both Chattanooga and Knoxville and responding to the appearance of a force of Yankees at Tazewell.[71]

After waiting three days, new orders finally arrived on June 24. Smith sent a two-gun section of the Cherokee Artillery back over Clinch Mountain to a location halfway down the opposite side of the heights as Stevenson attempted to thwart the threat at Tazewell. That same day, two guns, complete with horses, limber wagons, and equipment, arrived by train from Knoxville. Instructions followed for Yeiser to use the surplus manpower created by his unit's recent recruiting efforts to put them to profitable use. For the time being, at least, the Cherokee Artillery now had the distinction of being a six-gun battery.[72]

Occasionally a force of Federals would sally forth from the confines of Cumberland Gap to forage and probe the Confederate defenses. Stevenson and Smith deployed their troops to keep a close watch on the mountain defiles below Cumberland Gap. From there they could block Union troops from advancing on Knoxville or other important locations and keep the Yankees from raiding the country-

[70] *OR*, ser. 1, vol. 16, part 2, 683, 693, 705.

[71] Ibid., 696; WOC, June 24, 1862.

[72] *OR*, ser. 1, vol. 16, part 2, 705; WOC, June 24, 1862.

side. Except for those occasional alarms, the rest of June proved uneventful for the Georgia cannoneers as they continued to man their position on Clinch Mountain.

July, however, began on a decidedly somber note. On July 2, Yeiser's men marched to nearby Bean's station to witness the execution of a soldier whom a general court-martial had convicted of murder. Wesley Connor recorded the solemn event in his diary, along with a few thoughts on military discipline. "Yesterday marched over to Bean's Station," he wrote,

> and witnessed the military execution of a private of the 3rd Battalion, Tenn. Cavalry, condemned to die for killing a Lieutenant of the 11th Tenn. Regiment, who as officer of the guard had orders to arrest him for disorderly conduct. The prisoner took his seat upon his coffin, and after a short prayer by the minister in attendance, the white cap was drawn over his face. At a signal from the officer in charge, a volley of twelve guns was fired. The condemned man fell upon his coffin and died almost without a struggle. Upon examination, three balls were found to have entered his breast. As I looked at him, I thought it was hard that a man who voluntarily left his home to expose and, if necessary, sacrifice his life in the defense of his country, should be so severely dealt with for an act committed in the heat of passion, and that passion intensified by spirits,—but to take the right view of the matter, it is perhaps just, for an army would be worth but little without discipline, and from the commencement of the war, our commanders had been too lenient. Had army regulations been enforced from the beginning, much of the disorderly conduct seen every day would have been prevented.[73]]

The month of July also brought a number of changes that directly affected the Cherokee Artillery. Kirby Smith's efforts to secure reinforcements to defend Chattanooga and the rest of the Department of East Tennessee had finally begun to pay off. In preparation for the influx of troops, the district commander reorganized his army by combining his five brigades into two divisions. Carter Stevenson, his able

---

[73] WOC, July 3, 1862.

warhorse, would command the 1st Division and Brig. Gen. Henry Heth, a highly regarded career soldier newly arrived from the Department of Western Virginia, would lead the new 2nd Division.[74]

On July 3, after the rest of the Georgia battery had moved closer to Bean's Station, the cannoneers learned that they were now part of Stevenson's 2nd Brigade under the command of Col. Rains. Additionally, the unit's popular commander, James Yeiser, was promoted to the rank of major and reassigned to lead the 1st Division's artillery battalion. To replace Yeiser, Smith promoted the battery's Belgian-born first lieutenant, Maximillian Joseph Gustave Van Den Corput, to captain of the Cherokee Artillery.[75]

For nearly two weeks the gunners of the Cherokee Artillery and their new commander remained at Bean's Station. Then, on July 16, orders arrived for Rains's Brigade, including Van Den Corput's Battery, to proceed down the Knoxville Road to Powder Spring Road—approximately seventeen miles southwest of Bean's Station and twenty-three miles from Knoxville. By the night of July 17, they had reached the Knoxville Road, and Wesley Connor and several of his comrades spent the night in a graveyard. The diarist ruefully recorded that they used headstones for pillows, "thus to desecrate the last resting place for poor mortals." Marching on short rations, they reached Powder Spring Gap the following day. There they received orders to return to Bean's Station. To add to their misery, they had to trudge back in a drenching rain. Finally, on the night of July 21, the Georgia artillerymen—tired, hungry, and soaked to the skin—tramped back into Bean's Station. They never really learned why they had had to march to Powder Spring Gap in the first place. "Returned last night from Powder Spring Gap," Connor wrote in his diary. "Had a delightful march," he added sarcastically.[76]

Apparently, whether through soldiers' letters or via the newspapers, word reached the civilians back home in Floyd County that the

---

[74] *OR*, ser. 1, vol. 16, part 2, 719.

[75] Wesley O. Connor, Compiled Service Roster of the Cherokee Artillery, Fisher collection.

[76] *TWC*, July 29, 1862; WOC, July 17 and July 22, 1862.

Cherokee Artillery had been suffering from short rations. Led by Col. Daniel R. Mitchell and Cunningham Pennington, county leaders urged the citizens of Rome and the outlying areas to contribute food and other items for the "Soldier Car" to be sent to their hungry cannoneers in East Tennessee. "The Company is now on short rations," reported the *Rome Courier*, "and if the citizens of Floyd County permit this car to go off without being filled to the top with necessaries, it will be a shame and disgrace to the county. Never let it be said that Floyd County permitted her gallant sons to suffer, when it was in her power to relieve them." Leaving Rome on July 25, the railcar arrived in Morristown, Tennessee, on July 27. By that evening, its contents were in the hands of the grateful gunners of the Cherokee Artillery, who enjoyed the unexpected gifts from home immensely. "Good humor will be the order of the day for some time to come," reported the unit's correspondent to the *Courier*.[77]

On July 27, the same day the "Soldier Car" arrived, the situation northwest of them, near Tazewell, began to heat up. Federal troops from Cumberland Gap had ventured forth from their mountain fortress, driving the Confederate pickets before them and wounding several. The Rebel generals faced a quandary. They had to determine if the incursion represented only a foraging expedition to gather foodstuffs, since the dashing Confederate Col. John Hunt Morgan's cavalry had cut the Federals off from their supply bases during its extended raid through the Bluegrass State. Or the enemy foray might be merely a feint to cover an attack on the Rebel supply depot at Clinton. Adding to the uncertainty for Kirby Smith and Carter Stevenson, they had been receiving reports for the last several days that the Yankees planned to attack Knoxville. The Confederate leaders believed Don Carlos Buell's Army of the Ohio was marching up the Sequatchie Valley, southwest of Knoxville, to affect a junction with Morgan's bluecoats at Cumberland Gap. One thing the Rebels knew with certainty—a large number of Yankees had now positioned themselves between Tazewell and the Clinch River. From there they could either move on Clinton,

---

[77] *RC*, July 25, 1862; *TWC*, August 2, 1862.

Knoxville, or just assault the small Confederate force near the Clinch River.[78]

Reacting to this threat, on August 2, James Rains ordered the 3rd Georgia Battalion and one section of the Cherokee Artillery to move immediately to the Clinch River to help shore up the Confederate's defensive position. The following day he also dispatched the 42nd Georgia and the 4th and 11th Tennessee regiments to the Clinch. Finally, on August 4, Rains sent a second section of the Cherokee Artillery to join the strong contingent.[79]

Rains's troops first crossed the Clinch River toward Tazewell on the night of August 3. The Union troops retreated so precipitously that Rains feared his men might be drawn into an ambush. To prevent that, Rains ordered his graycoats to fall back across the Clinch that night. Advancing again the following day, Rains marched his troops, including the two sections of Van den Corput's Battery, toward Tazewell. Except for a brief skirmish between Federal pickets and Rains's horsemen, the Confederates advanced unimpeded.[80]

By that evening, Rains's men had trudged northward to within five miles of the town. As they approached Walden's Ridge, a plateau south of Tazewell, they came under fire from Yankee artillery strongly situated on the heights. Halting, the Confederates endured the Yankee shelling for several hours. "Have had a right lively time for a few hours," Wesley Connor noted in his diary. "Yankee shot and shell are passing over us, and occasionally we send one in return." While the Cherokee Artillery carried on this desultory duel with the Yankee batteries, Marcellus Stovall, their old commander, made an appearance on the field. He even took time to aim a few shots himself. A reporter from the *Columbus (GA) Sun*, traveling with Rains's Brigade, noted with approval "our firing was capital, particularly a few shots aimed by our gallant Col. M. A. Stovall. Our boys say the Yankees seemed to understand when the Colonel drew a bead, from the way they skedaddled."

---

[78] *TWC*, August 2 and 12, 1862; *OR*, ser. 1, vol. 16, part 2, 736–37.

[79] *TWC*, August 12, 1862.

[80] Ibid.

Despite the journalistic puffery, neither side inflicted any real damage on the other. Finally, at 2 A.M. on August 5, Rains ordered his troops to again withdraw across the Clinch.[81]

Advancing yet again at first light, Rains and his men crossed over the river and by 10 A.M. had arrived at Big Spring. The distant rumble of cannon fire announced that Carter Stevenson, moving forward with Taylor's and Barton's brigades in an effort to get between the bluecoats and Cumberland Gap, had made contact with the Yankees sixteen miles to the south at Powder Spring Gap. Rains, awaiting the arrival of two brigades, advanced his men no farther on August 5. They had once again come within range of the Federal guns mounted on nearby Walden's Ridge, and throughout the rest of the day, the Yankee artillery lobbed shells at Rains's men. Anxious to "show their teeth," the Cherokee artillery replied in kind while the rest of Rain's Rebels awaited their reinforcements.[82]

Unknown to Kirby Smith, Carter Stevenson, and the Confederate brigade commanders, the Rebel reports of Federal troop movements were greatly exaggerated. Far from being a large-scale coordinated attack by Buell's and Morgan's commands, the Confederates had instead run headlong into Col. John De Courcy's single brigade. Morgan had dispatched him to forage and gather intelligence on Rebels in the area. Having just sent 200 wagons to Cumberland Gap filled with supplies commandeered from the local populace, de Courcy and his men had been preparing to make a run for the Gap. Finding himself wedged between Barton's and Taylor's brigades, now moving to cut him off from Cumberland Gap, and Rains's Brigade, advancing from the south like a bulldog, de Courcy became increasingly alarmed.[83]

August 6 dawned with a dense, rolling fog that enveloped the entire countryside including Walden's Ridge, the site of the previous night's action. The plateau, covered with thick stands of cedar and

---

[81] *TWC*, August 12, 1862; WOC, August 4–5, 1862; Orderly, "Tennessee Correspondence of the *Columbus (GA) Sun*," newspaper clipping, Stovall scrapbooks, vol. 2, n.p., n.d.

[82] WOC, August 5, 1862.

[83] *OR*, ser. 1, vol. 52, 2, 269; *OR*, ser. 1, vol. 16, part 1, 835.

pine, contained a small gap through which the Morrisville Road meandered toward Tazewell. To the right of the gap stood a cleared knob, with another hillock on the left which was covered with corn stalks. Within the thick woods of the gap, the Federals had concealed two ten-pound rifled guns from Capt. Jacob T. Foster's 1st Wisconsin battery under the command of Lt. John D. Anderson. A small reserve force and the remaining companies of the 14th Kentucky (US) lurked in small encampments on the hills flanking the defile.[84]

By 10 A.M. thc fog had bcgun to lift. Firing at long rangc from their position at Big Spring, the Cherokee Artillery began hurling shells at the Federal troops as the Confederate attack got underway. To Rains's left, unseen in the morning fog, Stevenson launched Col. Thomas H. Taylor's brigade against the right flank of the Yankee position. As Taylor's 46th Alabama, 3rd Tennessee, 31st Tennessee, and 59th Tennessee regiments clambered up Walden's Ridge, they slammed headlong into two companies of the 16th Ohio on picket duty in advance of the main Federal line. The 16th Ohio, a weak regiment of only 400 men whose eight understrength companies had arrived only hours earlier to relieve the 14th Kentucky, reeled backward under the weight of the Rebel onslaught. Within minutes, Taylor's men had completely cut off and surrounded the two companies. After forty-five minutes of hand-to-hand fighting, the Rebels succeeded in overrunning the Buckeye unit's position. Anderson's Wisconsin gunners, reloading their guns as quickly as they could, fired round after round of grape and canister at the advancing Confederates with devastating effect. At the last second, as the troops of the 3rd Tennessee charged to within thirty paces of the guns, Anderson and his men limbered up their pieces and beat a hasty retreat downhill to a nearby orchard. There, the 14th Kentucky had formed a defensive line.[85]

---

[84] "Capt. J. H. Davidson letter," *Ironton (OH) Register*, August 21, 1862; "Capt. J. H. Ferry letter," *Louisville (KY) Daily Journal*, August 16, 1862. Little has been written about the Battle of Tazewell, but a valuable resource is Perkins, "The Battle of Tazewell," http://joepayne.org/battle/main.htm, which contains numerous news articles and letters written shortly after the engagement.

[85] "Capt. J. H. Davidson letter," *Ironton (OH) Register*, August 21, 1862; "Stein letter," *Wooster (OH) Republican*, August 21, 1862; *TWC*, August 14, 1862.

Taylor's regiments, determined to press home their assault, let out a loud cheer and swept down Walden's Ridge and around the right flank of the Federal position. As they raced forward "in splendid order," the Rebel units threatened to completely outflank the remaining companies of the 16th Ohio, whose stragglers were now streaming down the hills toward the line of the 14th Kentucky. As Taylor's men pushed forward, they received a momentary check by the fire of the 14th Kentucky and Lt. Anderson's Parrott rifles, which once again roared to life from their position in the orchard. The pause lasted just long enough to allow the survivors of the 16th Ohio to link up with their comrades in the 14th Kentucky.[86]

Despite the volleys of combined rifle and musket fire from the two Yankee regiments and the gaping holes that Anderson's guns had torn in their ranks, Taylor's graycoats reformed their lines and advanced. Lt. Anderson's guns limbered up and moved off, this time to a ridge a half a mile beyond Tazewell. The two Yankee infantry regiments, now under orders to fall back, retired in a disorderly fashion across the rugged, forested ground. Two large fences and the extreme heat made the retreat a trying ordeal. With Taylor's men in hot pursuit, the bluecoats skedaddled through Tazewell and rejoined the rest of de Courcy's brigade on the ridge behind the town. Checked by the fire coming from all six guns of Foster's Wisconsin battery, the Confederate infantry hesitated, and then fell back in confusion. Taylor's attack had run out of steam. The regiments, hot, thirsty, and exhausted from four hours of hard fighting in stifling heat, retreated to their newly acquired ridge line.[87]

Rains's Brigade, having advanced as part of the general assault, occupied positions on Walden Ridge. From their new location, the Cherokee Artillery enjoyed a spectacular view of Cumberland Gap, thirteen miles in the distance. The battle now became an artillery duel, as two guns from the Georgia battery traded fire with the six guns of Foster's Wisconsin artillery. For the rest of the afternoon, the Union

[86] "Capt. J. H. Davidson letter," *Ironton (OH) Register*, August 21, 1862.

[87] Ibid.

and Rebel guns lobbed shells over the town at each other. Although a lucky shot by one of the Federal guns snapped off a trail handspike of one of Van Den Corput's guns, neither side inflicted any meaningful damage on the other.[88]

After nightfall, de Courcy and his brigade made good their escape, returning to Cumberland Gap and leaving the Confederates in uncontested possession of the battlefield. The Battle of Tazewell had ended. Despite the intensity of some of the fighting, Federal losses proved to be relatively light; twenty-three men killed and wounded, along with fifty-two soldiers of the 16th Ohio taken prisoner. Although both the 16th Ohio and the 14th Kentucky lost all their knapsacks, blankets, overcoats, and ammunition, the Federals successfully returned to the Gap with all 200 wagonloads of "confiscated" supplies. Confederate casualty estimates varied greatly, but the carnage inflicted by the infantry and Foster's battery on the troops of Taylor's Brigade supports the contention that the Rebels suffered as many as 250 men killed and wounded. Kirby Smith's valiant infantry had paid a stiff price for their "victory."[89]

Edmund Kirby Smith had grown increasingly bored with his main objective—protecting Chattanooga from the threatened attack of Buell's Army of the Ohio. The Federals, creeping slowly eastward toward the Gateway City, followed the line of the Memphis & Charleston Railroad, repairing the tracks as they went. A competent strategist, Smith fully understood the necessity of defending this key city. Losing Chattanooga would not only sever the vital railroad to Virginia, but it would also leave Georgia vulnerable to invasion, and particularly, the vital Atlanta rail hub.[90]

---

[88] Ibid.; *TWC*, August 14, 1862.

[89] *OR*, ser. 1, vol. 16, part 2, 301.

[90] Connelly, *Army of the Heartland*, 189–92. A useful nonacademic source is J. H. DeBerry, "Kirby Smith's Bluegrass Invasion," *America's Civil War* 10/1 (March 1997): 54–60, 88–89.

Nevertheless, the aggressive, thirty-eight-year-old West Pointer, whom the Southern press had proclaimed the "Bluecher of Manassas," wanted greater glory than he could ever achieve commanding in the Department of East Tennessee. Even as events played out at Tazewell, Smith began putting the finishing touches on a grand plan that, if successful, would likely change the course of the war in the Western Theater. He planned to invade Kentucky and aid the inhabitants of the Bluegrass State in ridding themselves of their Union occupiers—thereby forcing the Yankees to abandon Tennessee. With one masterstroke, the Confederacy could regain the control over Tennessee and Kentucky they had lost during the preceding months, and Kirby Smith would add to his luster as a national hero. Indeed, the timing appeared to be perfect for such a venture. On July 4, Confederate authorities dispatched Kentuckian John Hunt Morgan and his partisan cavalry on a wide-ranging raid deep into the Bluegrass countryside. Morgan had orders to destroy Federal supply depots, disrupt Yankee communications, and recruit as many new men as possible for the Confederate cause. Morgan's incursion proved to be spectacularly successful. In less than a week, Morgan and his 1,500 troopers—many of them Kentuckians—had crossed half the state, deep behind enemy lines, sowing panic and confusion among the bluecoats, and electrifying the local population with their bold exploits.

Morgan dispatched a note to Smith on July 16, declaring, "The whole country [Kentucky] can be occupied, and 25,000 to 30,000 men will join you at once. I have taken eleven cities and towns very heavy with stores." Kentucky, indeed, appeared ripe for the taking. The Florida general forwarded a copy of Morgan's note to Carter Stevenson, optimistically directing him to move against the Gap and on into Kentucky if George Morgan sent a significant number of troops to pursue Morgan's raiders in Kentucky.[91]

Kirby Smith needed more men, or someone to take Chattanooga off his hands—or, preferably, both—to put his plan into play. At first, his requests for additional troops to defend Chattanooga fell on deaf

[91] *OR*, ser. 1, vol. 28, part 2, 733–34; Connelly, *Army of the Heartland*, 191; Hess, *Banners to the Breeze*, 24.

ears. Beauregard and Braxton Bragg, the Creole general's successor as leader of the Army of Mississippi, denied Smith's request because of their own impending operations and lack of transportation. Even the War Department in Richmond, fixated as usual on events in Virginia, seemed in no hurry to respond to the threat against Chattanooga. President Davis replied to separate appeals for help from two influential Knoxville citizens, simply expressing the hope that Bragg would dispatch troops to Smith "if it should be in his power to do so."[92]

Smith would not be denied. Alternately pleading, cajoling, and badgering, he continued to pester Bragg, Richmond, and even Georgia governor Joe Brown for more soldiers. Gradually, his persistence began to pay off. On June 25, Pres. Davis sent Brig. Gen. Henry Heth to Chattanooga, along with the promise that even more reinforcements than Smith had requested would soon arrive at the Gateway City.[93]

Braxton Bragg also relented. On June 26, Bragg ordered Brig. Gen. John P. McCown to Chattanooga with 3,000 men. Telegraphing his decision to Kirby Smith, Bragg informed him that he would also assume the offensive against the rear of Buell's army. Although Bragg seemed reluctant to further weaken his army, Smith continued prodding him for additional support. On July 20, the commander of the Department of East Tennessee sent Bragg a dispatch urging him to drive his army into Middle Tennessee and force Buell to pull his bluecoats away from Chattanooga. Four days later, Smith sent another plea for help, but this time he let slip a tantalizing suggestion—hinting at a broader plan. By cooperating, they might be able to regain not only Middle Tennessee but also wrench control of Kentucky from the Yankees. Smith even agreed to subordinate his command to Bragg if the dour North Carolinian would agree to such an undertaking.[94]

Little by little, Bragg began to warm up to Smith's proposals. He had, in fact, already made up his mind to take the fight into the Bluegrass State prior to receiving Smith's note of July 24. His Army of Mis-

[92] Connelly, *Army of the Heartland*, 191; *OR*, ser. 1, vol. 16, part 2, 695.

[93] *OR*, ser. 1, vol. 16, part 2, 707.

[94] *OR*, ser. 1, vol. 16, part 2, 730, 734; Hess, *Banners to the Breeze*, 18–24.

sissippi had been based in Tupelo ever since Gen. Beauregard abandoned Corinth following the defeat at Shiloh. Since then, Bragg's army had dwindled, primarily due to desertion, to only 31,000 men. If he sent additional troops piecemeal to defend Tennessee's Gateway City, which had to be held, his army would simply be too small to operate against Union Maj. Gen. Henry W. Halleck's 60,000-man army. The only logical answer involved moving his army to Chattanooga to defend that city against Buell's slow-moving Army of the Ohio. He could then move northward into Middle Tennessee. If successful, Bragg would regain that vital territory for the Confederate war effort, including the key city of Nashville. Success in Middle Tennessee would take pressure off of East Tennessee. Then, he could move into Kentucky with Smith if the situation warranted.[95]

On July 21, Bragg informed Richmond of his decision and ordered his army to begin what would become one of the most masterful troop movements of the war. His cavalry, artillery, and wagon train would proceed overland on a 430-mile loop around Buell's Army, crossing through Central Alabama and Northern Georgia before trudging north to Chattanooga. The infantry regiments would move by rail, first to Mobile, Alabama, then on to Atlanta before proceeding to Chattanooga.[96]

Bragg's foot soldiers began to arrive at Chattanooga on July 27. Three days later Bragg himself reached his destination. That afternoon, he and Kirby Smith met and hammered out plans for the campaign. Although senior in rank to Smith, Bragg hesitated to take overall command of their combined force. Indecisive by nature, he also saw himself as something of an interloper in the younger general's department. The resulting plan for the coming expedition was simple and well-conceived—as far as it went. Since Bragg's cavalry, artillery, and wagons had not yet arrived, Smith would immediately move on the Yankees at Cumberland Gap. If he successfully drove Morgan out of the Gap, the two Confederate armies would combine for a push into Middle Tennessee once Bragg's complete force arrived. They had not, however,

---

[95] Connelly, *Army of the Heartland*, 196–99.

[96] *OR*, ser. 1, vol. 16, part 2, 731; Horn, Th*e Army of Tennessee*, 158–60.

dealt with an overriding question in their otherwise straightforward plan. Rather than facing head-on the question of who would command the two combined armies, Bragg later said they merely "arranged measures for mutual support and effective co-operation." Though he likely did not realize it at the time, Bragg had agreed to a plan that remained just vague enough to allow Smith to free himself from the need to guard Chattanooga and permitted him to launch his Kentucky invasion. Bragg's failure to assume overall control of the operation would hamper the Rebel offensive during the coming weeks.[97]

Smith almost immediately began urging that he be allowed to put his Kentucky incursion plan in motion. Counting the fine brigades of Brig. Gen. Patrick Cleburne and Col. Preston Smith that Bragg had obligingly lent him, he now had more than 19,000 men—more than enough to deal with Morgan's 10,000 soldiers at Cumberland Gap. With that in mind, the Florida general had already decided to move at the earliest opportunity on Lexington, Kentucky. In letters to Pres. Davis and Braxton Bragg he explained his scheme: While waiting for Bragg's army to assemble and prepare to move, he would leave Carter Stevenson and his 9,000-man force to keep Morgan pinned down at the Gap. Smith would then advance with the rest of his army through Rogers Gap and sweep into the Bluegrass state. By occupying London and Barboursville, he would cut off Morgan from his source of supplies. If the Union general retreated to defend his supply lines, Smith's troops would pursue and overwhelm him; if he remained at Cumberland Gap, the graycoats would either starve him out or directly assault the American Gibraltar and retake the crucial position. The best option, Smith urged, involved bottling up Morgan while the Rebel commander moved his troops to Lexington. Kentucky, Kirby Smith asserted, was ripe for such a move, and it would allow him to threaten Buell's line of communications. Another opportunity for glory had arrived, and Kirby Smith determined to grasp it with both hands.[98]

---

[97] *OR*, ser. 1, vol. 28, part 2, 741; Hess, *Banners to the Breeze*, 22–25.
[98] *OR*, ser. 1, vol. 16, part 2, 748, 752.

Once again, Braxton Bragg failed to assert overall control over the proposed campaign. He seemed reluctant to voice his concerns regarding the plans of his strong-willed junior partner to bypass Middle Tennessee in favor of invading Kentucky. Instead, Bragg meekly replied that it would be a week before his troops could commence crossing the Tennessee River, and that it would be "inadvisable" for Smith to move too deeply into Kentucky with Morgan in his rear. Smith, choosing to take Bragg's lack of outright disapproval as concurrence with his plan, felt that the time to strike had come.[99]

Under orders from Smith to keep a close watch on Morgan's movements and attack aggressively should he attempt to retreat, Carter Stevenson moved his division north from Tazewell on August 16. The Cherokee Artillery left their position at Walden's Ridge around 2 P.M. After more than a week of enforced boredom spent greasing cannon wheels, polishing weapons, and grousing about lethargic generals and tardy paymasters, the men rejoiced at once more being on the move. In the distance they could hear the occasional booming of Yankee cannon at Cumberland Gap, firing on the Confederate cavalry patrols sent to probe the Federal defenses. The Georgia gunners had hardly marched a mile, however, before they received orders to halt.[100]

The Confederates quickly began tightening the noose around Morgan and Cumberland Gap. By August 18, Carter Stevenson's division had invested Morgan's position on three sides, steadily moving closer to the Gap and throwing up breastworks as they went. To the north in Kentucky, Kirby Smith's troops had occupied London, Barboursville, and Cumberland Ford, cutting the Lexington Road. The Rebels now had Morgan surrounded.[101]

One detachment of the Cherokee Artillery, along with two or three infantry regiments, had now been posted at an important observation post at Baptist Gap. The rest of the battery had moved to the upper end of Powell's Valley, only three miles below Cumberland Gap,

---

[99] *OR*, ser. 1, vol. 16, part 2, 748; Horn, *Army of Tennessee*, 165–66.

[100] *OR*, ser. 1, vol. 28, part 2, 755; WOC, August 17, 1862; *TWC*, August 19, 1862.

[101] Connelly, *Army of the Heartland*, 212–13.

taking a position along the Jacksboro Road. Although they exhibited high spirits and seemed pleased with the "energetic administration" of their new captain, the Georgia gunners, like the rest of Stevenson's troops, had grown weary of the tedious job of keeping watch over the besieged Yankees. They longed to join the rest of Smith's army on its Kentucky adventure. It now appeared clear to the men that their generals had no intention of assaulting the heavily fortified Federal position but had determined to starve them out instead. And they suspected that the enemy commander would be in no hurry to either surrender or attempt to break out. Upon receiving a demand from Smith to capitulate, Morgan replied, "If you want this fortress, *come and take it.*"[102]

So, day after day, the Cherokee Artillery and their comrades idly waited, hoping that either their generals would relent and allow them to attack, or that the Yankees would finally grow hungry enough to give up the fight. "Occasionally, we are greeted by a shell or two from the enemy's 30-pounder Parrott guns," Connor noted in his diary, "and now and then our pickets [would] get up a skirmish by way of variety." In between these minor scrimmages with the enemy, many of the cannoneers took time for letter writing to loved ones and friends in Georgia and Alabama, and comments about army life and the ongoing siege found their way into the missives. J. J. Brisendine, writing to Sarah Caroline Turner, his sweetheart, recounted a typical day in the lives of the men of the Cherokee Artillery: "Miss Caroline I haven't got any news to write to you that would be interesting or worth caulling your attention to read all tho I will scribble down something[.] I haven't got any thing to write only war news and I am getting very tired of war news[.] we have a little fight nearly every day with the pickets[.] the Yankees has bin shelling on us yesterday and today[,] but hasent hurt embody [anybody] as I no we got several of the [enemy] chaps and

---

[102] *TWC*, September 4, 1862; *RC*, September 19, 1862; W. C. Davis, "Cumberland Gap, 1862," 28.

killed several[.] I think we will get them all for we have got them surrounded and I think they will hav to [soon] give up the ghost."[103]

As August slowly turned to September, the news from Kentucky seemed promising. Braxton Bragg and his 27,000-man army had finally taken the field, leaving Chattanooga on August 28 to take the fight to the Bluegrass State. Moving by way of the lush Glasgow region of Central Kentucky, Bragg planned to rendezvous with Kirby Smith. His stratagem had already reaped benefits by forcing Buell to abandon his efforts to take Chattanooga and follow the Rebels northward. Meanwhile, on August 30, Smith's Army of Kentucky had won a decisive victory over the bluecoats at Richmond, Kentucky, and two days later occupied the city of Lexington. Three days later, Smith's Confederates raised the Confederate banner over Frankfort, the state capital.

The news from the Cherokee Artillery's own front near Cumberland Gap seemed equally favorable. The siege, it appeared, had begun to take its toll on the beleaguered Federals. Cpl. David Newton, commander of one of the unit's six guns, described the effectiveness of the Confederate blockade in a letter to his sister, Mary, writing,

> We have now advanced on Cumberland Gap, the enemy is in the Gap, and we got a force on both sides of them, we have had them surrounded over two weeks. We get more or less prisoners every day. The Yankees have sent reinforcements to the Gap, or started them there, but our forces in Bend captures them as fast as they come. And those in the Gap are very near starved out. We captured one of them this morning, and he was the hungriest man I ever saw.[104]

The situation for Morgan's Yankees had become quite desperate. Efforts to draw the Confederates into a fight in front of Cumberland Gap had failed. By September 14, they had only ten days of food left, and that at half rations. Faced with the choice of either surrendering

---

[103] WOC, September 20, 1862; J. J. Brisendine to Miss S. C. Turner, August 21, 1862, Special Collections, Rome-Floyd County Library, Rome, GA. (We have preserved the original spelling but added punctuation for clarity.)

[104] Connelly, *Army of the Heartland*, 215–25; D. O. Newton to Mary [Ann] Elizabeth Newton, September 9, 1862, transcribed copy in Cherokee Artillery papers, book 1, Anderson collection, Rome, GA.

his troops or abandoning Cumberland Gap and attempting to escape northward, Morgan and his officers chose to evacuate. The Federals set explosives as booby traps along the road through Cumberland Gap and its nearby cliffs and then spiked the thirty-pounder Parrott guns that proved too large and heavy to take with them. After that, Morgan dispatched a long train of supply wagons to make a break for freedom on the night of September 16. The following night at 8 P.M., exactly three months after they occupied it, Morgan and his men began quietly slipping out of Cumberland Gap. They headed for Manchester, Kentucky, intent upon reaching the village of Greenup on the Ohio River. Early the next morning, after giving the main force several precious hours head start, the small detachment left behind exploded the mines, ignited the arsenal and other buildings, and scurried north to join their comrades.[105]

Stevenson and his men, alerted by the smoke and fire billowing upward in the early morning sky, quickly realized what had happened. Reoccupying Cumberland Gap on September 18, Stevenson alerted Confederate forces in the area of Morgan's escape and opined that their route would take them to either Manchester or Boonville, Kentucky. Leaving Hilliard's Legion, Palmer's Regiment, and a section of the Cherokee Artillery at the Gap as a rear guard, the Rebels set out in pursuit of Morgan's retreating army. The rugged Kentucky terrain made the chase a slow, tiresome endeavor for the infantry. The artillery found the race even more difficult than did the foot soldiers and cavalry. The wild, barren mountains proved to be a cannoneer's worst nightmare. The gunners of the Cherokee, Eufaula, Rhett, and Anderson batteries struggled to handle their heavy guns and caissons along the rocky, steep paths through the dense undergrowth. Men and horses suffered intensely from the scarcity of water brought on by the drought from which the region had been suffering for weeks.[106]

---

[105] Morgan, "Cumberland Gap," 68–69; W. C. Davis, "Cumberland Gap, 1862," 28; *OR*, ser. 1, vol. 16, part 1, 991.

[106] *OR*, ser. 1, vol. 16, part 2, 652; *OR*, ser. 1, vol. 28, part 1, 1010; WOC, September 18, 1862.

Finally, by the night of September 19, Stevenson's Division of the Confederate Army of Kentucky, by hard toil and perseverance, reached the banks of the Cumberland River, where the exhausted soldiers made camp for the night. Somewhere miles ahead, the weary Rebel gunners reasoned, Morgan and his retreating columns must be as tired and thirsty as they.

For the better part of a week, the slow chase continued. Morgan and his bedraggled Yankees, now dogged at every turn by both Stevenson's Division and John Hunt Morgan's Cavalry, staggered through Boonville and headed toward the Kentucky River. Then, on September 25, Smith sent Stevenson new orders. Move as quickly as possible to Harrodsburg and report to Gen. Bragg, who faced a new threat from the large Federal armies now concentrating at Louisville. Brig. Gen. Humphrey Marshall, moving toward Mount Sterling with his Rebel divisions from Western Virginia, would now deal with Morgan.[107]

Braxton Bragg once again fell victim to his own lack of resolve. After proposing to Kirby Smith that they join forces at Bardstown for a campaign to take Louisville—the key Federal supply depot for all of Kentucky—he had allowed his army to become bogged down in a needless, two-day siege of the Union garrison at Munfordville. Buell, whose forces had shadowed Bragg's army along a parallel track into Kentucky, took advantage of Bragg's distraction at Munfordville to outflank the Rebels and march into Louisville unmolested.[108]

Bragg, still committed to bringing the two Confederate armies together at Bardstown, sent a messenger to Smith on September 20, reiterating his determination to consolidate the two armies there. He also requested that the Florida general send a supply train to Bardstown with rations for Bragg's famished troops. Arriving in Bardstown three days later, Bragg found neither Smith nor the requested supply train.

[107] "Dedication of Bronze Tablet in Honor of the Botetourt Battery in Vicksburg National Park," 35 (hereafter cited as "Botetourt Battery"); *OR*, ser. 1, vol. 52, part 2, 365.

[108] Connelly, *Army of the Heartland*, 229–32; Seymour, *Divided Loyalties*, 69.

Instead, he discovered a communiqué from Smith reporting that he had, in fact, never left Lexington. Fearing the growing enemy strength at Louisville and not knowing the direction of Morgan's retreat from Cumberland Gap, Smith had opted to remain at Lexington. There he could protect the valuable stores and supplies he had captured at Richmond. Three days later Smith sent another missive stating that he had moved his entire command eastward to Mount Sterling in an effort to cut off George Morgan's retreat. Rather than reinforcing Bragg's army, he had now positioned his army 101 miles east of Bragg's location.[109]

Bragg, after considering his situation, concluded that he would abandon any hope of further offensive operations in the Bluegrass State. First, the Federal forces at Louisville continued to grow with the arrival of the armies of generals Ulysses S. Grant, George Rosecrans, and Samuel Curtis to bolster Buell. Second, the "cooperative" command structure had clearly failed. Obviously, Kirby Smith seemed determined to pursue his own objectives. Third, instead of rallying fresh troops for the Confederate cause, most Kentuckians seemed content to wait and see which cause prevailed before taking sides. Bragg's army, in fact, had not enlisted a single Kentuckian, while the Florida commander, by his own admission, had enlisted less than a single brigade of volunteers.[110]

Arriving in Lexington on October 2, Bragg proposed a new plan. Since Kentucky had been admitted to the Confederacy in 1861, he would install Richard Hawes as the Confederate governor of Kentucky, in Frankfort, replacing the former Rebel chief executive, George W. Johnson, who had died in the bloodbath at Shiloh. This would hopefully encourage volunteers to join the Rebel armies, as well as establish a legal basis for Confederate conscription. Meanwhile, the combined armies of Bragg and Smith would prepare a strong defensive line some-

---

[109] Connelly, *Army of the Heartland*, 234, 237; *OR*, ser. 1, vol. 16, part 2, 862, 873.

[110] Hess, *Banners to the Breeze*, 116–17; Connelly, *Army of the Heartland*, 234–40; *OR*, ser. 1, vol. 16, part 2, 876.

where east of Bardstown and west of the Kentucky River. Once situated in such a formidable position, any bluecoat soldiers venturing forth from Louisville would dash themselves against the Confederate defenses before being overwhelmed by a Confederate counterattack. Kentuckians across the state, Bragg believed, would then rise for the victorious Confederacy.[111]

On September 27, after an eighty-mile march "through a mountainous country infested with bushwhackers, bad water, and inhospitality," Stevenson's Division arrived at the foot of Big Hill, south of Richmond. Tired and thirsty from what seemed to be a statewide drought, the men welcomed a chance to fill their canteens and store water for cooking. The gunners of the Cherokee Artillery, like most other soldiers in the division, believed that they were either still pursuing George Morgan's retreating Federals, or that they would soon turn north to join Smith's army at Lexington.[112]

Much to their surprise, orders came telling them to turn westward toward Danville and to report to Bragg. As they tramped along the fine turnpike—a welcome respite from the rocky, narrow mountain roads—the men admired the lush, fertile countryside and the friendliness of the largely pro-Confederate civilians. Passing through Lancaster on September 28, they continued marching, finally arriving in the Danville area later that evening. The next day the officers allowed the men to wash in the nearby river, after which the entire division passed in review before Bragg.[113]

The following morning, Stevenson detached a small infantry brigade and some cavalry to keep watch over the supply depot at nearby Bryantsville. Meanwhile, Stevenson and the rest of graycoats marched the fifteen miles to Harrodsburg. The inhabitants of Harrodsburg, a pleasant town about the same size as Rome, Georgia, at the start of the

---

[111] Connelly, *Army of the Heartland*, 242–45; Hafendorfer, *Perryville*, 88–89.

[112] "Botetourt Battery," 36; *TWC*, November 4, 1862.

[113] "Botetourt Battery," 36; *TWC*, November 4, 1862.

war, treated the passing Rebels cordially. Unfortunately, Stevenson and his men had scant time to enjoy the local hospitality. Stevenson received new orders to immediately proceed to Frankfort. There his division would beef up Bragg's defensive line, designed to protect Central Kentucky from any Yankee incursions originating from Louisville.[114]

Accordingly, the division left Harrodsburg on the morning of October 1. Passing through Salvisa on their way northward, Stevenson's troops marched on to Lawrenceburg, where they encamped for the night. The next morning, Stevenson received reports that Buell's army, heavily reinforced, had left Louisville, and had begun a march toward Frankfort. Additionally, rumors persisted that Federal cavalry had arrived in the region guarded by Stevenson's Division. Ordering the unit's supply wagons to the rear to move by another route, Stevenson pushed his infantry and artillery forward as fast as they could march. Crossing the Kentucky River, they hastened on to Versailles, and after a forced march of fifteen more miles, Stevenson's foot-sore troops reached Frankfort on the evening of October 2. It had now been exactly two weeks since they had left Cumberland Gap.[115]

The Cherokee Artillery and the other Confederate soldiers enjoyed their time at Frankfort. Situated in the heart of the beautiful Bluegrass region, the city provided plenteous amounts of food for man and beast, and the citizens proved gracious and friendly. Even during their forced march, the enthusiastic welcome of the locals made their exertion bearable. One of Stevenson's men wrote, "Our march was an ovation. The people crowded the roadside. Ladies (and very pretty are the Kentucky ladies) waved flags, huzzahed, took us by the hand, pressed us to go home with them, called us their friends, deliverers, and sweethearts! Altogether, the march was relieved of much of its tedium. Never was an army in such glorious spirits!"[116]

The men's enjoyment of Frankfort did not last long. The afternoon of October 4 witnessed the installation of Richard Hawes as the

---

[114] *TWC*, October 28, 1862; *OR*, ser. 1, vol. 16, part 2, 882.

[115] "Botetourt Battery," 36; *TWC*, October 28, 1862.

[116] "Botetourt Battery," 36; *TWC*, October 28, 1862.

new Confederate governor. An impressive list of army notables attended, including Braxton Bragg, Kirby Smith, and Kentuckians John Breckinridge and William Preston. Despite the cold rain outside, the pro-Confederacy crowd inside the chamber applauded enthusiastically as Hawes delivered his inaugural address. As the chief executive's oration progressed, the booming of artillery began reverberating in the distance. Assuming the guns were firing in Hawes's honor, the crowd continued wildly cheering their new governor. A short time later, however, messengers arrived and began hurrying to Bragg and his generals. Word spread—slowly at first, then with increasing speed—and panic began to register on more and more faces in the crowd. Reports speedily circulated that Buell's massively reinforced Army of the Ohio would soon reach the capital.[117]

Braxton Bragg, aware that Buell's bluecoats had left Louisville on October 1, had chosen to delegate military matters to his subordinates while he focused on placing Hawes in office. Even word that Shelbyville, only twenty miles west of Frankfort, had fallen to Buell's troops had not been enough to distract Bragg from his gala event. Now, desperate to understand the situation, Bragg finally concluded that the bulk of his opponent's army had just arrived outside of Frankfort. To counter this move, Bragg began hastily trying to locate the various pieces of his far-flung army. He hoped to reunite them at Harrodsburg, and then turn north and give battle somewhere in the vicinity of Versailles. After dithering about where Smith should place his troops, Bragg finally concluded he should keep his division north of the Kentucky River. Bragg would proceed to Harrodsburg to await the arrival of Rebel major generals Leonidas Polk's and William Hardee's corps from Bardstown. Then he would move to Versailles and consolidate the various units of his army.[118]

Within hours of Hawes's inauguration, Carter Stevenson received orders to march his division to Versailles. Destroying the bridges over

[117] *TWC*, October 28, 1862; Hess, *Banners to the Breeze*, 82–83; Connelly, *Army of the Heartland*, 250–52.

[118] *TWC*, October 28, 1862; Connelly, *Army of the Heartland*, 250–52; Horn, *Army of Tennessee*, 177–79.

the Kentucky River as they left, Stevenson evacuated Frankfort that night. Arriving at Versailles with the rest of Stevenson's soldiers, the Cherokee Artillery made camp and excitedly began trying to make sense of recent events. In high spirits, the Georgia gunners and their compatriots in the Georgia infantry regiments encamped nearby eagerly awaited an opportunity to take on the enemy. As additional units arrived and the size of the army swelled in numbers, the men felt certain that they would soon have a magnificent opportunity to strike Buell's bluecoats a crippling blow. They had no doubt a major battle would soon occur.[119]

The Georgians guessed correctly. A major battle would soon transpire, but it would commence entirely by accident, and neither side would choose the time nor place for the engagement. As it turned out, both Buell and Bragg suffered from mutual confusion as to the actual whereabouts of the enemy. Bragg incorrectly assumed that the Federals had set their sights on Frankfort and that the bluecoats harassing Hardee and Polk amounted to nothing more than a diversionary action. Buell believed with equal certainty that Bragg's entire army had gone to ground in the Bardstown-Perryville area. Although neither side recognized it, a huge mismatch had occurred. Polk and Hardee, with only 16,000 Rebel soldiers between them, now faced three Federal army corps—nearly 60,000 troops—near Perryville. Meanwhile, Bragg had assembled almost 36,000 Confederates near Versailles to defend against a feint by Brig. Gen. Joshua Sill's lone Federal division of 12,000 men.[120]

Bragg, concerned that the Federals near Perryville would either strike his Bryantsville supply depot or delay the Confederate concentration at Versailles, ordered Leonidas Polk to eliminate the threat. The next morning, unable to determine whether Polk had complied with the directive, Bragg arrived near Perryville around 10 A.M. to personally take command. Deciding to strike the Federal left, Bragg sent Maj.

---

[119] *TWC*, October 28, 1862; *TWC*, November 4, 1862; Connelly, *Army of the Heartland*, 252–57.

[120] Connelly, *Army of the Heartland*, 254–58.

Gen. Benjamin Cheatham's division forward around 1:30 P.M., along with the additional brigades of Brig. Gen. Patton Anderson's and Brig. Gen. Simon Buckner's divisions. Slamming into Maj. Gen. Alexander McCook's Federal 1st corps, the hard-fighting Rebels pushed the Yankees back nearly a mile. The Battle of Perryville had begun.[121]

All afternoon and into the evening, the engagement raged without letup. The soldiers from both sides suffered from the nearly 100-degree heat and severe lack of water. Despite their small numbers, the Rebels had control of the field by nightfall, mostly due to the savagery of their attack and blunders committed by Buell and his corps commanders. The casualties on both sides bore terrible witness to the battle's ferocity. The Federals had suffered 4,211 casualties, including 845 killed. The Rebels, despite being on the offensive most of the day, suffered only 3,396 casualties, including 510 fatalities. Bragg's veterans had won the day.[122]

Instead of celebrating a victory, Bragg started making plans to retreat. The prolonged engagement, plus information obtained from Alexander McCook's captured papers and the intelligence garnered from hundreds of Union captives, convinced Bragg he faced the entire consolidated Army of the Ohio. The Confederate leader felt he had no choice but to fall back and try to combine his scattered forces. He proposed consolidating his troops at Harrodsburg.[123]

In the early morning hours of October 9, Polk's and Hardee's troops abandoned the field at Perryville and marched to Harrodsburg. The following day, most of Kirby Smith's army, including Rains's and Barton's brigades of Stevenson's Division, joined Polk's and Hardee's units. For the first time in the entire campaign, the two Rebel armies had united under Bragg's overall command.

---

[121] Ibid., 258–61; Hess, *Banners to the Breeze*, 104.

[122] Connelly, *Army of the Heartland*, 262–65; Horn, *Army of Tennessee*, 182–85; *OR*, ser. 1, vol. 16, part 1, 1087.

[123] Connelly, *Army of the Heartland*, 266–67; Horn, *Army of Tennessee*, 186–87; *OR*, ser. 1, vol. 16, part 1, 1087.

While Bragg and Smith conferred on what to do next, a message arrived that Buell's army had left Perryville, apparently planning to attack the Confederates at Harrodsburg. Smith deployed his brigades south of town. The Cherokee Artillery, still assigned to Rains's unit, took up a position in support of the Rebel infantry. Even in the driving rain, the sight of nearly all of Smith's army deployed in line of battle was, in the words of one of the gunners in Capt. Joseph W. Anderson's battery, "a very pretty sight." Like the rest of the army, the Floyd County cannoneers felt elated by the previous day's victory. The gunners confidently waited, ready for a fight to the finish with their enemy. Buell, however, declined to attack. Bragg, for his part, found every excuse in the book to not renew the offensive. He worried about being outflanked, cut off from his line of retreat, or losing his supply depot in Bryantsville. Instead, late that night, the graycoats began their march eastward toward Bryantsville. Crossing the Dick River, the army spent the night at nearby Camp Dick Robinson, recently renamed Camp Breckinridge in honor of Kentucky's former vice president of the United States and present Confederate general.[124]

For the next two days, Bragg's army and supply trains arrived piecemeal at Camp Breckinridge, a strong defensive position at the junction of the Dick and Kentucky Rivers. The Cherokee Artillery, in buoyant spirits, prepared for one last decisive battle with Buell's Federals. The *Rome Tri-Weekly Courier* correspondent, traveling with Van Den Corput's Company, summed up the prevailing mood of his comrades, writing,

> For a number of days our troops and transportation were concentrating at Camp Breckinridge, and it was presumed that here the final stand would be made and that the decisive battle would be fought in the vicinity. Gen. Bragg had, probably, 70,000 or 80,000 men, who were in the highest spirits, and had conjectured that our series

[124] Connelly, *Army of the Heartland*, 266–67; Horn, *Army of Tennessee*, 186–87; *OR*, ser. 1, vol. 16, part 1, 1087.

> of backward movements were merely made to draw the enemy as far away from Louisville as possible, and then to offer battle.[125]

Bragg and his generals, however, lacked the optimism of their soldiers. They reasoned that army had only four days' rations left. To make matters worse, the autumn rains would surely come soon and would make the road through Cumberland Gap impassable to wagons and artillery. Finally, intelligence reached Bragg that Buell had begun swinging even farther south to outflank the Confederates and close the route to the Gap. Bragg's corps commanders all agreed. They had no option but to retreat.[126]

Early the next morning, October 13, the Rebel army began its slow, arduous withdrawal toward East Tennessee. In the words of historian Stanley Horn, the retreat appeared "a dismal but picturesque affair." A screen of cavalry led the way, followed by immense herds of cattle, sheep, and hogs, and the hundreds of wagonloads of supplies captured by Kirby Smith at Richmond. Behind the wagons marched the infantry brigades and artillery. Behind them trailed more horsemen serving as the rear guard. Arriving at Lancaster, the army split into two columns. Leonidas Polk would lead the Army of Mississippi to the right, toward Crab Orchard, while Smith's Corps would take the more circuitous route to the left and retrace its steps back toward Big Hill. Once near London, each column would then turn southeast toward Barboursville and enter Tennessee through the Cumberland Gap.[127]

Several days and nights of struggling to drag their cannon and equipment up and down the same steep, miserable roads that had proven so treacherous during the march into Kentucky left the gunners of the Cherokee Artillery completely exhausted. The rest of Carter Stevenson's worn-out troops, fast reaching the limits of human endurance, staggered and floundered along the same road. As the starving

---

[125] *TWC*, November 4, 1862; Hammond, "General Kirby Smith's Campaign in Kentucky," 72. According to Hammond, Bragg's army actually numbered only about 47,700 men present for duty.

[126] Connelly, *Army of the Heartland*, 279.

[127] *TWC*, November 4, 1862; Connelly, *Army of the Heartland*, 280; Horn, *Army of Tennessee*, 188–89.

mules began giving out, the men had no choice but to lift the loaded wagons by brute strength over the worst parts of the byways. Adding to their miseries, they also had to keep a sharp eye out for the increasingly aggressive Unionist bushwhackers who had begun preying on anyone who straggled. At one point, Smith requested that Polk protect the rear of his slow-moving columns, averring that he had never before seen worse roads. The going became so difficult, and his men so exhausted, that he fully expected to lose all of his captured supply wagons and most of his artillery to Buell's pursuing army. Fortunately, however, the commander of the Army of the Ohio conducted only a half-hearted pursuit of the Rebel armies and ceased altogether once Smith's troops passed London.[128]

Hungry, tired, and dispirited, the advance elements of Bragg's army reached Cumberland Gap on October 19. Wesley Connor, who had been left behind to command one of the Cherokee Artillery's guns at the Gap, captured the scene of the return in his diary: "Bragg's army, dusty, footsore, and hungry has been passing for several days," he wrote, "retreating from Kentucky. He brings out a considerable amount of jeans, beef cattle, horses, and mules, but will it satisfy the expectations of the people?" Two days later Kirby Smith and his Army of Kentucky, nearly dying of hunger, also began arriving at the Gap.[129]

The great Confederate expedition to liberate Kentucky had finally ended. The campaign, which had begun with so much early promise with the victory at Richmond, had deteriorated into a series of missed opportunities and poor command decisions. Neither of the Rebel commanders had provided the leadership crucial for success. Braxton Bragg, in his official report, put the best possible face on the operation, pointing out his successes but ignoring the bigger picture:

> With a force enabling us at no time to put more than 40,000 men of all arms and in all places in battle we had redeemed North Alabama and Middle Tennessee and recovered Cumberland Gap, the gateway to the heart of the Confederacy. We had killed, wounded,

---

[128] *OR*, ser. 1, vol. 16, part 2, 967, 949; Hammond, "Kirby Smith's Campaign in Kentucky," 75.

[129] WOC, October 23, 1862.

> and captured no less than 25,000 of the enemy; taken over 30 pieces of artillery; 17,000 small-arms, some 2,000,000 cartridges for the same; destroyed some hundreds of wagons and brought off several hundreds more with their teams and harness complete; replaced our jaded horses by a fine mount; lived two months upon supplies wrested from the enemy's possession; secured material to clothe the army, and finally secured subsistence from the redeemed country to support not only the army but also a large force of the Confederacy to the present time.[130]

Despite those supposed benefits, two unavoidable truths remained. First, Kentucky still remained in Union hands, and they could use the Bluegrass state as a base from which to threaten the Confederate heartland. Second, the people of Kentucky, despite having exhibited a certain amount of polite support for the Confederacy in some regions, had not risen *en masse* against their Federal oppressors. Judged against its primary objectives—creating a Confederate Kentucky and enlisting a large number of Bluegrass state residents into the Rebel army—the campaign had been a dismal failure.

After five weeks and over 400 miles of hard marching, the Cherokee Artillery had come full circle, returning to the steep cliffs and hills of Cumberland Gap. Dog tired, hungry, and disappointed, the men openly questioned why the army had gone into Kentucky at all. From their vantage point, it appeared that the entire campaign had been a series of missed opportunities, culminating in the failure to take the fight to the enemy. Worse yet had been the betrayal of those Kentuckians who had openly supported the Confederacy.[131]

The reunited Georgia battery did not remain long at Cumberland Gap. By October 25, they had crossed both the Powell and Clinch Rivers and arrived at Bean's Station. After a brief rest, the Georgia gunners marched back to the foot of Clinch Mountain where they made

---

130 *OR*, ser. 1, vol. 16, part 1, 1088.

131 *TWC*, November 4, 1862.

camp. An early snowstorm arrived the next day, dumping eight inches of snow on the artillerymen and, to their delight, the still-green trees.[132]

Two days later Van Den Corput's Battery and the rest of the brigade marched down the snow-covered Knoxville Road toward McMillan's Station. The cannoneers expected to stay there a while, resting and refitting from the long campaign. Marching through the snow, the gunners could not help noticing the number of barefoot soldiers among the infantry. "It is a disgrace to the officers of the army to have so much suffering in the ranks when there is evidently no necessity for it," an indignant Wesley Connor penned. "Pure neglect, on their part causes it all."[133]

Two days later, on October 29, the Cherokee Artillery and the rest of Rains's Brigade reached McMillan Station. Much to their disappointment, new orders arrived only a few hours after reaching their destination. The new directive instructed the company to leave the following morning and march to Lenoir, about seventeen miles below Knoxville on the East Tennessee & Georgia rail line. From there they would board a train bound for Murfreesboro, Tennessee, only thirty miles south of Nashville. Hitting the road the next morning, the Georgia gunners marched through Knoxville and finally reached Lenoir. There they found several brigades and their old comrades of the 3rd Georgia Battalion already encamped.[134]

Finally, a long-awaited chance to rest from six straight weeks of marching had arrived. For the next two weeks, the men of Carter Stevenson's division spent their time refitting and reorganizing. The army paymasters finally arrived, paying the men six months of back wages, and the quartermasters issued the soldiers new tents and clothing. The common soldiers experienced a growing expectation that a campaign would soon begin in Middle Tennessee, as Braxton Bragg's army had been passing by on its way to Murfreesboro for the last several days. Bragg, despite his earlier failures in Kentucky, now had command of

[132] WOC, October 25, 1862.
[133] WOC, October 27, 1862.
[134] *RC*, November 13, 1862.

the Rebel troops in Middle Tennessee with authority to borrow troops from Kirby Smith's Department of East Tennessee as he saw fit.[135]

Several notable events occurred while the Cherokee Artillery waited at Lenoir's Station. The War Department promoted Smith to the rank of lieutenant general and Carter Stevenson to the rank of major general. Colonels Rains and Taylor were both bumped up in rank to brigadier general. In addition, the high command in Richmond reassigned Van Den Corput's Battery from Rains's unit to Thomas Taylor's all-Georgian brigade.

The return of Sgt. Wilson Hammill brought a rare period of rejoicing for the Cherokee Artillery. Van Den Corput had earlier dispatched Hammill to Rome to collect winter clothing and shoes for the battery. He arrived in camp on November 7, accompanied by an entire train car loaded with donations from the concerned citizens back home. The thoughtful gifts and the knowledge that their loved ones in Rome had not forgotten them did much to raise the spirits of the grateful gunners. Although Hammill had tried to limit the gifts solely to footwear and garments due to the limited space, the people of Floyd County paid no attention to him. Intermingled among the boxes of necessities, the gunners found boxes containing everything from butter to sweet potatoes to tobacco. One gunner, William Baker, felt so certain that two bottles labeled "black ink" really contained whiskey that he insisted on sampling the contents of both jars. Unfortunately for Baker, the labels had not lied. Despite his blackened teeth, the comforter his sister had sent allowed him to sleep better than he had in a long time. He apparently used the ink to compose a letter thanking his sibling for her kindness.[136]

---

135 Ibid.; WOC, November 2, 1862.

136 *OR*, ser. 1, vol. 16, part 2, 984; *RC*, November 20, 1862 and October 23, 1862; W. H. Baker to Mrs. T. E. Roberts, November 8, 1862, Baker collection, KMNBP.

Kirby Smith had been under increasing pressure from Richmond to cooperate with Bragg in his planned Middle Tennessee offensive. Despite his misgivings about the dour North Carolinian's leadership, Smith reluctantly committed a corps, comprising brigades from Stevenson's and Maj. Gen. John Porter McCown's divisions, to the effort. Smith ordered Stevenson to send his wagons and artillery to Winchester, Tennessee, as soon as the batteries had been supplied with new horses to replace the ones lost or lamed during the Kentucky Campaign. There, they would supposedly rendezvous with the division's infantry, who had the good fortune of traveling by rail to their destination. The Cherokee Artillery, along with the Eufaula Artillery, left Lenoir Station on November 16, arriving late that afternoon in London after a march of eight miles.[137]

For the next five days, the artillery and wagons wended their way slowly to the southwest along the Chattanooga Road, finally reaching Tennessee's Gateway City on November 21. The following day the column marched to Kelley's Ferry, west of Chattanooga, intending to cross the Tennessee River. Connor noted that getting the six miles of wagons across the wide waterway took a long time. Fortunately, someone in the battery located a large quantity of whiskey, and, despite its being the Lord's Day, the gunners passed the day imbibing strong spirits. "Plenty of whiskey on hand," Connor wrote in his journal. "Most of the men got bricks in their hats."

Crossing the river took two days, but on November 25, the column marched another twelve miles, passing through the town of Jasper, the last stop before ascending the forbidding Cumberland Mountains. (Connor described Jasper as "Decidedly the hardest place I have ever seen.") The Cumberland range was fourteen miles wide at this point, and the gap through the heights proved every bit as torturous and miserable as anything they encountered on the retreat from Kentucky. In places, the path became so steep the artillerymen had to hitch as many as fourteen horses to each gun carriage just to move them. At

---

[137] *OR*, ser. 1, vol. 20, part 2, 396; *OR*, ser. 1, vol. 16, part 2, 984; *RC*, November 25, 1862; WOC, November 15–16, 1862.

one stretch of the journey, they managed to advance only four miles while struggling sixteen hours in wind-driven snow.[138]

Exhausted, cold, and hungry, the column finally marched into Winchester around 4 P.M. on Thursday, November 27, only to learn that the division's three infantry brigades had just been ordered to advance to Manchester, some twenty-six miles to the north. There, Smith's Corps had taken its position as the right wing of the newly named Army of Tennessee. The next morning the artillery column made their way through the hardscrabble countryside known locally as "The Barrens." At the pleasant little town of Manchester, they reunited that evening with the rest of Stevenson's Division.[139]

It appeared obvious to the soldiers that the battle for control of Middle Tennessee would soon begin. Rumors spread through the graycoats' camp that the Federals, now under the command of Gen. William Rosecrans, had crossed the Cumberland River and that skirmishing had already started east of Nashville. About a week later, Stevenson's men left Manchester, and the Cherokee Artillery plodded north some thirty miles to Readyville, a hamlet on the banks of Stones River and fifteen miles from Murfreesboro. The village, strategically situated on the turnpike between Murfreesboro and McMinnville, allowed Van Den Corput's unit to respond rapidly to any Union advance.[140]

The Georgia cannoneers set up their camp two miles east of the village. The Cherokee Artillery liked their new location. Though firewood proved somewhat scarce, they had plenty of clean water. President Jefferson Davis—known to the men as "Uncle Jeff"—reviewed Bragg's troops at Murfreesboro on December 13 and delivered a rousing speech asserting that his Rebels would not only take Nashville but redeem Kentucky as well. The Cherokee Artillery eagerly expected Davis to visit their camp, but the Confederate president failed to show.

---

[138] WOC, November 25 and 27, 1862; "Botetourt Battery," 37.

[139] WOC, November 28, 1862; *OR*, ser. 1, vol. 20, part 2, 411; *RC*, November 25, 1862.

[140] *RC*, December 26, 1862; WOC, December 7, 1862.

The pressures of his office caused him to return to Chattanooga on December 15, without ever making an appearance among Kirby Smith's troops.[141]

On December 18, new orders arrived with far greater import and lasting impact on the lives of the Cherokee Artillery than a politician's speech. Carter Stevenson's division would prepare to leave immediately for Mississippi to reinforce Lt. Gen. John Pemberton's Army of Vicksburg. Two days later, the Cherokee Artillery left camp, bound for Murfreesboro. There they would board a train for the long trip to the Magnolia State. It had been almost a year since the Cherokee Artillery had first arrived in Tennessee. Since then, they had been almost continuously on duty and had proven their mettle as soldiers on the battlefield. No longer raw troops, they had demonstrated the courage, skill, proficiency, and sheer grit that would one day make them, in the words of Confederate historian Joseph T. Derry, "one of the famous batteries of the Western Army."[142]

---

[141] *OR*, ser. 1, vol. 20, part 2, 449; WOC, December 10 and 15, 1862.

[142] WOC, December 20, 1862; *OR*, ser. 1, vol. 20, part 2, 453; Derry, *Georgia*, 145.

Chapter 3

"Another Display of Bad Generalship"

The Vicksburg Campaign (January–July 1863)

The Cherokee Artillery left Readyville and arrived at Murfreesboro, Tennessee, on Sunday, December 21, 1862. The battery established its camp two miles south of town near a large spring and the frame meetinghouse of the New Hope Baptist Church. The Union army occupied Nashville, twenty-eight miles to the north. Braxton Bragg, with his headquarters at Murfreesboro, had his army arrayed in a thirty-mile arc running from Triune and Eagleville on the left and to Readyville on the right. From this position, he could watch the enemy's movements and rapidly concentrate his forces wherever needed.[1]

Some of the Georgia artillerymen took the opportunity to visit Murfreesboro. After spending the previous year among the Unionists in the bleak mountains of East Tennessee, the gaiety of the Christmas season as celebrated by the loyal Southern citizens of Middle Tennessee lifted their spirits. The holiday in that region included the traditional doings of a Southern Christmas including horse racing, card playing, and other pleasant seasonal activities. The scene, however, had an opposite effect on Wesley O. Connor. In a melancholy mood, he wrote,

> Christmas Day! What hallowed associations come crowding upon us when this day rolls around. Visions of days long gone, when with candies, fire-poppers, rockets, we all were turned loose in search of fun. Those were bright spots in life's wastes which come but seldom, and are soon—to us, *gone forever*. Nonetheless, it is pleasant at times to recall the past, and reflect upon enjoyments *we had*.[2]

The business of war soon dispelled these dreary musings as the Cherokee Artillery prepared for the journey to Vicksburg, Mississippi.

---

[1] WOC, December 21 and 25, 1862; Horn, *Army of Tennessee*, 195.

[2] WOC, December 25, 1862; Horn, *Army of Tennessee*, 195.

The Georgia cannoneers spent the night loading railroad cars with their guns, horses, and baggage and the other accouterments necessary for the artillery service. Due to the deficiencies of the Southern rail system, the trip, with stopovers, would take twenty-nine days and cover a distance of 850 miles, almost doubling the actual distance between Middle Tennessee and Vicksburg. Van Den Corput's men bitterly complained about the Confederacy's transportation problems because each change to a new rail line necessitated unloading and then reloading their animals and equipment onto a new set of freight cars.

The unit also left one soldier, John W. Bowling, sick in the military hospital at Murfreesboro. Bowling soon "recovered" enough to slip through Union lines and sign the oath of allegiance, becoming the first known member of the Cherokee Artillery to desert to the enemy.[3]

Van Den Corput's Battery departed Murfreesboro at 7 A.M. on December 26. The unit boarded the Nashville & Chattanooga Railroad for the first leg of their journey. The men rested overnight at Chattanooga, before switching their equipment to the boxcars of the Western & Atlantic line for the short trip to Dalton, Georgia. On the morning of December 28, the Georgians left Dalton for the seventy-six-mile journey to Atlanta. The Floyd County company expressed keen disappointment because a large number of their friends and relatives had gathered at Kingston for a quick visit, but the engineer never even slowed down at the little depot.

From Atlanta, they clattered westward on the Atlanta & West Point Railroad to West Point, Georgia, a major rail hub on the Chattahoochee River near the Georgia-Alabama border. The artillerymen crossed into Alabama the next morning aboard a Montgomery & West Point train, arriving at the state capital on New Year's Eve. The highlight of this leg of the journey came during a brief rest stop at Opelika, Alabama. Connor noted: "[I] fell in love with the girls of Alabama,

---

[3] R. C. Black, *Railroads of the Confederacy*, 1–10 (esp. map on p. 5). Travel dates and routes are from the WOC, December 1862–January 1863; J. W. Bowling, Confederate Service Records, Georgia; Record Group 109, vol. 10911, National Archives, Washington, D.C.

especially those of Opelika. They gave us an abundance of potatoes, chickens etc.…Long may they live (to feed soldiers) and [may] Heaven's choicest blessings rest upon them."[4]

After a two-day hiatus at Montgomery, the artillerymen headed south on January 2, 1863, to the tiny hamlet of Pollard aboard the Alabama & Florida Railroad. Early in the war, the Confederacy had established a camp at Pollard, just north of the Florida state line. This allowed the Rebels to deal with Federal raids and foraging expeditions originating from Union-occupied Fort Pickens, near Pensacola. With nothing more than a ramshackle depot and three or four shacks scattered through the pines and wiregrass, it must have been the least memorable stopover of their journey.

The next morning, Van Den Corput's men rode about thirty miles on the Mobile & Great Northern Railroad to Mobile, Alabama. After reloading their gear onto the Mobile & Ohio rail cars, the Georgians tarried at Mobile three days and nights and enjoyed sightseeing in one of the South's larger cities. The first afternoon, the Georgia cannoneers visited the waterfront, noting that a blockade-runner had just arrived from Cuba with its cargo of arms, ammunition, salt, and dry goods. Later, four or five of the Floyd County troops rented a rowboat and went for a moonlight ride on Mobile Bay. Connor, the perpetually lovelorn bachelor, mused, "Had I had my dear and a guitar along, instead of these great rough soldiers…[the outing would have] transported me to an imaginary Paradise."[5]

On January 3, 1863, the unit headed northwest to Meridian, a village of about 700 residents in east-central Mississippi. The men stayed there overnight before continuing their journey to Jackson on the Southern Railroad of Mississippi. Settlers had founded Jackson in 1821 as a trading post along the west bank of the Pearl River, deep in the hills of the Choctaw Nation. The town had a pre-war population of about 3,000. Van Den Corput's men remained in the capital of the

---

[4] R. C. Black, *Railroads of the Confederacy*, 1–10; WOC, December 26, 1862 to January 6, 1863.

[5] R. C. Black, *Railroads of the Confederacy*, 1–10; WOC, January 2, 1863.

Magnolia State for three weeks before finally moving to Vicksburg, the great Confederate citadel along the Mississippi River.[6]

The Georgians established their encampment about a mile and a half from downtown Jackson, and the unit's life quickly settled into a now-familiar camp routine. Two topics always dominated the conversation of Rebel soldiers: the Confederacy's political and military situation, and wild conjectures regarding their next destination. As yet, there had been little in the way of a threat against Jackson, and rumors, great and small, circulated with the speed of a wildfire. William H. Baker reported, "There is a great talk of peace here now and many who did not believe that there would be any intervention by European Nations now say they think it will take place and they think we will have peace this spring....Papers are eagerly sought for and everything on the question eagerly read." The Floyd County artillerymen apparently thought the stop at Vicksburg would only be a temporary layover, and the soldiers' opinions regarding their next destination were split about equally among adherents for Corinth, Vicksburg, and Mobile. Rumors of a transfer to Texas also found some supporters, though all of the men in the Cherokee Artillery hoped that the army would not send them to the distant Lone Star State.[7]

Concerns regarding food also dominated the thoughts of Civil War soldiers, whether clad in blue or gray. Baker told his sister, "We get nothing but beef in the way of meat and the poorest beef I ever saw....I don't think you could get a thimble full of taller [tallow] off a single pot full." They ate red meat only once a day, however, and drank "sassafras tea and bread for supper and breakfast." Little did they realize that within six months they would view any daily ration containing meat and bread as a gift from heaven.[8]

The terrain in central Mississippi differed greatly from the hills and mountains of Floyd County, and many of the Georgians did not

---

[6] R. C. Black, *Railroads of the Confederacy*, 1–10; WOC, January 6–25, 1863 U.S. 1860 Census (Mississippi).

[7] W. H. Baker to Mrs. T. E. Roberts, January 1863, Baker collection, KMNBP.

[8] Ibid.

like the topography of the region very much. Baker spoke for most when he wrote, "[T]his portion [of the state] is not a very desirable looking portion at all....[I]t is too low in wet weather and there is to[o] much mud....It is nearly all swamps of magnolia and evergreens....I would not give Georgia for any state that I have seen yet."[9]

In addition to those complaints, the citizens of Jackson did little to endear themselves to the common soldiers defending their town. One Georgia graycoat carped, "We are not allowed to go to Jackson unless on Business and the citizens [recently] took a vote and come [came] within one vote of voting the private off the pavements; if they had carried it, they would have made us privates walk in the streets in the mud. This will show you what the people of Jackson think of us." The Cherokee Artillery shed no tears when, in late January, orders arrived directing them to head to Vicksburg.[10]

Union leadership had been fixated upon taking control of the Mississippi River since the beginning of the war. Northern forces quickly took possession of all of the major cities along "The Father of Waters," including New Orleans and Memphis, but Vicksburg and a few nearby strongholds still remained in Confederate hands. The Lincoln administration found that situation totally unacceptable. During the first year of the war, Lincoln had lectured Com. David Dixon Porter regarding the importance of the "Confederate Gibraltar." "We can take all the northern ports of the Confederacy," the chief executive explained, "and they can defy us from Vicksburg. It means hog and hominy without limit, fresh troops from all the states of the far South, and a cotton country where they raise the staple without interference." Confederate president Jefferson Davis concurred with Lincoln's assessment. The

---

[9] Ibid.

[10] W. H. Baker to "Dear Sister Tempy," January 1862[3], Baker collection, KMNBP.

Southern president had called the Bluff City "the nail head that held the South's two halves together."[11]

The first Yankee attempt to take Vicksburg occurred on May 18, 1862. Ships from the West Gulf Blockading Squadron arrived below the Bluff City, intending, with a show of force, to cow the Rebel defenders into capitulating. Post commander Lt. Col. James L. Autry rejected the demand to give up, snapping, "Mississippians don't know, and refuse to learn, how to surrender to an enemy." During their initial campaigns, Yankee gunboats intermittently bombarded the city's shore batteries for more than a month but failed to drive the Rebels from their bastion. As a result, Union political and military leaders concluded that taking the Confederate Gibraltar would require a large, coordinated operation using both land and naval assault forces. Lincoln quickly named Maj. Gen. Ulysses S. Grant, a hero of the Battle of Shiloh, to command Federal land operations along the Mississippi River. David Porter would direct the naval contingent.[12]

The Rebels wasted no time in turning the hilltop city into a proper citadel. In late July 1862, Confederate authorities charged Maj. Samuel H. Lockett with the responsibility for strengthening Vicksburg's defenses. An Alabama native and 1859 graduate of West Point, Lockett's official title was chief engineer of the Department of Mississippi and East Louisiana. The young engineer set out to make the bluffs and terrain surrounding Vicksburg as impregnable as possible. "Vicksburg was a natural fortress," historian Terrence J. Winschel reports,

> that he [Lockett] planned to make even stronger with the construction of field fortifications. The line as constructed consisted of nine major forts...made of earth and logs and connected by a continuous line of trenches and rifle pits. The line was more than eight miles in length and formed a huge semi-circle around Vicksburg, the flanks of which rested on the river above and below the city.

---

[11] Porter, *Incidents and Anecdotes of the Civil War*, 95–96; Winschel, *Confederate Gibraltar*, 13–16.

[12] Ballard, *Civil War in Mississippi*, 34–46; Winschel, *Confederate Gibraltar*, 13–22.

Almost 200 mounted artillery guns added firepower to the Rebel defenders' single shot rifles and muskets.[13]

By the time the Cherokee Artillery arrived at Vicksburg on January 26, 1863, Gen. Grant's initial attempts to capture the Confederate Gibraltar had ended in failure and frustration. In late December 1862, Grant commanded an army numbering almost 50,000 men strung out between Memphis, Tennessee, and Iuka, Mississippi. His opponent, Lt. Gen. John C. Pemberton, northern-born and with Quaker forebears, came north from Vicksburg with a Rebel infantry force of fewer than 20,000 men to confront the invaders. While the two armies jockeyed for position, Maj. Gen. Earl Van Dorn, a vain, flamboyant officer who had previously commanded the Confederate armies at the disastrous defeats at Pea Ridge and Corinth, led a Southern cavalry force behind Union lines, destroying Grant's primary supply depot at Holly Springs. Simultaneously, Brig. Gen. Nathan Bedford Forrest's horsemen conducted a series of raids on the Mobile & Ohio Railroad in West Tennessee. Forrest's depredations crippled the Union's ability to provision Grant's army with food, ammunition, and equipment unless the bluecoats resorted to slow and vulnerable wagon and animal transport. With his capability to feed and equip his troops compromised, Grant retreated back to Union-occupied Memphis.[14]

The second prong of Grant's initial attempt to capture Vicksburg fared even worse. Maj. Gen. William T. Sherman came south, using naval transport ships, with an army of 32,000, landing just north of the fortress city along the Yazoo River. The original Federal plan called for Grant to lure Pemberton away from the fortress city and keep him occupied north of Grenada. Meanwhile, Sherman's men would slip through the back door to take the lightly defended bastion. News of Grant's retreat finally reached Sherman several days after the fact, but Sherman determined not to leave without giving the entrenched Rebels a fight. Using particularly cold-blooded logic, Sherman announced, "We will lose 5,000 men before we take Vicksburg, and [we] may as

---

[13] Winschel, *Confederate Gibraltar*, 21–22.

[14] Ibid., 23–29; Arnold, *Grant Wins the War*, 23–46.

well lose them here as anywhere else." He ordered his troops forward against the Rebel fortifications, sustaining almost 1,800 casualties at Chickasaw Bayou and Walnut Hills. Combined Rebel losses during those engagements amounted to fewer than 200 soldiers.[15]

The one bright spot in the Union's early campaigns to occupy Vicksburg occurred on January 11, 1863, when a large force of Federals under Maj. Gen. John McClernand took the Rebel installation at Arkansas Post. That fortress had allowed Confederate vessels to slip down the Arkansas River, attack Federal boats in the Mississippi, and then retreat to the safety of the cannon at Arkansas Post. Grant likely viewed that success as a mixed blessing. Halting Rebel raids along the Mississippi certainly helped the Union cause; but McClernand, an Illinois politician and friend of Lincoln, had been lobbying to replace Grant as commander of the army operating against Vicksburg.[16]

A detachment of artillery from Van Den Corput's Battery would play an important role in foiling the next Yankee stratagem to take Vicksburg. About 175 miles north of Vicksburg, on the east bank of the Mississippi, lay a swampy labyrinth—a complex system of sluggish creeks, bayous, backwaters, and sloughs—that might have deterred a commander less bold and stubborn than Ulysses S. Grant. Where others saw insurmountable obstacles, the Union leader saw opportunity. Local collaborators informed Union officers that river steamers had used these waterways before the war to collect cotton bales from the plantations scattered throughout this fertile region. By blowing a gap in the levee along the Mississippi that protected the prime farmlands throughout the delta, Federal sailors and soldiers could proceed by ship through the Yazoo Pass and along a series of intersecting rivers to the Yazoo River just south of Greenwood. "A successful ascent via this

---

[15] Arnold, *Grant Wins the War*, 36–37; Lee, "The Campaigns of Generals Grant and Sherman," 15–36; Morgan, "The Assault on Chickasaw Bluffs," 467.

[16] Arnold, *Grant Wins the War*, 43–45; and see generally, Richard L. Kiper, *Major General John Alexander McClernand: Politician in Uniform* (Kent, OH: Kent State University Press, 1999).

route by Union forces," historian Michael Ballard stated, "would outflank Pemberton's position on the Snyder's Bluff heights overlooking the Yazoo northeast of Vicksburg."[17]

Union engineers blew the levee on February 3, unleashing a flood of near-biblical proportions throughout northwestern Mississippi. Shortly thereafter, gunboats and transports loaded with Federal infantry and sailors began a winding, month-long trip through the swamps toward Greenwood. Not only did the shallow, narrow waterways slow the flotilla's progress, but the Rebels also did everything in their power to delay the enemy fleet, including cutting thick trees to block passage through the bayou. It took two weeks for the Federals to reach the Coldwater River, but despite the Confederate's best efforts, the Union vessels continued their slow crawl through the swampy morass.[18]

A few days after the Yankees blew the levee, news of the new Union campaign reached Pemberton. At first, he considered the operation either a mistake or a massive diversion. A closer examination, however, revealed that the enemy just might be able to outflank the Rebel's outer defenses if they reached the Yazoo River. In response, Pemberton sent Maj. Gen. William Wing Loring to block the Yankee expedition. Loring took 2,000 infantrymen and eight cannon to the fortress his men had constructed near the confluence of the Tallahatchie and Yalobusha Rivers. (The convergence of the two rivers formed the Yazoo River.) The Rebels erected a bastion, which they called Fort Pemberton, using mud and cotton bales near the mouth of the Yazoo. To further strengthen the position, "large rafts were sunk in the Tallahatchie River, and the historic *Star of the West* [recently captured by Southern forces] was there scuttled and sank across the channel of the river." The Rebels completed the construction of Fort Pemberton during the first week of March.[19]

---

[17] Ballard, *Civil War in Mississippi*, 131–38; Woodworth, *Nothing but Victory*, 301–14.

[18] Ballard, *Civil War in Mississippi*, 131–38; Woodworth, *Nothing but Victory*, 301–14.

[19] Ballard, *Civil War in Mississippi*, 131–38; Woodworth, *Nothing but Victory*, 301–14; "Relics of War Times," *New Orleans Times-Picayune*, October 21, 1887, 7.

Various units provided artillery support for Fort Pemberton. Capt. W. L. Ritter, a Maryland cannoneer, recalled,

> The battery was composed as follows: two guns from Captain [Hiram Miller, Jr.] Bledsoe's Missouri artillery, commanded by Lieutenant [H. W.] Anderson; two guns from a Louisiana unit commanded by a Lieutenant [?] Cottenham; one gun of the Maryland Artillery, commanded by Sergeant Daniel Toomey; one gun from Captain Corput's Georgia Battery, commanded by Sergeant [Eber] Mitchell Johnston, which two latter pieces were commanded by Lieutenant T. J.[Jefferson] Bates, of [Captain James F.] Waddell's Alabama artillery. These six pieces were commanded by Lieutenant R. L. Wood, of Bledsoe's Missouri artillery.

Two larger siege guns completed the fort's armament. The detachment from the Cherokee Artillery also included "Privates W. J. [likely William Greene] Bennett, W. [William] C. Coney [or Couey], A. J. Dempsey, Thos. Griffin, J. [John] O. Henderson, E. N. [Eleazor Newton] McCurry, J. F. [or V.] Russell, R. [Robert] P. Scott, F. [Freeman] Wood." Cpl. McCurry served as Johnston's second-in-command. Van Den Corput's detachment took the three-inch rifled cannon cast at the Noble Brothers Foundry in Rome. Additionally, Lt. Col. Samuel W. Ferguson commanded the infantry (primarily Texans) along the Yazoo and a small troop of Mississippi cavalry.[20]

On March 11, the Federal fleet came within range of the Rebel fortress. Due to the narrowness of the Tallahatchie and the obstruction planted in the channel, only two boats at a time could attack Fort Pemberton. A reporter for a Northern journal described the situation: "Here at a sharp bend in the river, Fort Pemberton was erected. While the fort was hurriedly constructed and was nothing to boast of as a work of strength, its location and the nature of the ground on all sides, made it impregnable, and brought disaster to Grant's scheme."[21]

The U.S. naval ships *Chillicothe* and *Baron De Kalb* led the first assault on the stronghold. *Chillicothe*, an ironclad, drew fire while still

---

[20] Ballard, *Civil War in Mississippi*, 131–38; Ritter, "An Incident of the Deer Creek Expedition of 1863," 280–81; "From Mississippi," *RC*, August 7, 1863, 1.

[21] Ballard, *Civil War in Mississippi*, 135–37; Quad, *Field, Fort, and Fleet*, 290.

about a half mile upriver, and over the next two weeks the armored vessel received a terrible pounding. The Cherokee Artillery's gun apparently did excellent work as a Confederate participant recalled, "the enemy several times [were] compelled to retire before the rifle guns." A correspondent attached to the flotilla provided an eyewitness report of the damage done by the Rebel batteries. "The *Chillicothe* was disabled and compelled to return to Cairo [Illinois] for repairs," he wrote. "Her turret had been removed and replaced with a new one. The original armor on her turret was three-inch iron, but the reconstructed one was plated with five-inch [iron plates]." The brief initial exchange of gunfire killed four Yankee sailors and wounded nine before the vessels retreated out of range. The Rebels apparently emerged from the engagement unscathed.[22]

During a lull in the fighting, Sgt. Johnston sent James C. Browne back to Vicksburg to obtain supplies for the Cherokee Artillery contingent. Fighting in the bayou had been tough on the Georgians. The mosquitoes and vermin were largely dormant during that season, which proved a blessing, but sleeping on wet ground, enduring the hazards of battle, and walking through brush and brambles had left them tattered, bedraggled, and a couple of men short. A Floyd County correspondent reported, "Mr. Brown[e]...informs us that our boys have seen pretty hard service in that region, marching and fighting the Yankees almost daily, and they have lost most of their clothing and blankets, except what they have on.... Mr. Brown[e] returns [to Fort Pemberton] today with more men, clothes and money for our boys."[23]

After several more futile attempts to push past Fort Pemberton, the Federals set up a pair of batteries on some high ground nearby, but Confederate artillery easily kept the annoying guns in check. With twice as many Federal troops present as the graycoats could field, Brig. Gen. Leonard Ross and Lt. Cmdr. Watson Smith tried to unload Federal foot soldiers to flank the Rebels out of their mud citadel; but the bluecoats quickly discovered that the swampy terrain made effective

---

[22] Woodworth, *Nothing but Victory*, 306–309; William T. Keyes, "The River Flotilla," *National Tribune*, October 1, 1891, 1.

[23] *RC*, April 29, 1862[3], 2.

movement and maneuver impossible. A few hillocks rose from the marshes and muddy water, but these islands in the marsh proved too small for any significant infantry actions. The flotilla continued to hammer the Confederates, but the sailors and soldiers quickly deduced that only an act of God, or additional ships, troops, and artillery from Grant, could break the stalemate.[24]

Information reached General Grant that Rebel reinforcements from Vicksburg would soon arrive at Fort Pemberton, and the Union commander began worrying that his brown water naval force along the Yazoo might become trapped and overwhelmed. Cmdr. Smith, who had been battling a debilitating illness since the campaign began, decided to "throw in the towel." He turned over leadership of the expedition to his second-in-command and ordered a withdrawal to Yazoo Pass.[25]

Grant worried constantly that the politicians and desk officers in Washington would snatch away his command at Vicksburg on a moment's notice, so he sometimes overstated the results of his operations. On March 6, he had informed Maj. Gen. Henry Halleck, "I will have Vicksburg this month, or fail in the attempt." Unwilling to let the opportunity at Fort Pemberton slip away, he sent Brig. Gen. Isaac Quinby with a division from XVII Corps to reinforce the Union force along the Tallahatchie. Quinby met the ironclads retiring from Fort Pemberton and ordered them to turn around. The Federal infantry officer was determined to take a crack at Gen. Loring's citadel, so the combined expedition returned to its positions before Fort Pemberton. Quinby accomplished nothing, but continued his efforts until April 4 when Grant reluctantly directed him to return to the Mississippi River.[26]

Ulysses S. Grant, who was neither a coward nor a fool, recognized better than most that his various attempts to take Vicksburg had produced only a dismal litany of defeat. These included the direct invasion of Northern Mississippi in November and December 1862, Sherman's

[24] Woodworth, *Nothing but Victory*, 306; Winschel, *Confederate Gibraltar*, 39–40.
[25] Woodworth, *Nothing but Victory*, 306; Winschel, *Confederate Gibraltar*, 39–40.
[26] Woodworth, *Nothing but Victory*, 308; *OR*, ser. 1, vol. 24, part 1, 16.

blunder along Chickasaw Bayou, the attempt to bypass Vicksburg by constructing the De Soto Point Canal, the debacle at Yazoo Pass, and Steele's Bayou expeditions—all of which had been failures to a greater or lesser degree. Even more frustrating to Grant, the only clear-cut success in this region to date had been Maj. Gen. John A. McClernand's capture of Arkansas Post—and McClernand had now begun actively politicking to replace Grant.[27]

During the three months in the bayous, Van Den Corput's men suffered one dead (James F. Foster), two wounded (James C. Browne and Cooper Bennett), and two (William L. Scott and J. W. Scott) sick enough to be hospitalized. They also lost three horses killed. Union losses, on paper, seemed minimal, but the campaign may have had a far-reaching impact on many of the bluecoats. A veteran of the foray in the bayous later reported, "While they [Federal soldiers] did not lose many killed on this expedition, hundreds were disabled by exposure and died afterwards of disease."[28]

While Sgt. Johnston's detachment operated in the Yazoo River swamps, the rest of Van Den Corput's Battery had been busy in and around Vicksburg. A correspondent to the *Rome Courier* summed up the unit's activities: "Since we have been here we have been doing the various duties incumbent upon a soldier; marching and countermarching, from one post to another, on picket at various posts, watching the movements of our enemy, and preparing to meet him wherever he might choose to offer us battle." Wesley Conner's diary from February 1 through mid-March lists the Georgia artillerymen's various duty stations including Bovina, Warrenton, and along the Big Black River. The diarist also provided several examples of the caprices of a soldier's life. While scavenging for supplies one evening, he partook of the hospitality of a loyal Southern lady who offered hot food and a feather

[27] Joiner, *Brown Water Navy*, 127; Ballard, *Civil War in Mississippi*, 135–37.

[28] "From Mississippi," *RC*, August 7, 1863, 1; B. F. Gordon, "The Yazoo Pass Expedition," *National Tribune*, July 25, 1907, 6.

bed. The next night, however, found him camping—wet, cold, and hungry—in the middle of a muddy road.[29]

Around March 16, Gen. Pemberton finally located a position for Van Den Corput's men. Orders arrived directing them to emplace their guns at Warrenton, an abandoned town once known as Hopewell, five miles south of Vicksburg. A member of the Floyd County company described their new post as "breastworks, including an acre of ground, with a framework of heavy timbers extending along one side, fronting the river, and that covered with railroad iron, put up in a slanting position [to deflect incoming shells up and over the Georgians] behind which are our guns."[30]

Meanwhile, Grant, Sherman, and Porter had set in motion a new plan that would put the Cherokee Artillery in the thick of the action. Grant suggested moving all his forces back to Memphis to attempt another overland march; however, the three commanders quickly realized that Grant's detractors in Washington, D.C., would brand the move north as a retreat, which would almost certainly cost Grant command of the army. As a result, they agreed that the best option would be to move the Army of the Tennessee south of Vicksburg and deposit them on the Louisiana side of the Mississippi River. This would require the unstinting support of the brown water navy to transport the infantry past the gauntlet of Confederate batteries around Vicksburg.[31]

As a diversion, Grant sent Maj. Gen. Frederick Steele's division and part of Porter's fleet to northern Mississippi to capture or disperse Col. Wirt Adam's Rebel horsemen, burn Confederate supplies, drive out nests of Rebel bushwhackers, and generally clear the region of Confederate resistance. Meanwhile, Porter prepared the boats that would run the gauntlet of Rebel guns around Vicksburg by having the sailors stack row after row of cotton bales on the decks to absorb the shot and shell from the Confederate guns.[32]

---

[29] *RC*, April 29, 1862[3], 2; WOC, March 2, 1863.

[30] *RC*, April 29, 1862[3], 2.

[31] Joiner, *Brown Water Navy*, 129; Grant, *Personal Memoirs*, 240.

[32] Ballard, *Civil War in Mississippi*, 140–41; Joiner, *Brown Water Navy*, 129–31.

On the night of April 16, the Union boats successfully ran through the hail of gunfire at Vicksburg, suffering considerably less damage than the Federal commanders expected. Due to weather conditions, the Cherokee Artillery, waiting at Warrenton, got less advance warning of the approaching enemy than they had anticipated. An unnamed correspondent from the unit explained,

> We were aroused suddenly from our sleep, about twelve o'clock at night of the 16th inst., and ordered to the fort, which is about fifty yards from our quarters. From the way the wind blew that night the sentinels could not hear distinctly the guns at the city. They seemed further off, consequently the [enemy] boats were upon us sooner than expected. From the best information we could get, five gunboats and two transports passed our battery. We fired at them successively as they passed. Each [Federal] gunboat fired one shot at us. We could not tell what damage we did, as it was too dark. Our pickets below informed us, however, that we set one boat afire. After the boats had passed, we saw a large amount of burning cotton floating down the river, which we afterward learned was the remains of a gunboat sunk by the batteries at the city. On the [floating] cotton [bales] we heard some poor deluded Yankees crying for help.

Porter reported none killed and fewer than fifteen lightly wounded, which seems quite small when compared to accounts by the Confederates.[33]

On the next run, the U.S. Navy again successfully sailed past the fortress city, but this time they paid particular attention to the battery at Warrenton. A report published in the *Rome Tri-Weekly Courier* thrilled the civilians back home with this detailed account of the action:

> On the 22nd, a sloop of war, the *Hartford*, mounting twenty-six guns, and the gunboat *Albatross*, [with] sixteen guns, having passed our batteries below, at Port Hudson, came up and passed our batteries, throwing shot and shell at us. The two boats having passed above us, the *Albatross* remained and the *Hartford* returned and took position within cannon shot below. On the morning of the 25th about

[33] *RC*, May 21, 1863, 2; Joiner, *Brown Water Navy*, 131–33; *ORN*, ser. 1, vol. 24, 551–54.

> daylight, we heard heavy cannonading above, at the city....The *Hartford*, with steam up and colors flying, moved slowly up and began to fire at us with fearful precision. Piece No. 1, Sergt. I[saac]. W. Hume and Corp'l [G. A.] Hutchins, fired twenty shells. No. 5, Sergt. [Daniel] Millen and Corp'l [W. S.] Donahoo, 14 shots; No. 4, Sergt. [Sydney A.] Blassingame and Corp'l [David O.] Newton, fired none; No. 3, R. M. Jones and Corp'l [Wesley O.] Conner fired 5 shots. The first shots from the *Hartford* cut the railroad iron [used as protection for the gun ports] in two, and closed the porthole of No. 4, [and] partially [closed] No. 3, which prevented them [Guns #3 and #4] from firing as many shots as the others. The action lasted 1½ hours.... After the firing ceased we saw cotton bales and pieces of timber floating down the river.

In a spirit of unit pride the writer added, "Commodore Farragut reports to his government that our batteries at Warrenton did him more injury than any battery on the river."[34]

On a sadder note, the correspondent also reported the death of J. J. Brisentine, who succumbed to a case of smallpox. "He was," the writer reported, "a pious Christian and a good soldier....[T]he memory of...[his] noble and generous deeds, will be written with an iron pen upon the hearts of his comrades in arms."[35]

Max Van Den Corput's men gave him high marks, as well—at least in the public press. When the Belgian had originally assumed command of the Cherokee Artillery, he had brought with him the European attitude of soldiers as automatons who obeyed orders and did exactly as commanded without complaint or question. Confederate soldiers, he quickly learned, despite the best efforts of their West Point–trained officers, seldom abandoned the anarchistic belief that they were free men who knew better than anyone what they should do and how they should accomplish their purpose. Years later, Connor explained Van Den Corput's initiation into the Rebels' mindset. "[He] was a Belgian, a naturalized citizen who proved true to the Confederate cause. He was autocratic in his ideas of Military discipline which he

---

[34] *RC*, April 29, 1863; Joiner, *Brown Water Navy*, 133–35.

[35] *RC*, May 21, 1863, 2.

soon found out didn't suit the liberty-loving Southern boys, and they resented it and detested him. Having sense enough to realize the situation, he changed his methods and no officer in the army was more loved and respected by his men."[36]

The *Rome Weekly Courier*, on May 19, 1863, published an article from "the Ladies of Rome" excoriating Van Den Corput as a heartless, vindictive tyrant for failing to send home his sick cannoneers. In an epistle dripping with extreme ethnocentric bias, the writer (or writers) bemoaned the resignation of Captain Yeiser and ended with, "Oh, for a native born American Captain of the Cherokee Artillery." Van Den Corput responded, praising his men for their courage and sacrifices, and telling about some of the artillery duels in which his unit had been engaged. Then he got to the heart of the matter. "There are some [soldiers], however," he related, "whom I am sorry to say, invariably, when it looks as though we are going to be engaged, either take suddenly ill, or have friends whom they wish to see, or who hide coward-like, behind whatever is close enough for them to do so. I am happy to state that these are few in number. Did I have any favors to grant, those who stand like men, and do not want to avoid duty, would receive them." Having effectively "poisoned the well" by intimating that the family members of those who had written the letter were cowards, criticism from home apparently ceased.[37]

One soldier, W. S. Gray, had earned a reputation as a coward and a slacker, and a cruel trick played upon him made him the butt of many of the Cherokee Artillery's jokes. A soldier wrote,

> W. S. Gray, Cohen's [possibly referring to Bernard Kohn] clerk... was detailed to guard the baggage and [the] house we staid in. So when the yanks commenced shelling Gray left [quickly]...keeping behind the levee all the time. So when the boat left...the boys rized [razzed] him well...He knew the boat would pay them another visit soon and not willing to let the boys see him he got him a spade and dug him[self] a hole between two logs in front of the house after

36 WOC, p. 5 (no date listed).

37 *RC*, May 19, 1863, 2; see also letter from W. H. Baker to Mrs. T. E. Roberts, April 17, 1863, Baker collection, KMNBP.

> dark. This was to get in when the Yankees came. A great big Kentuckian named [John W.] Moore found Gray's breast works [and] knew what they meant—and being troubled with diarrhea used Gray's fort as a privey. That night the boat came steaming down before day. In the morning the boys went to the Fort and Gray went to his Fort. The rest you can imagine.... They [Van Den Corput's men] plague Gray badley.

Ironically, despite the ridicule W. S. Gray endured, he remained with the Cherokee Artillery until the end; Moore deserted to the enemy three months later and took the oath of allegiance to the Union.[38]

Grant's diversions in North Mississippi completely befuddled Pemberton, and he seemingly ignored the concentration of enemy troops south of Vicksburg. Brig. Gen. John Bowen, commanding the area south of the city, sent several warning notes to Pemberton, explaining that the Yankees had landed in force at Bruinsburg. Rather than resting and allowing the Rebels to concentrate opposition forces against his beachhead, Gen. McClernand, commanding the Union XIII Corps, ordered his commanders to begin a hasty advance toward Port Gibson. On May 1, Bowen, though badly outnumbered, attempted to use the wooded hills and ravines around Port Gibson to neutralize the Federal manpower advantage. After a hard, bloody fight, the bluecoats broke the Confederate line near nightfall, opening the road for an advance on the state capital.[39]

While Grant pursued his goal with a single-minded devotion, the Confederate commanders waffled and seemed incapable of deciding upon any coherent course of action. On May 9, orders from the War Department in Richmond reached Gen. Joseph E. Johnston, directing him to "take chief command of the forces [in central Mississippi], giving to those in the field, as far as practicable, the encouragement and

[38] W. H. Baker to Mrs. T. E. Roberts, April 13, 1863, Baker collection, KMNBP.

[39] Ballard, *Civil War in Mississippi*, 146–52.

benefit of your personal direction." This order, as it turned out, would have a dramatic—and disastrous—effect on the Confederate efforts to save Vicksburg.[40]

After the battle at Port Gibson, the bluecoats continued their advance northward, intending to cut the rail line between Clinton and Edwards Station. On May 12, the Federals brushed aside a rash attack by Brig. Gen. John Gregg's forces at Raymond, and McClernand's troops soon pulled within striking distance of Vicksburg's vulnerable supply line. Gen. Grant, however, decided to divert the expedition to the Mississippi capital city, and the bluecoats reached Jackson on May 14. Joe Johnston, sick, and with only about 6,000 troops, left Gregg's weary soldiers to cover his retreat and headed north toward Canton. Johnston's precipitous flight left the Mississippi capital in Union hands and had a major impact on the campaign. First, Jackson not only was an important communication and supply center but also housed arsenals, foundries, and large stockpiles of valuable stores and supplies. More importantly, Johnston's abandonment of Jackson cost the Confederates the strategic advantage: Johnston's troops were now scattered, and Confederate reinforcements bound for Jackson lost their rallying point. Seizing this splendid opportunity, Grant turned his attention westward.[41]

Pemberton now faced a real quandary. Should he try to halt the Union advance, hold Vicksburg, or comply with Joe Johnston's incessant demands to abandon Vicksburg and combine the two Rebel armies? On one hand, Johnston had earlier ordered Pemberton to "consolidate his army and attack the Federals, even if that meant risking the loss of Vicksburg." On the other hand, Jefferson Davis had earlier issued a directive to the Quaker general to protect the Confederate Gibraltar at all costs. That task seemingly fit his personality much better than aggressively mounting an offensive against the enemy. After a conference with his subordinates, Pemberton opted to scatter his army all

---

[40] *OR*, ser. 1, vol. 24, part 1, 215.

[41] Ballard, *Civil War in Mississippi*, 153–54; Bearss, "The Vicksburg Campaign: Grant Marches West—The Battles of Champion Hill and Big Black Bridge," 6 (hereafter cited as "Grant Marches West").

along the Big Black River, paying special attention to fords where the Yankees could cross. If Grant did turn west and followed the railroad toward Vicksburg, the Confederates could entrench along the bluffs on the west side of the Big Black River and let the Federals attack. However, on May 16, Johnston unequivocally ordered Pemberton to move his army to Clinton (a strange rallying point, as the department commander had taken refuge at Canton). Trying to make sense of Johnston's urgent orders to abandon the fortress city, a modern historian concluded, "He [Johnston] did not want to fight Grant, nor did he care if Grant took Vicksburg. Johnston was a disciple of the theory that armies mattered more than places.... His only goal seemed to be to get Pemberton's army out of Grant's way so that the two divided Confederate forces could unite."[42]

The men of the Cherokee Artillery remained at Warrenton until 6 P.M. on May 12. They seemed blissfully unaware of their commanding general's confusion and hesitancy in making a firm decision regarding his army's next move. Around twilight, the Georgians began marching eastward through the inky Mississippi night, stopping at noon the next day to feed and water their horses near Bovina. Wesley Connor took the opportunity to jot in his diary: "Destination not known. God grant that we are not evacuating Vicksburg. Movements very suspicious."[43]

Van Den Corput's unit was now the designated artillery support for Brig. Gen. Seth Barton's brigade. Barton, a native of Fredericksburg, Virginia, had entered West Point as a fifteen-year-old, and he graduated in the lower half of the class of 1849 because "he was fond of reading and gave more attention to the pursuit of general knowledge than to specific requirements of the course." After a lackluster career in the pre-war U.S. Army, he threw in his lot with the Confederacy, fighting in Virginia and present-day West Virginia. Transferred to East

---

[42] *OR*, ser. 1, vol. 24, part 2, 93–94; Ballard, *Civil War in Mississippi*, 153, 159.
[43] WOC, December 12–13, 1863.

Tennessee, he first served with the Cherokee Artillery during the Cumberland Gap campaign. In Mississippi, Barton commanded a Georgia brigade containing the 40th, 41st, 42nd, 43rd, and 52nd regiments.[44]

The lack of movement by Pemberton's army completely baffled the Georgia cannoneers. On May 14, they took a position near Edwards Station, a tiny community located along the Jackson Road just east of a bend in the Big Black River. The next day, Wesley Connor wrote, "Left our position near Edward's, marched two hundred yards, halted an hour or two, and then marched back to our [previous] position to await further orders." Just before nightfall, the battery joined the main body of Pemberton's army. The graycoats advanced a few miles to the east before finally turning southward and left the road when they reached the area near Champion Hill.[45]

Grant's Army of the Tennessee began the march toward Edward's Station at 5 A.M. on May 16. If he could vanquish Pemberton's army, Grant could then march on his ultimate objective, Vicksburg; thereby sundering the Confederacy and depriving the South of vital men, materiel, and foodstuffs from the Trans-Mississippi. The Illinois general had complete confidence in his ability to defeat Pemberton. Not only did Grant know the Quaker general's tendencies, but a Union spy had provided the Federals with a copy of Johnston's letter to Pemberton. (Unlike George McClellan at Antietam, who had obtained a copy of Robert E. Lee's plans before the battle, Grant would make good use of his prior knowledge.) "Today, we shall fight the battle for Vicksburg," he shouted, encouraging his advancing troops. As an added precaution, Grant ordered Sherman's corps, which had been occupying the Mississippi capital, to join the Union army's advance along the Jackson Road.[46]

Throughout the morning of May 16, the Federal force, consisting of seven divisions and totaling 32,000 men, continued their westward advance along three roads toward Edwards Station. The divisions of

---

[44] McDonald, "Seth Maxwell Barton," 18–19.

[45] WOC, May 14–15, 1863.

[46] Woodworth, *Nothing but Victory*, 370–71; "Jos. T. Derry," *Macon (GA) Telegraph*, August 28, 1888, 9.

Maj. Gen. A. J. "Whiskey" Smith and Maj. Gen. Frank Blair, composing Grant's left wing, moved west along the Raymond Road. The divisions of Brig. Gen. Eugene A. Carr and Brig. Gen. Peter Osterhaus proceeded along the Middle Road. To the north, the divisions of Brig. Gen. Alvin P. Hovey, Maj. Gen. John A. Logan, and Brig. Gen. Marcellus M. Crocker marched along the Jackson Road, approaching Edwards Station.[47]

Pemberton's army, which totaled about 23,000 officers and men (not counting the 10,000 men in the two divisions he had left behind in Vicksburg), had begun moving eastward the previous day (May 15), covering the same three roads. Maj. Gen. William Wing Loring, who had commanded at Fort Pemberton, advanced slowly along the Raymond Road; Maj. Gen. John Bowen's units wended their way along the Middle Road while Maj. Gen. Carter L. Stevenson's division moved cautiously eastward along the Jackson Road. In striking contrast to the Federal advance, delays and confusion plagued the slow Confederate advance. They spent most of the morning of May 15 waiting to draw supplies, and, once the march began, the army moved in fits and starts, with frequent orders to halt. To make matters worse, the men of Carter Stevenson's division were worn out, having already trudged ten hours through the muggy darkness before finally reaching the rest of the army about 5 A.M.

None of Pemberton's lieutenants had had the foresight to occupy Champion Hill, the key military position in the area, when they camped for the night. This seventy-five-foot, crescent-shaped bluff commanded the surrounding terrain four miles east of Edwards Station. According to Grant, this steep, heavily wooded position "[was] one of the highest positions in that section [region], and commanded all the ground in range."[48]

---

[47] Woodworth, *Nothing but Victory*, 370–71; Bearss, *Campaign for Vicksburg: Grant Strikes a Fatal Blow*, 571.

[48] Bearss, *Fatal Blow*, 577, 591; Hattaway, *General Stephen D. Lee*, 86; Grant, *Civil War Memoirs*, 178.

On the day of battle, Brig. Gen. Stephen D. Lee's Alabama brigade, composed of the 20th, 23rd, 30th, 31st, and 46th infantry regiments, moved east to occupy the heights. Brig. Gen. Alfred Cummings's Georgia brigade, composed of the 33rd, 34th, 36th, 56th, and 57th regiments, deployed south of S. D. Lee's position, covering the vital crossroads created by the intersection of the Jackson and Middle roads. Just south of the crossroads, Barton's Georgia Brigade and Van Den Corput's Battery had taken a position near the Isaac Roberts farmhouse.[49]

The battle of Champion Hill began about 7 A.M. when "Whiskey" Smith's Federal division stumbled onto Col. Edward Goodwin's 35th Alabama infantry regiment and a couple of companies of Mississippi horsemen. Fearing that his men might be marching into a trap, Gen. Smith carefully followed Grant's directive to move cautiously, using skirmishers to search out the enemy. A loud, steady artillery duel began, and Smith's bluecoats eventually pushed the Rebels across Jackson Creek.[50]

Along the Middle Road, Osterhaus's troops also proceded slowly and carefully. The Prussian-born general, who had previously proven his courage fighting in the European revolts during the 1840s and at Wilson's Creek and Elkhorn Tavern in the Trans-Mississippi region, likely chomped at the bit, anxiously awaiting orders to go on the attack.[51]

At the northern end of the field, Stephen Dill Lee waited nervously for the Federals to reach his position. From a Confederate perspective, the Yankees could not have picked a worse time to begin their attack. Johnston had just sent Pemberton yet another order demanding that he bring his army east so that the consolidated forces could destroy Grant's supply lines. Pemberton had apparently decided to comply with Johnston's orders and had already started sending brigades back toward Edwards Station, where a road led directly to Clinton. The

---

[49] Bearss, "Grant Marches West," 11; T. B. Smith, *Champion Hill*, 189–93.

[50] Bearss, "Grant Marches West," 9–10, 44–45; Hathaway, *Stephen D. Lee*, 88.

[51] Warner, *Generals in Blue*, 352–53; Arnold, *Grant Wins the War*, 152–53.

Quaker warrior first sent back Col. Alexander Reynolds's Tennessee brigade to guard the army's wagon train. The Volunteer State troops would be sorely missed in the coming hours.[52]

The conflicting orders and the Yankees' rapid advance may have addled Pemberton, but the crisis brought out the best in some of his subordinates. S. D. Lee moved his Alabamians into a strong position atop Champion Hill. Seeking any advantage they could find, the Deep South Rebels rested their rifles across the rails of a rickety wooden fence, awaiting the coming storm. Cumming moved two of his Georgia regiments—the 36th and 39th—and four companies of the 34th away from the crossroads to support Lee's right flank. Cumming, a West Pointer and veteran of some hard fighting in Virginia, knew what needed to be done, but his troops were rookies, about to "see the elephant" for the first time. With Lee's right covered, Maj. Gen. Carter L. Stevenson directed Seth Barton to move his brigade northeast to cover Lee's left. He also sent Van Den Corput's Battery, plus two guns from the 1st Mississippi Light Artillery, to add teeth to S. D. Lee's defensive line. Unfortunately, the reinforcements would not reach their new position until about 1 P.M.[53]

Around noon, Brig. Gen. Alvin Hovey's and Maj. Gen. "Black Jack" Logan's two Union divisions, totaling 10,000 men, bolted out of the woods and clambered up the ridge toward Lee's Alabamians and Cumming's Georgia regiments. Hovey's men struck first. The Federal general had been a prewar haberdasher in Ohio, but he had seen action in the Mexican War and had earned a reputation in Grant's army as "a glory-hound." The Georgians, in their first real battle, made the novice mistake of firing too high as the bluecoats charged up the hill. Before Cumming's Rebels could reload, the Yankees were upon them, shooting, clubbing, and bayoneting their foe. The Georgia general, who had previously battled in the Seven Days fight and at Sharpsburg, recalled with horror, "[A]n attack broke upon us with great impetuosity and vehemence, in overwhelming force, and in a manner wholly unexpected and unlooked for." This proved more than Cumming's untried

[52] Arnold, *Grant Wins in the War*, 154.

[53] T. B. Smith, *Champion Hill*, 192–93.

graycoats could stand, and many of them dropped their weapons and fled. Cumming rode forward, trying to stem the tide and rally his boys, but to no avail. A disgusted Georgia soldier wrote to an Atlanta newspaper that Cumming's men "[have] shown the white feather, and ran at the first fire. *This won't do for Georgia.*"[54]

Further to the left, Lee's Alabamians were either luckier, made of sterner stuff, or both. Crouching behind their rail fence to steady their aim, they held Logan's division at bay for half an hour, pouring a galling fire into the Midwesterners and covering the hillside with dead bluecoats. Soon, however, Lee realized that holding the fence line much longer would put his brigade in serious peril. Ordering his remaining regiments to pull back, they repositioned themselves along a new line running parallel to the Jackson Road. Four times during the long afternoon, the Federals broke the line of the men from Alabama, and four times Lee, despite having three horses shot out from under him, rallied his soldiers and held his rapidly constricting line together. When his men ran short of ammunition, he sent the 23rd Alabama Regiment and at least a portion of the 30th Alabama to deliver a bayonet charge to delay the onrushing enemy. The problem, as Lee well recognized, was that the much larger Union army kept overlapping his left flank, and Barton's men had not yet arrived.[55]

General Pemberton finally acted decisively, twice ordering William Wing Loring and John Bowen to move their troops to the left to support Stevenson's Division, but the two officers hesitated, apparently reluctant to obey. Loring and Bowen despised Pemberton, and earlier in the day a courier related how Loring and Bowen had sat in the shade of a tree making fun of their commanding officer. Around 1 P.M., with

[54] Ibid., 192–211; Arnold, *Grant Wins the War*, 160–64; Clint, "Letters from Georgia," *Atlanta Southern Confederacy*, May 30, 1863, 3; "Letter from Alfred Cumming to Stephen D. Lee," http://battleofchampionhill.org/history/cummings.htm.

[55] T. B. Smith, *Champion Hill*, 211–23; Arnold, *Grant Wins the War*, 164–65; Hattaway, *General Stephen D. Lee*, 86–88; Stephens, *Bound for Glory*, 205, 118; Calhoun, *42nd Regiment*, 32.

the bluecoats pressing hard against Lee and Carter Stevenson, Pemberton twice sent a courier with orders to "[t]ell General Bowen to move up at once to assist Stevenson and tell Loring to move his division…to the assistance of Stevenson, and crush the enemy." With Loring and Bowen still dragging their feet, Pemberton rode over and personally directed Col. Francis Marion Cockrell's Rebel Missouri brigade into the fray.[56]

The Cherokee Artillery's beef ration arrived early on the morning of May 16, with instructions to "jerk" it. They immediately began digging fire pits and building scaffolding from tree branches to dry out the meat. The boom of artillery, as McClernand began his tentative advance against Loring, signaled the end of that pleasant task, and the cannoneers apparently wolfed down their allotment of food almost raw. One of the Georgians wrote, "Movements immediately began, which from the hurry and confusion led them [his comrades] to believe that the Generals were not fully posted [prepared for the enemy advance]."[57]

As soon as the cannonading began between Loring and A. J. Smith's bluecoats, Seth Barton's Georgians, including the Cherokee Artillery, began moving to a position on the Ratliff Road south of the vital Crossroads and a little southwest of the Isaac Roberts house. There they waited as the artillery duel sputtered along to the south and the sound of a full-fledged battle raged along Stephen D. Lee's front.[58]

Barton, like his immediate superior, Carter Stevenson, hailed from Fredericksburg, Virginia, and had graduated from West Point. Barton, however, could not lay claim to the combat experience and savvy of his

---

[56] Bearss, *Fatal Blow*, 607–608; Arnold, *Grant Wins the War*, 160; Lt. William Drennan to his wife, Georgia Torrey Drennan, undated; shortly after May 16, 1863, www.battleofchampionhill.org/drennan/htm.

[57] WOC, May 16, 1863.

[58] *OR*, ser. 1, vol. 24, part 2, 99–100.

chief. Stevenson had seen considerable action during the Mexican War, in the West, and during the Third Seminole War in Florida.[59]

The Georgians did not have to wait long before they, too, joined in the desperate battle. Stevenson, realizing the danger now facing Lee's graycoats, immediately ordered Barton to hurry northeast to take a position to the left of the beleaguered Alabamians. Like a rising tide hitting a sandcastle, the Union battle line not only hit the obstruction in its front but also swirled in behind it. The disintegration of Cumming's Brigade had allowed Hovey's Federals to advance behind S. D. Lee's right flank while Logan's troops, with little opposition from the Alabamians' left, began to overlap the gray line to the west. If they managed to encircle and destroy Stevenson's entire division, Pemberton's only remaining option would be to take refuge inside the defenses of Vicksburg.[60]

Barton hurried his men, who had marched until 3 A.M. that morning before bedding down, as quickly as the broken, wooded terrain and human strength would allow. Barton later reported, "[T]he distance (about one and a half miles) was passed at the double-quick, and [the men] advanced as rapidly as the nature of the ground would permit." Van Den Corput's boys had few illusions regarding their immediate destination. They knew they were going into a full-fledged, deadly brawl. Connor noted in his diary, "Heavy fighting with infantry on the left and immediately to our right.... Firing of small arms still increasing on the left."[61]

By the time Barton arrived, only the remnants of Lee's Alabama regiments remained in line of battle, and even those hardy units were beginning to come apart at the seams. The Federals, having enveloped his position on both flanks, threatened to surround the graycoats. Barton came into line to the left of Lee, with his troops aligned left to right with the 40th regiment on the left, the 41st in the center, and the 43rd on the right. His left stretched to within 600 yards of the Bakers Creek

---

[59] Hewitt, "Carter Littlepage Stevenson," 8–9; *OR*, ser. 1, vol. 24, part 2, 93–99.

[60] *OR*, ser. 1, vol. 24, part 2, 93–99; T. B. Smith, *Champion Hill*, 213–14.

[61] *OR*, ser. 1, vol. 24, part 2, 99–100.

Bridge. The 52nd Georgia, stationed near the bridge as a reserve, kept watch over Barton's vulnerable left and supported the Georgia and Mississippi artillery batteries. More importantly, the regiment could keep open a line of retreat in the increasingly likely event that it would be needed.[62]

While the Cherokee Artillery waited, with firing all around them, one of those odd events happened that showed the human aspect of battle. "As an instance of how unconcerned men become in the presence of danger," Connor wrote, "our boys have cut bushes and built temporary shelters as a protection from the sun, and a few even have gone to sleep while we are expecting every moment to be ordered into battle."[63]

As soon as Barton's three regiments came into line, the Virginia commander ordered his Georgia boys to charge. They hit four unsuspecting Union regiments (the 20th, 31st, and 8th Illinois regiments and the 32nd Ohio) and drove them back a couple of hundred yards. The butternut reinforcements were too little, too late, but they momentarily threw the Federal assault off balance.[64]

Soon the tide turned, and the bluecoats roared forward again. Barton's Brigade, reflecting the fierceness of the fight, suffered 42 percent casualties, including Col. Skid Harris, commander of the 43rd Georgia. While the infantry onslaught sputtered to a close and the survivors fell into line beside Lee, Carter Stevenson sent his chief of artillery, Maj. Joseph W. Anderson, to make sure Van Den Corput's men had assumed the best position to support Barton's futile attack. Before he fell, mortally wounded, Anderson chose a position atop a slight ridge, in an open area (Connor called it a "rye field"), just north of the Jackson Road and west of the George Roberts house for Van Den Corput's four ten-pound Parrott rifles. Immediately to the west of the Georgia cannoneers, Anderson also emplaced two guns of the 1st Mississippi

---

[62] T. B. Smith, *Champion Hill*, 220–21; *OR*, ser. 1, vol. 24, part 2, 99–100.
[63] WOC, May 11, 1863.
[64] *OR*, ser. 1, vol. 24, part 2, 99–100; T. B. Smith, *Champion Hill*, 224–26.

Light Artillery. Capt. Samuel J. Ridley directed the section from the Magnolia State.[65]

They did not have long to wait before three regiments of Midwesterners belonging Union Brig. Gen. John D. Stevenson's brigade appeared in their front. The 8th and 124th Illinois and the 32nd Ohio had passed to the north of Barton's line when they came into range of the Southern cannon. Van Den Corput's and Ridley's guns roared their challenge at the approaching enemy and the bluecoats answered with rifle fire, aided by a Federal battery of four twelve-pounder Napoleon guns. Connor stated: "[I]t was hot work. Shot, shell, and shrapnel flew thick and fast around us. Here fell Hutchens [Thomas Hutchings],—killed, and [John T.] Lumpkin and [G. A. C.] Anthony mortally wounded." Each of the Floyd County guns, he noted, had fired fifteen to twenty rounds.[66]

As soon as their fellow Georgians in the artillery began taking casualties, the 52nd Georgia, commanded by Col. Charles D. Phillips, moved forward to protect their comrades. The regiment had been raised in Northeast Georgia, where strong Unionist sentiment would soon make that region virtually "enemy territory," so the 52nd Georgia may have felt it had something to prove. The unit's chaplain stated that his flock rushed into the "the thickest of the fight," and Barton reported, "It [Phillips's regiment] now moved up rapidly, and in handsome style engaged a brigade that was turning the [Rebel] left." As with Lee's Alabamians and Barton's other three regiments, the courage and sacrifice of Phillips's men came to naught as "Union muskets by the hundred leveled, took aim, and shot down the charging Southerners." Col. Phillips slumped to the ground, literally shot to pieces, and 18-year-old Capt. "Gus" Boyd, commanding Co. B, fell dead when a minie ball smashed into his forehead.[67]

---

[65] WOC, May 16, 1863; *OR*, ser. 1, vol. 24, part 2, 93–99; T. B. Smith, *Champion Hill*, 223–24; Calhoun, *42nd Georgia*, 32.

[66] WOC, May 16, 1863: T. B. Smith, *Champion Hill*, 225–27.

[67] T. B. Smith, *Champion Hill*, 227; *OR*, ser. 1, vol. 24, part 2, 99–100; William S. Kinsland, "A Band of Brothers: The Men and Legend of the 52nd Georgia Regiment," *North Georgia Journal* 2 (Summer 1985): 9–29 (part 1); 2 (Fall 1985): 18–39 (part 2).

The Confederate gunners used round shot as the bluecoats struggled up the briar-choked, brushy ravine toward the batteries. Several Union foot soldiers believed that the undulating terrain actually worked in their favor because the ridges and swales offered them a measure of protection. As the Yankees emerged onto more level ground, Van Den Corput's men switched to canister. (Canister rounds contained iron balls that dispersed when fired, much like birdshot from a shotgun shell.) A Federal participant recorded, "The rebels had been deficient in artillery throughout the battle but opened with rather heavy fire from four gun batteries, rifled six pounders, planted about four hundred yards back from the brow of the hill. The woods on both sides of the road…were filled with sharpshooters, supported by infantry." Despite taking heavy casualties from Van Den Corput's and Ridley's artillery, and the muskets of the 52nd Georgia, the Yankees kept coming.[68]

As the Floyd County artillerymen pounded the advancing Union soldiers, additional bluecoats came out of the woods less than 200 yards from Ridley's four-gun Mississippi battery. With most of his men dead, and the remainder fleeing for their lives, Ridley heroically manned the guns alone until he received a mortal wound. Van Den Corput ordered two of his guns to shift to the left to aid their comrades from the Magnolia State, but they had precious little time before the Federals were upon them. "[A] line of advancing [Federal] infantry emerged from the woods about two hundred yards in our front," noted Connor in his diary, "and as our infantry had given way, and the battery in that direction [Ridley's] already taken, no obstacle to their progress was presented. Two of our guns were unlimbered in the road, but only succeeded in firing one charge of canister."[69]

Max Van Den Corput realized the same fate would soon befall his men if they did not immediately flee. The problem, he quickly discovered, was that the enemy musket fire, that had wreaked such havoc

[68] WOC, May 16, 1863; "The Fighting at Vicksburg," *Junction City (KS) Smoky Hill and Republican Union*, May 30, 1863, 2; Arnold, *Grant Wins the War*, 167.

[69] WOC, May 16, 1863; Arnold, *Grant Wins the War*, 167–68.

with his troops, had also killed virtually all of their horses. An officer in Barton's Brigade later related, "Among the officers mentioned in the reports for gallantry...[was] Captain Max Van D. Corput. His horses and many of his men were killed, and finding it impossible to save his guns they were fired with double canister to the last. To this I can personally testify as I watched the destruction of the battery and some of his horses fell [with] in ten feet of me." That meant they would have to abandon their guns, but the Belgian knew that guns could be replaced easier than his dedicated band of warriors. Continuing his narrative, Wesley O. Connor wrote, "Capt. Corput brought us out into the road.... [T]he Yanks were close upon us. Capt. Corput told his men to take care of themselves, and we were not long in putting the order into execution. I felt so mortified [at retreating] that I stopped once or twice to make sure that I was not the first to leave the guns."[70]

From available records it appears that the Cherokee Artillery lost fifteen men killed, wounded, and captured at Champion Hill. G. A. C. Anthony, Thomas Hutchings, William M. Lloyd, and John T. Lumpkin died in the fighting, with Caleb Dempsey being so severely wounded that it took him two years to return to the unit. W. E. R. Anthony, S. J. Atwood, Henry W. Dean, Dempsey, Alex Franks, Solomon Fry, William V. King, Andrew R. Russell, H. C. Wilkinson and William J. Youngblood became captives near Bakers Creek. All but two would be paroled and would rejoin Van Den Corput's Battery. Franks and Fry both went over to the Union, signing the oath to remain north of the Ohio River.[71]

To the south, Bowen's men finally arrived, and his hard-hitting Missouri and Arkansas Confederates bought time for their comrades farther up the hill to retreat. Scavenging the field around the batteries they had just captured, the Federals discovered a scene of horrible carnage. "The rebels lay thick in the vicinity of the guns," one reported. "Their horses were more than half killed. Gun carriages and caissons

[70] WOC, May 16, 1863; Arnold, *Grant Wins the War*, 167–68; Calhoun, *42nd Georgia*, 32.

[71] Cherokee Artillery CSRs; see appendix, Cherokee Artillery roster.

were broken and overturned; while knapsacks, blankets, and small arms, and other debris attested to the death struggle for the ground."[72]

Pemberton's graycoats stumbled back to Edwards Station and then continued their retreat to the Big Black River. Many took a position along the east bank, but Carter Stevenson's battered division retreated all the way to Vicksburg. Southerners immediately began seeking a scapegoat for the debacle at Champion Hill. Connor found two easy targets for his wrath. "Had the Georgians and Alabamians stood up like men...," he wrote, "all would have been well, though Yanks outnumbered us three to one.... However...General Pemberton may have to shoulder it all [the blame]. He undoubtedly displayed bad generalship, and the day's work may have cost us Vicksburg."[73]

Without doubt, Pemberton made mistakes and would become the whipping boy for a generation of Southerners. But others deserved an equal share of the blame for the defeat at Champion Hill. Joe Johnston's orders to abandon Vicksburg and join him put Pemberton in the unenviable position of having to choose between defying a superior's direct order or ignoring his directive from President Davis. The insubordination of William Wing Loring and John Bowen also added to the Quaker general's woes, and the poor performance of Cumming's regiments, and others, certainly did not help the Rebels' performance at Champion Hill.

The following day, the disastrous campaign went from awful to horrendous. Pemberton placed his troops on the east side of the Big Black River, awaiting the arrival of Loring's men. Historian Edwin Bearss relates, "He [Pemberton] was holding the bridgehead for one reason, and one purpose only: to provide a haven for Loring's Division when it rejoined the army." All through the night, Pemberton held along the east bank of the Big Black, waiting for the arrival of the Florida general's troops even though crossing the "unfordable river" would have given Pemberton's defeated army the opportunity to rest and reorganize. Unbeknownst to the Vicksburg commander, Loring had

---

[72] Bearss, "Grant Marches West," 22–24; "The Fighting at Vicksburg," *Smoky Hill and Republican Union*, May 30, 1863, 2.

[73] WOC, May 16, 1863.

taken his division to join Joe Johnston's army. When Grant's army appeared before Pemberton's hastily constructed entrenchments, the graycoats could muster little in the way of a defense. Brig. Gen. John C. Vaughn's men, mostly conscripts from pro-Union East Tennessee, bolted at the first sign of Union troops. Though the Cherokee Artillery took no part in the day's fighting, they complained about their generals' perceived incompetence. The unit's diarist wrote, "Battle of the Big Black Bridge. Our forces defeated and falling back to the [Vicksburg] entrenchments. There was another display of bad generalship." Pemberton, with few other options, retreated into the citadel at Vicksburg.[74]

General Ulysses S. Grant, following his rather easy victory at Champion Hill and after gobbling up hundreds of disheartened stragglers after the fight at the Big Black and along the line of retreat, apparently thought taking Vicksburg would be simple. Unaware that Pemberton had fresh Rebel troops manning the works, the Union commander seriously underestimated the difficulty of the task before him. On May 19, from early morning until 2 P.M., Union artillery softened up the defenders with an intense artillery barrage before Grant sent one division of Sherman's corps in a wild charge against the Stockade Redan, situated at the northeast side of the city's defenses. The Vicksburg defenders bloodily repulsed the attackers. The Federals, stunned and chagrined, now knew the deadly truth: not only were the three Confederate divisions that had fought at Champion Hill not demoralized, but they had been augmented by two fresh divisions. The topography, consisting of ravines and gullies choked with felled trees, helped break any assault and hindered the approach to the earthworks as much as South-

[74] Bearss, *Fatal Blow*, 653–54; Bearss, "Grant Marches West," 45–52; WOC, May 17, 1863. The 60th and 61st Tennessee Regiments had more than 500 men "missing," but no casualties listed as killed and wounded (Bearss, *Fatal Blow*, 689).

ern shot and steel. The bluecoats lost almost 1,000 men—the Confederates less than 300. Sherman, in a letter to his spouse, averred, "This is a death struggle, and will be terrible."[75]

Grant's next attack on the Rebel citadel came on May 22. This time, the Union commander made careful preparations. The onslaught began with a terrific artillery barrage that lasted from daylight until 10 A.M., and then Grant's entire army clawed and scrambled up the wooded slopes, assaulting almost the entire Confederate line. The bluecoats enjoyed some local successes, particularly at the Railroad Redoubt, but by nightfall, the graycoats had again repulsed the Union soldiers. The Federal casualty lists on May 22 numbered 3,200 killed, wounded, or captured, while the Rebels lost about 500 men. The two battles convinced the Union commander that his only option was to besiege the citadel. The Southerners, heartened by the results of their successful defense, now believed that they could hold Vicksburg until relief arrived. Everything depended upon Gen. Joe Johnston, who had managed to collect an army of 30,000 men at Jackson, only about fifty miles to the east. Many Rebels fervently believed that their beloved "Old Joe" would soon arrive to lift the siege.[76]

Sgt. Johnston's detached gun of the Cherokee Artillery had done fine service at Fort Pemberton and Deer Creek. But when the bayou region no longer needed defending, they apparently wandered east, joining Joe Johnston's forces north of Jackson. The rest of Van Den Corput's men took refuge in Vicksburg, and since they had no guns, Pemberton immediately divided the remnants of the Cherokee Artillery.[77]

Shortly after the failed Federal attack on May 22, Pemberton ordered Van Den Corput to send a section of his unit to man a twenty-four-pound gun along the Mississippi River. The Georgia artillery detachment's new duty station was located about 200 yards north of what today is the intersection of North Frontage Road and Washington

---

[75] Woodworth, *Nothing but Victory*, 405; Sherman, *Home Letters*, 261.

[76] Winschel, *Confederate Gibraltar*, 90–94; Arnold, *Grant Wins the War*, 248–58.

[77] *RC*, August 7, 1863, 1; W. O. Connor to W. T. Rigby, Chairman, National Military Park Commission, May 4, 1903, CA file, VNBP; WOC, May 29, 1863.

Street. Sgt. "Reps" Jones commanded the detachment. Cpl. Connor served as Jones's second-in-command, assisted by privates J. Early Billups, Erasmus D. Cobourn, Caleb Dempsey, Sid H. Gattis, R. Marion Mathis, W. Jack Moore, Richard W. Rodgers, John V. Russell, Martin V. B. Wharton, and George H. Mathis. The change was not without problems. As Connor noted in his ledger,

> Wednesday night [actually, Tuesday, May 26] the gun came, but while on its way into the redoubt, through some awkwardness of the driver, it was overturned and dismounted. Next morning all was righted, and the gun ready to be put in position, when it was discovered that it was needed higher up the river. Thursday evening, the gun was placed in position upon the side of a knob in front of the "Gibbs House," so as to command the lowlands between the bluffs and the river.[78]

Capt. Van Den Corput and the remainder of his battery inherited one of the guns brought into the works when the Rebels abandoned Haynes's Bluff. The gunners protected part of the section of line assigned to Col. Alexander W. Reynolds's Tennesseans, located just southwest of the modern intersection of South Confederate Avenue and Hall's Ferry Road, near the North Carolina monument.[79]

After the timid actions of some of the East Tennessee troops at the Big Black River and the lackluster performance of Cumming's Brigade at Champion Hill, Pemberton apparently had lost confidence in those units. Col. Alexander Reynolds's regiments contained a significant number of mountaineers from the eastern section of the Volunteer State. As a result, Pemberton assigned Stevenson's brigades to defend a sector of the Confederate defenses that he thought unlikely to suffer a determined attack. Apparently, Stevenson's troops stretched from the Railroad Redoubt southward to the terminus of Lockett's defensive line, then northward along the Mississippi River to the point anchored

---

[78] W. O. Connor to W. T. Rigby, May 4, 1903, CA file, VNBP; WOC, May 29, 1863; Terrence Winschel email to Zack Waters, December 6, 2011.

[79] W. O. Connor to W. T. Rigby, May 4, 1903, CA file, VNBP; WOC, May 29, 1863.

by Sgt. Jones's twenty-four-pound siege gun. As the massive Federal attacks occurred against the Confederate lines farther to the north, Stevenson's graycoats spent most of their time "sharpshooting."[80]

Inside the citadel, conditions rapidly deteriorated to a hellish existence barely better than life in a fourteenth-century prison. One writer recounted, "Life in the Vicksburg trenches was brutal and violent. The stench of diarrhea, urine, gangrene, and filthy bodies was ever present. Fresh air did not exist. A wound that healed or health that was restored constituted a miracle." Food supplies diminished to the point that the Rebels faced literal starvation. Mule meat became a delicacy, and standard rations consisted of "one biscuit every twenty-four hours." Tales of soldiers and civilians consuming rats appeared so often in diaries and reminiscences that there must have been some truth to those stories.[81]

The men pinned their hopes for rescue upon Gen. Johnston's troops at Jackson, and news of victories in the east further strengthened the soldiers' resolve. Connor wrote in his diary, "We have glorious news this morning and quite encouraging to men cut off from the outside world as we are. The invincible Lee is again victorious in Virginia [likely referring to the Army of Northern Virginia's victory at Chancellorsville], and his [army has] driven the enemy back to Washington City." On another occasion, he reported, "Vicksburg is of vital importance to the Confederacy, and I believe our rulers will do all in their power to relieve the garrison here." But no orders, pleas, or entreaties seemed capable of goading "Old Joe" into moving toward the Confederate Gibraltar. Instead, he tarried at Jackson, badgering Richmond to provide him with even more troops and supplies.[82]

The two failed attempts to storm the works had convinced General Grant that a direct onslaught would cripple his army long before it ever took the city. Instead, he directed his engineers to begin digging assault trenches, moving the Union lines closer to Vicksburg yard by yard. From these advance positions, Union artillery devastated more

---

[80] Walker, *Hell's Broke Loose*, 85–90; Groce, *Mountain Rebels*, 101–102.

[81] Walker, *Hell's Broke Loose*, 85–90; Groce, *Mountain Rebels*, 101–102.

[82] WOC, June 5, 1863; Arnold, *Grant Wins the War*, 286–91.

and more of the city and its defenses, and the Yankees dug tunnels to detonate explosives beneath the Confederate defenses. Federal sharpshooters shot at any graycoat foolish enough to expose his head above the breastworks, while fire from the Federal artillery and howitzers caused serious damage both to the men and their morale. The Cherokee Artillery lost at least two men, Henry C. Penny and William M. Lloyd, to the sharpshooters, and the harassing fire also severely limited movement between Jones's detachment and Van Den Corput's main body.[83]

John S. Holland, of Van Den Corput's Battery, writing in a letter from Vicksburg on June 14, 1863, gave a rather rosy picture of life in the beleaguered city: "For twenty seven days," he wrote,

> we have stood the shock of battle. From the river the mortars are incessantly shelling us, while outside the artillery is at work night and day. Cannon balls are passing in all directions, and the nearer the trenches [are to the enemy] there is a perfect hailstorm of bullets from small arms. Our works have been assaulted time and again, but we have driven the enemy back in every attempt to take the place by storm; while from the river the [Union] gunboats have fared still worse. We have used them very roughly, sinking the best one [the U.S.S. *Cincinnati*, sunk on May 27] and crippling the others…There is some good deal of sickness among them [Van Den Corput's men] but none dangerous.

Holland refused to "picture our [living] conditions," likely fearing that his missive might fall into enemy hands.[84]

Human courage can last only so long, and it became obvious to Gen. Pemberton that his men had reached the breaking point. On July 4, the emaciated, filthy, and hungry Rebels marched out, laid down their arms, and accepted their parole from the Union troops. The Cherokee Artillery surrendered a total of ninety-two men. Connor

---

[83] W. O. Connor to W. T. Rigby, May 4, 1903, CA file, VNBP; WOC, June 5 and 27, 1863; Walker, *Hell's Broke Loose*, 88.

[84] John S. Holland, "From the Cherokee Artillery," unattributed, undated newspaper article in Stovall scrapbooks, vol. 3, n.p.

simply noted in his diary, "Vicksburg surrendered to the Yankees. Officers and men paroled and allowed to march out with their private property, officers retaining their side arms." Max Van Den Corput made good use of the "private property" clause. "By terms of the surrender of the Confederate forces at Vicksburg," a family history related, "…the officers were allowed to keep their private property. Captain Max Van Den Corput, considering the company flag as private property, took it from its staff, sewed it between the folds of his saddle blanket, and rode out of Vicksburg with it under his saddle."[85]

It took several days to parole all of the approximately 30,000 Confederate soldiers. There seem to have been few examples of animosity between the common soldiers in blue and gray; instead, an atmosphere of mutual curiosity existed between the opposing forces. One Georgian described what he observed while awaiting his oath:

> Since the surrender the Rebs and Bluecoats have been making themselves very familiar. In strolling around, one hears many spirited discussions going on, in reference to the merits of the two governments, the Rebs generally maintaining the grounds that we are not whipped. Now and then one strikes up with a low cur who whines out, "I knowed all the time we'd get whooped." And "I never would have been in it if I hadn't been conscripted." Heard a Yankee tell one of this class, he fought because he was [from the] north and believed he was right, and if he'd been [from the] south he might have been on the other side. You are South, your home is South, and I say damn a man that won't fight for his country and his home. It did me good all over. They [the "low curs"] generally wind up their whines by "Mister, can't you give me a little bread, a little coffee or a canteen…."

The writer concluded, "I'll eat peas another month, before I'd lower myself to lick hands and beg for bread or anything else."[86]

The bluecoats paroled the Rebs as quickly as they could after first searching each soldier's "outer works [clothing]" for contraband such

---

[85] WOC, July 4, 1863; "The Vicksburg Captures," *Savannah Republican*, August 17, 1863, 2; Boozer, *Long, Long Ago*, 231.

[86] WOC, July 7, 1863.

as medicines and percussion caps. While waiting to depart Vicksburg, the Confederate and Union soldiers apparently intermingled and conversed freely. Connor failed to mention any instances of animosity or vindictiveness from either side, though the sight of African Americans in blue uniforms caused some consternation among the Rebels. The Cherokee Artillery diarist noted, "[I] have seen as yet no regularly organized body of Negro troops." He seemed to take comfort in the fact that "…[n]one of the Yankees I conversed [with] would acknowledge them as equals."[87]

[87] WOC, June 28, July 7 and 9, 1863; "Memoirs of the Civil War: W. L. Truman," http://www.cedarcroft.com/cw/memoir/chapter15.html.

Chapter 4

"Nothing but the Hand of God Can Save Us"

Meridian to Dalton

(July 5, 1863–November 27, 1863)

On July 12, Carter Stevenson's division began hiking away from the Confederate Gibraltar. Almost to a man, Van Den Corput's cannoneers gave thanks that they had avoided confinement at Camp Douglas or one of the other Union prisons. The Rebels headed toward Meridian, Mississippi, where they hoped to get transportation home. Making good progress the first day, the Cherokee Artillery camped that night along the west bank of the Big Black River. As they hiked toward the parole camps at Meridian, Mississippi, and Demopolis, Alabama, they found many patriotic Southern civilians who willingly shared what little food and provisions they had with the gaunt soldiers.[1]

As the Vicksburg Confederates passed through Brandon, Mississippi, they observed Gen. Joe Johnston's army slowly retreating from Jackson. That army, numbering 30,000 men with seventy-eight cannon (including the Noble Brothers rifled gun of the Cherokee Artillery), had been occupying Jackson since mid-May. Johnston, however, had tarried until July 1 before finally beginning the march to lift the siege at Vicksburg. They had not gotten very far when the sudden silence of the artillery at Vicksburg signaled that the citadel had fallen. Perhaps with a sigh of relief, "Old Joe" turned his army around and retreated toward the state capital. As Pemberton biographer Michael Ballard concluded, "Johnston never had any intention of trying to save Vicksburg or its defenders. As usual, when a bold offensive maneuver was necessary, Johnston found every excuse not to move." President

---

[1] WOC, June 28–July 12, 1863; "Memoirs of the Civil War: W. L. Truman," http://www.cedarcroft.com/cw/memoir/ chapter 15, Demopolis.

Davis agreed. When he learned that Vicksburg had fallen because the men had nothing to eat, he bitterly quipped, "Yes, from want of provisions inside and a General [Johnston] outside who wouldn't fight."[2]

The Rebel soldiers and citizens, almost without exception, blamed the Quaker general for the capture of the fortress city. Both Northern and Southern newspapers widely reprinted a letter that averred, "The men [Confederate soldiers] had not the slightest confidence in General Pemberton, and since the surrender of Vicksburg express their determination of deserting rather than serve under Pemberton after they are exchanged." Perhaps a more telling comment regarding the common soldiers' attitude toward Pemberton (and Braxton Bragg), however, appeared in an old Mississippian's reminiscences. "I doubt," he wrote, "if the soldiers of Lee and Jackson ever entered into a battle with a thought of defeat; I doubt if the soldiers of Pemberton [and Bragg] ever entered into one with the hope of success." That sentiment goes a long way toward explaining the lack of success of the Confederacy's western armies.[3]

As the various units hiked along the route, they tended to separate into smaller squads. Most men chose friends they had served with for a long time. Wesley Conner's group consisted of Sgt. Isaac Hume, Erasmus Coburn, Arthur Sullivan, J. Early Billups, Eber Johnson, and J. J. Lloyd though other comrades, such as Lt. William S. Hogue, also traveled part of the way with them. Connor, plagued for nearly a month by an illness he had contracted during the final days of the siege, had been suffering from intermittent bouts of chills and fever. Due to his illness, the diarist had some trouble keeping up with his comrades. One night, after yet another bout of infirmity, he spent an evening at a blacksmith's shop, and a few days later he spent an entire day in a

---

[2] Arnold, *Grant Wins the War*, 286–91; Winschel, *Confederate Gibraltar*, 112–13; Ballard, *Pemberton*, 111–13; Strode, *Jefferson Davis*, 445.

[3] "Vicksburg: Its Siege and Fall," *Philadelphia Illustrated New Age*, August 5, 1863, 1 (quoting an unidentified Alabama journal); Jones, "The Rank and File at Vicksburg," 17.

hospital. Despite those delays, by July 21 most members of the Cherokee Artillery had arrived at the parole camp at Meridian, where they were to report before heading home.[4]

President Davis wanted to keep the Vicksburg army together and intact in the two camps until the men received their official paroles, but that proved to be a politician's pipe dream. Both Meridian and Demopolis lacked enough food, lodging, or supplies to accommodate 26,000 men, and the "tedium and inaction of a parole camp did not appeal to the men, already depressed by the siege and surrender at Vicksburg...[and] many began to absent themselves without leave and go home." Gen. Pemberton, realizing that the men had decided to leave, with or without official approval, began issuing thirty-day furloughs to soldiers from Mississippi, Alabama, the Carolinas, and Georgia until they could be officially exchanged. Troops from certain sections of Tennessee, Arkansas, Louisiana, and Missouri, states now largely under enemy occupation, would have to stay in the parole camps—or desert.[5]

Van Den Corput's Battery, being part of the lucky group Pemberton had furloughed, left Meridian and began walking to Enterprise, Alabama. There they boarded a train to Mobile. Late in the afternoon of Friday, July 24, the cannoneers left Mobile on the steamer *Georgia Sykes* and reached Tensas wharf at 7:30 P.M. An hour later they boarded a train to Camp Pollard. From there, they basically retraced the route they had followed on the trip to Mississippi seven months previously—from Camp Pollard, they passed through Montgomery, West Point, and on to Atlanta. Arriving at Kingston at noon on July 28, they changed trains for the three-hour ride to Rome. Then, individually and in small groups, they made their way home.[6]

Soldiers returning to the "City of Seven Hills" found it a far different place from the friendly, tight-knit community they had left two years before. Not only had the Noble Brothers Foundry transformed Rome into a major industrial center, employing dozens of skilled and

---

[4] WOC, July 13–19, 1863.

[5] Horn, *Army of Tennessee*, 220–21; Cheairs, *Old Reliable*, 158–61.

[6] WOC, July 12–28, 1863.

unskilled laborers, but the town had also become an important hospital center for sick and wounded Rebel soldiers. This change had also sparked a feeling of resentment among some Northwest Georgia residents. The editor of the *Tri-Weekly Courier* grumbled,

> Perhaps no people in the Confederacy...have submitted to the privations and yielded their hearty cooperation for the interest, prosperity, and success of the [Confederate] government with better grace than the people of Floyd County.... Now it is to be greatly regretted that the government has deemed it to its interest to occupy almost the entire city as a hospital. Nine-tenths of the important business houses are now occupied and laid off into four distinct hospitals...all crowded to overflowing with inmates.

Connor noted the change immediately, recording in his diary, "The place didn't look natural. All crowded with sick soldiers and streets full of strange faces."[7]

The harvest season had been good in North Georgia, and most of the returning soldiers rapidly began regaining their health and good spirits. After months of near starvation, each meal must have seemed like a feast, and life quickly settled back into familiar routines. The veterans spent time getting reacquainted with sweethearts, wives, and children, and later began visiting friends, extended families, and their churches. Wesley Connor especially enjoyed visiting churches and old friends as those activities offered a perfect opportunity for meeting pretty girls.

But even in relatively "safe" Northwest Georgia, the war occasionally reared its ugly head. Federal troops very nearly captured Connor while he visited friends in adjoining Chattooga County. Connor, who had accompanied a physician friend while the doctor made house calls, learned upon returning to his friend's residence that Union cavalry had paid a visit during their absence. Despite that close call, the corporal from Cave Spring was in no great hurry to return to the army.[8]

---

[7] WOC, July 12–28, 1863; *TWC*, February 12, 1863, quoted in Aycock, *All Roads to Rome*, 102–103.

[8] WOC, September 10, 1863.

Not all of the battery's sick and injured improved, however. William H. Baker, who had written so lovingly about Northwest Georgia, passed away at home. Likewise, C. W. Gattis never recovered from the disease he had contracted in Mississippi and also passed away at home. Two members of the unit, Alexander Franks and Solomon Fry, used their sojourn at a U.S. hospital in St. Louis as an opportunity to take the Oath of Allegiance. The two Tennessee natives decided to employ their training with the Cherokee Artillery by enlisting in Battery A of the Pennsylvania Light Artillery.[9]

Meanwhile, the Confederate government began hastily recalling the former members of the Army of Mississippi. Southern newspapers began running the following notice:

> Circular: The President of the Confederate States regarding the furloughs granted the paroled prisoners from Vicksburg of too great [a] duration in the present condition of the country…. [U]nder his instructions, all such furloughs are rescinded…. The furloughs of the troops from Georgia are reduced to twenty (20) days, those from Alabama and Mississippi to fifteen (15) days. At the expiration of their furloughs, all officers and men will report to this place [Demopolis or Meridian] in their former organization as far as practicable.[10]

On August 13, 1863, the circular appeared in the *Rome Weekly Courier*, to which Captain Max Van Den Corput appended a personal note to his men: "Our furloughs having by the above order been reduced to twenty (20) days, instead of thirty (30) days, I desire and earnestly call upon all officers and men belonging to the Battery, 'no matter when paroled or furloughed,' to return to Demopolis, Ala., at the time to which their furloughs have been reduced."

After assuring his boys that he realized this order was an extreme imposition upon their plans and desires, he noted, "your country…once more requires those services of which you [have] always so

[9] See appendix, Cherokee Artillery roster.

[10] *RC*, August 13, 1863, 2.

nobly acquitted yourselves." He asked them to meet at the Rome train depot on the morning of August 14 for the trip to Alabama.[11]

The stubborn individuality of the Cherokee Artillery once again reared its head, and the unit—almost to a man—ignored Davis's directive. As a result, Capt. Van Den Corput's plan to leave Rome in mid-August failed to materialize. The men, who had endured months of combat, siege, and deprivation, balked at any idea of cutting short their stay at home. Finally, on September 15, the *Tri-Weekly Courier*, "in tall headlines" ran the following notice: "ATTENTION TO CHEROKEE ARTILLERY: All Vicksburg prisoners regularly exchanged on the 12th inst. advise that Capt. Corput and his men are to meet at the Rome Railroad depot Saturday morning on the morning of the 19th to take the morning train, equipped for service. Capt. Corput has already secured another battery."[12]

This time, most of the members of the Cherokee Artillery arrived at the appointed time for the journey to Demopolis. They could not make up all the losses suffered during the Vicksburg Campaign, but they carried with them nine new recruits from Floyd County and nearby Cherokee County, Alabama. These men were William Barnett, Lafayette Emerson Camp, James Lumpkin Duke, James A. Dunn, Henry M. Gresham, John Harrison, J. M. Lovelady, Joseph R. Price, and J. W. C. Stewart.

Modern historians have generally concluded that both draftees and volunteers who enlisted after 1861 tended to be half-hearted in their devotion to the Confederacy, but only one of the new recruits—Lovelady—voluntarily went over to the enemy. Federal troops would capture two of the men (Camp and Gresham) at Salisbury, North Carolina, during the unit's last battle; one (Price) died in prison; and three (Barnett, Harrison, and Stewart) were listed as "present" on the last roll. James Duke, who enlisted despite having limited mobility due to a hip injury suffered as a child, was granted a medical discharge, but

[11] Ibid.

[12] *TWC*, September 15, 1863, 1; see also Aycock, "Old records tell trials of Rome Civil War prisoners," *Rome News-Tribune*, July 14, 1974, 8-B.

not before he had fought bravely during the Chattanooga Campaign. Eighteen-year-old Arkansas native James Dunn may have set the unit's record for stubbornness. Captured in Middle Georgia by Gen. James Wilson's Federal raiders in April 1865, the teenager refused to take the Oath of Allegiance until late August 1865.[13]

The men of the Georgia battery traveled by rail to the parole camp at Demopolis, Alabama, for their formal reinstatement into the Confederate States Army. Two days later, they again boarded the train and headed east to Atlanta to pick up their four new artillery pieces. From the records, it appears their newly acquired guns were twelve-pound "Napoleon" smoothbores. A few of the men, including Wesley Conner, straggled in later, having missed the train that left Rome on September 19. By the time the Cherokee Artillery received its replacement cannons and had assembled their entire command, the Army of Tennessee had won its one great victory.[14]

On September 19–20, Federal general William S. Rosecrans's Army of the Cumberland and Braxton Bragg's Army of Tennessee met in bloody combat among the heavily wooded hills and valleys of northwestern Georgia, adjacent to a small creek known by the Cherokee as Chickamauga—"River of Death." Despite significant reinforcements in the form of Lt. Gen. James Longstreet's 1st corps (which the War Department had temporarily transferred to Bragg from Gen. Robert E. Lee's Army of Northern Virginia), the Army of Tennessee was unable to break the Union line, and the first day's fighting devolved into a gory, inconclusive slugfest. The next day, Rosecrans, acting upon faulty intelligence, issued an order that opened a gap in the Federal lines. Longstreet's men poured through the opening, essentially cutting the Union defensive line in half. The Yankee left wing immediately dissolved, fleeing in disorder toward Chattanooga. Only a determined

---

[13] See appendix, Cherokee Artillery roster; see generally, Kenneth W. Noe, *Reluctant Rebels: The Confederates Who Joined the Army after 1861* (Chapel Hill: University of North Carolina Press, 2010).

[14] Aycock, "Old Records tell trials"; WOC, September 25–27, 1863.

defense by Maj. Gen. George S. Thomas's men, at Snodgrass Hill, prevented a total Federal rout.[15]

Rather than immediately pressing his beaten foe—despite fervent pleas from fiery Brig. Gen. Nathan Bedford Forrest, Longstreet, and several other generals—Bragg was in no hurry to pursue Rosecrans and his Army of the Cumberland and try to flank the Federals out of Chattanooga. Indeed, historians such as Earl Hess have rightly noted that Bragg faced significant challenges in any attempt to move his exhausted army across the barren, mountainous terrain and cross the Tennessee River to reach the Gateway City. Short of supply wagons, hopeful that recent signs indicated that Rosecrans was actually preparing to abandon the city, and deeply distrustful of his senior commanders, whom he viewed as insubordinate and inefficient, Bragg chose instead to move cautiously and limit the risk to his army, which had lost more than 18,000 men during the campaign. Nevertheless, as other historians have also pointed out with equal evidence, Bragg's cautious, methodical approach may well have frittered away a golden opportunity to annihilate Rosecrans's shattered army. Historian Edward G. Longacre bluntly asserted, "At long last having won a battle (thanks to Robert E. Lee's help), Bragg mounted a pursuit so slow and cautious as to ensure his inability to reap the fruits of victory." Just as he had been after the Battle of Perryville a year earlier, Bragg was simply unwilling to take the risks necessary to capitalize on a hard-won victory. By the time he finally reached the Gateway City, the opportunity to exploit the triumph at Chickamauga no longer existed.[16]

The men and guns of the Cherokee Artillery had left Decatur, Georgia, for Chattanooga on October 6. Once again, the Floyd County artillerymen would serve in Maj. Gen. Carter Stevenson's division. Not long after the Cherokee Artillery arrived on the outskirts of Chattanooga, the battery received orders to accompany Stevenson

---

[15] Connelly, *Autumn of Glory*, 201–24; see generally, Peter Cozzens, *This Horrible Sound: The Battle of Chickamauga* (Champaign: University of Illinois Press, 1996).

[16] Hess, *Braxton Bragg*, 169–72; Longacre, *Cavalry of the Heartland*, 242.

into East Tennessee to keep an eye on Federal Gen. Ambrose Burnside's army. The former commander of the Army of the Potomac directed a force numbering about 25,000 men and had established his headquarters at Knoxville. Recalling winter 1861–1862, spent in that icy, inhospitable region among a largely disloyal populace, the thought of a winter campaign in the Tennessee Mountains could not have been a pleasing prospect for the Georgia cannoneers.[17]

Wesley Connor noted in his diary that Van Den Corput's Battery camped at Sweetwater, Tennessee, on October 18, and the next day moved to Loudon. They emplaced their guns along the south bank of the Little Tennessee River and prepared to cover an attack or defend against an enemy assault. Luckily, neither event occurred. Connor observed that they saw "plenty of Feds" across the stream but neither side seemed anxious to bring on a battle. The Floyd County soldiers concluded that the two commanders had reached a tacit agreement to leave each other in peace. Even though the chance of action seemed minuscule, Bragg forwarded Brig. Gen. John K. Jackson's Georgia and Mississippi brigades as reinforcements for Stevenson's unit.[18]

No definition of "quiet" and "peaceable" applied to the furor and political in-fighting then occurring at Bragg's Headquarters near Chattanooga. It came to a head when generals Longstreet and Polk directed a scathing indictment of Bragg's failures to Confederate Secretary of War James Seddon. In part, Longstreet wrote, "Our Chief [Bragg] has done but one thing that he ought to have done since I joined his army—that was to order the attack upon the 20th [of September]. All other things that he has done he ought not to have done. I am convinced that nothing but the hand of God can save us or help us as long as we have our present commander." Lest Pres. Davis think that those opinions were the ravings of a couple of disgruntled generals, on October 4, a majority the Army of Tennessee's senior commanders wrote

[17] Connelly, *Autumn of Glory*, 263–64; *OR*, ser. 1, vol. 31, part 3, 576, 600–601; Seymour, *Divided Loyalties*, 103–104.

[18] WOC, October 18, 1863.

the chief executive a letter expressing their doubts about Bragg's leadership.[19]

Davis hurried to Chattanooga in a vain attempt to defuse the powder keg, but he only made matters worse. Realizing that his only viable options to replace his friend, Bragg, were either Joe Johnston, whom the chief executive loathed; or James Longstreet, who was only on loan from the Army of Northern Virginia, Davis took the path of least resistance. He condemned those who had expressed doubts regarding Bragg's competency and reiterated his support for the dour North Carolinian. Bolstered by the president's support, Bragg began purging his enemies even before Davis returned to Richmond. He banished Forrest and Polk to Mississippi and dispatched Longstreet to East Tennessee to deal with Burnside. As if to further punish Longstreet, Bragg refused to provide the leader from the Virginia army with adequate transportation, provisions, or even maps of the region. Longstreet requested that Bragg assign Stevenson to his corps, but Bragg refused. (Seemingly, the Army of Tennessee commander hoped Longstreet would fail, even if the Confederate cause suffered as a result.) At the same time, Bragg realized that he could not easily replace the 17,000 men in Longstreet's Corps, so he recalled Carter Stevenson's and John K. Jackson's troops from East Tennessee. The Cherokee Artillery reached Chattanooga on November 12.[20]

Stevenson's artillery battalion consisted of four batteries commanded by Capt. William W. Carnes. Carnes, a Tennessee native, had been ready to graduate from the United States Naval Academy at Annapolis, Maryland, when he resigned in 1861 to throw in his lot with his home state. Only twenty-one, he "was beyond a doubt the youngest captain of artillery in the Confederate States Army." Despite his youth, Carnes clearly had the respect of his superiors and men. His batteries

---

[19] Seymour, *Divided Loyalties*, 96–102; *OR*, ser. 1, vol. 30, part 2, 65–66; *OR*, ser. 1, vol. 30, part 4, 705.

[20] Seymour, *Divided Loyalties*, 96–102; Connelly, *Autumn of Glory*, 260–66; WOC, November 12, 1863; Woodworth, *Six Armies in Tennessee*, 138–41.

included Max Van Den Corput's Cherokee Artillery; Capt. E. D. Baxter's Tennessee unit; Carnes's Tennessee Artillery (severely understrength, due casualties suffered at Chickamauga), and Capt. John B. Rowan's Marylanders (often listed as a Georgia battery). Due to seniority, Van Den Corput served as Carnes's second in command.[21]

After exiling Longstreet, Polk, and Forrest, Bragg finally turned his attention to driving the bluecoats out of Chattanooga. Author Wiley Sword concluded: "Bragg now had...three alternatives: cross the Tennessee [River] and outflank Rosecrans, attack the Federal defenses headlong, or starve out the Federals by establishing a siege line." He chose the latter tactic. Unfortunately, the Rebel commander "failed miserably in implementing his new strategy," and on October 27, 1863, Brig. Gen. William F. "Baldy" Smith's Union troops drove the Confederates away from the west bank of the Tennessee River at Brown's Ferry. Shortly thereafter, the Federals stretched a pontoon bridge across the waterway, allowing Ulysses S. Grant, who had replaced Rosecrans, to open the so-called "Cracker Line." Regular shipments of food and military supplies now flowed into the Yankees' camps, and Bragg's slender hope of starving the enemy into retreat or submission vanished like the morning mist.[22]

After Stevenson's Division returned to the Gateway City, his units had assumed a position on the Confederate left at Lookout Mountain. Bragg rode over to inform Stevenson that his men had responsibility for holding Lookout Mountain and personally instructed Stevenson on the positions he expected his units to occupy. The Army of Tennessee's commander also took the opportunity to test whether Carnes's Artillery Battalion could fire effectively on the Union supply line at Brown's Ferry. "One of the heaviest [guns] of our battalion of four batteries was driven to the point [of Lookout Mountain]," Carnes later wrote. "A

---

[21] Lindsley, *Military Annals of Tennessee*, 824 (hereafter cited as *MAT*); Head, *Campaigns and Battles of the Sixteenth Regiment*, 238; Mathes, *Old Guard in Gray*, 288.

[22] Sword, *Mountains Touched with Fire*, 112–22; Cozzens, *Shipwreck of Their Hopes*, 48–65.

lieutenant with the gun detachment made the trial under my direction, and having found that none of our field pieces could throw shot to the bridge, the gun was at once returned to its battery in our lines of investment, below the mountain."[23]

Gen. Stevenson's position provided a magnificent view of the countryside, but also allowed Bragg to keep an eye on his own troops and the enemy as well. On the evening of November 23, Stevenson sent a message to Lt. Gen. William J. Hardee that he suspected that the Yankees would soon attack the Confederate left near Tunnel Hill. Stevenson's assessment made sense. Grant had shown a propensity for spearheading his assaults, as he had done at Vicksburg, with Maj. Gen. William T. Sherman's Army of the Tennessee. He usually chose the red-haired general, a reliable combat officer, rather than Maj. Gen. Joseph Hooker, whose actions at Chancellorsville had revealed a tendency to crack under pressure. Unknown to the Rebel high command, the Federals had recently decoded the Confederate flag system, which allowed the Union commanders to translate Stevenson's message almost as quickly as the intended recipients.[24]

Early on the morning of November 24, Hooker's Yankees, numbering 10,000 men, launched a surprise attack on the Rebels east of Lookout Creek. Spanning the stream by using felled trees and jerry-built pole bridges, the Federals advanced in two columns over terrain described as "rugged, heavily timbered, and full of chasms." One of Hooker's units moved to the northeast along the western slope of Lookout Mountain, while another force pushed due east toward Missionary Ridge. Confederate Brig. Gen. Edward C. Walthall had previously deployed two of his Mississippi regiments as skirmishers, defending the lowlands east of Lookout Creek. Walthall's other two regiments

[23] Cozzens, *Shipwreck of Their Hopes*, 117–18; W. W. Carnes to J. B. Pound, October 28, 1931, Carnes file, CCNMP.

[24] Sword, "The Battle Above the Clouds," 44.

held a line of hastily dug entrenchments along the western slope of Lookout Mountain.[25]

The Magnolia State skirmishers were under orders to fall back fighting if a heavy force attacked them, but the speed and ferocity of the enemy onslaught almost overwhelmed them. A Federal soldier recalled, "The Rebels seemed to be behind every rock and tree, and poured lead like hail, but it was useless." While it likely appeared to be a stubborn defense to the bluecoats pushing forward under enemy fire, one Mississippi officer saw the situation differently. Col. W. F. Dowd, stationed at the Craven House plateau defenses, believed that Hooker's men pursued the graycoats retreating from the creek bank so quickly that his men's initial fire killed some of their own skirmishers. Shells from Union artillery near Moccasin Bend added to the misery of the Mississippians. Walthall, one of the finest brigadiers in the Army of Tennessee, hastily got his remaining troops into a line of battle to slow Hooker's advance. He directed his Magnolia State warriors that he expected them to "hold until Hell freezes over." The Mississippi commander, however, quickly realized he could not hold the Federals long without help. Sorely pressed, Walthall appealed for help from Carter Stevenson and nearby brigades. Until aid arrived, Walthall would have to fight a delaying action and pray that help would arrive quickly.[26]

On the night of November 23–24, Van Den Corput's Battery had replaced Capt. James Garrity's Alabama artillery near the northern tip of Lookout Mountain. Capt. Van Den Corput positioned a two-gun section at the point of the peak, and they began raining shells on the Federal troops advancing against Walthall. Completely blinded by the clouds and fog, Van Den Corput reported, "[W]e could hear his [the enemy's] march and [the] sound of the guns and guided by this, and the sound of the musketry, ours [fire of the Cherokee Artillery] was

---

[25] Ibid., 44–54; H. V. Boynton, "Second Day's Operations—Battle of Lookout Mountain," Carnes file, CCNMP; Dowd, "Lookout Mountain and Missionary Ridge," 397; Smartt, "Walthall on the Battle of Lookout [Mountain]," 562–64; Bohannon, "He exhibited the highest soldierly qualities: General Edward C. Walthall's Confederate Army Service," unpublished, undated manuscript, personal collection of Zack Waters, Rome, GA.

[26] *OR*, ser. 1, vol. 31, part 2, 728; Cozzens, *Shipwreck of Their Hopes*, 175.

directed." Col. D. R. Hundley, commanding the 31st Alabama Regiment, provided a vivid postwar account of the Georgia battery's fight. "The [Cherokee Artillery] guns," he wrote,

> were placed close to the brow of the mountain. Not a word was being spoken by the officers and men, but the latter loaded their pieces in silence and fired with great deliberation and regularity. They saw nothing below them but a seemingly fathomless abyss of lurid darkness, but into this darkness they poured their live thunders with a right good will. In the distance, from Federal batteries on Moccasin point, came the answering boom, and occasionally a shell went screaming over our heads, while minie balls were spinning past us continually. Below us the battle raged unabated....[27]

In the only document by the Belgian commander that appears in the *Official Records*, Van Den Corput wrote,

> About 10:00 A.M. the fog on the side of Lookout Creek had disappeared enough to show us the Federals moving in three different bodies from the foot of Raccoon Mountain toward Lookout Creek. The pickets had been firing from about sunrise toward the creek.... The longest fuse that I had with my guns was 7", which time would carry my shells only 1 mile. The position of the Federals being far over that distance, I did not open fire on them then. After their first charge on our infantry—who instantly gave way, the enemy pursuing them—I opened fire on the Federals, having brought my section in position on the left of the mountain. I fired 33 shells, doing in many instances good execution. The Federals were, however, soon under cover of the rocks, [and] being unable to depress my guns enough [I ceased firing].... Unable to do anything more, I waited for further orders.

Initially, the Confederate fire caught Col. David Ireland's New Yorkers of Howard's XI Corps, in the open. Lying prone to escape the

[27] *OR*, ser. 1, vol. 31, part 2, 728–29; Wilder, *Seventh Regiment OVI*, 38.

fire from Walthall's regiments, they also suffered briefly from the Georgia battery's shelling, but they quickly scurried into the rocks closer to the base of Lookout Mountain to escape the fire from above.[28]

At about 12:30 P.M., Brig. Gen. John C. Brown, directing a brigade of Tennesseans in Stevenson's Division, ordered a section of the Cherokee Artillery to move back toward division headquarters but soon rescinded the directive. According to Van Den Corput, "[A]t about 2 p. m. General Brown gave me orders to fire towards the Craven House if I could ascertain the direction [in the clouds and fog], the enemy being reported in force in that direction. I obtained from the signal corps the position of the house, and fired about thirty times at intervals in that direction and toward the right."[29]

It is difficult to determine the effectiveness of the afternoon barrage. The Belgian commander stated that both he and Gen. Brown felt the two guns' efforts had been effectual, but a Union soldier sarcastically reported the artillery section really did little more than shoot the tops off the trees, causing them to rain down upon the Federal troops below. An early historian wrote that the fire from the Georgia guns "was of little consequence." He further stated, "The day was foggy and misty throughout, and the firing from the summit was of necessity inaccurate."[30]

About 3:45 P.M., Gen. Stevenson sent orders for the Georgia gunners to bring the battery away from the point overlooking the Craven House plateau, proceed to the foot of the mountain, and then move to the rear. This the Cherokee Artillery did with alacrity. Although they were virtually unscathed, the battery had been on the receiving end of heavy, long-range shelling from Federal artillery, as well as musket fire, and the men were more than ready to move to a less exposed position.[31]

---

[28] *OR*, ser. 1, vol. 31, part 2, 728–29; Wilder, *Seventh Regiment OVI*, 38.

[29] Sword, *Mountains Touched with Fire*, 221; Sword, "Battle Above the Clouds," 54.

[30] Connelly, *Autumn of Glory*, 270–71; Cozzens, *Shipwreck of Their Hopes*, 211.

[31] *OR*, ser. 1, vol. 31, part 2, 729.

Braxton Bragg seemed completely unconcerned by the loss of Lookout Mountain. It had been expendable all along, despite the 1,251 Rebel casualties sacrificed in the defense of the worthless rock. Walthall's Brigade alone suffered more than 800 men killed, captured, and wounded.[32]

First light on the morning of November 25 found the Confederate defenses stretched along the spine of Missionary Ridge. The plateau extended south to north for eight miles from Rossville (just below the Georgia state line) to Tunnel Hill on the north. Bragg felt confident that his position could be easily defended. The eminence rose 500–600 feet above the valley floor, and enemy attackers would be forced to scale those heights to reach his troops. Confederate artillery was emplaced to cover the approaches from Chattanooga and a line of rifle pits at the base of the ridge offered additional protection. Two high hills just north of Tunnel Hill, where railway workers had blasted a passageway through the ridge in 1849 to accommodate rails for the Chattanooga & Cleveland Railroad, represented the apex of the Rebel line. Maj. Gen. Patrick Cleburne, with his combat veterans from Texas, Arkansas, Tennessee, Alabama, and Mississippi, held that vital position. Bragg considered this northern sector of his line to be the weakest point. As a result, he sent all the reinforcements he could reasonably spare to the Irish general.[33]

Concern regarding the safety of Cleburne's position led Bragg to hurry Carter Stevenson's division to bolster the Confederate position at Tunnel Hill. He had good reason for his anxiety. As Stevenson had previously predicted, Grant now called upon William T. Sherman to lead the primary Federal assault. Writing to his brother, Sherman explained the Yankee's plan. "The whole philosophy of the battle was that I should get by a dash, a position on the extremity of the Missionary Ridge from which the enemy would be forced to drive me, or allow his [major supply] depot at Chickamauga Station to be in danger. I expected Bragg to attack me at daylight, but he did not, and to bring

---

[32] W. W. Carnes to Randolph, November 20, 1931, Carnes file, CCNMP.

[33] Cozzens, *Shipwreck of Their Hopes*, 205–10.

matters to a crisis quickly…Grant ordered me to assume the offensive." Flanking the Rebels from their position should have been a relatively easy task, but Sherman concluded that a quick frontal assault could to drive the graycoats from their entrenchments.[34]

At daylight the next morning (November 25), Stevenson's Division commenced the march to reinforce Cleburne's position. The batteries of Carnes's Battalion followed behind them as quickly as possible along the rugged ridge road. Carnes hurried ahead to confer with Cleburne, and Van Den Corput, as the senior captain, brought Stevenson's batteries to the front. The Cherokee Artillery led the way, followed by the batteries of Rowan, Baxter, and Marshall. Even before reaching Cleburne's position, the sounds of heavy firing arose in the distance, and Carnes learned that the Confederates had just beaten back the initial Federal attack. Cleburne ordered Carnes to get artillery in position quickly. Carnes found a Missouri battery—probably Capt. Hiram Bledsoe's battery from Maj. Gen. William Walker's division—and ordered them to move up in support of Cleburne's troops. Shortly thereafter, Carnes's four batteries arrived and also took up positions near the tunnel.[35]

That first Union attack, by Brig. Gen. John Corse's brigade—two Illinois regiments and one each from Iowa, Ohio, and Michigan—had begun shortly after 10 A.M. with a total of about 950 men. Corse's bluecoats had charged from the north and had actually reached Cleburne's breastworks before the Rebels drove them back. Rebel artillery and small arms fire had cut wide swaths in Corse's ranks before halting the assault, and rather than run the gauntlet of fire back their lines, many of Corse's men hunkered down in relative safety at the base of the hill.[36]

---

[34] Ibid., 205–10, 224–25; W. W. Carnes to Randolph, November 20, 1931, Carnes file, CCNMP.

[35] Cozzens, *Shipwreck of Their Hopes*, 205–10, 224–25; W. W. Carnes to Randolph, November 20, 1931, Carnes file, CCNMP; Byers, *With Fire and Sword*, 106–107; WOC, November 25, 1863.

[36] W. W. Carnes to Randolph, November 20, 1931, Carnes file, CCNMP.

About the time the initial Yankee attack faltered, Carnes's Battalion began filing into line. Somewhat surprisingly, Lt. Gen. William J. Hardee directed Carnes "that no artillery firing should be done, as no demonstration against our position was being made." Whether by luck or design, the location Carnes selected allowed the Rebel artillery to throw a raking, enfilading fire into Sherman's columns that moved in from the west. That was exactly the route taken by Col. John M. Loomis's Illinois, Indiana, Iowa, and Missouri soldiers of Brig. Gen. Charles L. Matthies's brigade, as they followed Corse's initial assault. The Federals soon found themselves in something like "artillery hell." An Iowa officer recalled that his unit's "bayonets glittering in the sun made an excellent mark for the enemy's artillery. The first shot struck close to my line, ricocheted and skipped over the men; the second struck directly in the ranks of the regiment to my left, [and] several others plowed the ground immediately in our front and rear." Having found the range, the Rebel gunners poured a hail of fire upon the unfortunate bluecoats.[37]

Lt. Samuel Byers of The Fifth Iowa left a vivid description of the damage the Confederate batteries inflicted upon them. "In front of us was a rail fence," he declared,

> and being in direct line of fire, its splinters and fragments flew in every direction. "Jump that fence, men! Tear it down!" cried the colonel. Never did men get over a fence more quickly. Our distance was nearly half a mile to the Rebel position. We started on a charge, running across the open fields. I had heard the roaring of heavy battle before, but never such a shrieking of cannonballs and bursting shell as met us on that charge. We could see the enemy working their guns, while in plain view other batteries galloped up, unlimbered, and let loose on us.... It sounded as if the end of the world had come.

With rapid, accurate fire, the Confederate guns first staggered and then scattered the Yankee formations and drove them back in confusion.[38]

---

[37] *OR*, ser. 1, vol. 31, part 2, 736–38; Cozzens, *Shipwreck of Their Hopes*, 236–43.

[38] W. W. Carnes to Randolph, November 20, 1931, Carnes file, CCNMP; *OR*, ser. 1, vol. 31, part 2, 753; Cozzens, *Shipwreck of Their Hopes*, 345–46.

Gen. Hardee, apparently believing his command had been flouted, approached Stevenson's position with fire in his eyes. According to the artillery battalion commander,

> Genl. Hardee came rapidly riding back to find why his order to do no artillery firing was disobeyed. Our General [apparently Carter Stevenson] pointed to the Federal line which our concentrated cannon fire had broken up, and Hardee, after watching the effect of our unexpected artillery attack, said it was a line of battle broken into disordered fragments as quickly as he had ever seen done.

Hardee quickly returned to his previous position.[39]

Loomis's and Matthies's Union brigades, who had taken cover in the killing ground by sheltering in a roadbed, kept up a steady, deadly fire on the Confederates on Tunnel Hill. Cleburne quickly gave permission to Brig. Gen. Alfred Cumming, whose Georgia brigade now bore the brunt of the Union fire, to lead a bayonet charge to drive off the annoying bluecoats. The Irish commander not only gave approval for the attack but also joined in the assault, leading Brig. Gen. James A. Smith's Texans. The sudden onslaught scattered Matthies's men. With his flank now uncovered, Loomis joined Matthies in a hasty retreat. In this action, the graycoats captured between 300–500 Federals. Shortly thereafter, Sherman essentially called an end to the attempt to take Tunnel Hill. All total, he had lost about 2,000 men in killed, captured, and wounded and left modern historians to debate why he failed to flank Cleburne from his position at Tunnel Hill.[40]

Despite the successes at Tunnel Hill, disaster loomed further south along the Confederate line. Several individuals claimed credit for delivering the news of the incredible collapse of Bragg's veteran troops at Missionary Ridge. William Carnes, writing more than fifty years after the fact, averred that he first informed Stevenson and Cleburne, but the shocking news did not cause the Irishman to panic. He held his men in position at Tunnel Hill until about an hour after nightfall. He then sent Brig. Gen. Mark Lowery's Alabama and Mississippi brigade

[39] WOC, November 25, 1863.

[40] Cozzens, *Shipwreck of Their Hopes*, 372; *OR*, ser. 1, vol. 31, part 2, 321.

toward Sherman's lines in a noisy foray designed to hold the enemy in place. Col. Hiram Granbury's reliable Texans drew the unenviable assignment of serving as Cleburne's rear guard. The Irish Confederate reported, "By 9:00 P.M. everything was across [Chickamauga Creek] except the dead and a few stragglers lingering here and there under the shadow of the trees for the purpose of being captured, faint-hearted patriots succumbing to the hardships of war and the imagined hopelessness of the hour."[41]

Van Den Corput's men, despite spending several hours under heavy fire, again escaped the engagement virtually unscathed, and they soon became the recipients of another stroke of good fortune. The Cherokee Artillery, along with the rest of Carnes's Battalion, marched away from Tunnel Hill and soon put the South Chickamauga Creek between themselves and the Yankees. Once across the creek, the Georgia cannoneers quickly bedded down and went to sleep. At about 4 A.M., the battery arose and began marching toward Chickamauga Station. Before Bragg's retreating army arrived to destroy the warehouses, Van Den Corput's men took the opportunity to refill their haversacks, loading up on sacks of meal, flour, and rice. After this rare stroke of good fortune, the Georgians resumed their retreat until they reached Ringgold, Georgia, where they again encamped for the night.[42]

Just as Braxton Bragg lost a golden opportunity after his triumph at Chickamauga, so Ulysses S. Grant squandered his chance to cripple or even demolish the Army of Tennessee following the incredible victory at Missionary Ridge. The Rebel horde that halted at Dalton certainly seemed ripe for the picking, and conditions in Dalton gave Southerners little cause for optimism. According to a civilian who witnessed the retreat, Bragg's army was "sorely pressed, his animals exhausted, and his army hopelessly demoralized. In a small portion of it only had the officers been able to preserve regimental and company

[41] W. W. Carnes to Randolph, November 20, 1931, Carnes file, CCNMP; *OR*, ser. 1, vol. 31, part 2, 697, 752; Sword, *Mountains Touched with Fire*, 315; Connelly, *Autumn of Glory*, 270–76.

[42] WOC, November 25, 1863.

formations, many of the men having thrown away their arms. A still greater number were open and violent in their denunciations of the Confederacy." Less than 28,000 graycoats stumbled into the rallying point at Dalton.[43]

Cleburne's Division, covering the army's disorderly flight, seemed to be one of the few Confederate units that maintained its esprit and will to fight. The Army of Tennessee's supply train and artillery trailed the Rebel troops and made a tempting target for Joe Hooker's pursuit force, but the Irish general sprang a trap on Hooker's Federals at Ringgold Gap. The four-hour fight cost the Union an additional 500 men while Cleburne suffered 200 casualties, but only twenty dead. Grant arrived as the fight flickered to a close and called off the chase.[44]

Scores of the Confederate survivors of the fight near Chattanooga, seeing the condition of the army at Dalton, soon slipped away under cover of darkness and went home. Wesley Connor, a true believer in the Confederate cause, had no intention of deserting the Southern army. No matter how low the South's hopes sank, he had determined to remain faithful to the end. The final 1863 entry in Connor's diary, before a month of silence, read, "Received orders to build stables for the horses. Indications are that we winter here, though we will be governed entirely by Grant's movements."[45]

---

[43] Cozzens, *Shipwreck of Their Hopes*, 372; *OR*, ser. 1, vol. 31, part 2, 321.

[44] Sword, *Mountains Touched with Fire*, 335–46.

[45] WOC, November 27, 1863.

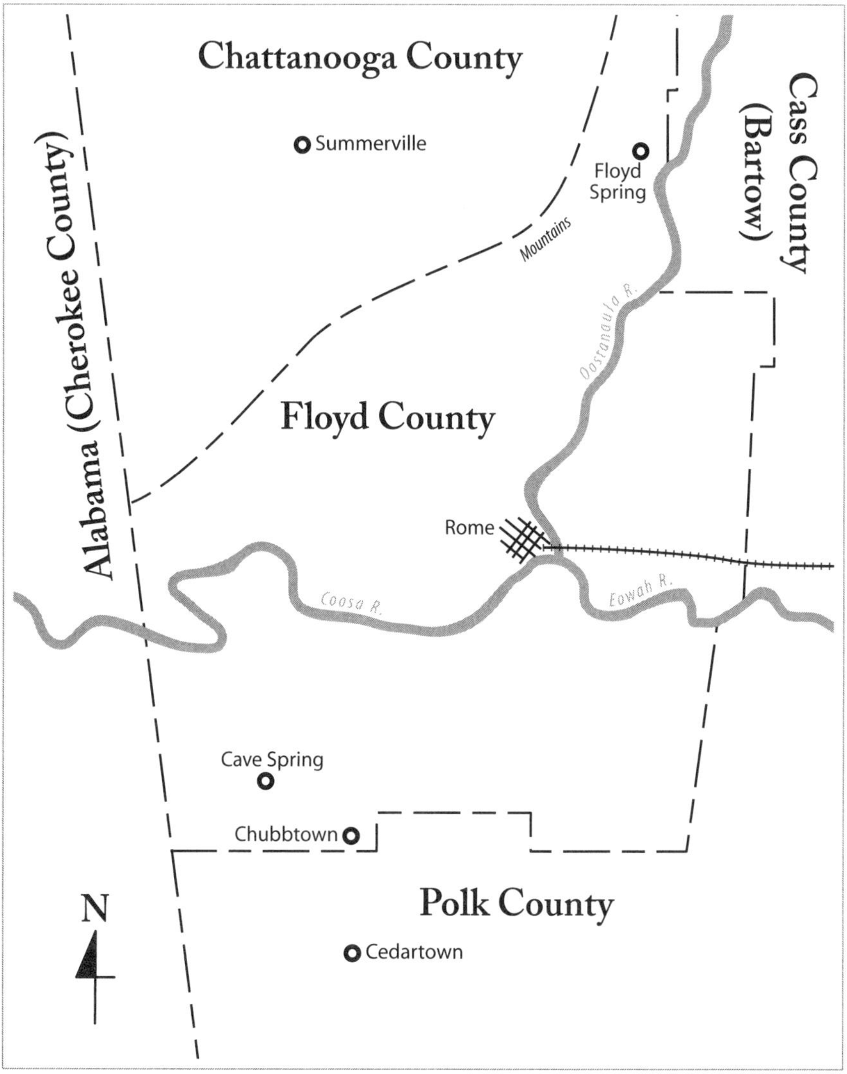

Northwest Georgia in 1861.

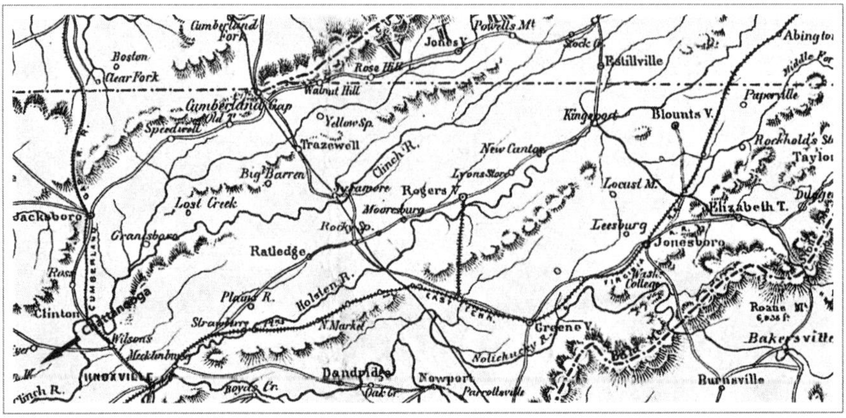

Contemporary Map of Cherokee Artillery's Eastern Tennessee Area of Operations. Detail of 1862 map of Kentucky and Tennessee by O. Lederle. Note the misspelling of Tazewell, Tennessee, as Trazewell. (Courtesy of Library of Congress.)

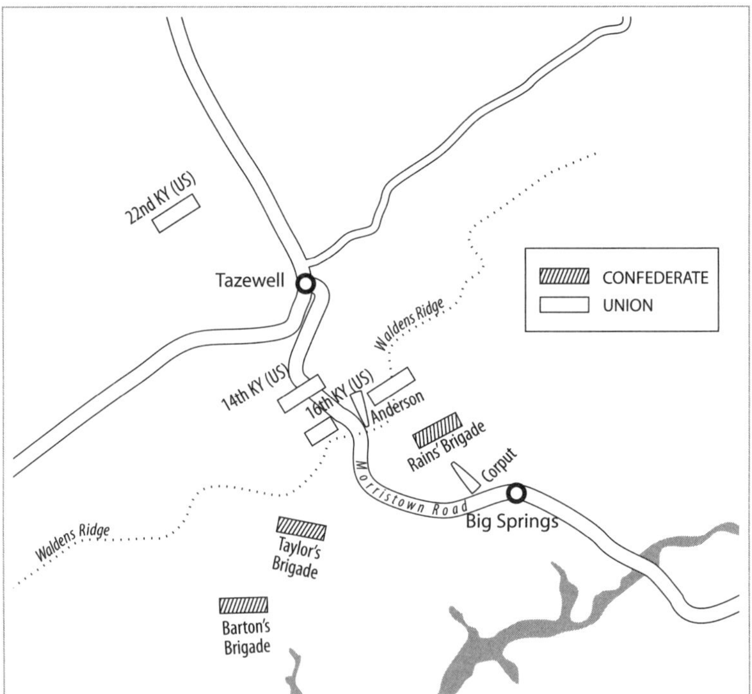

Battle of Tazewell, Tennessee.
August 6, 1862. Positions as of 10:00 a.m.

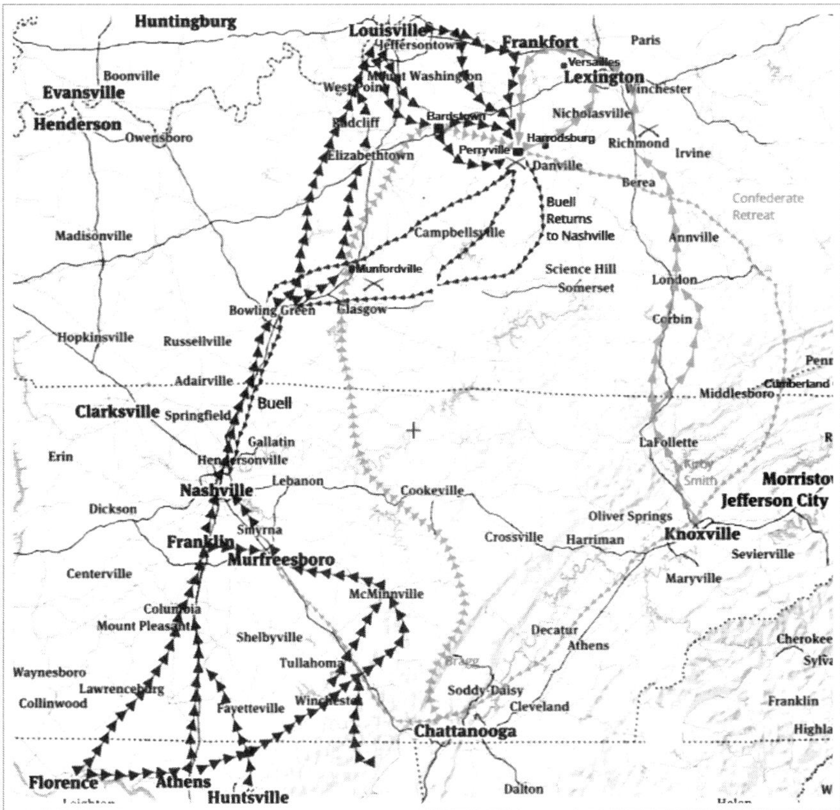

1862 Confederate Invasion of Kentucky.
August 14, 1862–October 10, 1862 (Map by G. Fisher.)

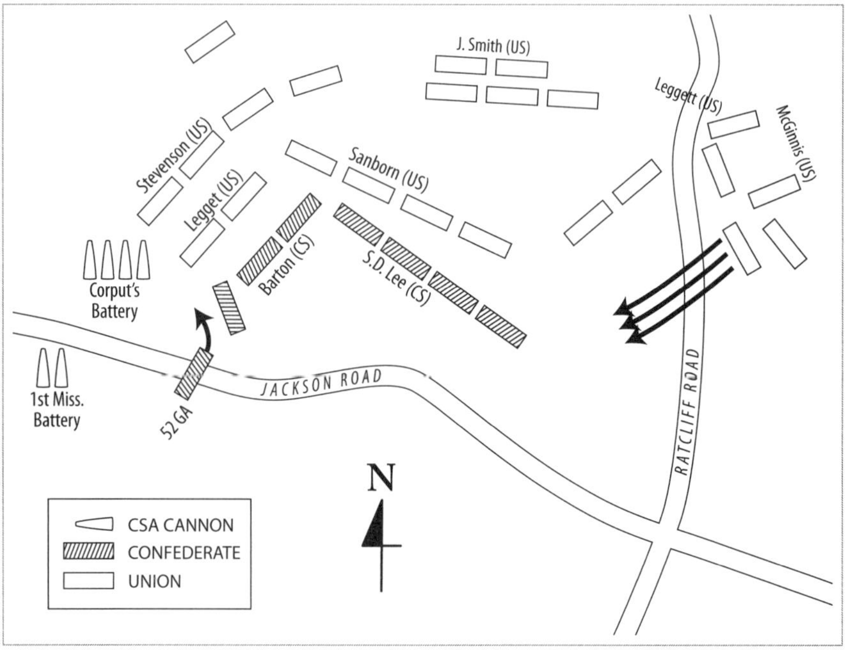

Champion Hill.
May 16, 1863. Positions as of 12:45 p.m.

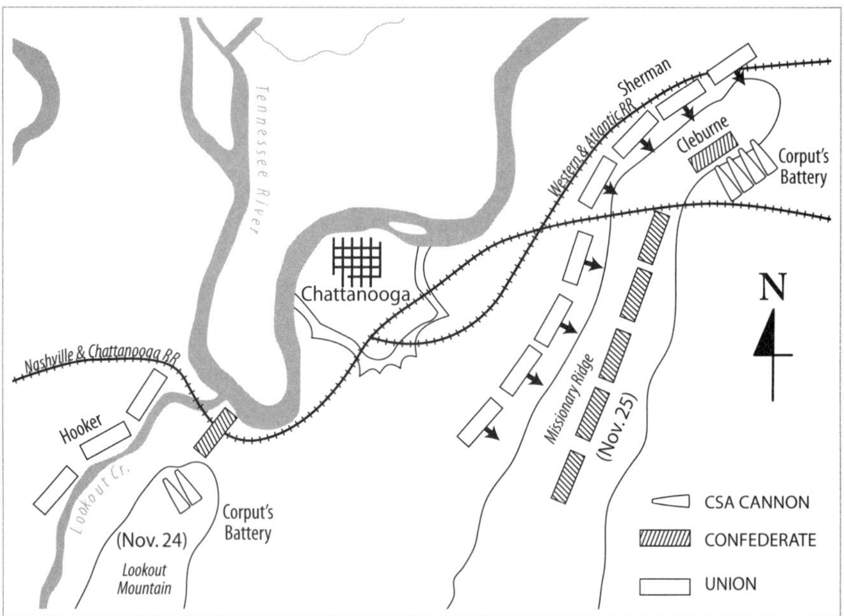

Chattanooga.
November 24–25, 1863.

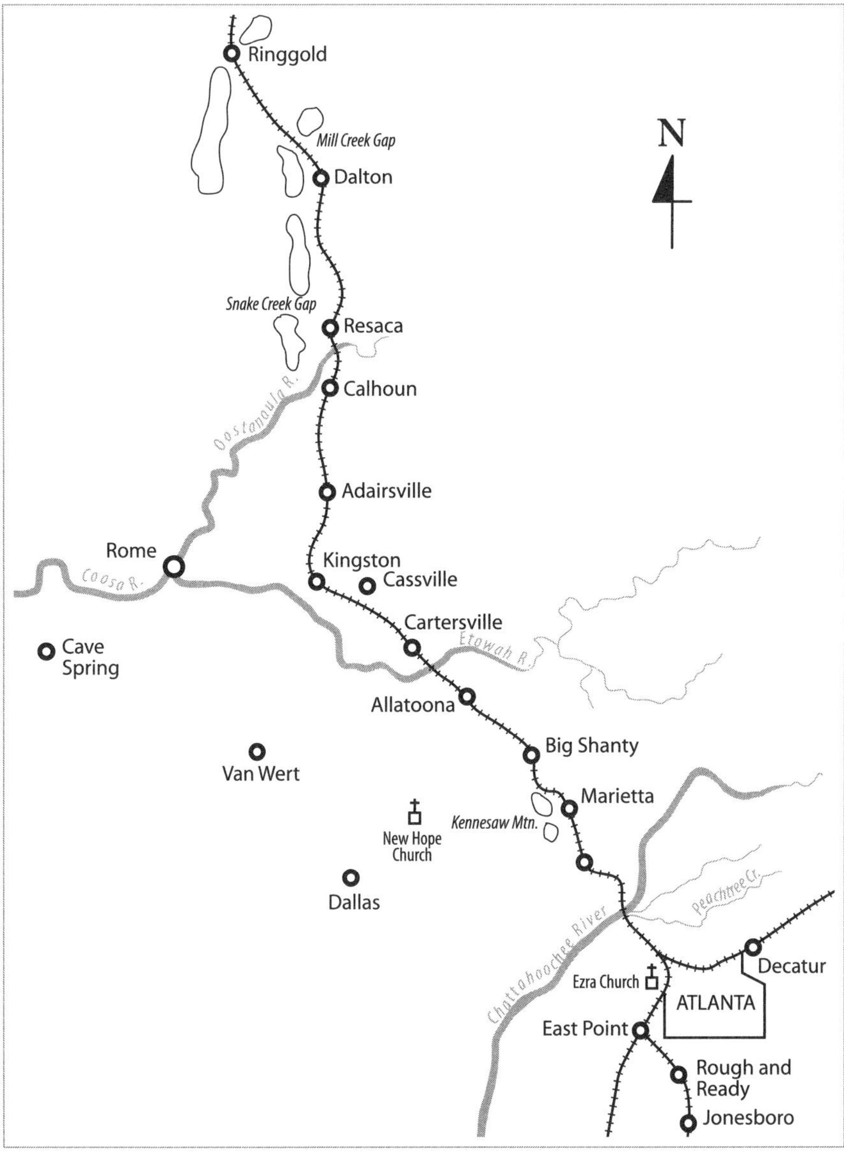

The Atlanta Campaign.
May–September, 1864.

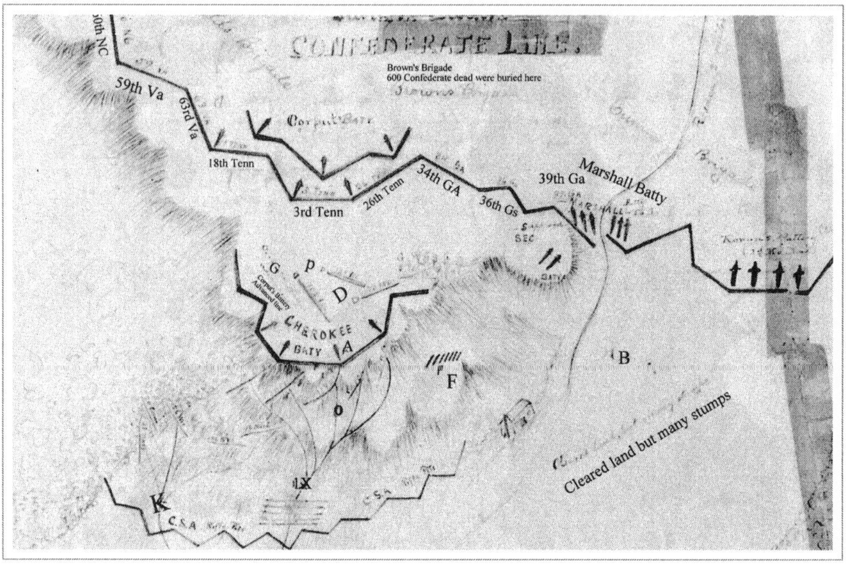

Blakeslee/Corput Map.
Probably drawn by Captain Max Van Den Corput or one of his brothers, this detail shows the locations of the Cherokee Artillery and surrounding units at the Battle of Resaca, May 15, 1864. (Courtesy Rome Area History Museum.)

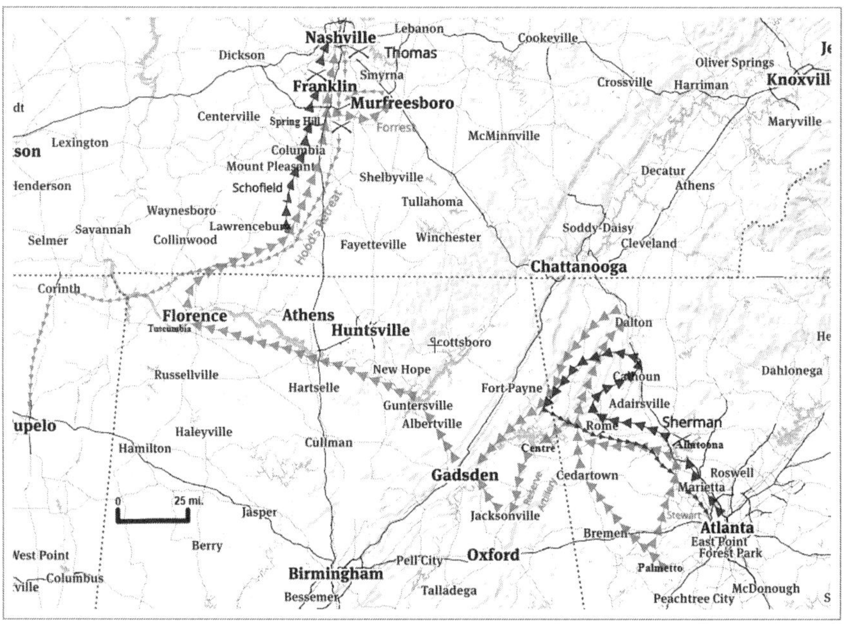

1864 Nashville Campaign.
September 29, 1864–December 27, 1864. (Map by G. Fisher.)

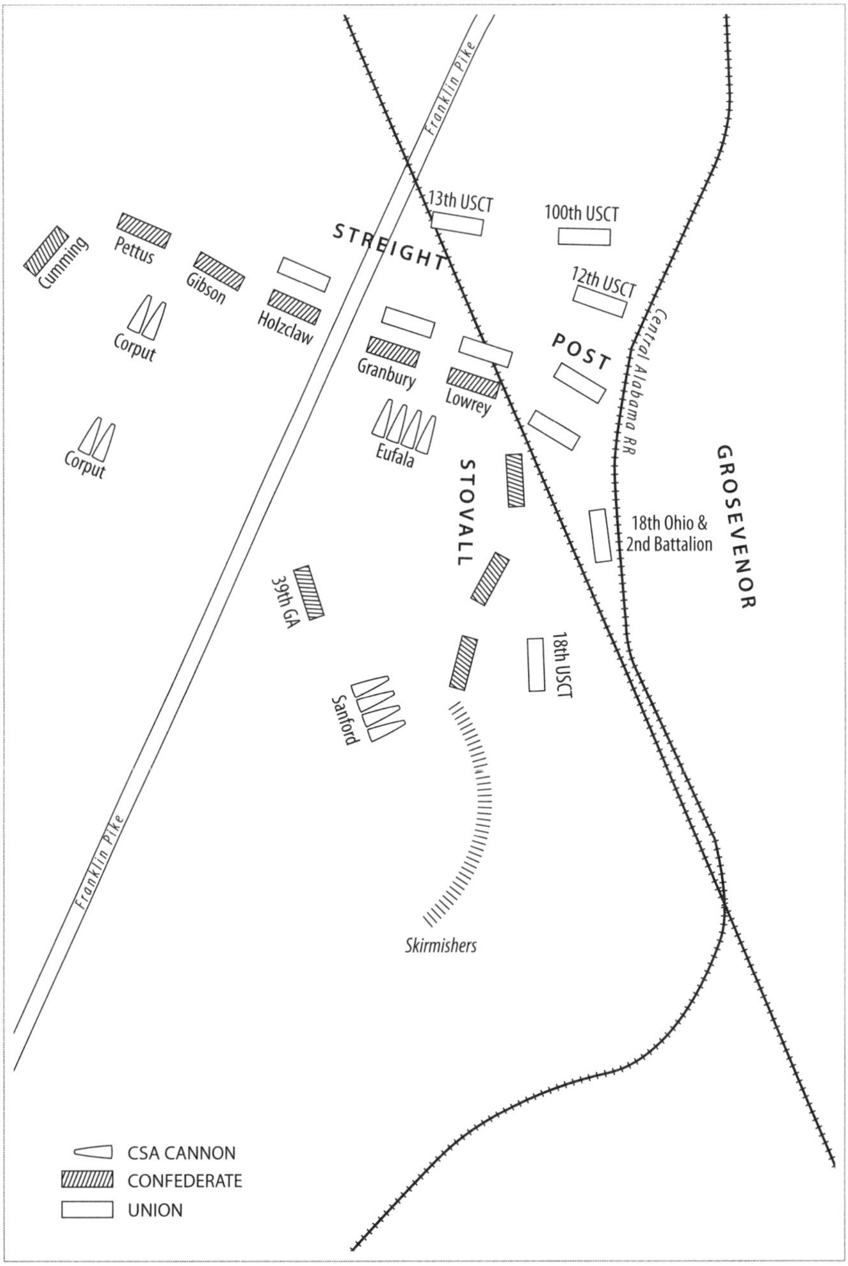

Attack on the Confederate Right.
December 16, 1864. Based on a map of Nashville, Tennessee, by J. R. Willett and O. M. Poe showing units and positions from O.R. Atlas, 73-1; O.R. 45-1, and regimental reports.

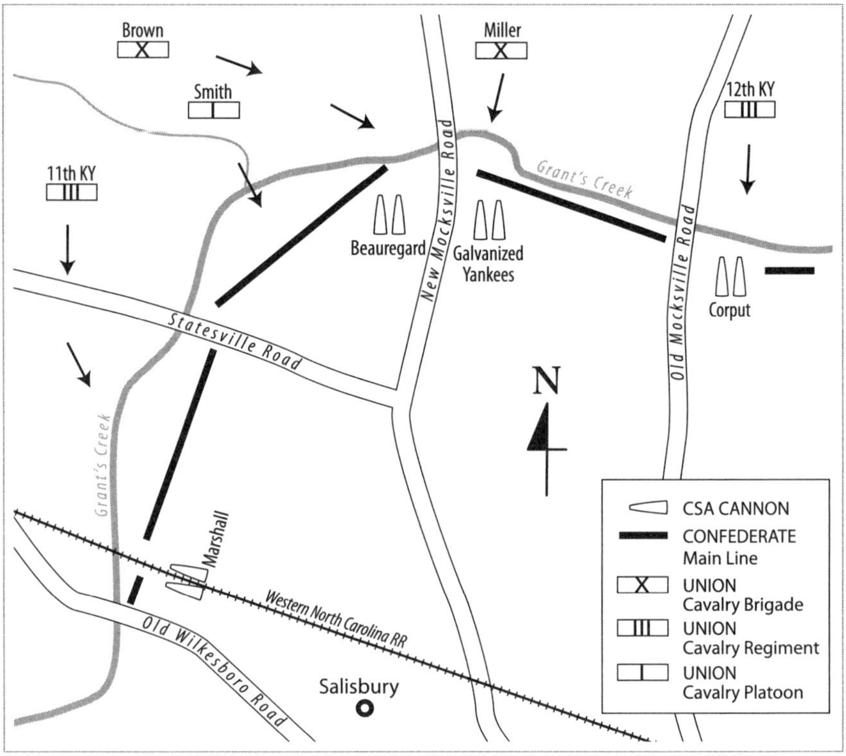

Battle of Salisbury, North Carolina.
April 12, 1865.

Captain Maximillian Van Den Corput.
Loved and respected by his men, Corput would lead them for most of the war. (Courtesy Bob Anderson; Rome, Georgia.)

Officers with Battery's New Flag, July 4, 1861.
From left to right, the battery's officers (with arms crossed) are tentatively identified as 1st Lt. Max Van Den Corput, Capt. John G. Yeiser, 2nd Lt. George W. Bowman, and 3rd Lt. C. Oliver Stillwell. (Courtesy Bob Anderson; Rome, Georgia.)

Cherokee Artillery Training Encampment at Big Shanty, Georgia.
Photograph was probably taken in either June or July 1861.
(Courtesy Bob Anderson; Rome, Georgia.)

Battery Members Gathered at Big Shanty.
Photograph was probably taken in either June or July 1861.
(Courtesy Bob Anderson; Rome, Georgia.)

Aging Artillerists.

Photograph of some of the surviving members of the Cherokee Artillery taken at the 1904 annual reunion. (Courtesy Margaret Hollingsworth and Hargrett Rare Book and Manuscript Library/University of Georgia Libraries.)

Reunion Photograph (Undated).

At the left is W. O. Connor, whose diary captured the battery's exploits throughout the conflict. The flag is the original one presented to the battery on July 4, 1861, by the ladies of Rome, Georgia. (Courtesy Margaret Hollingsworth and Hargrett Rare Book and Manuscript Library/University of Georgia Libraries.)

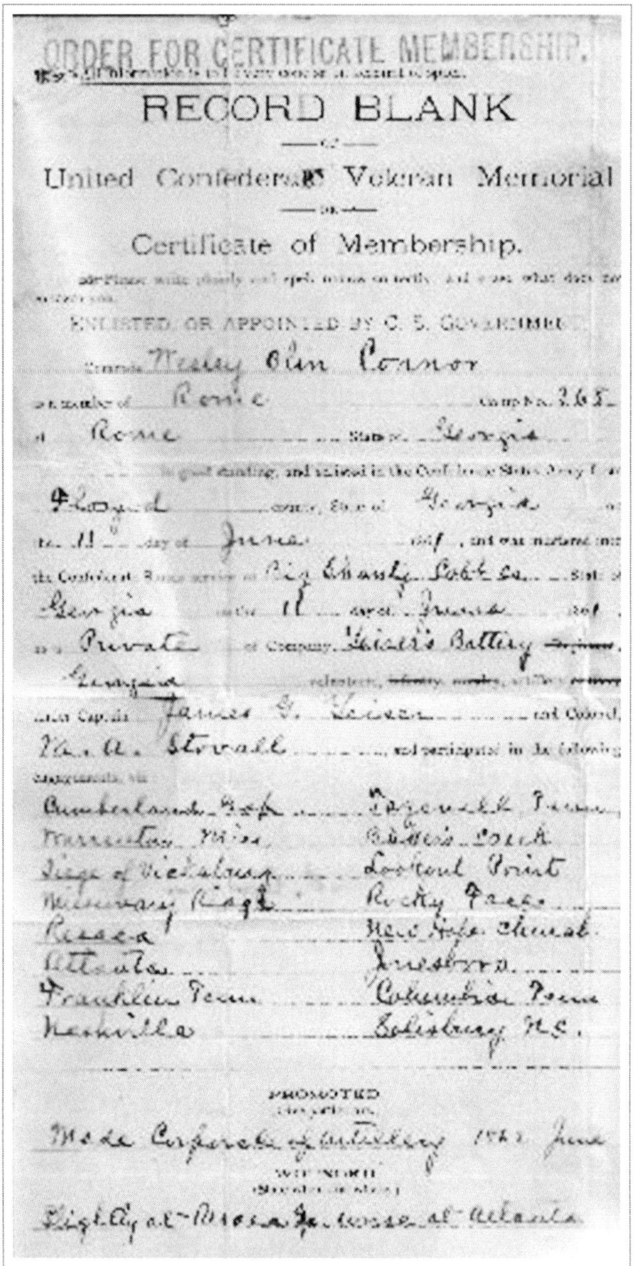

ORDER FOR CERTIFICATE MEMBERSHIP.

RECORD BLANK

—of—

United Confederate Veteran Memorial

—or—

Certificate of Membership.

ENLISTED OR APPOINTED BY C. S. GOVERNMENT

Comrade Wesley Olin Connor

a member of Rome Camp No. 368

of Rome State of Georgia

[illegible] in good standing, and enlisted in the Confederate States Army from Floyd county, State of Georgia on the 11 day of June 1861, and was mustered into the Confederate States service at Big Shanty Cobb Co. State of Georgia on the 11 day of June 1861 as Private of Company Yeiser's Battery Georgia volunteers, under Captain James G. Yeiser and Colonel M. A. Stovall, and participated in the following engagements, viz:

Cumberland Gap — Tazewell Tenn.
[illegible] Miss. — Baker's Creek
Siege of Vicksburg — Lookout Point
Missionary Ridge — Rocky Face
Resaca — New Hope Church
Atlanta — Jonesboro
Franklin Tenn — Columbia Tenn
Nashville — Salisbury N.C.

PROMOTED

Made Corporal of Artillery 1862 June

WOUNDED

Slightly at [illegible] worse at Atlanta

W. O. Connor's United Confederate Veterans Membership Certificate Application.

Like many ex-Confederates, Connor was active in post-war organizations dedicated to preserving the South's Confederate legacy. (Courtesy Margaret Hollingsworth and Hargrett Rare Book and Manuscript Library/University of Georgia Libraries.)

Cherokee Artillery Veteran.

Lacy H. Lott served three and a half years as a private in the Cherokee Artillery. Photograph taken shortly before his death in 1929 at age ninety-five. (Courtesy Linda Babuscio.)

Reunion Photograph (Undated).

Both W. O. Connor and Max Van Den Corput appear in this photograph. Notice the deterioration of the battery flag over time. (Courtesy Margaret Hollingsworth and Hargrett Rare Book and Manuscript Library/University of Georgia Libraries.)

CONFEDERATE STATES OF AMERICA

SOUTH CAROLINA NORTH CAROLINA MISSISSIPPI GEORGIA TEXAS FLORIDA ALABAMA LOUISIANA

FIRST CAMP AT BIG SHANTY.

OFFICERS WITH THE FLAG.

GROUP AT PANCHEN'S TENT.

MEMBERSHIP CERTIFICATE

IN THE

Corput Battery, C. S. A., of Rome, Ga.

ORIGINALLY CHEROKEE ARTILLERY.

This Certifies, that Lacy Howard Lott was a member of the CORPUT BATTERY, old CHEROKEE ARTILLERY; that he was enlisted at Rome Georgia June 16, 1862, and that he rendered faithful service in the CONFEDERATE CAUSE until he was honorably discharged from said service by release from the Military Prison of Camp Chase near Columbus Ohio, June 13, 1865.

W. O. Connor.
Sec'y C. A. Survivor's Ass'n.

Capt. Max Van Den Corput
President of the Association

CAPT. VAN DEN CORPUT—1862.

VIRGINIA TENNESSEE ARKANSAS KENTUCKY MISSOURI

Cherokee Artillery Survivors Association Certificate.
Survivor's association membership certificate of Lacy H. Lott. (G. Fisher Collection.)

Reunion Photograph (Undated).
Max Van Den Corput (white shirt) is at the center of the photograph; W. O. Connor (holding hat), is to his left on the lower step. (Courtesy Margaret Hollingsworth and Hargrett Rare Book and Manuscript Library/University of Georgia Libraries.)

Reunion Photograph (Undated).
Identified on the photograph: (1) Felix Van Den Corput, (2) W. O. Connor, (3) Max Van Den Corput. (Courtesy Margaret Hollingsworth and Hargrett Rare Book and Manuscript Library/University of Georgia Libraries.)

Wesley Olin Connor as a Young Man.
Photograph probably taken prior to his enlistment in the Cherokee Artillery in 1861. (Courtesy Margaret Hollingsworth and Hargrett Rare Book and Manuscript Library/ University of Georgia Libraries.)

Wesley Olin Connor in Later Life.
Undated photograph probably taken while Connor was still principal of the Georgia School for the Deaf. (Courtesy Margaret Hollingsworth and Hargrett Rare Book and Manuscript Library/University of Georgia Libraries.)

Chapter 5

"Some Frightfully Wicked Work"

The Atlanta Campaign
(November 28, 1863—September 1864)

Despite the victory at Chickamauga, 1863 had been a disastrous year for the Confederacy. Robert E. Lee's defeat at Gettysburg had stymied the South's efforts to take the war to the North. Even worse, the loss of Vicksburg was a crushing blow that had split the young nation in two. Federal naval vessels now sailed with impunity along the entire length of the mighty Mississippi River, depriving the Confederacy of men, materiel, and foodstuffs from the Southern states west of the river. Nevertheless, the Southern nation still had formidable armies in the field and public support for the war effort. Across the South, one great hope emerged. If they could just deny the Union a major military victory before the North's presidential elections in November 1864, they might very well be able to grind down the Northern public's support for the war and foment the election of an administration and Congress committed to ending the war and accepting Southern independence.[1]

Jefferson Davis's first opportunity to strengthen the South's hand was not long in coming. On November 28, Gen. Braxton Bragg sent a letter to Davis requesting to be relieved as commander of the Army of Tennessee. The cantankerous North Carolinian likely hoped that the president, Bragg's most ardent supporter, would retain him as leader of the Confederacy's Army of the Heartland. The chief executive realized, however, that he had no choice but to dismiss his old friend in favor of a leader more acceptable to the army and Southern civilians. Anger and vituperation against Bragg had reached a fever pitch as the public, newspapers, and Rebel Congress grasped the true immensity of

---

[1] Castel, *Decision in the West*, 24–27.

the debacle at Chattanooga. Worse yet, hundreds of soldiers in gray began leaving the Dalton encampment without orders, and even those who remained exhibited a spirit of utter demoralization. Wesley Connor noted in his diary, "Everything now has a gloomy aspect. The soldiers are disheartened, and deserting in large numbers. Some course should be adopted to encourage the army."[2]

Finding a suitable replacement for Bragg proved more difficult than Davis might have imagined. He first offered the command of the Western army to Robert E. Lee, the legendary leader of the Army of Northern Virginia. Lee, however, adamantly refused the position. Next, he offered leadership of the Army of Tennessee to Lt. Gen. William J. Hardee. The Georgian seemed the perfect candidate to replace Bragg. A modern historian described him as "A West Pointer, veteran of the Mexican War, author of *Hardee's Tactics* [the standard drill book for both the North and South], and a corps commander in all the Army of Tennessee's major battles except Chickamauga; the tall, sinewy, forty-eight-year Georgian seemed a most appropriate choice." To Davis's surprise, Hardee also declined the appointment.[3]

Historians have long debated the factors that led to the Georgia general's decision to refuse the promotion, but a recent Hardee biographer suggests three possible factors. Hardee apparently believed that Davis should have first offered Gen. Joseph E. Johnston the opportunity to lead the army. The Georgian considered "Old Joe" both his friend and mentor, but Hardee apparently had also concluded that Johnston was the best man to lead the Rebels' most important western army to victory. Additionally, Hardee felt he could be "more useful as a Corps Commander than [as] the commander of the army." Finally, the Georgian's courtship of Alabama widow Mary Foreman Lewis, "who worshiped Hardee..., had distracted him from military matters."[4]

---

[2] Horn, *Army of Tennessee*, 305–306; Castel, *Decision in the West*, 27–29. Davis "kicked Bragg upstairs," naming him the president's military adviser.

[3] Horn, *Army of Tennessee*, 305–306; Castel, *Decision in the West*, 27–29; Woodworth, "Command Options," 5–7.

[4] Cheairs, *Old Reliable*, 181–87; Woodworth, "Command Options," 5–7.

In the president's opinion, this left him with only two legitimate options—Joseph E. Johnston and P. G. T. Beauregard. Davis loathed both officers. Beauregard, a Louisiana Creole, had become a hero to the Southern people by his early victories at Fort Sumter and First Manassas. But Davis believed his failures at Shiloh and Corinth indicated a lack of skill necessary to lead the Army of Tennessee. The president also despised Joe Johnston, a Virginian and West Pointer. Davis correctly blamed him for the failure to lift the siege at Vicksburg, and the president believed that Johnston—despite his reputation for brilliance—specialized in retreating. Johnston, however, possessed one important military asset. The common soldier in the Army of Tennessee loved "Old Joe." They believed that he would not sacrifice them needlessly in battle and would do everything in his power to see that they received adequate food and weaponry. Reluctantly, Davis appointed Johnston to replace Bragg.[5]

The new commander immediately set about rebuilding the Confederacy's battered Army of Tennessee. He badgered Richmond to supply his men with uniforms, shoes, weapons, and—more important to his men—food to rebuild strength and morale. He ordered a number of underutilized units, such as Brig. Gen. Philip D. Roddey's North Alabama cavalry, to Dalton to replace the men killed and captured at Missionary Ridge. "Old Joe" declared a blanket amnesty for deserters, and many men voluntarily returned to the army. In what must have been a calculated gamble, Johnston issued furloughs to some veteran troops, thereby indicating the faith he had in his men. His efforts soon bore fruit. "I doubt whether a volunteer army could be more perfect in its organization than the Army of Tennessee," an officer wrote approvingly to his wife that April. "General Johnston seems to have infused a new spirit into the whole mass, and out of chaos brought order and

---

[5] Woodworth, *Davis and His Generals*, 256–60; Castel, *Decision in the West*, 28–31.

beauty. Our men are better clothed than at any previous time, while their food is better than one would have anticipated two months ago."[6]

The concentration of the large army at Dalton, a town with a prewar population of only about 1,600 people, taxed the mountainous region's ability to provide forage for the cavalry and artillery horses and mules. As a result, Johnston dispersed those units to smaller towns throughout Northwest Georgia. On January 19, Van Den Corput's Georgia, Marshall's Tennessee, and Rowan's Maryland batteries received orders to relocate to Kingston, in Bartow County. The artillerymen loaded their horses and equipment aboard the train and reached their new quarters the following day.[7]

Three days later, they again moved, this time to a plantation about a mile from Kingston. Kingston proved an ideal place for the Floyd County cannoneers. Located only fourteen miles from Rome, and with a railroad connecting the two towns, they could easily exchange visits with their family and friends. Many, like Wesley Connor, also had friends in Kingston and the Rebel soldiers received frequent invitations to parties and festivities. They would stay there for almost a month.[8]

A pleasant mood prevailed while the unit stayed in Bartow County, but the killing of a member of the Cherokee Artillery temporarily spread a spirit of gloom over the unit's camp. The *Memphis Daily Appeal* reported,

> Capt. Corput, of the Cherokee Artillery, now encamped near Kingston, sent out a squad of men to find and bring to camp if possible, a man by the name of Heidle [Hydle] who had deserted [for] the third time. He was found secreted in some woods. As soon as he discovered [his] pursuers, he attempted to make his escape. He was reportedly ordered to halt and [warning] shots were fired on either

---

[6] Horn, *Army of Tennessee*, 311–13; Castel, *Decision in the West*, 28–33; Dubose, *General Joseph Wheeler and the Army of Tennessee*, 275; WOC, January 1, 1864.

[7] WOC, January 19–February 25, 1864; U.S. Census Records, Georgia, Whitfield County (1860), GDAH.

[8] WOC, January 19–February 25, 1864; U.S. Census Records, Georgia, Cass County (1860), GDAH.

> side of him, but all to no effect. Finally, Neal [likely George W.] Duke aiming directly at him shot him through.

Hydle had served with Van Den Corput's Battery through the Vicksburg and Chattanooga Campaigns, but those disastrous operations, along with news of his father's death in Confederate service in Virginia, had apparently sapped his will to fight. Connor noted that Hydle's "mother and sister were with him in his last moments. He was an only son. How his mother must have felt for him, dying thus in disgrace."[9]

While Joe Johnston attempted to get the Army of Tennessee in fighting trim, news from other battlefields gave Confederate sympathizers new reasons for optimism. Union forces conducted a series of campaigns throughout the Rebel hinterlands during the first four months of 1864, and two of the three expeditions were unmitigated disasters for the Federals. The Olustee expedition in North Florida in mid-February and the March and April Red River campaign in the Trans-Mississippi both ended in defeat and retreat for the bluecoats.[10]

However, Maj. Gen. William T. Sherman's Meridian campaign, begun on February 3, swept through the Magnolia State and devastated a wide swath of the state's vital agricultural heartland. Because Nathan Bedford Forrest, the Confederate "Wizard of the Saddle," defeated Sherman's cavalry after the main Union force had begun its return to Vicksburg, most people, North and South, considered the expedition a third Federal failure. In fact, it had been chillingly effective and provided a test run for the tactics that Sherman would use in both the Atlanta Campaign and the March to the Sea.[11]

---

[9] "A Deserter Killed," *Memphis Daily Appeal*, February 25, 1864, 1; WOC, January 25, 1864.

[10] "The Way to Independence and Victory," *Augusta (GA) Daily Constitutionalist*, May 5, 1864, 1. For information on the two campaigns see Gary D. Joiner, *Through the Howling Wilderness: The 1864 Red River Campaign and Union Failure in the West* (Knoxville: University of Tennessee Press, 2014), and William H. Nulty, *Confederate Florida: The Road to Olustee* (Tuscaloosa: University of Alabama Press, 2014).

[11] Woodworth, *Davis and His Generals*, 259–60; Ballard, *Civil War in Mississippi*, 172–94.

While Sherman's veterans laid waste to the Mississippi's farms and fields, Lt. Gen. Leonidas Polk, commanding Confederate forces in Mississippi, hounded Richmond to send reinforcements to his hard-pressed army. Pres. Davis immediately ordered Joe Johnston to send troops from Dalton to assist Polk. Sherman anticipated that move and directed Maj. Gen. George H. Thomas, at Chattanooga, to keep Johnston occupied by attacking his northern outposts. For two days—February 23 and 24—the Federals drove in "Fighting Joe" Wheeler's horsemen near Tunnel Hill but made little headway against Brig. Gen. Daniel Govan's entrenched Rebel infantry. Both sides claimed victory, of course, but the repulse of Thomas's men cheered the Army of Tennessee. A Rebel general officer (likely Brig. Gen. M. A. Stovall) wrote, "I never saw [our] men more eager for a fight. Our men were burning to avenge Missionary Ridge, and can never be in better humor for a fight than they are now." Connor echoed that sentiment, jotting in his diary, "The health and spirits of the army were never better. The prompt manner in which Johnston offered battle to the Yanks, in their late advance, did more toward inspiring confidence in the troops than any move since the battle of Chickamauga. All seem to think that 'Joseph' [Johnston] is the right man in the right place."[12]

The day after the Union attack ended and the bluecoats retreated toward Chattanooga, Van Den Corput received orders for his battery to leave Kingston. The Cherokee Artillery quickly obeyed, moving to a point east of the Western & Atlanta Railroad midway between Dalton and Kingston. Apparently this put the new camp near a place called Five Springs. Since the rocky region could only briefly sustain the number of horses and mules the Rebel cannoneers used, Van Den Corput regularly sent wagons into the surrounding countryside to collect fodder. The men also prepared for the spring campaigning, shoeing their animals and putting their weapons in good order.[13]

---

[12] "From General Johnston's Army," *Augusta (GA) Daily Constitutionalist*, March 6, 1864; Ballard, *Civil War in Mississippi*, 172–94; WOC, March 13, 1864; *OR*, ser. 1, vol. 32, 3, 9–11.

[13] WOC, February 25–29, 1864.

Several activities and events occurred during this time that had a profound effect upon the morale of Johnston's troops. Best known of these was the snow battle that found almost the entire Confederate army at Dalton squaring off against their comrades in mock combat. On the morning of March 22, the camps awoke to find several inches of snow on the ground. Men will often be boys, and snowballs soon filled the air. A member of Van Den Corput's Battery recalled, "Hoxton's Battalion charged our camp this morning. Our boys fought gallantly for a short time, but having no intimation of the attack, were soon compelled to give up." By making—and breaking—alliances with various battalions, as it fit each unit's self-interest, the mock fight raged back and forth throughout most of the day. The Cherokee Artillery got their revenge, eventually capturing Hoxton's camp, horses, and artillery. Many soldiers noted in diaries and letters that the day's snow battles were one of the greatest scenes they had ever witnessed.[14]

A religious revival had also been sweeping through the Confederate armies almost since the war began, but it reached a fever pitch during the army's encampment at Dalton in 1863 and 1864. A Texas chaplain reported, "I have never seen such a spirit as there is now in the army. Religion is the theme. Everywhere you hear around the campfires sweet songs of Zion." The chaplains generally ignored Protestant denominational differences and a spirit of sectarian unity prevailed. Connor thought it a wonderful development, but he noted a certain irony in the scene.

> The congregation were seated upon the ground and upon the gun carriages. This was a sight long to be remembered, that of strong and brave men listening to words of wisdom, seated upon their guns which are, in a few days to deal death and destruction into the ranks of our enemies, and near which some of them are destined to yield up their lives,—a sacrifice upon the altar of liberty. We have had services every Sabbath and prayer meetings during the week.[15]

---

[14] WOC, March 22, 1864; S. Davis, "The Great Snow Battle of 1864," 32–35.

[15] Daniel, *Soldiering in the Army of Tennessee*, 119–25; WOC, April 30, 1864.

Warm weather meant the beginning of the campaigning season, and around May 1 Johnston had stationed his men in their prepared defensive positions. Although historians vehemently disagree on the exact numbers at the beginning of the campaign, the Army of Tennessee seemingly had less than 50,000 men to confront Sherman's 110,000 soldiers. Like an overmatched boxer, "Old Joe" planned to rely upon a strong defense and counterpunch when his opponent made a mistake. This tactic seemed to be the wisest plan, under the circumstances, and the best fit for Johnston's personality, but some revisionist historians have written him off both as fainthearted and a failure. Historian Steven E. Woodworth summed up the prevailing revisionist opinion, writing, "Johnston seemed to be skillful, but he lacked nerve. Obsessed with his reputation, Johnston would not risk it on the outcome of a battle unless the conditions were perfect, and success seemed certain. Since such situations rarely occur in warfare, the reputedly brilliant Johnston made a specialty of retreating."[16]

The Confederate commander established his defenses along the highlands west of Dalton. Rocky Face Ridge towered 1,500 feet above Crow Valley to the east and the lowlands to the west. The terrain appeared virtually impregnable to direct assaults. Only three gaps allowed easy passage through the mountain range, and small numbers of Rebel troops could easily defend those openings. The Western & Atlantic rail line snaked through Mill Creek Gap, a couple of miles north of Dalton, and Dug Gap bisected the ridge about the same distance south of the town. Further to the southwest, narrow Snake Creek Gap twisted through the highlands for five miles before opening into Sugar Valley near the village of Resaca. Blocking these gaps would allow Johnston, at least temporarily, to hold Sherman at bay and neutralize the Union manpower advantage.[17]

---

[16] Woodworth, "Command Options," 5. For various estimates of the Army of Tennessee's military strength in April 1864, see, McMurry, *Atlanta 1864*, 194–96; Johnston, *Narrative of Military Operations*, 302; Scaife, *Campaign for Atlanta*, 3–4.

[17] McMurry, *Atlanta 1864*, 42–45; Scaife, *Campaign for Atlanta*, 7–15 (including Plates III and IV).

Sherman may have been, at times, rash and erratic, but he was not stupid. He had no intention of wasting his army with futile attacks against the heavily fortified Rebel positions. Instead, he sent Maj. Gen. George Thomas's Army of the Cumberland and Maj. Gen. John Schofield's Army of the Ohio to create a diversion to hold Johnston's graycoats in place. Meanwhile, Maj. Gen. James McPherson, with his Army of the Tennessee, would march through Snake Creek Gap, cut the railroad at Resaca, and trap the Southern army at Dalton. As the Federal commander wrote in his memoirs, "The position [at Rocky Face Ridge] was very strong, and I knew that such a general as was my antagonist [Johnston]...had fortified it to a maximum. Therefore, I had no intention to attack the position seriously in the front, but depended on McPherson to capture and hold the railroad to its rear."[18]

On May 8, Thomas's bluecoats began probing attacks against the Confederate defenses along Rocky Face Ridge. They met with little success. The Rebels on the high ground and had constructed strong barricades using the boulders that littered the area. Despite being the obvious avenues of assault, the Rebel commander had apparently placed only tiny caretaker forces to guard two of the vital openings in the mountain range. At mid-afternoon, Brig. Gen. John Geary's Federals pushed hard against a small detachment of Arkansas infantry and Kentucky horse soldiers guarding Dug Gap. Providentially, Maj. Gen Patrick Cleburne arrived with a couple of regiments of hard-fighting Texas infantrymen just in time to prevent a breakthrough. Geary pulled back in the face of the stiffening resistance, suffering about 350 casualties.[19]

The following day, Gen. Thomas made stronger forays all along the line in an attempt to find a weak point in the Confederate defenses. Van Den Corput's Battery was located on the crest of a hill near a tiny font known locally as Poplar Spring, supporting Carter Stevenson's division. Small skirmishes erupted early that morning as the Yankees probed the Confederate line at Rocky Face Ridge. A Federal artillery

---

[18] Castel, *Decision in the West*, 121–23; Scaife, *Campaign for Atlanta*, 7–15.

[19] McMurry, "The Atlanta Campaign," 20, 23; Castel, *Decision in the West*, 132–35.

battery wheeled into position approximately two and a half miles from the Cherokee Artillery, but it remained silent. The Georgia cannoneers were situated on the right-center of the Rebel line, about two miles from the Western & Atlantic Railroad. After sitting silently most of the day, Van Den Corput's Battery received orders around 4:45 P.M. to fire a few rounds at a column of bluecoats. The Union troops opposing the Floyd County artillerymen were members of Brig. Gen. Nathaniel McLean's brigade, and the historian of the 25th Michigan recalled, "They [the graycoats] opened on us with artillery. We halted and not being within effective range of musketry, were ordered to lie down so as to give the least exposure to their guns. The guns came quite lively for a while, and were aimed mostly at the flag. The shells were well aimed, for as we lay on the ground they just grazed [our position] and passed [overhead]." After a while, the men from the Wolverine State, finding they could make no real headway, fell back.[20]

On the afternoon of May 9, McPherson's corps began debouching from Snake Creek Gap near Resaca. Joe Johnston had ordered a mere company of Georgians to guard the mouth of the gap, but the bluecoats initially found no Rebels in the immediate area. For once, however, good fortune smiled on the Army of Tennessee. Brig. Gen. James Cantey, the advance guard of Polk's army from Mississippi (which Pres. Davis had recalled to North Georgia), held Resaca with about 4,000 men. As the bluecoats approached the village, a hail of enemy musket and artillery fire greeted McPherson's men. The Union commander—generally one of Sherman's most aggressive officers—now hesitated in the face of the unexpected Confederate resistance. Fearful that Johnston's troops would cut him off if the Rebels advanced down any of the roads running off to the north, and without cavalry to screen his movements, McPherson chose the path of caution and withdrew to the mouth of the gap.[21]

Perched atop Rocky Face Ridge on the morning of May 10, the men of the Cherokee Artillery knew nothing of the threat to Johnston's line near Resaca. The Floyd County cannoneers threw a few more

[20] WOC, May 9, 1864; Travis, *Story of the Twenty-Fifth Michigan*, 192–93.

[21] McMurry, "Atlanta Campaign," 20; Castel, *Decision in the West*, 136–41.

shells toward the Union lines during the morning, but otherwise remained inactive. They complained bitterly when raw Georgia troops, commanded by Brig. Gen. Hugh Mercer, left them without infantry support during the night; but the arrival next morning of a regiment from Cleburne's Division alleviated their concerns.[22]

The following day, nothing much happened atop Rocky Face Ridge except dodging a few Union shells. Unknown to the men of Van Den Corput's Battery, both Sherman and Johnston had begun withdrawing from their respective positions near Dalton. On May 10–12, all of Sherman's troops, except those of Maj. Gen. Oliver Howard's IV corps, were trudging southward on the few available roads. The trip was neither easy nor quick. The narrow mountain roads, choked with men, horses, wagons, and artillery, slowed the Federal advance to a crawl. A sudden spring rain made matters even worse, turning the dusty roads into knee-deep quagmires of churning, sticky mud. Forced to manhandle their wagons and heavy equipment through this morass, Sherman's weary soldiers progressed as fast as they could.[23]

By early afternoon on May 12, Maj. Gen. Joseph "Fightin' Joe" Wheeler's horsemen brought news to Johnston that the enemy had evacuated their position. Johnston had a shorter route over good roads and access to the Georgia & Atlantic Railroad to move men and equipment. "Old Joe," always a careful and conservative leader, eschewed any offensive operations and conducted a skillful retreat to protect his railroad lifeline.[24]

The arrival of Lt. Gen. Leonidas Polk, with the remainder of his corps, relieved immediate concerns about defending the rail lines at Resaca. Polk, a West Point graduate who had abandoned a military career to serve as the pre-war Episcopal bishop of Louisiana, along with Lt. Gen. John Bell Hood, rode the train to Dalton to confer with Johnston. Apparently not all their discussion centered on military matters,

---

[22] WOC, May 12, 1864.

[23] McMurry, "Atlanta Campaign," 23; WOC, May 12, 1864; Scaife, *Campaign for Atlanta*, 12–13; Miles, *Fields of Glory*, 40.

[24] McMurry, "Atlanta Campaign," 20–23; Horn, *Army of Tennessee*, 323–25.

for late that evening Polk administered the rite of baptism to the Confederate commander by sprinkling him with water from an oaken bucket. The arrival of the reinforcements from Mississippi now gave Johnston about 66,000 men to confront Sherman's 120,000 troops.[25]

The town of Resaca took its name from Resaca de la Palma, site of an early victory for Gen. Zachary Taylor's American army in the Mexican War; but the combat about to occur in the North Georgia hills would make the earlier fight resemble a mere skirmish. The hamlet sat on a spit of land created by the confluence of the Conasauga and Oostanaula rivers. The Army of Tennessee occupied a position along a line of hills overlooking a valley created by the twisting route of Camp Creek. Polk's Corps, with its left flank resting on the north bank of Oostanaula, comprised the southern section of Johnston's army. Hardee's Corps held the center, and Hood's troops guarded the north, with his defensive line curving back to the bank of the Conasauga. The placement of the Rebel commander's army at Resaca involved considerable risk. The two rivers, swollen to flood stage by recent rains, would prove an insurmountable obstacle if Johnston's army had to flee the battlefield.[26]

The Cherokee Artillery left their position atop Rocky Face Ridge near nightfall on the afternoon of May 12. The men pushed along through the inky darkness, leading the teams that strained to pull the four twelve-pounder guns, ammunition, and camp equipment. By the afternoon of the following day they went into position supporting Carter Stevenson's division in Hood's fortified section of the line.[27]

Maj. John W. Johnston, commanding the three-company artillery battalion, received a serious wound on May 14. Capt. Van Den Corput, as senior captain, assumed the leadership of the artillery battalion in Johnston's absence. Lt. John E. Stillwell took command of the Cherokee Artillery, now deployed in a position about fifty yards in

---

[25] Castel, *Decision in the West*, 147–48; Miles, *Fields of Glory*, 40–41.

[26] McMurry, "Atlanta Campaign," 46; Scaife, *Campaign for Atlanta*, Plate VI; *OR*, ser. 1, vol. 38, part 1, 63–64.

[27] WOC, May 12–14, 1864.

front of Brig. Gen. John C. Brown's brigade of Tennesseans. To their left stood the other two batteries of the battalion: Capt. Lucius C. Marshall's Tennessee battery and Rowan's Maryland battery, now under the command of Lt. William Ritter.[28]

Throughout May 13–14, Johnston's and Sherman's regiments sought to find a weak point in their opponent's lines, making only limited gains while the casualty rates soared. Gen. Johnston's skillful use of the terrain near Resaca contributed to the Federal's lack of success. In front of the Rebel positions lay a large open field that sloped downward to a creek that ran roughly parallel to the Federal front through dense brush and felled trees. In many places the stream was too deep and full of muck and undergrowth to be easily fordable. On the afternoon of May 13, Brig. Gen. Charles R. Woods's Iowa, Missouri, and Ohio troops assailed Brig. Gen. Thomas M. Scott's graycoats, pushing back their skirmishers, but failing to make any headway against the main line. The next day, attacks by the Union XIV and XXIII corps also ended in failure. Late on the evening of May 14, John Bell Hood ordered an attack on a supposed gap in the Union line. The hard-charging Southerners achieved some initial success, but stout fighting by Joe Hooker's XX corps halted Hood's assault and ended the fighting for the day.[29]

On the morning of May 15, a stalemate of sorts settled over the battlefield at Resaca, with only some skirmishing and long-distance cannon fire disturbing the Gordon County woodlands. Maj. Gen. Thomas Hindman's Rebel division occupied a bend in Hood's trenches. A Union battery had found the range and had begun lobbing shells among his men with increasing regularity. About 11 A.M., Hood ordered Carter Stevenson to emplace a battery outside the trenches to drive off the enemy artillery which was "annoying General Hindman's line." Stevenson ordered Lt. Stillwell to move the Cherokee Artillery's four twelve-pounder Napoleons to a wooded hill fifty to eighty yards

---

[28] Ibid.; "Maj. John William Johnston," 116–17; *OR*, ser. 1, vol. 38, part 3, 812; John E. Stillwell to E. A. Carmen, September 15, 1890, Carmen papers, LOC.

[29] McMurry, "Atlantic Campaign," 46; Scaife, *Campaign for Atlanta*, 16–23.

in front of the Confederate entrenchments. Stevenson reminded Stillwell, "Gen. Hood gave the order for the commander of the battery to stay at his guns until he and all his men were killed. They were not to leave the guns under any circumstances."[30]

Stillwell quickly found an excellent location for the Cherokee Artillery. On the high ground, approximately eighty yards in front of the Confederate breastworks, he discovered a flat area fronted by a chest-high mound of Georgia clay. His troops, numbering only about fifty-five men because of furloughs, quickly cut four notch-like openings in the embankment to create a half-moon-shaped *lunette* with embrasures for their twelve-pounders. The Georgia cannoneers planned to dig a series of rifle pits from the lunette to the Confederate entrenchments, which would provide Van Den Corput's men some infantry support. Stevenson, however, could not wait. "Before the necessary measures for the protection of the artillery could be taken," Stillwell explained, "I received repeated and peremptory orders [from Hood] to open it upon the battery before alluded to."[31]

Stevenson wrote, "It [Van Den Corput's Battery] had hardly gotten into position when the enemy hotly engaged my skirmishers, driving them in and pushing the assault with great impetuosity." The columns of bluecoats came primarily from Maj. Gen. Daniel Butterfield's 3rd Division of Hooker's XX Corps. According to Butterfield's battle plan, Col. James Wood's brigade would assail the high ground on the left side of the Dalton—Resaca Wagon Road, while Brig. Gen. William T. Ward's 1st brigade, on the right side of the byway, would charge the hill with Stillwell's four-gun battery. Col. John Coburn's 2nd brigade served as a reserve for Ward.[32]

In addition to the entrenched graycoats, the Yankees had to deal with two additional obstacles. Historian Albert Castel, writing in the

---

[30] WOC, May 15, 1863; Secrist, "Resaca," 33–34; F. Anderson, "A Courier at the Battle of Resaca," 297.

[31] John E. Stillwell to E. A. Carmen, September 15, 1890, Carmen papers, LOC; *OR*, ser. 1, vol. 38, part 3, 812; Kilpatrick, "The Fifth Ohio Infantry at Resaca," 246–54.

[32] *OR*, ser. 1, vol. 38, part 3, 812; Castel, *Decision in the West*, 174; Perry, *Touched with Fire*, 239.

present tense, described the challenges facing the advancing Federal troops: "The Federals," he wrote,

> from Hooker down to the rawest private, have only an approximate idea of the location of the Confederate lines and none whatsoever of their strength. The Federals simply plunge ahead through the underbrush and dense clusters of pine trees, up and down hills, across and through ravines. With each step their ranks become more and more uneven and broken, companies and regiments wander off course, brigades get mixed up with other brigades...and some commanders lose contact with their units, in fact, they cannot even see them. Adding to Hooker's woes, many of these soldiers have never experienced combat before—which might prove either a blessing or a curse.[33]

Even as old men, Butterfield's veterans recalled the charge they made with justifiable pride, but neither did they forget the terror of that half hour of battle and sacrifice. Virtually all agreed that the combination of fire—from the Cherokee Artillery, Marshall's and Rowan's Batteries and the Southern infantrymen in the trenches—resembled the fires of Hell. A Wisconsin trooper, referring to the devastating fire laid down by the Cherokee Artillery, averred, "That 4-gun battery was playing on us as fast as it could fire, and did some frightfully wicked work." A member of Harrison's regiment recorded, "As we struck the road (pike) we were in plain view of the Rebs and they let loose on us about 30 rods away. We were staggered and the men were going down like tenpins. We obliqued to the left and gained the [thicket of] red cedar.... [A]nd up the hill for that battery we went. We finally got the four guns but we were in the jaws of Hell." Another bluecoat claimed that his division had suffered a loss of 963 officers and men in twenty minutes.[34]

---

[33] *OR*, ser. 1, vol. 38, part 3, 812; Perry, *Touched with Fire*, 239; Castel, *Decision in the West*, 174.

[34] G. H. Blakeslee, "Harrison at Peach Tree Creek," *National Tribune*, July 5, 1906, 6; R. C. Clawson, *National Tribune*, April 4, 1895, 3; Harvey Reid, "Recitals and Reminiscences," *National Tribune*, July 11, 1907, 6. Excellent material, taken from the [W. O.] Connor–[G. H.] Blakeslee letters, at the Rome Area History Museum, Rome, GA, is presented in Roper, "I Know the Place," 4–6.

Inside the small fort, the men of the Cherokee Artillery began furiously firing as soon as they discovered the danger. The sudden appearance of the Federals rushing from the dense underbrush came as a shock to the Rebel artillerymen. Holding their fire until they had nearly closed on the little fort, the Yankee attackers let loose with a murderous volley. Inside the lunette, the gunners in gray began to fall. One of the first casualties was J. S. Magnus. A thirty-year-old merchant in 1861, he had moved to Georgia from Germany ten years earlier. Magnus had been part of Rome's small but thriving Jewish community and a relative of Ralph Moses, a planter who had pioneered the growing of peaches in Georgia. Magnus left behind a wife and several children. Working furiously, the rest of the men continued loading and firing their twelve-pounders with double-shotted canister. Despite working furiously to fire and reload, the Rebel gunners were only able to get off four or five rounds per gun before Hooker's men swarmed over them.[35]

Further to the south, along the Confederate trenches, the Tennessee and Maryland cannoneers added their fire in a vain effort to save their comrades from Georgia. "The batteries of Rowan and Marshall had already open[ed] fire," Van Den Corput wrote in post-war correspondence with one of the Federal commanders,

> when I received notice of the [Union] advance and I had just left my old battery to go to them, passing around the breastworks and I sent them word to concentrate their fire on your advancing columns hoping to cause you [the Federals] to retreat[.] My battery after commencing fire kept such a constant fire that it, with the fire of your men[,] put fire to the woods[.] We double shot [fired double-shotted canister] several times, and I know that the batteries of my command made your side pay dearly for the four guns you captured from me.[36]

---

[35] John E. Stillwell to E. A. Carmen, September 15, 1890, Carmen papers, LOC; Max Van Den Corput to E. A. Carmen, June 17, 1892, Carmen papers, LOC; Sullivan, "Magnus," www.preprowhiskeymen.blogspot.2014/09/magnus-fathers-death-and-sons-redemption.html.

[36] Max Van Den Corput to E. A. Carmen, June 17, 1892, Carmen papers, LOC.

Despite the Confederates' best efforts, the bluecoats kept coming, taking casualties with every step. One of Hooker's infantrymen recalled, with obvious pride, "the hill tangled of underbrush caused some disorder in the ranks, but the brave boys from Indiana and Illinois kept steadily on. In a breathless rush, [they pushed forward] until the battery was reached and the gunners struck down or driven to the shelter of their entrenchments in the rear." In the heat of battle, the men of the Cherokee Artillery ignored Hood's order to stand to the last man. In his diary entry for that day, Wesley Connor noted that the Rebel cannoneers had "stood to their guns till the Yanks were inside the embrasure, when they [the Confederate gunners] were forced to leave, having no support nearer the entrenchments." Stillwell explained it even more succinctly, "When the enemy captured the battery we ran out."[37]

One of the best-known incidents of the capture of the lunette involved a member of the Cherokee Artillery. According to the only known account of the incident, one of Van Den Corput's gunners, a large, red-headed man, crawled shirtless from beneath one of the guns, begging for quarter. The bluecoats, enraged upon seeing the words "Fort Pillow" tattooed in big letters on his arm, shouted "No quarter for you!" and bayonetted and shot the man to death on the spot. The incident likely never happened, but if it did, it made the Union warriors guilty of the same crime they apparently found so repugnant about Fort Pillow—killing a surrendered enemy in cold blood. A second occurrence paints a far different picture of the Floyd County soldiers and their captors. A captain of the 70th Indiana related,

> I remember that after the gallant Confederates had done their best, one brave fellow would neither run nor surrender, but stood there laying about [swinging] with his ramrod. I fired the last two shots of my revolver at him and begged him to surrender, but his only reply was a swinging sweep of his ramrod, which was dodged. Then a hand reached over my shoulder, somebody said, "Captain, let me at him," a pistol was fired close behind me, and turning I saw [Maj.] Merrill,

[37] Reid, "Recitals and Reminiscences"; WOC, May 15, 1864; John E. Stillwell to E. A. Carmen, May 15, 1890, Carmen papers, LOC.

> smoking revolver in his hand. In a few minutes the gunners were overcome, and the battery and position was ours.[38]

Of the fifty-five men present, Lt. Stillwell reported that the Cherokee Artillery lost twenty-one men either killed, wounded, or captured. Due to the scarcity of records for the unit after April 1864, it is impossible to compile a complete list of the casualties. The three confirmed Resaca battle deaths were J. S. Magnus, Lewis H. Newton, and a newcomer to the unit remembered only as "Summerhill." The known prisoners included B. F. Burnett, Sidney A. Blassengame, William W. Brice, James H. Champion, David Davidson, George W. Duke, Archibald C. Leary, Thatcher R. Smith, Leonidas B. Stillwell, and Henry C. Wilkerson. Of the captured, Burnett, Brice, Champion (who had been severely injured in the torso by a large piece of shrapnel), Duke, Stillwell, and Wilkerson all died in Union prisons. (Far into the postwar years, Lt. Stillwell and his brother sought to bring Leonidas's body home, though whether they succeeded is unknown.) James Dunn was one of the lucky cannoneers. Though seriously wounded, he somehow made it to the Confederate lines. Sent to a hospital in a small South Georgia town, he eventually recovered.[39]

With the Rebel gunners out of the small fort, the men of Carter Stevenson's division turned their full firepower upon the victorious bluecoats. The Federals had bravely carried the works, but keeping them became a more difficult matter. The Confederate infantry behind the rear of the fort raked the inside of the lunette with rifle fire. Unable to drag out the guns or turn them on their attackers because of the galling fire, all the Yankees could do was hunker down in the shelter of the hill below the little fort. The Confederates, for their part, were equally unable to retrieve their lost guns because of the fire of the Union troops opposite the lunette. With the enemy pinned down and nightfall quickly approaching, Wesley Connor traveled along the trench line for a final look at the little fort. "Went up a few minutes

---

[38] Strong, *A Yankee Private's Civil War,* 16; Perry, *Touched with Fire,* 239–40.

[39] John E. Stillwell to E. A. Carmen, September 15, 1890, Carmen papers, LOC; see appendix, Cherokee Artillery roster; W. O. Connor, "The Martyr Roll," *Rome (GA) Weekly Courier,* August 15, 1877, 3.

ago," he entered in his diary, "to see the battery—everything is as we left it except that the stars and stripes are floating over it. Neither party has possession of it. The Feds cannot remove it till night...." What happened that evening frustrated the men of Harrison's brigade until the day the last member of the unit died. The 5th Ohio came, after dark, to relieve the brave troops who had overrun the small fortress. Under cover of darkness, the Buckeye soldiers removed the four guns, and thereafter claimed credit for capturing them.[40]

Though neither Hooker's nor Stevenson's men knew it, the battle for Resaca had already been decided. Federal Brig. Gen. Thomas G. Sweeny, a one-armed, profane, old-Army Irishman, had taken his division across the Oostanaula River late on the afternoon of May 15, effectively outflanking Joe Johnston and the Army of Tennessee. Maj. Gen. W. H. T. Walker's Rebels had attempted to dislodge Sweeny but failed. As a result, the Confederates started evacuating their positions late on the afternoon of May 15. That night, they crossed the Oostanaula River using a newly constructed pontoon bridge. At around 3:30 A.M. that next morning, the retreating Confederates set fire to the nearby railroad bridge over the river just as their last units completed crossing the pontoon bridge. During the fight at Resaca, the Federals had lost approximately 4,000 men; the Confederates about 3,000 combatants.[41]

Initially, the men of the Cherokee Artillery seemingly maintained a cheerful, positive attitude. They still had their horses, caissons, and gun carriages, and they tagged along with Marshall's and Rowan's cannoneers in the battalion ordinance train. Despite their losses and the retreat from a strong position at Resaca, Connor still retained his faith that the Army of Tennessee would prevail in the end. Four days after

---

[40] Perry, *Touched with Fire*, 239–40; WOC, May 15, 1864; Reid, "Recitals and Reminiscences."

[41] Castel, *Decision in the West*, 168–78; McMurry, "Atlanta Campaign," 23. Sweeny had earlier crossed the Oostanaula but retreated when he received incorrect information that a large Rebel force was approaching the Union bridgehead at Lay's Ferry.

the bluecoats captured the unit's guns, he wrote, "Don't know where we will [next] meet the Yankees, but when the issue comes, [I] think the Confeds will tell a tale for themselves. In every engagement [our retreat was] caused by flanking movements of the Yanks. Our forces [are] nearly equal to theirs, and if we can't whip them we best quit fighting. 'Old Joe' is awake and knows a thing or two."[42]

Sherman declared the Etowah River to be "the Rubicon of Georgia," and Gen. Johnston wanted very much to hold the enemy north of the waterway. The Confederate commander set an ambush for Union forces near Cassville, but for unknown reasons—still hotly disputed by historians—the battle failed to materialize. Old Joe blamed Hood for the failure because he left his assigned position before springing the trap. Hood reported that a large enemy contingent threatened his flank, forcing him to retreat. However, even historian Richard McMurry, who is frequently critical of Joe Johnston's generalship, suggests that, while there were some Federal troops east of Hood that morning, there simply were not enough of them to impede his advance. The Confederate leader tried again to waylay the Yankees two days later, but after a conference with Hood and Polk, the Army of Tennessee retreated across the Etowah to the virtually impregnable position at Allatoona Pass.[43]

If Wesley Connor's journal is an accurate indication, the period between May 15 and May 25 represented a time of confusion and discontent for the soldiers of the Cherokee Artillery. Confederate soldiers began to whisper that Sherman might indeed succeed in taking Atlanta after the army's failure to engage the Yankees at Cassville. "God knows what will become of us if we go [fall back] much further," Connor penned in his journal. Additional concerns gnawed at the men of the battery as well. Reports that the Federals had captured Rome appeared in both Northern and Southern newspapers. Most of the cannoneers hailed from that area, and they naturally worried about friends and

---

[42] WOC, May 18, 1864.

[43] McMurry, "Atlanta Campaign," 54–57, presents the evidence most critical of Johnston, while Scaife, "Waltz between the River," 269–92, makes Hood the "villain" of the failed ambush.

family at home. Equally distressing, the cannoneers feared that the army would break up the battery and parcel out the men to other units. In their midst, they had an example of just such an occurrence. E. R. King, from neighboring Polk County, had organized and captained King's Georgia Light Artillery; but orders had come down from on high to break up the battery and disperse its gunners to other companies. King now served as a lowly private in Van Den Corput's unit. "Members of the Cherokee Artillery becoming demoralized," wrote Connor. "Most of them believe we will not get a battery, and the men will be put into Rowan's and Marshall's Batteries. Should that be the case, I venture the assertion that in a month there will be not thirty men of the [original] 150."[44]

Desertions served as a reliable barometer of soldiers losing hope, and the Cherokee Artillery suffered a rash of men taking "French leave" after the Resaca fight. William J. Cooper allowed himself to be "captured" by Federals, at Adairsville, on March 18. He, like most of the deserting Rebels, claimed to be a conscript who had always opposed secession. Deserters usually took the oath of allegiance to the Union, agreeing to remain north of the Ohio River until the war ended; but Cooper immediately enlisted in the Union Navy. A few of the other deserters from Van Den Corput's unit joined the U.S. Army, requesting service on the frontier.[45]

The majority of the Floyd County cannoneers seemed to be made of sterner stuff. Federal horsemen captured Charles M. Gattis, Sidney H. Gattis, and Angus M. Lassiter at Euharlee Creek as they returned from the veteran's furloughs they had received from Gen. Johnston at Dalton. The three men spent a long, cold winter at Camp Morton and Johnston's Island, refusing to sign the oath. In March 1865, Federal authorities finally forwarded the three diehards to Maryland for transfer back to the Confederacy.[46]

---

[44] WOC, May 19–26, 1864; Daniel, *Cannoneers in Gray*, 210; "Latest News from the Georgia Front," *Augusta (GA) Daily Constitutionalist*, May 21, 1864, 1.

[45] See appendix, Cherokee Artillery roster.

[46] Ibid.

Capt. Van Den Corput, still serving as the head of Stevenson's artillery in the absence of Maj. Johnston, learned of his unit's despondency and set to work to procure another battery of guns. The men left the Army of Tennessee's position near New Hope Church late on the afternoon of May 26. They traveled slowly, being burdened with their caissons, equipment, and wagons, but Van Den Corput's efforts soon paid dividends. Near Stone Mountain they received four twelve-pound "Napoleon" smooth-bores to replace the ones lost at Resaca. After getting the guns, they went to the armory in Atlanta to have the front sights attached. On the evening of May 29, they headed back to the front.[47]

Along the way, they met a former Rome resident, living near Marietta, who invited the cannoneers to stay with him for supper. They must have found some liquor too, as a few of the boys got drunk. They camped for the night at Camp Brown, where the Floyd County volunteers had learned the craft of war two years previously. "The question is how long we can keep them," Connor fretted as they made their way back to the killing fields. "Not long, if we are placed in such positions, as we have been heretofore. I hope we may pass through the struggle without losing another gun."[48]

The Cherokee Artillery arrived back at the front on June 1. The fighting along the New Hope Church-Pickett's Mill-Dallas line had ended in a stalemate, and Gen. Sherman, in another of his patented flanking movements, began pushing his troops toward Marietta, while Rebel cavalry harassed them every step of the way. By June 5, Gen. Johnston had established a new series of entrenchments twelve miles long called the Mountain Line. It stretched from Lost Mountain, on the left, to Brush Mountain, on the right. Carter Stevenson's division occupied a section of the barricades near a rustic house of worship known as Gilgal Church.[49]

---

[47] WOC, May 26–29, 1864.

[48] Ibid.

[49] WOC, July 1, 1864; Hess, *Kennesaw Mountain*, 5–6; Kelly, "Kennesaw Mountain," 11–12.

The Confederate commander knew he lacked the numbers to adequately man the Mountain Line, but likely hoped he could shift troops to meet any isolated Union advances on threatened points. Apparently, Johnston had second thoughts, for twice he shortened the length of his fortifications. On June 15, Old Joe pulled his left off Lost Mountain to Gilgal Church, and two days later retracted his defenses again to a point along Mud Creek. Finally, on June 19, he withdrew to Kennesaw Mountain, the highest mountain in that region. The southernmost point of his new barricade was anchored on Olley's Creek, while the northern terminus of the new defensive position looped around the crest of the mountain to protect the Powder Springs and Marietta Road.[50]

Two weeks of almost constant rain compounded the hardship the common soldiers suffered during the constant shifting of positions. The downpours limited the Federals' ability to mount large-scale offensives because the red clay roads, usually only a pair of unpaved ruts, mired artillery and supply wagons up to their axles in mud. It also wore down the Confederate cannoneers. A member of Marshall's Tennessee Battery explained,

> Nearly every day the rain poured in torrents, and still the sun shone hot and burning; still the artillery fought night and day, threw up intrenchments night and day, and men snatched what sleep they got under the roar of contending guns. Movements were always made at night, or at least begun at night, and whenever and wherever a designated position was reached then began at once the digging and building of earthworks, which had to be from ten to fifteen feet thick to resist the enemy's fire.

"In addition," he continued, "the works were often protected by abatis. The mere labor of fortification was beyond what prudent masters would demand of robust slaves.... The strain of constant vigilance

[50] Hess, *Kennesaw Mountain*, 8–15.

was perhaps harder to bear than the digging, marching, and fighting all combined; but neither could be relaxed for an hour."[51]

Despite the inclement weather, Sherman ordered limited attacks against the Rebel fortifications on June 14, 16, and 17. These assaults accomplished little, but on June 14 a Union artillery shell struck Lt. Gen. Leonidas Polk in the chest, killing him instantly. Though Polk had the habit of sending reports disparaging his superiors to his friend Jefferson Davis, the common soldiers loved the bishop-general from Louisiana and grieved his death.[52]

Sherman's first significant move to dislodge the Confederates from the Kennesaw Mountain Line came on June 22, at the Kolb Farm. The Union commander ordered Maj. Gen. Joseph Hooker's XX corps and Maj. Gen. John Schofield's XXIII corps to advance north along the Powder Springs Road. This put them south of the Kennesaw Mountain Line, where they could easily attack the Rebels from the rear. Gen. Johnston reacted promptly, ordering Hood's Corps to move south to block the Federals' flanking movement.[53]

Ever aggressive, as soon as his troops arrived at their destination, Hood ordered Stevenson's and Maj. Gen. Thomas C. Hindman's divisions to assault the bluecoats. The directive almost guaranteed failure. "The engagement, spoken of by General Sherman, as the '*Affair of Kulp's* [Kolb] *House*,' was a disgrace to the officer who planned it [Hood]," wrote Brig. Gen. A. M. Manigault shortly after the war had ended, "and showed an amount of ignorance of the enemy's position, and the difficulties to be overcome before it could be reached, for which there could be no excuse. The ground had been ridden over by

---

[51] Ibid.; Lindsley, *MAT*, 826–28. Abatis are fortifications formed by tying or wiring sharpened tree branches together to present the enemy with a dense tangle of sharpened sticks.

[52] Castel, *Decision in the West*, 275–78; Col. W. S. Dilworth, "Statement of the Death of Gen. Polk," *Memphis Daily Appeal*, June 28, 1864, 1.

[53] Hess, *Kennesaw Mountain*, 34–46; Kelly, "Kennesaw Mountain," 22–24; McMurry, "The Affair at Kolb Farm," 20–27.

many officers the day before, at the latest, and ought to have been thoroughly understood by General Hood, the greater part of his staff, and particularly his engineers."[54]

Stevenson's Rebels never stood a chance. His troops charged through an area of dense forest before entering into an open field, where waiting masses of strongly entrenched enemy infantry and artillery tore them apart. Stevenson's Division lost almost 1,000 men killed and wounded in less than an hour of combat. A short distance to the west, Maj. Gen. Thomas C. Hindman's men struggled through a dense forest and undergrowth, becoming badly disorganized, as Yankee artillery and infantry poured fire into the graycoats. The ill-advised assault added an additional five hundred Confederate casualties to the butcher's bill. The Confederate's attack did, at least temporarily, halt the Federal advance south of the Kennesaw Mountain Line. But the price had been too dear.[55]

Their general's failure to employ his cannon at the Battle of Kolb's Farm dumbfounded the members of Carter Stevenson's artillery battalion. "On the 22nd, at Marietta," a member of Rowan's Third Maryland Battery wrote, "the battery was ordered out on the field with General Stevenson's division, to charge the right wing of the enemy's line. It [their artillery] was placed on a hill half a mile from the Federal forces, there to await further orders, but it was not sent forward.... The Maryland battery lost none, though under a severe artillery fire the whole time." W. O. Connor expressed similar consternation that the army's long arm failed to get into action:

> Stevenson's Division heavily engaged.... Loss heavy in killed and wounded. It was said when Stevenson ordered his Brigadiers to charge, he shed tears knowing what a hazardous undertaking he was about to perform, and the loss of life that must necessarily ensure

---

[54] Hess, *Kennesaw Mountain*, 34–46; McMurry, "The Affair at Kolb's Farm," 20–27; Tower, *A Carolinian Goes to War*, 192.

[55] Hess, *Kennesaw Mountain*, 35–42; Scaife, *Campaign for Atlanta*, 42–43. Estimates of Rebels killed, wounded, and missing vary widely, but the losses were likely as high as 1,000–1,500 men.

> [ensue]. The men acted gallantly, but were unable to stem the torrent of canister and minnies which were hurled against them. The artillery moved out to within supporting distance but were not engaged.

Why Hood, or Stevenson, failed to utilize the army's "long arm" to cover the assault remains a mystery.[56]

The fight at Kolb's Farm presented additional evidence that many members of the Army of Tennessee would rather desert than continue to fight. Scores of Rebels, their hands high in the air, sprinted through the smoke toward Federal lines. Others hid in the woods until their comrades had withdrawn some distance, and then surrendered themselves to the Yankees. Most of them claimed to have always been loyal to the Union, joining the Confederate army only to avoid conscription. Desertion had been a major problem with the Army of Tennessee since Chattanooga, but it increased significantly south of the Etowah. For example, a couple of weeks prior to the action at Kolb's Farm, all but three men of a company of the 54th Virginia Infantry had deserted to the enemy. There were plenty of good reasons for making that decision. The Western army's almost unbroken string of defeats, unpopular generals, conscription, the suffering of their families at home, and a general feeling of despair led many to leave the army. Still, most persevered and continued to fight.[57]

Following Hood's ill-advised assault at the Kolb Farm, he ordered his corps to pull back a mile or so and dig trenches, thus extending Johnston's Kennesaw Mountain Line to a point below Olley's Creek. The Confederate fortifications now extended seven miles, from Olley's branch on the south to the Powder Springs-Marietta Road north of the mountain's crest. Hood's troops occupied the southern sector of Johnston's entrenchments, Lt. Gen. William J. Hardee's corps the middle

---

[56] Ritter, "Sketch of the Maryland Artillery," 191–92; WOC, June 22, 1864.

[57] Baumgartner and Strayer, *Kennesaw Mountain*, 84; Stephens, *Bound for Glory*, 250; Weaver, *54th Virginia Infantry*, 112. Weaver points out that the three men from the company who stayed with the regiment "seemed to try harder than the rest of the regiment to make up for their comrade's disloyalty, and before the war ended all three became casualties" (6).

region, and Maj. Gen. William Wing Loring's divisions the north. Wheeler's horsemen guarded the small section of the barricades located between the Bell's Ferry and Marietta roads.[58]

Rather than employing the flanking methods that had worked so well throughout the Georgia campaign, on the evening of June 25, Sherman issued Special Field Order No. 28. In it, he directed Gen. McPherson to attack the southern slope of Johnston's line on June 27; Thomas's Army of the Cumberland would simultaneously assault south of the Dallas Road. Meanwhile, John Schofield's men would create a diversion near Olley's Creek to hold Hood's troops in position.[59]

The Federal frontal assault accomplished nothing but another slaughter of brave men. The bluecoats slammed into Maj. Gen. Samuel French's division of Texans, Missourians, and Mississippians—the works held by Brig. Gen. Francis M. Cockrell's and Brig. Gen. Mathew D. Ector's brigades—near the center of the Confederate line. The blue columns reeled from the storm of shot and shell thrown at them and attempted to take refuge in a nearby valley. Exposed to Rebel fire from both flanks, the Yankees either fell where they stood or melted away in confusion. As Schofield's diversionary attack on Hood began, Yankee shells directed at a Confederate battery on the skirmish line in front of the Cherokee Artillery's position occasionally over-shot and smashed into the Georgians' defensive works. At about 11:30 that morning, a percussion shell from a Yankee Parrott gun badly damaged the limber on the Cherokee Artillery's number one gun. Miraculously, the shot did not injure a single member of the battery. The Federal assault also hit elements of Hardee's Corps hard, especially the divisions of Patrick Cleburne and Maj. Gen. Benjamin Cheatham. Despite the determined Federal attack, the two Rebel divisions put up a stout resistance, throwing the Yankees back all along the line. By the time the fighting had

[58] Hess, *Kennesaw Mountain*, 51–55; Kelly, "Kennesaw Mountain," 25; Scaife, *Campaign for Atlanta*, 42–47 and Plate XII.

[59] Castel, *Decision in the West*, 303–305; *OR*, ser. 1, vol. 38, part 4, 588–90; Kelly, "Kennesaw Mountain," 25.

petered out, anywhere from 3,000 to 8,000 bluecoats had become casualties, compared to fewer than 600 Rebels in the assault at Kennesaw Mountain.[60]

Gen. Sherman had learned his lesson. In the early morning of July 2, all along the Kennesaw Mountain Line, the Union artillery roared into action, and soon the skirmishers added musketry to the cacophony of fire and shot. This demonstration was designed to cover the withdrawal of Maj. Gen. John Logan's XV corps as they moved to the southeast to flank Johnston's Rebels from the "Gibraltar of Georgia." It proved to be an exercise in futility, as Joe Johnston had already abandoned the Kennesaw Mountain Line. His three corps had stolen a march to the newly constructed Smyrna Line, leaving behind only his cavalry to cover his retrograde movement.[61]

The next week and a half followed a predictable pattern. The Confederates would fall back to prepared positions and within a few days the Yankees would flank them out of their entrenchments. The first position was the Smyrna Line, a series of barricaded ridges running east to west on a small ridge just north of the town of Smyrna. From there, the Confederate army fell back to Johnston's line along the west bank of the Chattahoochee River, which 1,000 conscripted slaves had constructed under the direction of Brig. Gen. Francis A. Shoup, the Army of Tennessee's Chief of Artillery. Sherman later described the fortifications as "the best line of field entrenchments I have ever seen," but it took the Union commander only four days to get his army across the Chattahoochee. On July 9, the Cherokee Artillery left its position at Turner's Ferry and crossed the Chattahoochee on two pontoon bridges. Since rejoining the Southern army on June 1, if the Floyd County battery had fired a single shot in anger, neither Wesley Connor nor Gen. Stevenson reported it in their writings.[62]

---

[60] WOC, June 27, 1864; Hess, *Kennesaw Mountain*, 206–207; Connelly, *Autumn of Glory*, 358–60; Kelly, "Kennesaw Mountain," 27–30, 46–55.

[61] WOC, July 9, 1864; Castel, *Decision in the West*, 332–34.

[62] Kelly, "Kennesaw Mountain," 53–58.

Allowing Sherman's troops to cross the Chattahoochee virtually guaranteed Gen. Johnston's termination as leader of the Army of Tennessee. The people of Middle Georgia shook in terror at the thought of the Yankees' approach and issued urgent appeals to Richmond for relief. A letter taking Johnston to task for his Fabian tactics appeared in the *Augusta Daily Constitutionalist* and received a wide reprinting in other Southern journals. It read in part,

> The people have seen enough of Johnston's retreats…to satisfy them that if left alone by the Government, he has no idea of making a stand this side of the Gulf of Mexico. If he could not hold the strong position at Kennesaw Mountain, much less would he have held the weak one about Atlanta. The people do not generally know that while Johnston has been retreating before Sherman, he has an army approaching nearer in numbers to that of his adversary [and greater] than Lee ever had when he won his great victories.

Add to that article President Davis's intense dislike of Johnston, plus reports from Gen. Hood finding fault with his commanding general's every decision, and it should have come as no surprise that on July 17, 1864, the chief executive ousted Johnston from command. In the same document, he placed the fate of the Army of Tennessee, and Atlanta, in the hands of John Bell Hood.[63]

W. O. Connor's opinion of the decision to remove Johnston seemed to express the general view of the Army of Tennessee's common soldiers. Connor wrote in his diary,

> Gen. J. E. Johnston was today relieved from command of the Army of Tennessee, which event has cast a universal gloom over the whole army. No commander of an army was ever more loved or honored than was Gen. Johnston. The confidence of the troops in his ability while on the retreat from Dalton, instead of diminishing, has daily increased, and it seems to me that to relieve him (as everyone thinks)

---

[63] *Augusta (GA) Constitutionalist*, July 28, 1864, 1; Castel, *Decision in the West*, 360–65. A recent book by a descendant of Gen. Hood, apparently designed to salvage his ancestor's reputation, admits Hood "may have been scheming to replace Gen. Johnston as commander of the Army of Tennessee…[but] there is no conclusive evidence to support the charge" (Hood, *John Bell Hood*, 19).

> upon the eve of a great battle, fraught with such momentous interests to our country, was injudicious....

Recent claims by some revisionist historians that most of the Rebel army embraced the change of leadership are largely unsupported. A soldier of a Tennessee unit wrote, "Great stalwart sunburnt soldiers by the thousands would be seen falling out of line, squatting down by a tree or fence corner, weeping like children. This act of the War Department threw a damper over this army from which it never recovered, for 'Old Joe,' as we called him, was our idol."[64]

Hood lost no time in going on the offensive. On the afternoon of July 20, he discovered three Union corps—Maj. Gen. John M. Palmer's XIV corps, Maj. Gen Joseph Hooker's XX corps, and Maj. Gen. Oliver O. Howard's IV corps—stretched along a high ridge south of Peachtree Creek. Hood sent Lt. Gen A. P. Stewart's and Lt. Gen. William J. Hardee's corps plunging through a densely wooded thicket in an effort to kill, capture, or scatter the bluecoats. Despite some initial successes for the Confederate infantry, Hood's men were soon driven back. The Union lost less than 2,000 men to the Rebels' 4,800 casualties.[65]

The three sister batteries—Van Den Corput's Georgians, Rowan's Marylanders and Georgians, and Marshall's Tennesseans—did not participate in the fight along Peachtree Creek. Hood had other plans for those units. On July 23, the three batteries took up positions in the defensive line surrounding Atlanta. The heavily fortified city would not be an easy nut for the Yankees to crack. The protective barrier consisted of ten miles of entrenchments, including nineteen redoubts on the main line, each containing five cannon. Besides the guns in the redoubts, there were five exterior artillery batteries and several interior

---

[64] WOC, July 18, 1864; McMurry, *History of the Twentieth Tennessee Regiment Volunteer Infantry, C. S. A.*, 319. For the revisionist viewpoint, asserting that the vast majority of common Rebel soldiers welcomed replacing Johnston with Hood, see McMurry, "Confederate Morale in the Atlanta Campaign of 1864," 226–43.

[65] Castel, "The Heavens and Earth Had Suddenly Come Together," 23–47; S. Davis, "July 10 to September 2, 1864," 12–18.

batteries (such as the three commanded by Capt. Van Den Corput). The Confederates had cleared a field of fire 900 to 1000 yards wide in front of the works, obliterating fruit orchards, barns, and even houses to provide an unimpeded field of fire. Additionally, elaborate abatis protected each artillery position.[66]

Marshall's Battery was positioned just to the right of a roadway that is today Peachtree Street—just north of North Avenue. Rowan's Marylanders took up a position about 600 yards to the left of Marshall's Battery, near the streetcar rails that ran toward Ponce de Leon Springs. Van Den Corput's Battery was posted 600 yards to the right of Marshall's Battery in the direction of Ponce de Leon Springs. This alignment positioned the cannoneers in the center of the northernmost barricade protecting Atlanta.[67]

If any of the Rebel artillerymen thought that their new post would be an easy assignment, they quickly learned otherwise. Previously, the unit's orders had been to fire only upon advancing enemy formations. Their new orders now allowed them to shoot at any target they could find. "Here, for thirty-five days, the employment was shot and shell night and day," wrote the historian of Marshall's Battery, "[and] during this considerable period the firing ceased not for an instant." Shelling from Federal batteries besieging the city was so intense that the Confederates had to keep their artillery horses over a mile and a half from the batteries to protect them from injury.[68]

Conditions inside the Atlanta fortifications boggled the imagination. On August 9, the Federals fired over 5,000 shells into the city, "smashing buildings and taking lives." Though the combat occasionally caused damage to civilian property and inflicted civilian casualties, military targets were under constant bombardment and infantry assaults. Historian Stephen Davis described the siege, noting, "Out in the trenches…as soldiers of both armies dodged 'bum shells' and bullets, mortality was much worse. Among the Confederates, [Carter] Stevenson's Division…lost in a month and a half of skirmishing more

[66] Lindley, *MAT*, 828; Daniel, *Cannoneers in Gray*, 156.
[67] Lindley, *MAT*, 828.
[68] Ibid.; WOC, July 22, 1864.

men than at Resaca, and almost as many as were lost at Kolb's farm." One particular "vidette pit" in front of Van Den Corput's Battery became known as the "dead hole," because Federal sharpshooters shot and killed seventeen Rebel soldiers there—each one by a shot in the head. But the fighting was not confined to just shelling and sniping; the cannoneers were often involved in repulsing frequent Yankee attacks on Hood's outer line of rifle pits.[69]

The Cherokee Artillery suffered as much or more than Hood's infantry soldiers. An obituary of W. O. Connor recalled that he suffered a dangerous trauma about a week after entering the Atlanta defenses. "[H]e was severely wounded," it noted, "and was borne unconscious and bleeding from the field to the hospital. He surprised his comrades, many of whom thought him dead, by appearing on the battlefield in a few weeks; and though still weak, he refused to retire again, but stood fast by the gun to the end." When Connor returned to his unit, he discovered that enemy fire had killed both P. J. Lumpkin and Bud Loyd and wounded Erasmus D. Cobourn and W. C. Bennett. Two families, he noted, had now lost both sons serving in the battery: John T. Lumpkin had died at Baker's Creek, and William Loyd had lost his life during the siege of Vicksburg. Now their two brothers had died defending Atlanta—a single enemy shell having killed both of them. In addition, Capt. Van Den Corput fell, severely wounded, during this period. Capt. Ritter, of the Maryland battery, now assumed command of the artillery battalion.[70]

On the morning of August 25, the Confederates in the trenches on the north side of Atlanta awoke to absolute silence. No artillery fire, nor skirmishers, nor snipers disturbed the early morning air. The cannoneers immediately raided the enemy's former camps, securing all the loot and equipment they could carry. Though Hood sent Wheeler's cavalry in pursuit of the foe, Wesley Connor had already correctly deduced that Sherman had begun another flanking move. The Floyd

---

[69] S. Davis, "July 10 to September 2, 1864," 46.

[70] WOC, August 17, 1864; Ritter, "Sketch of Maryland Artillery," 192; "W. O. Connor," 349.

County soldier confided in his diary that Sherman would move south of the beleaguered city to cut the Rebel's railroad supply line.[71]

Later that day, Ritter's three artillery units received orders to move toward Jonesboro, south of Atlanta, where another battle seemed to be brewing. The Federals of Maj. Gen. Oliver Howard's IV corps, and parts of the XV, XVI, and XVII corps, had assumed a strong position on hills overlooking the Flint River. A deep gully, created by a tributary of the Flint, ran along the southern part of the Yankee barricades, and would play an important role in the first day of what became the Battle of Jonesboro. William Hardee, tasked by Hood with dislodging the Federals, arranged his corps just west of the Macon & Western Railroad line.[72]

At about 4 P.M., Hardee's Rebels charged the Federal lines, but the onslaught seemed doomed to fail from the onset. Many of the Confederates leaped into the ravine fronting the Union defenses and found themselves in a trap. Hundreds of graycoats, realizing they could neither retreat nor advance without being gunned down, meekly surrendered. Like the fight at Kolb's Farm, Ritter's three batteries were stationed within easy range to support the attack but seemingly did not fire a shot. At 1 A.M., Hood, without notifying Gen. Hardee, recalled Lee's Corps to Atlanta.[73]

The next day, Hardee remained in position near Jonesboro. He arranged his seriously depleted line in the shape of an inverted "V," or like "a half-opened jackknife," as the soldiers described the defensive alignment. Late in the afternoon, Sherman's men attacked Hardee's graycoats, and at first it looked as if the Southern line would break. The Yankees hit the Rebels' defensive configuration at the apex, capturing Gen. Daniel Govan and 600 men of his hard-fighting Arkansas Brigade and taking prisoner dozens of men from the famed Kentucky

---

[71] WOC, August 25, 1864; S. Davis, "July 10 to September 2, 1864," 49–51.

[72] WOC, August 25, 1864; Scaife, *Campaign for Atlanta*, 108–15; S. Davis, "July 10 to September 2, 1864," 51–52.

[73] Cheairs, *Old Reliable*, 234–39; WOC, September 1, 1864; Scaife, *Campaign for Atlanta*, 108–15; S. Davis, "July 10 to September 2, 1864," 59–61.

"Orphan Brigade." Luckily, Confederate reinforcements from the southern part of Hardee's line arrived in time to plug the breakthrough. As night fell, a second band of bluecoats attacked the back of the "V," but the Rebels drove them off with considerable casualties.[74]

Stevenson's Division and Ritter's three batteries had camped at a church three miles north of the Jonesboro battlefield on the morning of September 1. When Hardee retreated six miles south to Lovejoy Station shortly after the battle, Stevenson's soldiers followed them. Hood now faced a momentous decision. Pres. Davis had ordered him to protect Georgia's industrial hub, but he no longer had the troops necessary to defend Atlanta. With his army divided and his supply line broken, Hood decided to evacuate Atlanta and left his cavalry to destroy a large munitions train and delay pursuit while he moved his army to Lovejoy Station. On the morning of September 3, Sherman wired the U.S. War Department in Washington: "So Atlanta is ours, and fairly won."[75]

The Federals made one attack against the Rebel fortifications at Lovejoy Station, but found the entrenchments too strong to take without months of preparation and the loss of tens of thousands of lives. Gen. Sherman fell back to Atlanta to regroup and resupply. He had other plans for his army.[76]

During the lull in the fighting, W. O. Connor moved about freely, observing, and recording his thoughts. On September 6 he listened as Lt. Gen. Stephen D. Lee, their corps commander since Hood had assumed command of the army, addressed Carter Stevenson's division. "He [Lee] intimated that his corps had not been fighting, as it ought to do. Hope it will do some good, as it was entirely [the fault of] Lee's corps that Atlanta had to be evacuated. Had the men gone forward at Jonesboro, Sherman would be now, instead of in Atlanta, on his way

---

[74] Castel, *Decision in the West*, 510–21; Scaife, *Campaign for Atlanta*, 108–15.

[75] WOC, September 1–3, 1864; Castel, *Decision in the West*, 510–21.

[76] Castel, *Decision in the West*, 534–42.

to Chattanooga." The Floyd County cannoneer had already concluded, "We can only look to the interposition of Providence in our [the Confederacy's] behalf."[77]

On September 11, the diarist visited the battlefield at Jonesboro. He expressed shock at how little remained of the fierce battle fought there only ten days previously. Except where Cleburne's troops had fought, there was precious little to suggest that there had been a fierce engagement there. Nevertheless, Connor was convinced that Hardee and his troops had fought well. "Impartial history," he wrote in his diary, "will accord to Gen. Hardee the credit of having on the 1st of September 1864 made one of the most gallant fights of the war." The Georgia artilleryman found where the Union troops had hastily buried his comrades, leaving inscriptions such as "51 dead rebels buried in these two trenches." Upon one such "headstone" a Rebel sympathizer had inscribed the tribute: "Tread lightly for here sleep the brave." It would be sad, he observed, "to think their lives were sacrificed in vain."[78]

On September 26, W. O. Connor reported that at Palmetto, Georgia, Confederate president Jefferson Davis rode in review, with Hood and his corps commanders, past the assembled troops. The soldiers drew up and gave the president three cheers as he passed. Some regiments, Connor observed, cheered only feebly, and it was clear that their hearts were not in it. Other units bluntly screamed "Give us Johnston! Give us our old commander!" In an attempt to defuse the possible powder keg, Davis named Gen. P. G. T. Beauregard as commander of the new military division of the West. Despite his grand-sounding title, Davis authorized Beauregard only the power to advise his nominal subordinates, including Hood. He had no right to issue direct orders to the Army of Tennessee commander. The president's attempt to appease Hood's critics neither fooled nor placated the common soldiers. "I suppose he will," Connor wrote, "as usual, return to Richmond and report everything [is] in excellent condition."[79]

---

[77] WOC, September 1 and 6, 1864.

[78] WOC, September 12, 1864.

[79] WOC, September 26, 1864; Castel, *Decision in the West*, 550–52.

Chapter 6

"One of the Most Melancholy Sights a Person Ever Saw"

Hood's 1864 Tennessee Campaign

The loss of Atlanta, with its rail yards, foundries, warehouses, and machine shops represented a devastating blow to the Confederate war effort; but the Atlanta Campaign had proven equally ruinous to Southern morale. Summing up the prevailing mood of both the soldiers in Hood's army and the people of the Confederacy, Wesley Connor wrote, "Feel more despondent than at any time since the beginning of the struggle. We can only look to an interposition of Providence in our behalf."[1]

The battles before Atlanta and the subsequent siege had inflicted terrible losses on the Army of Tennessee. The Confederacy's Western army began June 1864 with just over 82,000 men, but the army had lost 42,000 soldiers by mid-September. This included over 10,300 taken prisoner and at least 13,000 deserters. By September 10, Hood's entire army numbered only slightly more than 39,000 effectives.[2]

The loss of supplies and equipment proved almost as critical as the loss of men. Between May and August, Sherman's troops captured four-dozen Rebel cannon and more than 13,000 small arms. To make matters worse, the army's reserve ordnance train, trapped in Atlanta after the Yankees seized the Macon Railroad, had been destroyed by the retreating Confederates. This resulted in the loss of the Southern army's entire ammunition reserve, huge quantities of ordnance and equipment, and vast quantities of sorely needed foodstuffs.[3]

The campaign had been especially hard on the artillery. In addition to the loss of their captured guns and reserve ammunition, the army's "long arm" had also suffered heavy losses in equipment, horses, and men.

---

[1] WOC, September 1, 1864.

[2] *OR*, ser. 1, vol. 38, part 1, 171–72; Connelly, *Autumn of Glory*, 467.

[3] *OR*, ser. 1, vol. 38, 1, 171–72; Connelly, *Autumn of Glory*, 467–69; Sword, *Embrace an Angry Wind*, 35.

The remaining artillery horses had become so feeble that Capt. Charles Swett, the Army of Tennessee's acting inspector general, ordered each battery to turn in two caissons to the Ordnance Department in exchange for mule wagons. This allowed a sizable portion of the remaining horses an opportunity to rest. The Cherokee Artillery, along with the other two batteries in Johnston's Battalion—Rowan's Maryland and Marshall's Tennessee batteries—had no more than four worn-out horses per gun. The situation with the men proved almost as bad. Johnston's units had only about sixty effectives in the ranks for each battery. Since the evacuation of Dalton, each of the three batteries had lost around thirty-five men due to various causes. Now, they needed several weeks to rest. That would, hypothetically, permit Hood an opportunity to replace men, horses, and equipment in order to allow the Rebel artillery to operate at peak efficiency.[4]

More importantly, Hood's army suffered from something much more insidious and difficult to remedy than the loss of soldiers, animals, and weaponry. His troops exhibited low morale and a loss of faith in their commander. Unlike his predecessor, Joe Johnston, John Bell Hood devoutly believed in the efficacy of aggressively attacking the enemy whenever possible. He had become an instant Southern hero in 1862, when his famed Texas Brigade pierced the center of the Federal line in a vicious and bloody frontal assault at Gaines Mill, Virginia. During the recent campaign, Hood continued to rely heavily on frontal attacks, but unlike the success at Gaines Mill, these recent onslaughts had been costly failures. First at Peachtree Creek, then at Ezra Church, and again at the Battle of Atlanta, Hood's divisions had made courageous but futile attempts to dislodge entrenched Federal troops, some of whom were now armed with repeating rifles. Confederate desertions began to increase, and Hood complained to Braxton Bragg, now Davis's military adviser, that the men in the ranks had begun to demonstrate a palpable timidity when ordered to assault fortified Federal positions.[5]

---

[4] Lindsley, *MAT*, 829; *OR*, ser. 1, vol. 38, part 3, 683.

[5] Sword, *Embrace an Angry Wind*, 44; *OR*, ser. 1, vol. 39, part 2, 893; McDonough and Connelly, *Five Tragic Hours*, 4–5. Sword sardonically refers to Hood's headlong assault obsession as "Gaines Mill syndrome."

Jefferson Davis, the Confederate president, found himself astride the horns of a dilemma. John Bell Hood, his hand-picked choice to replace Joe Johnston, had not only squandered the lives of thousands of irreplaceable soldiers, but had also lost the politically and strategically important city of Atlanta. Abraham Lincoln's re-election as the Federal president now appeared to be a virtual certainty, negating any realistic hope of a negotiated peace. Davis's critics within the Confederate government began stridently demanding that Hood be relieved. Many of these malcontents, aware from sources within the army of the tensions between Hood and his senior commanders, clamored to have Hood replaced as leader of the Western army. Davis, a proud man not given to flexibility, simply could not admit the possibility that he had been wrong in removing "Old Joe." He would have to find a different solution—one that would improve Southern morale, placate his critics, and assuage his pride.[6]

While Davis searched for solutions to his difficulties, "Sam" Hood tried to deal with his own problems. Despite the relative calm, the Army of Tennessee was in a precarious situation. Too weak to push the Yankees out of Atlanta, the Army of Tennessee could also not sit idly by until Sherman's army, fully rested and recovered, came after them with a vengeance. Hood's only viable option, he believed, involved taking the offensive. He determined to move to the northwest to cut Sherman's supply line between Chattanooga and Atlanta. On September 6, Hood communicated his intentions to Pres. Davis, indicating that his army would move "as soon as practicable."[7]

Over the next twelve days, the army continued its respite from the rigors of the recent campaign. The army had enough supplies and a pleasant location, and the men and horses rapidly recovered their strength. Thanks to Hood's emergency appeal to the president, the soldiers, who had not been paid for months, received their back pay in an effort to help stem the rising tide of desertions.[8]

---

[6] Connelly, *Autumn of Glory*, 470–76; Sword, *Embrace an Angry Wind*, 44–46.

[7] *OR*, ser. 1, vol. 38, part 2, 864; Sword, *Embrace an Angry Wind*, 46; Connelly, *Autumn of Glory*, 476–79.

[8] Lindsley, *MAT*, 829; Sword, *Embrace an Angry Wind*, 44.

During this time, an event transpired that was, in some ways, only a footnote in the history of the Atlanta Campaign but served as a portent of the changing nature of warfare. On September 7, Sherman sent Hood a bluntly worded message stating his intention to remove the remaining inhabitants of Atlanta from the city. Atlanta would become a Union military post and logistical base. In preparation for this change, Sherman sought to expel Atlanta's civilian population. The move would eliminate the need to feed and care for the noncombatants, thereby reducing the number of troops needed to garrison the city. The Federal army would provide conveyance to the civilians who wished to go north. Those who decided to go south would receive transportation as far as Rough and Ready (modern Mountain View, Georgia). From there, they would become the responsibility of Hood's army. Over the next several days, a flurry of heated messages flew between the two headquarters—Hood aghast at the very notion of Sherman's proposal, and Sherman adamant upon Hood's agreement. Further inflaming the situation, Hood allowed several of his responses to Sherman to be printed in the *Macon (GA) Telegraph*. Reaction across the South was swift and angry. W. O. Connor noted, "[Federal Gen. Benjamin "Beast"] Butler at New Orleans only exiled the registered enemies of the U.S. while Sherman makes a sweep of the whole population. As Gen. Hood says, 'it [the order of exile]. stands pre-eminent in the dark history of war for studied and ingenious cruelty.'" Hood, realizing he had no other real choice, reluctantly agreed to Sherman's terms. On Monday, September 12, a ten-day truce began, culminating in the wholesale removal of Atlanta's citizens.[9]

As the armistice neared its end, Hood put his army in motion, positioning it to attack Sherman's supposedly vulnerable supply lines. (The Union commander had been stockpiling supplies for months, and his army could have survived almost indefinitely without receiving a single biscuit or bullet.) Starting on the morning of September 18,

[9] *OR*, ser. 1, vol. 39, part 2, 414; "Correspondence Between Gens. Hood and Sherman," *Macon (GA) Telegraph*, September 14, 1864; WOC, September 10, 1864; Castel, *Decision in the West*, 548–49; Cox, *Atlanta*, 220–21.

the lead elements of the Army of Tennessee began moving to the northwest. For most of the Rebel soldiers, their destination remained a mystery. "Left camp for somewhere," Wesley Connor wrote in his diary that day. "Have less idea what course we will take than at any previous move." Bivouacking that night at Glass Mills, by 10:00 the following morning the Cherokee Artillery was once again on the march. Rumors began spreading through the ranks that they were headed for the town of Palmetto, on the West Point Railroad. The purpose of this move, to the common soldier, remained unclear.[10]

After reaching Palmetto on the morning of September 20, the battery established its camp at a point about a mile northeast of town. There, the Army of Tennessee formed a defensive line shaped like an arc, with its left flank resting on the Chattahoochee River and its right extending past the West Point and Montgomery Railroad. Breaking camp the next day, the cannoneers moved to a new position, a half-mile behind the infantry. Still not sure what Hood had in mind, the gunners spent the rest of that day, and much of next, digging defensive works.[11]

At 6 P.M. on September 27, Pres. Davis and his advisers—still trying to find a way to placate Hood's detractors—left the Army of Tennessee's Palmetto encampment. Davis and his entourage boarded a train bound for Montgomery, Alabama. The president appeared satisfied with Hood's plan to destroy Sherman's supply line and directed him to establish a defensive position near Gadsden, Alabama. There, supplied by the Alabama and Tennessee Rivers Railroad, the Army of Tennessee could give battle on ground of their choosing. If Sherman, as expected, followed Hood's army northward to defend his supply and

---

[10] *OR*, ser. 1, vol. 39, part 2, 863; WOC, September 19, 1864; McDonough and Connelly, *Five Tragic Hours*, 12–18.

[11] *OR*, ser. 1, vol. 39, part 2, 862; Connelly, *Autumn of Glory*, 476–78; Sword, *Embrace an Angry Wind*, 47.

communication lines, the Rebels could strike the widely scattered Federals. On the other hand, if Sherman chose to ignore Hood's move and continue his march across Georgia, the Army of Tennessee would be able to follow and assault the Union general at his weakest point. Prior to leaving, Davis also advised Hood that he would soon render a final decision regarding whether he would continue in command of the Confederacy's Western army.[12]

Hood didn't have to wait long to learn his fate. The following day, Davis sent Hood word that he would relieve Gen. Hardee, Hood's most vocal critic in the army. Hardee would be reassigned to Charleston, South Carolina. Hood would retain command of his army, with one important proviso. Davis planned to appoint Gen. Pierre G. T. Beauregard, the popular "hero of First Manassas," as commander over the Department of Tennessee and Lt. Gen. Richard Taylor's Department of Alabama, Mississippi, and East Louisiana. Despite his strong dislike for the fiery Creole, Davis hoped that placing Hood under Beauregard's command—at least on paper—would appease the growing chorus of critics across the South. The president seemed pleased. He had found a way to placate his detractors without admitting that his appointment of Hood to command of the Army of Tennessee had been a grievous mistake.[13]

With his position at the head of the Army of Tennessee secure, Hood named hard-fighting, hard-drinking Maj. Gen. Benjamin Cheatham to replace the contentious Hardee. On September 29, the Army of Tennessee left Palmetto and began marching westward toward Moore's Ferry, where they would cross the Chattahoochee River. The fateful campaign had begun.

Ordered to make ready to move out by 2 P.M., the Cherokee Artillery harnessed its horses, hitched caissons and wagons, and prepared for the march. At 4 P.M., they finally began moving "in a tremendous

---

[12] Connelly, *Autumn of Glory*, 472; *OR*, ser. 1, vol. 39, part 2, 879–80; WOC, September 19–27, 1864.

[13] Hughes, *Old Reliable*, 246–49; Roman, *Military Operations of General Beauregard* 2:277–80; *OR*, ser. 1, vol. 39, part 2, 879–80; McDonough and Connelly, *Five Tragic Hours*, 6–11.

hurry" toward the Chattahoochee. They had barely covered two miles when new orders arrived directing them to stand down and be ready instead to move again the next morning. No sooner had the cannoneers made camp and drifted off to sleep than the bugle blared "Boots and Saddles." Roused from their rest, they once again prepared to march. They had just completed their preparations when yet a third set of orders arrived, countermanding the previous ones. The weary gunners unhitched and unharnessed their critters and again lay down to sleep.[14]

Early on the morning of September 30, the Cherokee Artillery crossed the Chattahoochee at Pumpkin Town and marched on until making camp one mile west of Skinned Chestnut (modern-day Douglasville). Wesley Connor seemed to sense the singular importance of this event. "The Rubicon is crossed," he noted. Two days later, the battery tramped along, with the rest of Johnston's Artillery Battalion, passing through Villa Rica before making camp seven miles from Dallas.[15]

Hood now began to execute his plan to disrupt Sherman's communications along the West Point and Atlantic Railroad. Leaving Lee's Corps near Lost Mountain to protect the army's left flank, he ordered Gen. A. P. Stewart to march northward to begin the attack. By the afternoon of October 3, Stewart's Corps took Big Shanty (modern-day Kennesaw), tearing up the rail line as they moved. The next morning, the Federal garrison at Acworth surrendered to Maj. Gen. Loring's division.

Late that same afternoon, Maj. Gen. Samuel French's division had trudged from Big Shanty and prepared to attack Sherman's supply depot and the railroad bridge at Allatoona. French began his assault around 10 A.M. on October 5. After a hard fight, French withdrew when he received intelligence that Federal reinforcements were moving against his exhausted division. Only later, after having incurred nearly

---

[14] *OR*, ser. 1, vol. 39, part 2, 879–80; Sword, *Embrace an Angry Wind*, 47; WOC, September 19–27, 1864.

[15] WOC, September 30–October 2, 1864; *OR*, ser. 1, vol. 39, part 1, 802, 813, and 814; Scaife, "Sherman's March to the Sea," 12–20.

1,000 casualties in a vain attempt to dislodge the stubborn enemy, did he learn that the information about advancing Federals had been incorrect.[16]

So far, Hood's move had accomplished its primary goal. On October 4, Sherman left Slocum's XX Corps behind to guard Atlanta and the Chattahoochee rail bridge. He then directed his remaining brigades to march northwestward toward Stewart's Confederate corps, moving first to Smyrna Campground, and then on to a strong position near Kennesaw. After Corse's successful defense of Allatoona, Sherman pushed his troops toward Dallas on October 6 and 7, only to find that Hood had withdrawn farther westward. Concerned now that Hood would attack the rail line near Kingston, Sherman wheeled his army northward. The Union commander quickly realized that he was doing exactly what he had tried to avoid—chasing the erratic, unpredictable Hood around Northwest Georgia instead of sweeping eastward across Georgia.[17]

Leaving Dallas on October 7, Hood's army marched farther west to Van Wert, in Polk County. The following day, the reunited Rebel army continued moving west, arriving at Cedartown, not far from the Alabama border. The men of the Cherokee Artillery, camping that night at McMeekin's place, about three miles north of Cedartown, felt their excitement growing as they moved closer to home. Many of the cannoneers hailed from Cave Spring, only a few miles away. Granted permission to go on ahead to visit family and friends, the Cave Spring

---

[16] Sword, *Embrace an Angry Wind*, 54–56; *OR*, ser. 1, vol. 39, part 1, 813–14; Scaife, "Sherman's March to the Sea," 12–20. See generally, Brad Butkovich, *Battle of Allatoona Pass: Civil War Skirmish in Bartow County, Georgia* (Mt. Pleasant, SC: Arcadia, 2014).

[17] *OR*, ser. 1, vol. 39, part 1, 580–84; Sword, *Embrace an Angry Wind*, 58–62; Scaife, "Sherman's March to the Sea," 12–20.

boys found that word of their pending arrival had preceded them. Several of the area's young ladies came out to meet them and provided a wild, joyous welcome. When the soldiers arrived, the citizens of Cave Spring gave their war-weary sons an equally merry reception.[18]

All that day, and on into the next morning, the Cave Springs artillerymen spent as many hours as they could among family, friends, and sweethearts. No one knew when, or if, they might return to their hometown. In some ways, it seemed like little had changed in their absence. Indeed, it did not appear as if the inhabitants had suffered much under Yankee occupation. But, subtle signs of time's passing soon became apparent. The children they remembered had blossomed into gallant young men and graceful young women. The gunners discovered that in the eyes of the townsfolk they, too, had changed. The raw, boisterous young men who had eagerly left more than three years ago had returned hardened, and much matured, by their wartime experiences. All too soon, orders arrived directing the gunners to return to camp and prepare to move out.[19]

The men from the Cherokee Artillery had not been the only ones having a reunion in Cave Spring. Gen. Beauregard, the theater commander and Hood's immediate superior, arrived at the general's headquarters to see the Army of Tennessee's progress for himself and to discuss Hood's plan. After a brief consultation, Beauregard approved Hood's scheme to draw Sherman farther away from Atlanta by continuing to tear up the railroad track from Kingston to Dalton. The Creole general warned Hood not to try to engage Sherman unless numbers, or terrain, favored an offensive, or the safety of the Army of Tennessee required it.[20]

When at Cedartown, Hood had notified Braxton Bragg, in Richmond, of his next move. In orders to his corps commanders, Hood stressed that the army would move in "marching order." The infantry would draw three days rations and be accompanied by only one battery

---

[18] WOC, October 8–10, 1864.

[19] Ibid.

[20] WOC, October 8–10, 1864; *OR*, ser. 1, vol. 39, part 1, 796; Scaife, "Sherman's March to the Sea," 17–20.

from each artillery battalion. Soldiers without shoes, the baggage train and supply wagons, and the rest of the artillery would move west under Hood's recently appointed chief of artillery, Maj. Gen. Arnold Elzey. Once they had torn up the railroad line as far as Dalton, the infantry divisions would turn to the southwest and rendezvous with Hood's force near the army's supply depot at Jacksonville, Alabama.[21]

On Monday, October 10, the Army of Tennessee marched northward to Coosa, about ten miles due west of Rome. Although Lt. Meshack McWhorter, now the acting commander of Van Den Corput's Battery, had ordered the men of the Cherokee Artillery to remain with the guns, "it didn't amount to much," noted Wesley Connor. Arriving in Cave Spring at 8 A.M., he and the other hometown men managed to slip away and spend a few parting moments with family and friends before moving out with the rest of the battery. After marching only a short distance, the battery received orders to halt. Directed again to remain in camp, this time the men from Cave Springs could only look wistfully toward home and recall memories of their visit. As noon approached, the arrival of Gen. Hood alleviated some of the boredom of waiting for orders. Buoyed by the army's success thus far, the battery "gave him a hearty cheer, such as does one good to hear." Maybe, the common soldiers hoped, they had been wrong about their commander.[22]

By mid-afternoon, the Cherokee Artillery began the march again. As they turned their backs on home, many of the gunners couldn't help feeling a twinge of sadness. For most, it would be a long time before they returned. Moving with the rest of the reserve artillery, the battery reached Centre, Alabama, the next day. By October 15, they had marched south from Centre—first to Goshen, and then to within three and a half miles of the army's new supply base at Jacksonville. What news they received from the rest of the army did not seem particularly important. The Rebel soldiers had torn up more of the railroad track

[21] *OR*, ser. 1, vol. 39, part 3, 804, 812; Ritter, "Third Maryland Artillery," 537.
[22] WOC, October 10, 1864.

at Dalton, as planned, and had captured a large number of United States Colored Troops at Dalton.[23]

Four days later, on Thursday evening, October 20, Elzey's forces moved north and rendezvoused with Hood's scattered infantry divisions at Gadsden, Alabama. For the first time the men of the Cherokee Artillery observed a large number of black soldiers among the captured Yankees. Some actually hailed from Floyd County, and their masters soon began arriving to reclaim their "property." The Confederate soldiers found the sight of black men in the uniform of the United States both sobering and disturbing. Some of the Rebels, after further reflection, concluded that the black men had simply been deluded by the enemy, and therefore deserved charitable treatment by their captors.[24]

Over the next couple of days, the army rested and refitted. From the stores that Beauregard had marshaled at Jacksonville, the army received badly needed clothing and shoes. The break in activity also allowed several members of the Cherokee Artillery the opportunity to explore Nachalula Falls, which lay about three miles north of Gadsden. Once a popular resort area, the men found that it no longer bore any resemblance to the thriving, pleasant amusement place they remembered. Nearly four years of war had taken a desperate toll on the spa. Saddened, they gave a sigh for the "days of yore," and returned to camp.[25]

While the army rested and the members of the Cherokee Artillery explored the surrounding countryside, on October 21 a frustrated and confused Beauregard arrived at Hood's headquarters. Based on their discussion at Cave Spring, Hood had led the Creole general to believe that the Army of Tennessee would continue operating in the Jacksonville area as a threat to Sherman's rear. Expecting to find Hood near Alpine or Summerville, Georgia, he had ridden as far as the Round Mountain Ironworks, near Centre, Alabama, when he learned, almost

[23] WOC, October 10–20, 1864.

[24] Ibid.; *OR*, ser. 1, vol. 39, part 3, 832.

[25] WOC, October 22, 1864.

accidentally, from Maj. Gen. Joseph "Fighting Joe" Wheeler's cavalry, that his headstrong subordinate had moved north to Gadsden.[26]

Hood had again changed his plans. If his troops moved northward into Middle Tennessee, Hood explained to the impatient Beauregard, Sherman would be compelled to follow him to protect and repair his supply lines, which his forces had badly damaged in their recent sweep through North Georgia. Either way, Hood reasoned, he would win. If Sherman attempted to advance into Tennessee, or continued his effort to subdue Georgia, the Army of Tennessee could defeat each Union contingent in detail. On the other hand, if Sherman opted to follow Hood into Tennessee with his entire army, Georgia would be freed from Yankee occupation. Despite his misgivings, Beauregard reluctantly agreed. Hood would have his way.[27]

On Saturday, October 22, the Army of Tennessee began its march northwest toward Guntersville, Alabama, where Hood planned to cross the Tennessee River. At 2 P.M., the Cherokee Artillery hitched up, expecting to move out. Instead, they found themselves idly waiting for orders. Finally, at around 5 P.M., they moved out "and traveled the great distance of a half mile." Ordered to unhitch, the battery made camp in an old field without so much as a twig of wood for evening fires. To make matters worse, the Rebels had received strict orders not to burn any wooden fence rails. Soon, however, unsubstantiated rumors began swirling that Maj. Johnston, their battalion commander, had commandeered some of the fence rails and built a large fire. Encouraged by this supposed duplicity, the entire battalion began dismantling the nearby wooden fences, and numerous fires were soon burning merrily throughout the artillery camp. Only after the most strenuous efforts by the battalion's officers did they manage to extinguish the blazes. With the damage already done, the men received orders reiterating the original directive.[28]

Without informing Beauregard, Hood changed his plan yet again. The general later claimed that he moved farther westward along the

[26] *OR*, ser. 1, vol. 45, part 1, 646–48; Connelly, *Autumn of Glory*, 483–84.
[27] *OR*, ser. 1, vol. 45, part 1, 652, 662; Sword, *Embrace an Angry Wind*, 63–64.
[28] WOC, October 22, 1864.

Tennessee River to effect an eventual link-up with Nathan Bedford Forrest's cavalry division. Beauregard had recently sent orders to the "Wizard of the Saddle" to rendezvous with the Army of Tennessee. His veteran horsemen would replace Wheeler's cavalry, which had been left behind to protect Georgia. With insufficient cavalry to guard his vulnerable flanks and supply trains, Hood later explained, he could not yet risk crossing the Tennessee. Instead, the Army of Tennessee would have to move farther west to Tuscumbia, Alabama, its new supply base, and there link up with Forrest. Only then could they safely cross the Tennessee River and begin the campaign to liberate the Volunteer State. This explanation did not stand up to close scrutiny. Forrest, away raiding in West Tennessee, had not yet received orders from Beauregard to meet up with Hood. Instead, the reason he gave Beauregard, when the furious Creole finally caught up with the army at Decatur, Alabama, on October 27, likely came closer to the unvarnished truth. Guntersville, and other river towns in Northeast Alabama, had simply been too heavily defended by enemy troops to allow an easy crossing. The only reasonable solution, Hood concluded, involved moving farther west.[29]

Hood's erratic advance had not gone unnoticed by the bluecoats. Sherman, whose army had been encamped at Gaylesville, Alabama, for several days, had been keeping a close eye on Hood, hoping to get an accurate assessment of his intentions. Hood's continued movement to the west convinced Sherman that the Rebel commander did indeed plan to invade Middle Tennessee. The Union leader had had enough. All along he had reasoned that chasing Hood away from the Federal supply line was a fool's errand. Sherman planned to abandon Hood to his fate and move eastward. Ulysses S. Grant had finally approved Sherman's plan to march across Georgia to the sea. "Let him go north," the

[29] *OR*, ser. 1, vol. 39, part 1, 801; Connelly, *Autumn of Glory*, 485–87; McDonough and Connelly, *Five Tragic Hours*, 17.

red-bearded general told a council of his senior commanders. "Our business is down South."[30]

On October 26, Sherman dispatched Maj. Gen. David Stanley's IV corps to report to Maj. Gen. George Thomas, at Nashville. Four days later Sherman committed additional troops to the defense of the Volunteer State, ordering Maj. Gen. John Schofield to also move north with his corps and report to Thomas. Satisfied that he had now provided Thomas with sufficient resources to defend against Hood's likely invasion of Middle Tennessee, Sherman returned to Georgia and began preparations for his March to the Sea.[31]

Meanwhile, the Cherokee Artillery and the rest of Army of Tennessee continued their trek westward. On October 29, after trudging nearly ninety hard miles over roads that were often slippery and muddy, the men of the battery found themselves passing through the pleasant little town of Courtland, Alabama. Unlike many of the other towns along the line of march, the citizens of Courtland—especially the ladies—gave them a warm welcome. They seemed genuinely happy to see the ragged rebels and "glad of [for] an opportunity of getting up a conversation with even a private." Encouraged by that reception, the Georgia gunners continued their march westward, stopping that night ten or twelve miles west of Courtland on the Memphis & Charleston Railroad. By noon the following day, they neared Tuscumbia, the army's new supply depot. Hood had finally decided to cross the Tennessee River, near Tuscumbia, and begin his offensive. The Georgia gunners had heard rumors that some of the Confederate infantry had already crossed the river, into nearby Florence, to oust the small force of Yankees stationed there. With artillery fire rumbling in the distance, they made camp that evening in the nearby woods.[32]

---

[30] *OR*, ser. 1, vol. 39, part 1, 580–84; *OR*, ser. 1, vol. 39, part 3, 202; "Sherman's Campaign," Augusta *(GA) Chronicle*, November 22, 1864, 2; Scaife, "The March to the Sea," 17–18.

[31] Horn, *Army of Tennessee*, 380; WOC, October 29–30, 1864; "From Hood's Army," *Richmond Examiner*, November 1, 1864, 3.

[32] Lindsley, *MAT*, 829; WOC, November 5, 1864; Lee, "Lieutenant-General S. D. Lee's Report of the Tennessee Campaign, Beginning September 29th, 1864," 66 (hereafter cited as "S. D. Lee's report").

As October gave way to November, the weather, which had been mostly favorable, turned cold and rainy. Hood's lackadaisical attitude toward the establishment of an efficient supply system now proved to be another pivotal mistake. The inclement weather hindered efforts to repair the Mobile & Ohio and Memphis & Charleston rail lines, seriously delaying efforts to resupply the tattered, ill-shod graycoats, who were now subsisting almost entirely on parched corn. Hood no longer spoke boldly of living off the fat of the land in Middle Tennessee. Instead, short of supplies and anxiously awaiting the arrival of Forrest's cavalry, Hood had to delay his offensive for an additional three weeks. Although Hood didn't know it at the time, this delay would prove critical. It gave Gen. Thomas the time he needed to organize the Federal troops, now hastening through Middle Tennessee, into a formidable fighting force.[33]

The Cherokee Artillery, along with the rest of Johnston's Artillery Battalion, crossed the nearly mile-long pontoon bridge spanning the Tennessee River on November 5. S. D. Lee's corps, the vanguard of the Army of Tennessee, had crossed the river on the previous Saturday and had easily chased away the 1,000 or so enemy horse soldiers posted in Florence. Meanwhile, the Cherokee Artillery, assigned to support their old comrades in Stevenson's Division, took up a position east of town on the Shoal Creek Road. Federal cavalry still prowled the area, and the battery witnessed a sharp exchange of fire between the Yankee horsemen and the infantry of Maj. Gen. Edward "Old Allegany" Johnson's division. In short order, the Yankees "skedaddled," leaving Florence firmly in Confederate hands.[34]

The next couple of weeks passed without incident, allowing the Georgia cannoneers time to explore the pleasant town of Florence. They were also fortunate enough to draw some captured Yankee horses and blankets from the booty captured by S. D. Lee's troops. Despite

---

[33] WOC, November 6 and 17, 1864.

[34] *OR*, ser. 1, vol. 45, part 1, 65; WOC, November 5–17, 1864; "Day of Prayer and Thanksgiving," *Augusta (GA) Daily Constitutionalist*, November 15, 1864, 2.

the quiet, the Floyd County artillerymen knew that they would be moving out soon. In addition, a nervous tension filled the air. The next day, Sunday, May 6, was Election Day in the North. Like their fellow citizens throughout the Confederacy, the troops held their breath, anxiously awaiting the results. Would George "Little Mac" McClellan, the general turned politician, win and sue for peace with the Confederacy, or would the North re-elect Abraham Lincoln and ensure that the war would continue? "Our sky is o'ercast with dark clouds," Wesley Connor wrote. "I can see no bright ray to illumine our horizon, but there is time yet." Perhaps attempting to focus the Confederate nation's anxiety into an appeal for Divine intervention, Pres. Davis appointed Wednesday, November 16, to be a national day of prayer and fasting.[35]

Hood's preparations to take the offensive continued to slowly take shape, but a constant deluge of rain hampered his efforts. The Tennessee River, at near flood stage, made crossing on the army's rickety pontoon bridge a dangerous feat. Nevertheless, by November 19, Cheatham's and Lee's corps had safely reached the north side of the river, with Stewart's Corps poised to cross the next day. Forrest's troopers had also arrived earlier that week. Although rations continued to be in short supply, they would wait no longer. Hood's proclamation to the army, issued on November 20, urged the men to meet the privations and hardships of the coming campaign with a "cheerful, manly spirit," and to envision "the fruitful fields of Tennessee [that] are before us." After weeks of moving in slow motion, Hood's campaign to retake Tennessee had finally begun in earnest.[36]

At 5 A.M. on November 20, Lee's Corps began marching toward Columbia, Tennessee, passing through Henryville and Mount Pleasant. They exhibited high spirits and a little of their old swagger as they prepared to drive the Yankees out of the Volunteer State. Stewart's

---

[35] *OR*, ser. 1, vol. 45, part 1, 652; WOC, November 5–17, 1864; "Day of Prayer and Thanksgiving," 2; *OR*, ser. 1, vol. 45, part 1, 652; Sword, *Embrace an Angry Wind*, 87–88.

[36] Ritter, "Third Maryland Artillery," 538; WOC, November 21–24, 1864; Sword, *Embrace an Angry Wind*, 83–86.

Corps, on Lee's right, advanced along the Lawrenceburg Road. Beyond them, screening the Confederate right flank, rode Forrest's cavalry. To Lee's left, Cheatham's Corps would follow early the next morning along the Waynesville Road. Cutting off a large body of Federal troops under Gen. John Schofield at Pulaski, Tennessee became Hood's immediate objective. Then, the graycoats would move rapidly to take Columbia.[37]

Four days later, after marching nearly seventy-five miles over difficult terrain, the Cherokee Artillery reached a point about seventeen miles northwest of Mount Pleasant, Tennessee. There the three corps of the army and Forrest's cavalry planned to reunite. It had been a difficult journey for both men and animals. The artillery horses, in particular, suffered acutely, having already been completely worn out by the time the army arrived in Tuscumbia. Both rations and forage had been scarce, and the atrocious weather served to temper the men's initial enthusiasm. If anything, the conditions had deteriorated, as the rain gave way to biting, icy winds, alternately mixed with snow or sleet. Even the locals whom they met along the way appeared less enthusiastic than the civilians they had earlier passed in Alabama. Perhaps the inhabitants shared the general apprehension that accompanied news that Abraham Lincoln had been re-elected.[38]

Hood's attempt to cut off Schofield's troops, stationed near Pulaski, came within a hairs-breadth of success. Schofield somehow sensed the noose tightening around his neck, and quickly withdrew his 25,000 men to Columbia, on the south bank of the Duck River. Forrest's troopers harried and harassed the bluecoats every step of the way as they fell back to their new position. Hood followed the enemy to the Duck River and ordered his army into battle alignment a mile and a half south of Schofield's hastily constructed entrenchments. The Union general, recognizing that the Rebels could easily cut off his force by

---

[37] S. D. Lee's report, 66; Ritter, "Third Maryland Artillery," 538–39; WOC, November 28, 1864; Sword, *Embrace an Angry Wind*, 83–86.

[38] S. D. Lee's report, 67; WOC, November 28, 1864; Lindsley, *MAT*, 830; Stevenson, "Report of Major-General Carter L. Stevenson," 161 (hereafter cited as "C. L. Stevenson's report").

throwing a pontoon bridge farther north over the Duck River, withdrew his forces from Columbia. Schofield burned the bridges over the Duck and took a new position on the northern side of the river.

The Cherokee Artillery received orders to reunite with Carter Stevenson's division as it entered Columbia. The Floyd County cannoneers moved into a suburb southwest of the city and halted. All around them, confusion, panic, and disorder reigned. Wesley Connor described the frenzied scene that swept around the battery:

> Officers, soldiers, women, children, and Negroes could be seen rushing to and fro with arms full of plunder of all imaginable descriptions. One soldier told me I could get anything I wanted downtown. A squad of us struck out although orders were strict to remain with the guns. Met our Major [John W. Johnston] who ordered us back. Waited until he was out of sight and pushed on. Had not gone far when we saw a large college building from which emanated numberless soldiers with all sorts of goods. Went in and saw any quantity of hospital clothes such as shirts, drawers, dressing gowns, etc. Saw nothing I wanted. Came to a door which was locked, opened it and found stacks of new blankets, coverlets, sheets—secured seven splendid blankets and went back to the battery. Divided out [the bedding]—desired much to secure a hat and a pair of shoes, neither of which I could find.[39]

Hood once again set a trap to capture Schofield's force. He positioned the Army of Tennessee, which consisted of more soldiers than either Schofield's or Thomas's forces separately, to defeat the bluecoats in detail. Hood left Lee at Columbia, with Carter Stevenson's and Maj. Gen. Henry Clayton's divisions and the bulk of the artillery, to keep Schofield's troops pinned down. The Yankees soon began trading shots with Lee's Rebels from the opposite side of the Duck. Hood, and the rest of his army, planned to swing northeast toward Spring Hill, ford the Duck, and come upon Schofield from behind. Late the night of November 28, Forrest's intrepid cavalry forded the river, driving off

[39] McDonough and Connelly, *Five Tragic Hours*, 28–35; Sword, "Hood's Desperate Hour," 12–13; Scaife, *Hood's Campaign for Tennessee*, 19–23; WOC, November 28, 1864.

the Federal cavalry screening the ford. Early the next morning, Hood, with Stewart and Cheatham's corps, and Johnson's Division of Lee's Corps, forded the waterway and moved toward the town of Spring Hill. Hood felt confident that he had the Federals within his grasp. All he had to do was spring the trap.

Until 4 P.M. on November 29, the Cherokee Artillery's four twelve-pound Napoleon cannons, along with the guns of five other Confederate batteries, hammered away at the Yankee infantry and artillery arrayed along the northern bank of the Duck River on a large hill overlooking the town. During the exchange of fire, Col. Robert F. Beckham, Lee's chief of artillery, received a mortal wound when a Federal shell exploded next to a large boulder, sending a chunk of granite into his temple. Gen. Lee barely escaped becoming a casualty when an enemy shell exploded a nearby caisson, killing or wounding all the men and horses around it. Lee held Schofield fast, doggedly laying a pontoon bridge across the river despite a "galling fire" from the bluecoats. Lee then deployed three regiments of Edmund Pettus's brigade, which successfully drove the Yankee skirmishers back to Schofield's main line.[40]

Schofield, who had earlier ignored reports of Confederate troops headed for Spring Hill, suddenly awoke to the danger he faced. He sent Maj. Gen. David Stanley northwards toward Spring Hill with two divisions. After one infantry brigade reached Spring Hill and succeeded in successfully fending off Forrest's cavalry, the Federals received reinforcements when the rest of Brig. Gen. George Wagner's division arrived. No sooner had Stanley and Wagner arranged their troops and artillery in a defensive arc around the town than Hood arrived on the scene around 3 P.M. with Cheatham's Corps. Confident that Cheatham's veterans, who outnumbered the Federals 2 to 1, would win the day, Hood launched his assault at around 4 P.M. The attacks, however, did not go as planned. Lack of reconnaissance to pinpoint the exact location of the Federal positions, coupled with confusion on

---

[40] Lindsley, *MAT*, 830; Daniel, *Cannoneers in Gray*, 172–73; *OR*, ser. 1, vol. 45, part 1, 338.

Cheatham's part after Hood changed the original plan without informing him, caused the Confederate attack to misfire. By sundown, Hood nevertheless remained confident that he had Schofield in the bag. Though hurting from a fall from his horse, the Confederate commander ordered his troops, now augmented by Stewart's Corps, to bivouac in place. They would finish the job the next morning.[41]

Hood and his generals did not realize that they had left the road between Spring Hill and Franklin completely unguarded. Hood's infantry, spread out along the southeastern edge of the town, had ended up parallel to road when he had ordered them to bivouac in place. Not a single unit actually overlapped the road. Schofield, now fully awake to the peril of being cut off from Nashville, hurried his remaining troops northward, arriving that evening in Spring Hill. The Federals soon discovered the open road, stretching toward Franklin. Ordering his army to march with as much stealth as possible, Schofield's entire force slunk past the Confederates, who were no more than a stone's throw away. Despite a few isolated brushes with Confederate sentries, the Federals managed to slip the noose. By dawn the next morning, the Yankees assumed a defensive position at Franklin, eight miles north of Spring Hill. Schofield, meanwhile, hurried his supply trains over the Harpeth River, on the outskirts of Tennessee's capital city. Schofield and his little army had lived to fight another day.[42]

The next morning, upon learning that Schofield had slipped through his grasp, Hood, became "wrathy as a rattlesnake." He bitterly vented his spleen at Maj. Gen. John C. Brown and his senior officers after summoning them to an early breakfast. Furiously complaining about his subordinates' failure, Hood blamed everyone but himself for the failure of his carefully laid trap. In his mind, the ineptness of those

---

[41] McDonough and Connelly, *Five Tragic Hours*, 44–46; Horn, *Army of Tennessee*, 385–89; *OR*, ser. 1, vol. 45, part 1, 652–53; Dodd, "Reminiscences of Hood's Tennessee Campaign," 520–24.

[42] Hattaway, *General Stephen D. Lee*, 134–36; Woodworth, *Jefferson Davis and His Generals*, 299; *OR*, ser. 1, vol. 45, part 1, 338; Ritter, "Third Maryland Artillery," 539; Dodd, "Reminiscences of Hood's Tennessee Campaign," 520–24.

around him had cost him the single-biggest opportunity of his career to destroy a Federal army. Gen. Cheatham, whom Hood blamed for having made only a feeble attempt to carry out his orders to take Spring Hill, seize the pike, and cut off Schofield, also caught the full force of Hood's anger.[43]

Immediately after daybreak on November 30, an angry and frustrated Hood directed Stewart's and Cheatham's corps northward toward Franklin. S. D. Lee, with Stevenson's and Clayton's infantry divisions and artillery, acted as the Rebel army's rear guard. He and his men would move north after the last remnants of Schofield's men had withdrawn from his front. The Cherokee Artillery, along with the rest of Johnston's Artillery Battalion, pushed to within six miles of Franklin, at which time they received orders to remain in place as Hood's reserve.

Hood, burning with desire to exact revenge upon Schofield for eluding him the night before, chose not to wait for Lee's infantry and the artillery to deploy. Instead, at about 4 P.M., he ordered an all-out infantry assault upon the entrenched Federals holding Franklin. Again and again, Cheatham's and Stewart's gallant veterans dashed themselves against the Federal defenses along a two-mile front, seizing the enemy's outer works in places but unable to break the stubborn Yankees' line. By 10 P.M., shot to pieces and exhausted, the Confederates ended their attacks. A short time later, the Yankees began an uncontested withdrawal toward Nashville. The terrible battle for Franklin had ended.

Although he could claim possession of the field, Hood had squandered the lives of 1,750 of his men in a Pyrrhic victory that had torn the heart and soul out of the Army of Tennessee. It also shredded any remaining confidence his men had had in their commander. Six of his generals numbered among the dead or mortally wounded, including Maj. Gen. Patrick Cleburne, the hard-fighting Irishman renowned as

---

[43] Woodworth, *Jefferson Davis and His Generals*, 299; McDonough and Connelly, *Five Tragic Hours*, 49–59; S. D. Lee's report, 68; Dodd, "Reminiscences of Hood's Tennessee Campaign," 523–24; *OR*, ser. 1, vol. 45, part 1, 652–53; *OR*, ser. 1, vol. 45, part 2, 211; WOC, November 30, 1864.

the best division commander in the Army. Six other general officers were either wounded or captured. Fifty-four regimental commanders had also become casualties. In all, the Army of Tennessee had suffered nearly 7,000 killed, wounded, and captured on that fateful November evening.

The following day, Wesley Connor visited the battlefield. In his diary that day, he vividly described the terrible carnage: "The ditches on either side of the Yankee works were literally filled with the dead and wounded—Yankees on the inside, and Confederates on the outside. In some places would be found Yankees and Confederates piled upon each other.... I had long desired to visit a battlefield, but my curiosity is now fully satisfied." While neither Connor nor the rest of the Army of Tennessee could know it, their dance with disaster had just begun.[44]

On December 1, Hood, seemingly unwilling or unable to recognize the shattered condition of his army, renewed the march northward toward Nashville. Lee's Corps led the advance, followed by Stewart's Corps, with Cheatham's Corps bringing up the rear. In his after-action report—remarkable for its brevity, given the intensity of the Battle of Franklin—Hood sounded as if he had won a convincing victory. The South rejoiced. But even he couldn't gloss over the loss of so many men and officers. Soon, despondency began to replace the initial elation of the Southern people as they realized the magnitude of the army's losses. Bitter and discouraged, the soldiers of the once-great Army of Tennessee—now numbering barely 23,000 effectives—limped toward Nashville.

By around 2 P.M. the following day, December 2, Hood's men began arriving at the Brentwood Hills overlooking Nashville. Hood placed his troops in a shallow arc around the southern side of the city opposite the Federal's formidable works. Lee's Corps, with its center

[44] Daniel, *Cannoneers in Gray*, 175; Ritter, "Third Maryland Artillery," 540; WOC, December 2–5, 1864; Woodworth, *Jefferson Davis and His Generals*, 299–301.

on the Franklin Pike, occupied the middle of the army's new position. Stewart's Corps, located on Lee's left, stretched west to the Hillsboro Pike. Cheatham's Corps made up the right wing of the army, extending just beyond the Nolensville Pike. In its entirety, Hood's line barely stretched four miles and covered only four of the pikes running southward out of Nashville. By contrast, Thomas's Federals, numbering around 70,000 men, occupied a line of strong fortifications across a ten-mile front that covered all eight major roads emanating from the city and easily overlapped the Confederates breastworks. While he had wanted to ground each of his flanks on bends in the Cumberland River, Hood ended up relying on cavalry screens and a series of five redoubts on his left flank (only three of which were ever finished) to extend his line. Hood no longer had enough infantry available to extend his lines that far.[45]

The soft, wet soil played havoc on the Rebel artillery as the army marched on Nashville. In places, gun carriages sank up their axles in mud. The starving horses, already struggling, sometimes had to be abandoned because they simply could not continue. By around 8 P.M. on December 2, the Cherokee Artillery arrived at its assigned position and dug in. The next evening, following the retreat of Federal skirmishers from their front, Lee's infantry and artillery advanced approximately three-quarters of a mile. The Cherokee Artillery pushed forward again and began entrenching in a small valley about 300 yards to the left of the Franklin Pike. Parallel to them on the opposite side of the pike, Rowan's battery of Marylanders and Georgians began entrenching on another small hill. The next several days proved relatively calm as the artillerymen focused on strengthening their entrenchments and trying to augment their meager rations. Adding to their woes, the weather now grew increasingly colder. On December 9, the worst storm of the season covered the ground with sleet, measuring up to five inches deep. Ill-fed, ill-clothed, and short of tools, all the gunners of the Cherokee Artillery and Rowan's Battery could do was attempt to

---

[45] *OR*, ser. 1, vol. 45, part 1, 32; Scaife, "Hood's Desperate Hour," 15–16; Hattaway, *General Stephen D. Lee*, 137–40.

dig even deeper into the frozen soil for protection from the elements and the ubiquitous Federal artillery.[46]

It had become increasingly apparent that Thomas would soon lash out at the Confederate army arrayed against him. Although Hood had further weakened his army by ordering Forrest to take two cavalry divisions and a pair of infantry brigades to invest Murfreesboro, he still remained hopeful that he could repel Thomas and take Nashville. Hurrying his men to put the finishing touches on their entrenchments, Hood made the final adjustments to his perilously thin lines. Skirmishes with Federal troops became more frequent, especially on the right of the Confederate line, held by Cheatham's troops, as the moment of truth rapidly approached.

Hood and his men didn't have long to wait. Thomas had been receiving tremendous pressure from his superiors to launch an all-out assault on Hood and complete the destruction of the Army of Tennessee. Ever thorough, the stolid "Rock of Chickamauga" had now gathered his strength and put the finishing touches on his plan. He intended to jump-start the operation with a large diversion designed to pin the Confederate right in place. He then planned to launch a violent assault on the Confederate left, striking the flank held by Stewart's Corps, swinging around Stewart's position, and rolling up Hood's entire army from left to right. At 8 A.M. on Thursday, December 15, the "Rock of Chickamauga" launched his long-awaited attack on the Army of Tennessee.[47]

During the interlude, the men of the Cherokee Artillery had been incessantly toiling to improve the new works. All morning, the air had been filled with the not-so-distant rumbling of heavy musketry and artillery fire as the Federal attack unfolded. Under orders to be ready to fight or retreat at any moment, the Georgians now discovered that they had constructed their works in the middle of an ancient Native

---

[46] WOC, December 15, 1864; *OR*, ser. 1, vol. 45, part 1, 55, 678; S. D. Lee's report, 68; Ritter, "Third Maryland Artillery," 541.

[47] Ritter, "Third Maryland Artillery," 541; WOC, December 15, 1864; Connelly, *Autumn of Glory*, 509–10; Daniel, *Cannoneers in Gray*, 175–79; *OR*, ser. 1, vol. 45, part 1, 39.

American burial ground. The deeper they dug, the more macabre the trenches became as they began unearthing a number of human skeletons and clay burial pots. Reports began circulating that heavy fighting was underway on the left. Stewart's Corps, already badly battered at Franklin, desperately tried to hold the line with 5,300 men against the onslaught of the nearly 46,000 Federal troops. The Union attackers came from Maj. Gen. Andrew J. Smith's divisions, detached from the Federal Army of the Tennessee; Brig. Gen. James H. Wilson's Cavalry corps; John Schofield's XXIII corps; and Brig. Gen. Thomas J. Wood's IV corps.[48]

Despite heroic efforts to defend them, the redoubts the Confederates had constructed to protect their left flank began to fall one by one. With Wilson's Yankee cavalry freely roaming in their rear and the masses of Federal infantry pressing in their front, Stewart's outnumbered divisions slowly crumbled and fell back in confusion. Around 3 P.M., Hood ordered Lee to move his corps to the support of Stewart's retreating troops and occupy a series of hills a mile to the left and rear of his current position. Moving with the rest of their battalion, the Cherokee Artillery arrived at their new location just in time to see Maj. Gen. Edward Walthall's division, Stewart's only reserve division, "flying in disorder from the field." The gallant Mississippians had vainly tried to hold the rock wall between Redoubts 3 and 4 against the blue tide washing away the Confederate left. Despite that pressure, Stewart's veterans made a fairly orderly withdrawal. Aided by the early setting of the December sun, Hood's troops managed to blunt the Federal advance and avoid an outright disaster. George Thomas, satisfied with the day's success, ordered his bluecoats to bivouac in place and pick up the fight in the morning. The first day of the long-awaited Battle of Nashville had ended.[49]

---

[48] Ritter, "Third Maryland Artillery," 541; WOC, December 16, 1864; *OR*, ser. 1, vol. 45, part 1, 169.

[49] Ritter, "Third Maryland Artillery," 541; WOC, December 16, 1864; *OR*, ser. 1, vol. 45, part 1, 169; Sword, "Hood's Desperate Hour," 42–44; S. D. Lee's report, 68.

Despite the evidence supplied by his fleeing troops, Hood still clung to the illusion that his army could drive the Yankees from Nashville. Seemingly oblivious to the rapidly deteriorating spirits of his army, Hood moved to consolidate the Confederate position and fashion a new, shorter line of defense about two miles south of where they had started the previous day. Cheatham's relatively fresh corps moved into position on the army's left flank. The line now curved around Compton's Hill (now dubbed Shy's Hill, in honor of Lt. Col. William Shy, who would soon die courageously defending it) just west of the Granny White Pike, and stretched eastward to anchor on Stewart's Corps. Stewart's weary men now held the army's center. The barricades of Lee's Corps, on the army's right, ran eastward across the Franklin & Columbia Turnpike, with its right anchored on a 300-foot-high hill known variously as Peach Orchard Hill or Overton's Hill.

By 11 P.M., after hours of digging new fortifications, the Cherokee Artillery and the rest of Johnston's Battalion received orders from Hood to move to a new position. Hood directed the battalion to shift to the left of the Franklin & Columbia Pike, to support Stevenson's Division. There, they bivouacked on the same line they had occupied on their initial advance on Nashville. The Cherokee Artillery's right section received a directive to relocate to a position near the right of Brig. Gen. Edmund Pettus's brigade. (Pettus's graycoats had dug in to the left of Brig. Gen. Randall Gibson's brigade, of Clayton's Division.) The left section of the Floyd County battery had been designated to serve as the artillery reserve for Lee's Corps. That part of the battery occupied a position several hundred feet to the rear of the right section.[50]

Friday, December 16, dawned wet and cold, and a light fog clung to the trees and hollows. The Federal infantry began a wary advance over the shattered landscape toward Hood's new line, slowly pushing

---

[50] WOC, December 16, 1864; S. D. Lee's report, 68; *OR*, ser. 1, vol. 45, part 1, 692, 130, 505; Clayton, "Report of the Operations of Clayton's Division North of the Tennessee River in the Campaign of the Winter of 1864," 86 (hereafter cited as "Clayton's Division report"); "Report of Brigadier-General R. L. Gibson of Operations in Vicinity of Nashville," 140; Sword, *Embrace an Angry Wind*, 357–63.

back the determined Confederate skirmishers. By 9 A.M., Gen. Thomas's Union artillery began a blistering close-range bombardment of the Army of Tennessee's new positions. For the most part, the Confederate batteries waited in silence. Lt. Col. Llewellyn Hoxton, Stephen D. Lee's chief of artillery since December 10, ordered his cannoneers to conserve their limited ammunition and not fire unless large bodies of enemy troops threatened their location. He later remarked on the intensity and accuracy of the Federal artillery fire in his after-action report: "During the whole day the batteries were subjected to a terrible artillery fire, which destroyed a large number of horses, in the best cover I could obtain, and exploded two limber chests."[51]

Horses and limber chests were not the Federal artillery's only victims. The Cherokee Artillery's sister battery, Capt. John Rowan's 3rd Maryland battery, ordered to harass the enemy in their front, moved forward to occupy a small hill a third of a mile to the left of the Cherokee Artillery. Immediately, the battery came under thunderous artillery fire as the men attempted to build some semblance of fortifications during the intervals between the firing of the eighteen Federal guns trained on the Maryland battery. As the battery's four twelve-pound Napoleons began bravely responding to the enemy's fire, the men bringing up ammunition to the guns were quickly cut down as they tried to move forward. Around 12:30 P.M., enemy cannon fire killed Capt. Rowan, who was directing his men, and wounded one of the gunners. The same shell fragment hit both men, exploding after entering through the embrasure for the battery's Number 2 gun.[52]

Despite the Federal artillery fire, the Cherokee Artillery's cannoneers in the right section renewed their efforts to dig new gun emplacements, and by 1 P.M. had managed to throw up some rudimentary fortifications. Shortly thereafter, Thomas's Army of the Tennessee attempted to roll up Hood's right flank and cut off its escape route via the Franklin-Columbia Pike. The weight of the Yankee assault fell upon Lee's line on Overton's Hill. Two brigades from Woods's Federal

[51] L. Hoxton Report, OR, ser. 1, vol. 45, part 1, 692.

[52] WOC, December 16, 1864; *OR*, ser. 1, vol. 45, part 1, 704 and 691; Clayton's Division report, 86; Sword, *Embrace an Angry Wind*, 357–63.

IV Corps, along with Col. Charles Thompson's 2nd colored brigade and Lt. Col. Charles Grosvenor's 3rd brigade of Maj. Gen. James Steedman's command, launched a series of furious assaults designed to wrest Overton Hill from the Rebels. Waiting until the Yankees had advanced into easy range, Stevenson's and Clayton's infantry poured a devastating series of volleys into the blue-clad ranks. The Cherokee Artillery and the other batteries of Johnston's and Eldridge's artillery battalions aided the infantry, laying down a withering fire with their twelve-pounder Napoleons that Connor averred "did most splendid execution upon them [the Federals] with canister, killing and wounding large numbers." On and on the blue ranks rose and struggled bravely toward the Confederate defenses. The Rebel fire flashed on the enemy's bayonets as they advanced. At a few points along the line, a handful of the Yankees managed to clamber atop the Confederate works before being shot down in a literal hail of lead. The Rebels' withering fire staggered the Federal troops before most could come any closer than seventy-five yards to the Confederate defenses and sent them reeling back down the hill.[53]

By 4 P.M., the Federal attacks had petered out. Confederate losses, thus far, had been relatively light. During the fight, Pvt. Martin V. B. Whorton, in the Cherokee Artillery's right section died, killed by the concussion of an enemy shell that exploded directly on the opposite side of the breastworks against which he was leaning. Miraculously, he would be the only fatality the battery suffered during the entire campaign. Federal casualties, on the other hand, numbered in the thousands, with the bodies of black and white soldiers mingled indiscriminately in piles before the Confederate works. The men in blue—black and white—bravely fought and died. The 13th U.S. Colored Infantry, an inexperienced African American regiment composed mainly of former slaves, advanced again and again, with the courage and steadiness of veterans. The 13th finally lost their colors after the men of Gen. M. A. Stovall's brigade killed five color-bearers in rapid succession just a few feet in front of their works. The sight of so many dead appalled

[53] S. D. Lee's report, 69; Connelly, *Autumn of Glory*, 510–11; Sword, *Embrace an Angry Wind*, 373–74.

even the toughest veterans. Brig. Gen. James Holtzclaw, a brigade commander in Clayton's Division, wrote afterward,

> I have seen the most determined charge on my right. Placing a Negro brigade in front they gallantly dashed up to the abatis, forty feet in front, and were killed by [the] hundreds. Pressed on by their white brethren in the rear they continued to come up in masses to the abatis, but they came only to die. I have seen most of the battle-fields of the West, but [I] never saw dead men thicker than in front of my two right regiments.[54]

Despite S. D. Lee's success at repelling the Yankee attack on the army's right, the situation on the left flank of Hood's army had begun to deteriorate rapidly. Hood mistakenly believed that Cheatham, and not Lee, faced an overwhelming concentration of Federal troops, and he grew concerned lest the Federal attacks on Lee's line should succeed. Around 2 P.M., he dispatched two brigades of Cheatham's old division, now under the command of Brig. Gen. James Smith, to Lee's assistance. Maj. Gen. William B. Bate, whose sorely weakened division, short of shoes and clothing, had only arrived on the field from Murfreesboro after midnight, had no choice but to shift his depleted brigades further to the left to cover the northern and western approaches of Compton's Hill. This weakened Cheatham's already thin line at its most exposed and vulnerable point. To make matters worse, Hood's earlier decision to detach Forrest's cavalry to take Murfreesboro came back yet again to haunt the army, as Federal cavalry now ranged nearly unopposed in Cheatham's rear.[55]

Stephen Lee sent Smith's unneeded brigades on their way around 3:30 P.M. with orders to return to Cheatham's sector. They would not arrive in time to help prevent a breach in the Confederate line. At approximately 4 P.M., with the low December sun already beginning to set on the rain-soaked field, George Thomas dropped the hammer on the Confederate left. In a replay of his strategy of the previous day,

---

[54] *OR,* ser. 1, vol. 45, part 1, 40; Connelly, *Autumn of Glory*, 510–11; Sword, *Embrace an Angry Wind*, 373–74.

[55] Connelly, *Autumn of Glory*, 510–11; Sword, *Embrace an Angry Wind*, 373–74.

Thomas launched the combined might of Schofield's Corps and A. J. Smith's divisions against the left. Smith's 1st Division, led by impetuous Brig. Gen. John McArthur, stormed downhill, across the narrow valley, and began swarming up the steep slopes of Compton's Hill even before Thomas had officially ordered the attack to commence. Thomas, upon seeing McArthur's troops scrambling up Compton's Hill, ordered the rest of his troops to push forward to support McArthur and commence their assault on Cheatham.[56]

There is an old military maxim that every soldier (and, by extension, every group of warriors) has a breaking point. It is the point at which discipline, training, experience, and pride evaporate, leaving behind only the naked human instinct to survive. For the men of Bate's depleted division, that dreadful moment had arrived. Charged with holding Compton's Hill, they now found themselves under attack on their front, left, and rear as McArthur's men overwhelmed the Confederate line just east of Compton's Hill. Below and to their rear, Bate's men could now see Brig. Gen. Daniel Govan's Arkansans fleeing in disorder through the fields. It proved too much for mortals to stand. Bate's brigades dissolved into a chaotic mass of frightened, beaten men. With their comrades falling dead and wounded all around them as bullets found them from every direction, the survivors threw down their weapons and hastily retreated toward the Granny White Pike. Their only goal seemed to be to escape southward, out of the Yankee vise. With the bluecoats now pouring through the huge gap in the Rebel line, the rest of Cheatham's Corps also dissipated into a panicked rabble. They joined their comrades, rushing pell-mell for the pike, only to find that their escape had been cut off by Wilson's troopers.[57]

Now the broken remnants of Cheatham's Corps began fleeing south and eastward, intent on reaching the Columbia & Franklin Pike—the army's last available escape route. Stewart's Corps, holding the center of the Confederate line, seeing Cheatham's men fleeing the

---

[56] Connelly, *Autumn of Glory*, 511; Sword, *Embrace an Angry Wind*, 374–75; *OR*, ser. 1, vol. 45, part 1, 710–11.

[57] S. D. Lee's report, 69–70; Clayton's Division report, 87–88; WOC, December 16, 1864.

field, and now under frontal attack themselves, began collapsing from left to right, as each brigade found its left flank dangling in the air. Within minutes, Stewart's Corps, already mauled on the previous day's battle, dissolved, and joined Cheatham's men, as tangled mobs of frightened soldiers ran toward the safety of the Franklin & Columbia Pike.[58]

The men of the army's right wing had been, in Stephen Lee's words, "in fine spirits and confident of success." After all, they had ably held their ground and, just minutes earlier, had repulsed all the attacks the bluecoats had launched against them. Suddenly, through the mist and rain came the incredible sight of fleeing mobs of Confederate soldiers sprinting to their left and rear toward the pike with cheering Yankees hot on their heels. As Lee and his men watched in horror, they also came under renewed attack by the pursuing Federal troops. Striking first at the left-most units of Johnson's Division, Johnson's men initially checked the bluecoats' attack. But, the unstoppable tide of charging Federals, along with the spectacle of Confederate troops now fleeing behind them, caused Lee's divisions to also begin wavering. Moments later, at around 4:30 P.M., Cumming's Brigade, the leftmost of Carter Stevenson's two brigades on line, began to crumble. Soon, only Lee's right-most division under Henry Clayton, and part of Stevenson's Division, Pettus's Brigade, and the 39th Georgia Regiment from Cumming's Brigade—remained reasonably intact.[59]

Everything had happened so quickly that the Confederate batteries seemed to be in grave danger of simply being left behind, or overrun, as their infantry support melted away. Desperately, the batteries struggled through the chaos around them. They hastened to bring up their surviving horses, which had been taken back to relative safety, limber up, and flee from their exposed positions. At 4:30 P.M., with everything around them dissolving in panic and disorder, the cannoneers of the Cherokee Artillery hitched their horses to their guns and

[58] *OR*, ser. 1, vol. 45, part 1, 692; WOC, December 16, 1864; C. L. Stevenson's report, 164–65.

[59] *OR*, ser. 1, vol. 45, part 1, 692; WOC, December 16, 1864; C. L. Stevenson's report, 164–65; D. Smith, *In the Lion's Mouth*, 87–89; S. D. Lee's report, 69.

wheeled about in a desperate attempt to churn through the boggy soil and bring off their guns to safety. Nearby, they could see the men of Rowan's Battery starting to abandon their guns. Like the Cherokee Artillery, they had remained at their guns, firing until the last possible moment. Unable to bring up their horses in time, the gun crews of Rowan's Battery had no choice now but to flee on foot. Driving at full speed, a crew of the Cherokee Artillery's right section slammed the Number 2 gun into a large stump, shattering the gun carriage. Nothing remained for the gunners to do but cut loose the horses and abandon the weapon. The entire scene presented, in the words of Wesley Connor, "one of the most melancholy sights a person ever saw—that of a beaten and panic-stricken army...the scene beggars description."[60]

S. D. Lee quickly realized that he would lose all his men if he could not restore some semblance of order. The veteran officer rode among his fleeing troops, urging them to make a stand. "Rally, men!" he shouted at one point, as his men continued their confused withdrawal down the Franklin & Columbia Pike, "for God's sake, rally! This is the place for brave men to die!" His calm, courageous example finally began to stiffen his men's resolve. Here and there, pockets of graycoats rallied just long enough to allow large numbers of Hood's beaten army to make their way unmolested down the pike.

About a mile to the rear, in an area of the Brentwood Hills, a few of Lee's units turned to make a stand. While the remaining gun of the Cherokee Artillery's right section continued down the pike toward Franklin, the left section, with its two serviceable guns, unlimbered, began blazing away at their pursuers. This attempt at forming a new line lasted only a few minutes. Hood sent a note to Lee telling him that the Federals were closing in on the pike several miles behind him, near the village of Brentwood. Now charged with being the rear-guard of the army, Lee began withdrawing the men from Clayton's Division and part of Stevenson's, southward down the pike.[61]

---

[60] WOC, December 16, 1864; S. D. Lee's report, 69–70.

[61] Sword, *Embrace an Angry Wind*, 382–83; *OR*, ser. 1, vol. 45, part 1, 689–90; WOC, December 16, 1864.

By 2 A.M., the three remaining guns of the Cherokee Artillery, along with their crews and surviving horses and equipment, had all arrived in Franklin. There they spent the night on the same campground on which they had bivouacked only weeks earlier on the way to Nashville. Signs of an army in chaos greeted the new arrivals as men, guns, and wagons of various commands scattered haphazardly wherever they found an empty space. Bloody footprints in the snow and slush silently attested to the truth that as many as half of the men had no shoes. An equal number shivered in inadequate clothing that consisted of little more than rags.[62]

The army set out on the pike toward Columbia by 5 A.M., having partially regained some sense of organization during the night as men began to find their units. The Cherokee Artillery's left section obeyed orders to accompany the rear guard under S. D. Lee. The single gun of the right section, and what was left of Johnston's Battalion, moved south with the rest of the army.

Over the next several days, Hood's men marched south in either pouring rain, snow, or howling wind. At the same time, Federal infantry from Wood's IV Corps and Wilson's Federal cavalry troopers harried and harassed the army's rear guard nearly every step of the way. After fording the Duck River and passing through Columbia on December 19, the army neared Pulaski on December 20, where the Cherokee Artillery's left section rejoined the rest of the battery. The Confederate soldiers staggered forward, exhausted from the lack of sleep, the terrible weather, and the strain of almost constant marching. Only the determined rearguard efforts of Nathan Bedford Forrest, with infantry support from Gen. Edward Walthall's Mississippi and Tennessee regiments, kept the Army of Tennessee from being captured. The finest tribute for Forrest and Walthall came from the pen of Gen. Thomas: "With the exception of his [Hood's] rear guard, his army became a disoriented and disorganized rabble of half-armed and barefoot

[62] Sword, *Embrace an Angry Wind*, 382–83; *OR*, ser. 1, vol. 45, part 1, 689–90; WOC, December 16, 1864.

men....The rear guard, however, was undaunted and firm, and it did its work bravely to the end."[63]

Wesley Connor provided a brief anecdote illustrating just how much men desperate can endure: "Rained about 12 hours, which froze all our blankets," the diarist wrote. He continued,

> Bivouacked at 7 P.M. without rails or wood near [for fires]. Blankets all wet. Spread a [canvas] fly over a wagon and crawled in and slept well, considering that my blankets were wet, rain sifting down upon me, a horse pulling at my head and two mules at my footing. Rose next morning and found two mules had pulled one shoe and sock off and tramped them in the mud, also my saddle and the haversack and canteens of my bedfellow.[64]

On December 20, the Army of Tennessee resumed its retreat toward the Tennessee River, and the relative safety on the south side of the waterway. With Forrest skillfully fending off the Yankees snapping at their heels, Lee's Corps, temporarily led by Carter Stevenson after Lee suffered a severe foot wound on December 17, marched in the van of the army. They reached Pulaski after dark during a terrible sleet storm. The next morning, December 21, dawned intensely cold. The two surviving batteries of Johnston's Artillery Battalion, the Cherokee Artillery and Marshall's Battery, had a momentary stroke of luck, running across some "splendid" beef that the infantry, unable to carry, had left behind. Although they had no cook wagons, the hungry cannoneers nevertheless made the best of their good fortune.[65]

---

[63] Available sources contain no references to the Cherokee Artillery's left section having seen actual combat as part of the rear guard. It seems likely that it was the rear guard's artillery reserve. *OR*, ser. 1, vol. 45, part 1, 692; S. D. Lee's report, 71; Ritter, "Third Maryland Artillery," 170; Lindsley, *MAT*, 831; Clayton's Division report, 88; Wigginton, "Nashville Cavalry Operations," 143.

[64] *OR*, ser. 1, vol. 45, part 1, 692; S. D. Lee's report, 71; Ritter, "Third Maryland Artillery," 170.

[65] Scaife, *Hood's Campaign for Tennessee*, 69; *OR*, ser. 1, vol. 45, part 1, 673; WOC, December 20, 1864; John C. Holland to Dr. William Forelle, January 20, 1865, Atlanta History Center; McNeilly, "The Retreat from Tennessee," 305.

Leaving Pulaski by way of the Lambs Ferry Road, the battalion forded Richland Creek and marched southwest, crossing into Alabama. As they marched mile after muddy mile, the Georgia gunners everywhere observed the abandoned wagons, pontoons, and ammunition littering the roadside, signaling the passing of a desperate, beaten army. By Christmas Eve, the Cherokee Artillery had passed through Lexington, Alabama, and encamped eight miles outside of town. Early on Christmas Day, the battery forded treacherous Shoal Creek. This involved manhandling the three Napoleons across the rock-strewn creek in icy water up to four feet deep in places. Wesley Connor averred that the unit never had a harder river crossing during the entire war.[66]

The badly crippled Army of Tennessee had abandoned their pontoons and virtually everything else that hindered their flight. Luckily, the Alabama horse soldiers of Gen. P. D. Roddey found some floats the Union army had abandoned at Florence a month earlier. Aware that the pontoons might be in short supply, Lt. Col. Francis Marion Windes, of Roddey's Cavalry, hauled them to Bainbridge, the point chosen for the army's crossing of the Tennessee River. Meanwhile, Llewellyn Hoxton, the corps' chief of artillery, sent orders to the Cherokee Artillery and Marshall's Battery to take up defensive positions along the high bluffs on the north side of the Tennessee. Several Federal gunboats, under Rear Adm. Samuel Lee, had reportedly begun patrolling the river near Florence. The flotilla included two "tin-clads" with drafts shallow enough to approach Bainbridge. The batteries had to prevent those ships from destroying the vital pontoon bridge. That one rickety bridge was all that stood between the Army of Tennessee's escape and being trapped on the wrong side of the river.[67]

The Cherokee Artillery coaxed their three worn-out teams over the muddy soil and took up a position about a half-mile below (west of) the pontoon bridge. A mile farther downstream, Marshall's Battery struggled through the mire and unlimbered their four twelve-pounder Napoleons. The men of the two batteries realized they constituted the

---

[66] *OR*, ser. 1, vol. 45, part 1, 673; WOC, December 21, 1864; Lindsley, *MAT*, 831.

[67] *OR*, ser. 1, vol. 45, part 1, 673; Lindsley, *MAT*, 831–32; WOC, December 21, 1864.

last line of defense should any Federal gunboats run the gauntlet of Confederate guns farther downstream. Exposed and without infantry support, they also realized their highly vulnerable position should marauding Yankee cavalry make a quick dash through the fluid lines. In the end, there was nothing to do but man their posts and hope for the best.[68]

By daybreak on December 26, the Confederate engineers finally finished laying the pontoon bridge over the swiftly flowing Tennessee River. Around 10 A.M., two Federal tin-clads emerged through the mist. From their closer vantage point, the men of Marshall's Battery could actually see the three gun ports on the side of the lead tin-clad. A member of the Tennessee artillery unit reported the aft deck "[was] black with people gazing intently, it seemed, at the pontoon-bridge...." About fifty yards behind the ship came another identical vessel. Closer and closer the two tin-clads silently steamed until the Confederate gunners on shore could hear the water breaking on their bows and the splash of their paddle wheels. Suddenly, the lead vessel yawed hard to the right, apparently preparing to fire a broadside at the pontoon bridge, whose occupants started scurrying toward the safety of dry ground. In unison, the two remaining ten-pound Parrot rifles of Cowan's Mississippi Battery, and the one surviving gun of Hoskins's Magnolia State Battery, suddenly roared to life. Upon his corps' arrival, A. P. Stewart had prudently deployed those cannoneers farther downstream to protect the approach to the bridge. Moments later, the guns of Marshall's battery joined in, sending booming rounds of solid shot at the two Federal vessels. A brief but spirited exchange of fire ensued between the two ships and the shore batteries. The gunners of the Cherokee Artillery stood at the ready, in case the two vessels somehow managed to blast their way upstream. At length, however, the two Federal ships withdrew, and the pontoon bridge remained unmolested.[69]

---

[68] WOC, December 25, 1864; *OR*, ser. 1, vol. 45, part 2, 357; Lindsley, *MAT*, 831–32.

[69] WOC, December 26, 1864; Lindsley, *MAT*, 832–34; Dabney, "Gen. A. P. Stewart on Strong Topics," 31.

That night, the men of the Cherokee Artillery and their comrades in the other batteries scattered along the riverbank kept a close watch lest the Federal gunboats make another run at the pontoon bridge. The enemy vessels, however, never reappeared, and the army's crossing of the Tennessee River proceeded unhindered. Over the next two days, the tattered remnants of the once-mighty Army of Tennessee made their way across the floating bridge. Lee's and Cheatham's corps traversed the span on December 26, followed by Stewart's and the rear guard the next day. As December 27 wore on, the Georgia gunners grew increasingly concerned about being left behind. Maybe—just maybe—someone had in mind to make them a sacrifice to save the rest of the army. Finally, around 4 P.M., orders arrived telling them to harness and hitch and move across the bridge. "All was joy and gladness," Wesley Connor noted in his diary. Then another order arrived, countermanding the first one. Finally, at midnight on December 27, 1864, the Cherokee Artillery marched across the pontoon bridge to safety.

John Bell Hood's audacious, if wrong-headed, attempt to invade Tennessee had ended disastrously. A recent study of the winter invasion of the Volunteer State put Hood's losses at "perhaps 23,500 casualties from a total strength of about 38,000 men." Union casualties amounted to fewer than 6,000. The campaign had been "a spirited if futile attempt by a desperate man to turn the course of the war." It had failed—and virtually destroyed the Army of Tennessee in the process.[70]

[70] Lindsley, *MAT*, 832–34; Dabney, "Gen. A. P. Stewart on Strong Topics," 31; *OR*, ser. 1, vol. 45, part 1, 674; WOC, December 26–27, 1864; Sword, *Embrace an Angry Wind*, 425.

Chapter 7

"Four Long Weary Years"

The Last Hurrah

(December 31, 1864—June 19, 1865)

New Year's Eve found Van Den Corput's Battery camped three miles south of Iuka, Mississippi. On the first day of 1865, the Cherokee Artillery marched with the remnants of Johnston's Battalion westward to Burnsville, Mississippi. Shortly thereafter they received orders to continue on to Rienzi, some thirteen miles to the southwest. The artillerymen tramped to the Burnsville railroad depot, unhitched their horses, and proceeded to load the guns and limber chests onto the waiting train cars. After lingering near the station for several hours, word finally came that a train farther down the line had run off the track. They would have to march instead of traveling by rail. The horses and their wranglers, already well down the road toward Rienzi, began retracing their steps and arrived back at Burnsville around 10 P.M. Meanwhile, the cannoneers manhandled the guns and caissons off the train. Hitching up the horses and moving away from the tracks, the gunners returned to their campground and settled in for the night.[1]

The next day, the Floyd County unit received orders to march thirteen miles northwest to Corinth. There, to their delight, they found full commissaries and accommodating guards who let the hungry soldiers fill their bellies and replenish their supplies. After breakfasting the next morning on biscuits, salt pork, and real coffee, the men loaded the battery's guns and equipment onto the waiting train cars. Knowing that they would not leave for Columbus, Mississippi, until the following morning, some of the Georgians spent the balance of the day attempting to buy fresh meat from civilians in the nearby countryside. The locals, however, wanted nothing to do with the soldiers' nearly worthless Confederate currency. Taking matters into their own hands,

[1] WOC, January 1, 1865.

the "John C. Martin Committee" (named for its leader, Cpl. John Martin) conducted a daring nighttime sortie and "confiscated" a large black hog they had spotted earlier that day. The unfortunate swine, in the soldier's vernacular, "entered the Confederate service" that night.[2]

Crowded onto the overloaded train, "which stalled at every grade," the Cherokee Artillery slowly made its way south. Over the next few days, they passed through Baldwyn and Okolona, finally arriving in Columbus, Mississippi, at around 4 P.M. on Saturday, January 14. Moving out the next morning, the battery marched two or three miles west of town and set up camp with the rest of Maj. Johnston's artillery battalion.[3]

At Columbus, the "long arm" units had a chance to rest themselves and their horses, replace and refurbish equipment, and obtain additional supplies. Despite a shortage of cannon in Hood's army, the Cherokee Artillery managed to obtain a replacement for the gun they had lost at Nashville. Rumors of their destination ran rife throughout the camp. Some men felt certain the signs pointed to a move to Charleston, South Carolina; others seemed equally sure they would next head for Macon, Georgia. Still, others felt that the battery's ultimate destination would be Mobile or Montgomery, Alabama, or even out West, to serve in the Trans-Mississippi Department.[4]

While the dejected remnants of Hood's army rested and refitted, Gen. Beauregard began to discover the true magnitude of the disaster that had befallen the Army of Tennessee at Nashville. Unable to hide the truth any longer and unwilling to suffer the humiliation of being removed as commander of the army, Hood telegraphed John Seddon, the secretary of war, on January 13, stating that he wished to be replaced and reassigned. On January 23, 1865, Seddon obliged Hood, relieving him as leader of the Army of Tennessee. Seddon appointed Lt. Gen. Richard Taylor as the unit's temporary leader.[5]

---

[2] WOC, January 3, 1865.
[3] WOC, January 4–14, 1865; Lindsley, *MAT*, 835.
[4] WOC, January 18, 1865; Daniels, *Cannoneers in Gray*, 183.
[5] *OR*, ser. 1, vol. 45, part 2, 805; Sword, *Embrace an Angry Wind*, 428–31.

The Confederacy now faced a daunting strategic challenge. Gen. Sherman, having rested after his "march to the sea," in mid-January, began moving northward from his base at Savannah. His plan seemed to be to first "punish" South Carolina, the cradle of the secession movement. That completed, he would move north to unite with Ulysses S. Grant's forces near Richmond for a final campaign to destroy the rebellion.

Beauregard began a desperate scramble to assemble a force large enough to oppose Sherman, utilizing the various Confederate units scattered throughout Georgia and the Carolinas. He first directed the infantry of S. D. Lee's and Cheatham's corps to move into South Carolina by way of Augusta, Georgia. He also ordered the six batteries of Johnston's and Key's battalions—the only serviceable artillery battalions remaining in the Army of Tennessee—to move with them. He then sent the rest of the army's artillerymen south to Mobile, Alabama, to man the defenses there. (These troops included their former comrades in Rowan's Battery, who had suffered so grievously at Nashville.) At Gen. Beauregard's specific request, a South Carolina battery, commanded by his son Rene, took the place of the Maryland cannoneers.[6]

On Saturday, January 21, word reached the men of the Cherokee Artillery that they would travel by river and rail to Macon, Georgia. Preparing to depart, the men moved the guns down to a boat landing on the Tombigbee River. Three days later, after being paid a full year's wages, the gunners moved their guns and equipment onto a newly arrived steamer, the *Gertrude*, and clambered aboard. Moving downriver at a rate of about 125 miles per day, the gunners enjoyed a "delightful" trip, passing first by Demopolis, Alabama, where many of them had waited to be exchanged after the Battle of Vicksburg. From Demopolis, they went by rail to Selma. Finally, on February 4, the three batteries of Maj. Johnston's battalion arrived in Columbus, Georgia. The following day, the cannoneers traveled by rail to Macon.[7]

---

[6] *OR*, ser. 1, vol. 45, part 2, 802; Daniel, *Cannoneers in Gray*, 183; Horn, *Army of Tennessee*, 422–24.

[7] WOC, January 21–26, 1865; Daniel, *Cannoneers in Gray*, 183.

The batteries remained in Macon nearly a week while their horses, which had been driven overland over bad roads, recovered somewhat from their arduous trip. The men mounted the guns on their carriages and made various repairs to their equipment.

At Macon, the Cherokee Artillery's interim commander, Lt. William S. Hoge, tendered his resignation. In a letter dated February 10, 1865, Hoge stated that personal matters precluded his being able to discharge his duties as the unit's commander. He further noted that he wished to reenlist "as a private soldier, in which capacity I am satisfied, and can render better and more profitable service to the country." The reasons for Hoge's sudden withdrawal from the Cherokee Artillery remain a mystery, but he ended the war serving as a private in an Alabama cavalry company.[8]

Finally, orders came to hitch up and move out toward Augusta, by way of Milledgeville, Georgia. Upon reaching Milledgeville, however, it became clear that the horses, in their weakened state, could not pull the guns, caissons, and wagons all the way to Augusta. Once again, the men loaded the guns onto trains, while the unit's wranglers herded the beasts overland. After arriving in Augusta, Johnston's Battalion crossed the Savannah River and made camp about three miles east of Hamburg, South Carolina.

The batteries spent the next three weeks there, procuring additional horses and needed equipment. They even participated in a military review held by the post's commander, Maj. Gen. Daniel Harvey Hill. While in camp, the Cherokee Artillery experienced yet another change in its leadership. Near Hamburg, the men joyously welcomed back their beloved commander, Capt. Max Van Den Corput, who had been on convalescent leave since being seriously wounded during the defense of Atlanta.[9]

The war soon interrupted this pleasant interlude. Jefferson Davis faced a difficult decision. He had an army, battered though it might

---

[8] Lindsley, *MAT,* 836; Hoge to Cooper, February 10, 1865, Compiled Service Records of Confederate Soldiers, Georgia, Record group 109, roll 10911.

[9] Lindsley, *MAT,* 836; Bradley, *Bentonville,* 28–29.

be, but no commander. He still despised "Old Joe" Johnston, and reinstating the dapper general would amount to an admission that he had made a mistake in appointing John Bell Hood. But he had to face reality. Johnston was the only experienced leader he had whom the men would follow into battle. Biting the bullet, Davis directed Johnston to take charge of what remained of the Army of Tennessee.

The situation in the Palmetto State gave Rebel sympathizers little reason for optimism. The Confederates had finally been forced to evacuate Charleston, and Sherman's "bummers" left Columbia a burned, gutted ruin as they marched north. "Old Joe" began pulling his scattered forces together to confront Sherman in North Carolina. On March 18, Beauregard ordered Johnston's Artillery Battalion to move north and complete its long-delayed rendezvous with Lee's Corps, near Charlotte, North Carolina.[10]

All things considered, the citizens of South Carolina gave the Rebel troops an enthusiastic greeting as they marched through the Palmetto State. "The column was ardently welcomed by the citizens along the route through South Carolina as the Army of Tennessee," noted L. G. Marshall, commander of the battalion's Tennessee battery, "though much of the command was from Mississippi.... There were fragrant flowers and tasteful mottoes, hundreds of which garlanded the fences, gateways, and buildings." By April 1, Johnston's Battalion began arriving at Salisbury, North Carolina, where they halted again, under orders from Gen. Beauregard.[11]

Salisbury, the fifth-largest town in the state, had assumed an outsized level of importance to the shrinking Confederacy for several reasons. Not only did it sit astride an important junction of the Western North Carolina and North Carolina Railroads, but it also was home to

---

[10] Lindsley, *MAT*, 836, 837; WOC, March 25, 1865; *OR*, ser. 1, vol. 47, part 2, 1132; Bradley, *Bentonville*, 24.

[11] Lindsley, *MAT*, 837; *OR*, ser. 1, vol. 47, part 3, 738. L. G. Marshall, of Marshall's Battery, states that the battalion arrived on April 3, but Featherston reported to Beauregard that he expected the battalion to arrive on the morning of April 1. This latter date seems to square better with Marshall's assertion that they remained at Salisbury "eight or ten days," since an April 3 arrival would seem to conflict with the battalion's orders to leave for Yorkville, SC, on April 7.

a large foundry and military arsenal. More importantly, it had become the Confederate Army's single largest remaining supply depot. Rebel authorities had stockpiled supplies from North Carolina and Virginia at Salisbury to provision both Robert E. Lee's Army of Northern Virginia and Joe Johnston's motley collection of troops. These reasons alone provided enough incentive to make the city an important target for the advancing Federal forces; but there was another, more visceral reason that made Salisbury a prime objective for the Yankees. Since December 1861, Salisbury had also housed a large prison camp for captured Federal soldiers, individuals judged disloyal to the Confederacy, and common criminals. Until 1864, conditions in the camp had been satisfactory. However, once the Union stopped exchanging captured soldiers with the Confederacy, conditions at Salisbury had rapidly deteriorated. The horribly overcrowded prison became a deathtrap, filled with disease and death as available food and medicine dwindled. Only after prisoner exchanges resumed in early 1865 did conditions begin to improve. Confederate authorities had by then decided to close the prison permanently. On February 22, Rebel officials released the remaining 3,000 prisoners into Federal hands, but tales of the mistreatment of Union captives incensed the Yankee soldiers.[12]

On January 31, 1865, prior to the Confederate release of the camp's prisoners, Lt. Gen. Ulysses S. Grant had directed Maj. Gen. George Stoneman, commander of the Federal District of East Tennessee, to launch a raid into North and South Carolina. Stoneman's objectives would be to destroy "railroad and military resources" ranging "well down toward Columbia." On his return to East Tennessee, Grant suggested, he might be able to go "by way of Salisbury, N.C., thus releasing some of our prisoners in rebel hands." Stoneman, who had once been held captive at the Confederate prison at Andersonville, Georgia, was only too ready to oblige. His career had been in a downward spiral since 1863, and he welcomed the opportunity to redeem

[12] Hartley, *Stoneman's Raid 1865*, 28; Mason, "Stoneman's Last Campaign," 23–29.

himself. His failures as commander of the Army of the Potomac's cavalry, during the Chancellorsville campaign, and as leader of a cavalry division under Sherman during the Atlanta campaign, had been well publicized, and this raid offered an opportunity for redemption.[13]

On March 26, Stoneman's force of 4,000 cavalry troopers, under the direct command of Brig. Gen. Alvan C. Gillam, swooped into western North Carolina. Encountering only scattered resistance, Stoneman split his force at Boone, North Carolina, taking one brigade with him north of the Yadkin River, through Deep Gap, toward the town of Wilkesboro. Gillam led the remaining two brigades and the horse artillery along the south bank of the Yadkin. He first struck southeast, but then turned to complete a pincer movement targeting Wilkesboro. After reuniting his command at that city, on March 29, Stoneman and his raiders galloped east toward Jonesville. The Yankee raiders then veered to the northeast, striking Mount Airy before riding into southern Virginia on April 3.[14]

Gen. Beauregard, who had the responsibility of defending against Stoneman's incursion, had suspected that Salisbury, Greensboro, or Danville (Virginia) would be Stoneman's ultimate objective when the bluecoats had initially entered North Carolina. On March 30, Beauregard ordered Stephen D. Lee, whose understrength corps was approaching Chester, South Carolina, to speed as many troops as he could northward to defend Salisbury. Meanwhile, the Creole leader kept a watchful eye for any enemy movements toward either Greensboro or Danville. When Stoneman made his turn northward toward Virginia, a relieved Beauregard changed his focus. He moved troops away from Salisbury, first to reinforce the weak Confederate garrison

---

[13] *OR*, ser. 1, vol. 49, part 1, 616; Bradley, *This Astounding Close*, 132–33. An excellent account of Stoneman's record during the Atlanta Campaign can be found in David Evans, *Sherman's Horsemen: Union Cavalry Operations in the Atlanta Campaign* (Bloomington: Indiana University Press, 1999).

[14] Hartley, *Stoneman's Raid 1865*, 78; Beall's account of Stoneman's Raid, Cornelia Phillips Spencer Papers, 1; Trowbridge, "The Stoneman Raid of 1865," 195–96.

at Danville, and then repositioned the remainder of his troops to defend Greensboro. As Stoneman penetrated farther into southern Virginia, Beauregard also began releasing additional troops to reinforce Joe Johnston at Smithfield, North Carolina. Only a token force remained at Salisbury.[15]

Beauregard had guessed wrong. Gen. Stoneman, recalling Gen. Grant's admonition to "visit" Salisbury, had every intention of returning to North Carolina. On April 9, the same day Gen. Robert E. Lee surrendered the valiant Army of Northern Virginia, the Union raider and his troopers crossed back into the Tar Heel State. He split his force at Germanton, dispatching Col. William Palmer's brigade to raid as far south as Salem. There, the Federals destroyed the textile factories before burning all the bridges at Danville and Greensboro, as well as those spanning the Yadkin River. With his other two brigades, Stoneman moved toward Salisbury. By 8 P.M. on April 11, they had gone into camp only twelve miles north of Salisbury. Stoneman's prize appeared to be nearly within his grasp.[16]

After arriving at Salisbury on April 1, the Cherokee Artillery and the other batteries of Johnston's Battalion went into camp on the edge of town. Like tourists, the Rebel gunners spent the next few days exploring the historic old town. On April 5, with Stoneman's Union cavalry raiding the southern Virginia countryside, Johnston's cannoneers received a directive to proceed south to Yorkville (modern York), South Carolina. There the battalion was to receive fresh horses and new orders.

Owing to the poor condition of the unit's animals, the battalion delayed their departure until the following morning. After marching for two days, they made camp for the night on the outskirts of Charlotte, about forty-five miles southwest of Salisbury. During the night,

---

[15] Hartley, *Stoneman's Raid 1865*, 97–100, 112–13, 133–34.

[16] *OR*, ser. 1, vol. 49, part 1, 323, 330; Trowbridge, "The Stoneman Raid of 1865," 195–96.

a courier arrived from Beauregard. The Creole officer had received intelligence that Stoneman had indeed turned south and now seemed to be heading toward Salisbury. The men hurried to comply with the directive to return to Salisbury, but the wretched condition of their critters slowed their return. However, the evening of April 10, found the batteries again encamped on the outskirts of Salisbury.[17]

By the next morning, little doubt remained that Stoneman had set his sights on Salisbury. Maj. Johnston and captains Van Den Corput and Marshall reported to acting post commander Brig. Gen. William M. Gardner. Also present was Lt. Col. (formerly Lt. Gen.) John C. Pemberton, now serving as Gardner's inspector general of artillery and ordinance. After some discussion, the officers decided to defend the town, and Gardner instructed the artillerymen to "put your batteries on the ground selected by the engineer."[18]

About a mile and a half north of the town, they established a defensive line that ran in a two-mile arc along the south bank of Grant's Creek. The deep creek, with its steep embankments, provided a good natural barrier upon which to establish the city's defenses. Van Den Corput's Cherokee Artillery had orders to defend the bridge across the creek at the Old Mocksville Road. They would anchor the far right of the Confederate line. About a half a mile to the left, René Beauregard's battery guarded the bridge over the creek at the New Mocksville Road. (The two roads both ran directly into downtown Salisbury.) Several contemporary sources suggest that a battery manned by "Galvanized Yankees" made up the third Rebel artillery unit. (Galvanized Yankees had been primarily recruited to fight for the Confederacy from the immigrant Irish Yankees held at the prison.) The Rebel commanders had apparently positioned them near the younger Beauregard's guns so that regular Confederate troops could keep a close eye on these dubious

---

[17] WOC, April 10, 1865; Lindsley, *MAT*, 837; *OR*, ser. 1, vol. 47, part 3, 756, 761.

[18] Lindsley, *MAT*, 838; Hartley, *Stoneman's Raid 1865*, 229–31; R. L. Beall's account of Stoneman's Raid, 4. The "engineer" referred to appears to have been an unnamed officer who had just arrived from Lee's Army of Northern Virginia.

allies. Together, those two batteries formed the center of the Rebel line. Located on the far left, Marshall's Battery guarded the Western North Carolina Railroad span. By 11 P.M., the batteries had all assumed their positions.[19]

Conspicuously missing from the alignment was the presence of enough infantry support to prevent the artillery from being overrun. The majority of the prison's defenders had accompanied Gen. Bradley Johnson to Greensboro, where Gen. Beauregard had initially expected Stoneman's primary attack to occur. He left behind a ragged collection of "troops" scraped from the very bottom of the Confederacy's manpower barrel. These included a few companies of Col. John Hoke's 4th regiment, North Carolina Senior Reserves; three companies of Freeman's Battalion, North Carolina Prison Guards; and Col. A. G. Brenizer's 1st regiment, North Carolina Detailed Men, composed of clerks, mechanics, and government workers. Almost all of these men were unfit for front-line service although some would participate in the battle. A few small companies of invalids pressed into service from the local hospital, another tiny detachment of "Galvanized Yankees," and a small number of citizen volunteers rounded out the collection of available troops. All told, William Gardner probably had at his disposal around 2,500 men. Virtually none of the men detailed as infantry support for the artillery had ever been in combat. Gardner appears to have assigned around 1,000 men of his force to the Grant's Creek defense line. The rest he detailed to guard another important bridge over the Yadkin River.[20]

The men of the Cherokee Artillery and their comrades from the other two batteries of Johnston's Battalion bivouacked that night, keeping a sharp lookout for enemy cavalry. Their horses remained in

---

[19] Lindsley, *MAT*, 838; Hartley, *Stoneman's Raid 1865*, 227; Chastain, "When Yankees Fought Yankees." Confederate prisoners who switched sides and fought for the Union were also called "Galvanized Yankees," and former Federals who joined the Rebels were called "Galvanized Confederates." We have used the more commonly applied phrasing.

[20] Hartley, *Stoneman's Raid 1865*, 228–32.

harness in case a quick departure was required. Too far from Beauregard's Battery for mutual support, and painfully aware of their feeble infantry support, the gunners waited in the darkness with a growing sense of foreboding. Writing around midnight, Wesley Connor captured the mood of the men in his diary: "Our battalion is gone, if it remains [here], and Maj. Johnston is fool enough to try to defend the place with artillery alone. Nothing authentic from [Gen. Robert E.] Lee since the evacuation of Richmond. Things look dark. A crisis is undoubtedly upon us."[21]

As dawn broke at 5:30 on April 12, the gunners heard scattered firing from the convalescents detailed as pickets a few hundred yards in front of their position. As the outposts fell back to the main defense line, the rising sun revealed glimpses of Yankee horsemen moving here and there through the timberline. Capt. Van Den Corput, hearing the cannonading of Marshall's Battery on the left, gave the order to open fire. For the next twenty minutes, the Cherokee Artillery and the other batteries kept up a lively fire at the enemy maneuvering in front of them. As Stoneman's raiders deployed for action, a section of Lt. James Reagan's Union horse artillery battery galloped up, unlimbering its two ten-pounder Parrott rifles. Whether by choice or chance, the bluecoats concentrated their fire on the batteries of René Beauregard and the Galvanized Yankees. Unable to dislodge the Confederates, and having taken a number of casualties, the Yankee gunners eventually decided to retire. With his two cavalry brigades now ready for action, Stoneman launched a general assault, attacking the Grant's Creek line simultaneously at five places. The Confederate artillerymen continued blazing away at their attackers, holding their line for over an hour.[22]

A battalion of the 12th Kentucky Cavalry (US) made the first contact with the Rebel gunners. The unit had orders to "make a determined demonstration of crossing Grant's Creek two miles from Salisbury, and if successful to attack the forces defending the upper bridge in rear." As the gunners of the Cherokee Artillery continued laying

[21] WOC, April 11, 1865; Lindsley, *MAT*, 383.

[22] Lindsley, *MAT*, 383; Mason, "Stoneman's Last Campaign," 25–29; Trowbridge, "Stoneman's Raid of 1865," 195–96.

down a brisk fire on the Federals in their front, the sudden noise of hundreds of hooves off to their right signaled impending disaster. The men of the 12th Kentucky had managed to cross the creek farther upstream and were now thundering down on the battery's unprotected right flank. As the artillerymen had feared, their infantry support "bolted at the first sight of the Yankees." W. O. Connor, writing many years later, recalled, "Having no fortifications, of course this force offered but little resistance to the impetuous onslaught of Stoneman's disciplined cavalry. The [Galvanized] Yankees threw down their arms and refused to fight as soon as the Yankees made the charge on our lines."[23]

With drawn sabers, pistols, and Spencer repeating rifles glinting in the morning sun, the Kentucky Yankees surged forward in a mad gallop, intent on destroying the Georgians. It was too late to hitch up the guns and limbers and attempt to move off to safety—it was now every man for himself. The Cherokee Artillery's mounted officers managed to make good their escape by riding hell-for-leather back through Salisbury. There they joined the mass of retreating Confederates who dashed into the woods to avoid capture. Most of the men serving the guns were not that lucky. Forty-five of them—over half the members of the battery—surrendered to the advancing Federal cavalrymen.[24]

Having turned both Confederate flanks and overrun and captured all of the enemy's artillery, Stoneman's troopers made short work of the rest of the Salisbury defenses. Although a handful of veteran Confederates attempted to continue the fight, most of the Rebel defenders, routed and disorganized, dispersed in a desperate effort to evade being taken prisoner. By 9:30 A.M., the battle had ended.

Stoneman and his troopers triumphantly entered the town. Despite finding the prison empty, they did take 1,364 prisoners. Over the

---

[23] WOC, April 12, 1865; Mason, "Stoneman's Last Campaign," 25–29; R. W. Black, *Cavalry Raids of the Civil War*, 188–90.

[24] *OR*, ser. 1, vol. 49, part 1, 332; WOC, April 12, 1865; Connor, "Sixteen Faithful Confederates," 505; Hartley, *Stoneman's Raid 1865*, 235–36.

next two days, the Federals destroyed the prison and a veritable mountain of ammunition, supplies, and equipment desperately needed by Joe Johnston's army. It had, indeed, been a rich haul.[25]

Later that day, the men of Van Den Corput's Battery who had not managed to escape began the long trek to a Union prison. As they marched through East Tennessee, they passed through several hamlets they had occupied during 1862. The Rebel gunners had little time for sight-seeing, however, as their guards pushed the Georgia cannoneers hard, sometimes forcing them to cover as much as twenty miles a day through the rough, mountainous region. Confederate accounts contain no suggestions of mistreatment by their guards, and the civilians seem to have ignored the ragged, hungry prisoners. Connor and his battery mates continued hearing unconfirmed reports of the surrender of the Army of Northern Virginia, but they hoped the rumor amounted to nothing more than Yankee propaganda. At Greenville, however, the diarist met a man he had known while stationed there in 1862, who confirmed that Lee had indeed capitulated. He also informed the ragged Rebels that Pres. Abraham Lincoln had been assassinated.[26]

On April 27, the men taken captive at Salisbury limped into Chattanooga. Almost immediately the guards put the graycoats aboard trains bound for the infamous Camp Chase prison in Ohio. From Tennessee's "Gateway City," the Salisbury captives rode the rails through Nashville, Louisville, and Indianapolis, and then on to Columbus, Ohio. On May 4, 1865, the men disembarked and marched to the prison, five miles outside of the town.[27]

---

[25] *OR*, ser. 1, vol. 51, part 1, 324; Mason, "Stoneman's Last Campaign," 25–29; Trowbridge, "Stoneman's Raid of 1865," 195–96.

[26] WOC, April 12–22, 1865. Since Capt. Van Den Corput escaped uninjured, he likely commanded his unit until the surrender. One source, however, indicates that Sgt. John S. Panchen led them until the end of hostilities, but a review of Panchen's service record makes this seem unlikely. See "Reminiscences of the Third Georgia Battalion," *Atlanta Sunny South*, March 10, 1894, 10.

[27] WOC, April 27–May 4, 1865.

Many of the Confederate prisoners, particularly those who had been in the penitentiary for two years or more, wanted only to take the oath of allegiance and go home. With Lee and Johnston's armies surrendered and Pres. Davis captured, there seemed to be little realistic hope for the Confederacy to somehow survive and carry on the war for independence. This sense of defeatism upset the new prisoners. Connor wrote, "The roll of prisoners has been called for the purpose of giving an opportunity (to all who wished to do so) to subscribe for the oath of allegiance. A very few chose to put down their names for exchange."[28]

For the next two months, the numbers of the Cherokee Artillery dwindled as unit members signed the oath. Only sixteen holdouts remained by mid-June. The guards, bored and with little supervision by officers, began playing cruel tricks on the Rebel prisoners. One jailer threatened to shoot Connor for failing to sign the oath. Another time a sergeant lined up all the remaining prisoners at the main gate and ordered the soldiers to march. Most of the men thought they had been transferred to another camp, but "upon marching two or three hundred yards were suddenly turned to the right into Prison 1." Finally, on June 13, the diarist wrote that he and his remaining comrades had bowed to the reality of their situation and signed the Oath of Allegiance.[29]

The next day the Floyd County soldiers began the long journey home. Like many Southerners, Connor observed the North's stunning wartime prosperity. Everywhere, affluent-looking people were going about their daily lives, seemingly unaffected by the recent conflict. At Louisville, local ladies met the trains and gave the former Rebels food and clothes. By contrast, the citizens of Nashville treated the returning graycoats with thinly veiled contempt. The Tennesseans passed the wretched men without even a smile for those who had sacrificed so much for them.[30]

---

[28] WOC, May 19, 1865.

[29] WOC, May 21–June 13, 1865; Connor, "Sixteen Faithful Confederates."

[30] WOC, June 10–13, 1865; Connor, "Sixteen Faithful Confederates," 506.

On June 19, the train carrying the members of the Cherokee Artillery reached Kingston, Georgia, about midafternoon. They disembarked and boarded the cars for the short trip to Rome. A storm enveloped the countryside, but the train made the trip in about one hour. As Connor's entry for the day reported, "As the train stopped [in Rome] a heavy rain fell, which I suppose drove what few inhabitants there were into their houses, at any rate, the streets were deserted; and Rome indeed was a desolate looking place."[31]

After almost four long years of fighting, marching, and suffering, their great adventure had ended. It had begun with so much excitement and enthusiasm in summer 1861 but had terminated with a skirmish in the Rebel hinterlands, surrounded by Yankee turncoats, graybeards, and the walking wounded. The war had ended for the Cherokee Artillery—but something yet remained.

[31] WOC, June 13–19, 1865.

Chapter 8

“The Damnedest Set of Fellows You Ever Saw”

Postwar

Rome and Floyd County had suffered great devastation during the last year of the war. Union occupation forces arrived at the City of Seven Hills on May 18, 1864, and departed on November 7, 1864. Brig. Gen. John M. Corse, commanding the bluecoats at Rome, zealously obeyed Gen. Sherman’s orders to destroy “all public property not needed by your command, all foundries, mills, workshops, warehouses, railroad depots or other storehouses convenient to the railroad, together with all wagon shops, tanneries, and other factories useful to the enemy. Destroy all bridges immediately, then move your command tomorrow to Kingston.”[1]

As soon as the bluecoats departed, bushwhackers and marauders quickly filled the vacuum. With no organized military force to defend the region, the irregulars began robbing, pillaging, and torturing victims to make them reveal the location of hidden valuables; they murdered on a whim. Most of the civilians who had remained now left their homes for safer locations. The memoirs of William Towers, who had served with Gen. Nathan Bedford Forrest’s escort, revealed how well Corse and the pillagers had done their work. “When I arrived at the city,” Towers wrote,

> I found the bridge burned, and had to cross in a ferry boat at the forks of the river. The bridge across the Oostanaula was also burned, along with quite a number of storehouses, the Old Etowah House, the depot, etc., [and] the remaining storehouses looking desolate, all the doors standing open, and the shutters flapping in the wind. None

---

[1] *OR*, ser. 1, vol. 39, part 3, 628–29; Aycock, *All Roads to Rome*, 111–17.

> were occupied, and there was not a living thing in sight when I arrived at Broad Street.[2]

Families who had taken refuge elsewhere and former Confederate soldiers began returning to Rome as soon as the war ended. Among the last group of ex-soldiers to arrive were W. O. Connor, James C. Browne, and a few other die-hard members of the Cherokee Artillery. They had steadfastly refused to take the Oath of Allegiance until not a single Confederate army was still in the field.[3]

During the period of Reconstruction, which lasted from 1865 through 1876, the new social order often inflamed tensions between the white and African American citizens of Rome and Floyd County. In particular, the local Freedman's Bureau, responsible for everything from furnishing rations to the former slaves and establishing schools and hospitals for them to setting up a contract labor system, seemed to act as a lightning rod for racial tensions in the community.[4]

One of the first directors of the Freedman's Bureau in Rome was Capt. Carlos A. De La Mare, whom local white residents disparagingly described as a mercenary and tyrant who "encouraged the Negroes to all kinds of lawlessness." At one point, events during De La Mare's tenure created such animosity between the city's white residents and the bureau that many feared the tensions might lead to violence. However, the combined efforts of Bishop Henry Thomas of the African Methodist Episcopal Church and local white leaders defused the potentially volatile situation.[5]

---

[2] Aycock, *All Roads to Rome*, 124–33; Waters, "Gartrell's Georgians," 14.

[3] See appendix, Cherokee Artillery roster; W. O. Connor, "Sixteen Faithful Confederates," 505–506. The unit's record for the ultimate holdout belongs to a teen from Arkansas, James A. Dunn, who did not swear fealty to the United States until late August 1865.

[4] Battey, *A History of Rome and Floyd County*, 243–44; Hatfield, "The Freedmen's Bureau," www.georgiaencyclopedia.org/articles/history-archaeology/freedmens-bureau. The Rome Freedmen's Bureau office occupied the present location of the historic DeSoto Theater on Broad Street.

[5] Battey, *A History of Rome and Floyd County*, 242–45; "Rome, Georgia Treason," *Memphis Daily Avalanche*, February 3, 1867, 2; "Dr. E. C. King," *Memphis*

Shortly thereafter, the Ku Klux Klan, an organization composed primarily of disaffected Confederate veterans, began terrorizing the African American community and disrupting Reconstruction policies in Northwest Georgia. Though the extent of violence by the Northwest Georgia Klan never equaled the level of terror that enveloped some regions of South Carolina and Tennessee, the threat hung like the Sword of Damocles over the African American citizens of Rome and Floyd County. In 1876, with the removal of Federal troops from the former Confederacy, the South gradually settled into the state-sponsored "Jim Crow" system of racial discrimination that would last for almost 100 years.[6]

Rebuilding Rome's economic base ranked as the highest priority for many of the returning veterans, and transportation seemed to be the key to industrial growth in Northwest Georgia. City fathers had long dreamed of a rail connection that would allow local merchants to convey their products to markets in the Northeastern United States. Work on a rail line from Selma, Alabama, to Dalton, Georgia, had progressed as far as Blue Mountain, Alabama, before the outbreak of war halted further construction. Work on the railroad resumed soon after the war ended, and in 1869, the Selma, Rome & Dalton Railroad began operations. Max Van Den Corput apparently served as an engineer for the railroad during the construction of the rail line. (The former leader of the Cherokee Artillery would later establish a successful architecture firm in Atlanta. He died in 1911, and is buried in Atlanta's Oaklawn Cemetery.) Steamboats also began plying the Coosa River again, picking up cotton bales at various landings along the waterway and transporting them to Rome's "Cotton Block." By using the Coosa and Alabama rivers, the steamboats could deliver goods from Northwest Georgia to Mobile, Alabama. By 1870, products from Rome

Daily Avalanche, January 24, 1868, 1; "Rome, Georgia," *Memphis Daily Avalanche*, May 25, 1867, 1; "Negro Character," *Atlanta Sunny South*, July 29, 1893, 16.

[6] Aycock, *All Roads to Rome*, 151–56.

could be shipped to both the major Northeastern cities and the Gulf Coast.[7]

Not content with the area's merely becoming a transportation hub, legendary journalist Henry Grady (at that time—1869—the associate editor of a Rome newspaper) proposed a train excursion and business fair to publicize the industrial and commercial opportunities to be found in Northwest Georgia. Newsmen from throughout the state arrived at Rome and were dazzled by the area's potential. A typical article read, "Rome, before the war, was Lilliputian in dimensions, but now is a growing, enterprising city of six thousand inhabitants.... Rome has four churches for whites and two for the blacks, two steam flour mills...one foundry, one lumber and furniture mill, a female college, a large male academy, three newspapers, two steam fire engines, plenty of pretty girls; [and] accommodating and polite citizens." The financial outlook for the area seemed extremely promising.[8]

Meanwhile, veterans of the Cherokee Artillery began picking up the pieces of their pre-war lives. W. O. Connor, for example, settled at Cave Spring and tried for two years to make his sister's farm into a paying enterprise. In 1867, the trustees of the Georgia School for the Deaf asked him to serve as the institution's principal, and Connor would spend the rest of his life supervising the education of hearing-impaired students. The next year, he married a local girl, Editha Simmons. The loving couple had six children together. Connor never forgot his service with Van Den Corput's Battery and helped keep memories of the unit alive by organizing reunions of the battery's members, founding a social version of the Cherokee Artillery, corresponding with various early historians, and even penning an article about his time at

---

[7] Ibid., 165–69, 184–87; Max Van Den Corput to E. A. Carmen, June 17, 1892, Carmen papers, LOC.

[8] Aycock, *All Roads to Rome*, 142–47; "Letter from Rome," *Augusta (GA) Daily Constitutionalist*, October 29, 1869, 2.

Camp Chase for *Confederate Veteran* magazine. He passed away on February 18, 1920, and is buried in the Cave Spring Cemetery.[9]

Felix Corput (he apparently dropped "Van Den" from his name) may have been the best-known member of the Cherokee Artillery in postwar Georgia. He had surrendered at Macon and remained in the Middle Georgia city for many years. Corput served several terms as Macon's mayor and took an active interest in the Farmer's Alliance, a grange movement created to help Southern planters deal the loss of slave labor and the difficulty in obtaining bank credit. After about twenty years, Corput moved back to Cave Spring, where he planted a vineyard, reputed to be the finest in the South. He represented Floyd County in both the Georgia House and Senate, acted as a trustee for the Georgia Experiment Station, and served on the Board of the Georgia School for the Deaf. In addition, he often hosted the Cherokee Artillery's annual reunions. He passed away on July 7, 1916, and is buried in the Cave Spring Cemetery.[10]

Many Confederate veterans, upon returning to find their homeland ravaged by war and (in their view) prostrate under the heel of an occupying Federal army, chose to leave Georgia and take advantage of cheap land and new opportunities in the West. The men of the Cherokee Artillery were no exception. Two veterans of the battery, with prewar ties to the "Show-Me State," returned to Missouri and became prominent citizens. Benjamin Franklin Jones served as the director of the Kansas City, Missouri, waterworks, and Jefferson Lemmon practiced medicine in Polk County for many years. Lacy Howard Lott, after returning to Cave Spring in 1865, uprooted his growing family around 1869 and settled into life as a prosperous farmer in Gentry, Arkansas. Two of his three brothers-in-law with whom he had served

---

[9] "Veteran Educator of Deaf Succumbs at Cave Spring," *Macon (GA) Telegraph*, February 20, 1920, 10; Montgomery M. Folsom, "The Cherokee Artillery," *Atlanta Sunny South*, March 10, 1894, 10; Connor, "Sixteen Faithful Confederates," 505–506; W. O. Connor file, CA file, VNBP.

[10] "Captain Felix Corput Passed Away Yesterday at His Cave Spring Home," *Rome (GA) Tribune-Herald*, July 8, 1916, 1; Northern, "Felix Van Den Corput," 334–37.

in the Cherokee Artillery, Isham and William "Claiborne" Couey, eventually left Cave Spring to resettle in Texas, as did Sidney Hampton Gattis, Harvell Dempsey Griffin, David O. Newton, and Lemuel B. Rumsey. J. M. Penney seemingly relocated to the Indian Territory (present-day Oklahoma).[11]

The end of Reconstruction in 1876 witnessed a resurgent pride among Northwest Georgia residents for the sacrifices of Georgia's ex-Confederates. On May 11, 1879, Governor A. H. Colquitt, a former Rebel major general, and large contingents of veterans from Floyd County and Atlanta assembled atop Myrtle Hill for the unveiling of Rome's Confederate monument. A local historian described it as a "heroic marble monument," facing to the west and standing atop Myrtle Hill's "topmost peak" while flowers peeked from the lush grass. The state's chief executive delivered a fiery speech, ministers offered prayers, and brass bands played songs of the Southland while representatives of various Floyd County units deposited mementos of their service into the base of the statue. W. O. Connor represented his unit, depositing the muster roll of the Cherokee Artillery, from the unit's beginning on July 11, 1861, to their final battle at Salisbury, North Carolina, on April 12, 1865.[12]

A couple of weeks later, a number of Floyd County's leading citizens began discussing the possibility of reforming Van Den Corput's Battery as a social and fraternal organization. On June 5, 1879, a local newspaper reported that the Cherokee Artillery "was reorganized last Tuesday night by the election of the following officers: John E. Stillwell, Captain; J. G. Yeiser, First Lieutenant; J. J. Seay, Second Lieutenant; W. O. Connor, Third Lieutenant; Jack [John T.] King, Orderly Sergeant." All of the officers except Seay had been members of the battery during the war. Mr. Seay had served with Cobb's Legion in

---

[11] See appendix, Cherokee Artillery roster; "Lacy Howard Lott Is Called by Death," *Journal-Advance and Benton County (AR) Gazette*, January 10, 1929.

[12] Battey, *A History of Rome and Floyd County*, 621–22; "The Confederate Monument," *TWC*, May 13, 1879, 3.

the Army of Northern Virginia until he was severely wounded at Knoxville, Tennessee, in 1864. Postwar, Seay owned the White Star Line, running steamboats up and down the Coosa, hauling crops and passengers between Central Alabama and Rome.[13]

Acquiring cannon would be the first step in putting the fraternal artillery company back in service. Luckily for the group, the North Georgia representative in the U.S. Congress was William Harrell Felton. Felton, a Methodist minister, medical doctor, former Confederate surgeon, and Independent Democrat from Bartow County, managed to obtain four guns from the War Department. Bitter opposition to Felton's request came from Rep. Omar D. Conger, a Michigan Republican who had seemingly sat out the Civil War without ever hearing a gun fired in combat. Felton had no intention of caving to Republican obstacles. An Atlanta newspaper reported, "Felton succeeded in getting a battery for the Cherokee Artillery. The original bill would have cost Georgia $7,000, but Felton amended it to be considered 'an indefinite loan.'"[14]

By the time the big guns arrived, the unit had more members than they took into their final fight at Salisbury. The roster included some of the elite of Floyd County. The members, listed in the *Tri-Weekly Courier* were as follows: J. G. Yeiser, J. E. Stillwell, C. O. Stillwell, G. W. Bowen, J. J. Seay, W. W. Seay, S. C. Caldwell, F. H. Caldwell, W. M. Towers, J. R. Butt, A. E. Williams, R. T. Hoyt, M. McLauren, J. H. Elliot, H. D. Cothran, W. S. Cothran, W. M. Gammon, P. C. McNulty, E. R. Smith, J. W. Roundsaville, J. C. Sproull Jr., W. W. Martin, E. M. Ross, R. V. Allen, J. W. Ewing, J. A. Cooley, S. Gregory, J. A. Smith, R. Hume, K. S. Simmons, W. Shafer, C. Omberg, W. L. Omberg, F. J. Cohen, D. O. Newton, John Kerr, H. W. Deem, W.

---

[13] "Cherokee Artillery Re-organized," *TWC*, June 5, 1879, 3; Southern Historical Association, "John J. Seay," 679–80.

[14] "The Patriots on a Hegira," *Atlanta Weekly Constitution*, December 23, 1879, 2; "Georgia in Congress," *Atlanta Weekly Constitution*, March 23, 1880, 2; "Felton, William Harrell," http://bioguide.congress.gov/scripts/biodisplay.pl?index=F000070. For more on Felton see, George L. Jones, "William H. Felton and the Independent Democratic Movement in Georgia," Ph.D. diss., University of Georgia, 1971.

W. Noble, W. O. Connor, Coke W. Stewart, A. J. King, R. T. Logan, C. Hosking, E. T. Morrison, J. J. Thompson, I. Donkle, A. A. Hardwick, R. Wright, C. A. Hanson, R. Campbell, H. Landstell, J. C. McKenzie, W. C. Enwright, W. Arnot, A. J. Johnson, __ Rucker, J. W. Mathews, R. Stephens, C. Dempsey, E. M. Johnson, and F. M. Carwile. Though several members of the new unit had never fired any weapon larger than a pistol, enough of the veterans of Van Den Corput's Battery remained to teach the rookies the rudiments of firing cannon.[15]

One of the first events the reconstituted Cherokee Artillery sponsored was a four-day muster at Camp Lee, near Rome. Military units from as far away as Savannah arrived, and they slept in tents, paraded, and engaged in target practice and military maneuvers. The Floyd County company impressed a writer for an Atlanta newspaper, who wrote, "The last company in the procession was the Cherokee Artillery, commanded by Captain J. G. Yeiser, whose fine military presence, together with the handsome uniforms and bearing of his men attracted universal admiration. The company numbered twenty-five." The local unit finished in the middle of the pack in the various competitions, and the hosts wound up awarding a silver cup to the famed Chatham Artillery of Savannah for accuracy in target shooting.[16]

An accident that occurred in 1884 may have led to the dissolution of the artillery company. Grover Cleveland, one of only two Democrats who would occupy the nation's highest office between 1860 and 1932, won the presidential election that year. Across the Democratic "Solid South," joyous whites celebrated the news. In Floyd County, bonfires ringed the seven hills, people danced in the streets, and the Cherokee Artillery joined the merriment, firing volley after volley near Broad Street. During the gaiety, Ellston Morgan, the young son of Maj. Sam Morgan, "had a portion of his right arm blown off by a premature explosion" fired by the Cherokee Artillery. Thereafter, mentions of Yeiser's battery in the local and Atlanta papers ceased, and

[15] "Reorganization of Cherokee Artillery," *TWC*, May 31, 1879, 3.

[16] "The Glittering Steel," *Atlanta Weekly Constitution*, July 20, 1880, 1.

within three years their four guns had been emplaced at Grant Park in Atlanta.[17]

When the fraternal version of the Cherokee Artillery disbanded, the unit members began a routine of holding annual reunions. Luckily, Montgomery M. Folsom, a respected writer from Atlanta and a friend of W. O. Connor, provided colorful details of the get-togethers, as did several other journalists.[18]

The business portion of the reunion usually began in Connor's office at the School for the Deaf. Folsom recounted, "In the office of Superintendent Wesley O. Connor, veterans will meet and transact such business as brought before them." Those present at these "business meetings" were usually Connor, Max Van Den Corput, Felix Corput, and J. S. Panchen. No one knows the exact nature of the matters discussed, but they likely included such things as assisting impoverished veterans or their widows, aiding comrades with pension applications, and responding to calls for information on the unit's various battles and campaigns. At the first reunion, the old comrades had formed the Cherokee Artillery Survivors Association, and they likely spent part of each business meeting preparing the handsome membership certificates for first-time attendees.[19]

The presentation of the unit's old flag always ranked as the highlight of every reunion. "That old banner, frayed and worn," one newsman recalled, "was exhibited this morning and tears glistened in those aging eyes as the members of the old artillery gazed upon that faded relic." At the first reunion, held at Noble Hall in downtown Rome, the public display of the flag created a sensation. "Major J. G. Yeiser, bearing the tattered flag of the battery...," a journalist wrote, "entered the

---

[17] "Rejoicing in Rome," *Atlanta Constitution*, November 11, 1884, 4. Samuel Morgan, Elston's father, had been the mayor of Rome in 1881. Atlanta's Grant Park was the original location of "The Battle of Atlanta" Cyclorama.

[18] Montgomery M. Folsom, "The Cherokee Artillery," *Atlanta Sunny South*, March 10, 1894, 10; "Montgomery Morgan Folsom," https://www.findagrave.com/memorial/45599528/montgomery-morgan-folsom.

[19] Montgomery M. Folsom, "The Cherokee Artillery," *Atlanta Sunny South*, March 10, 1894, 10; "Valiant Veterans," *Rome Tribune*, December 30, 1891.

hall, and as he did so the men rose with one accord and with uncovered heads, gave three cheers, the Rebel yell, and the sight of their honored banner brought tears to the eyes of these sturdy veterans, and their hearts beat with emotions, many fondling it and looking upon the tattered shield of silk. They valued it more than had it been gold."[20]

The get-togethers often included a musical interlude courtesy of Connor and his children. The *Rome Tribune* observed, "In the parlors of the Institution [School for the Deaf] the party was treated to some delightful music consisting of 'Auld Lang Syne,' 'Dixie,' 'Girl I Left Behind,' and other pieces, the performers being W. O. Connor, Sr., on the fiddle, W. O. Connor, Jr., on the guitar, and Miss Hattie Connor on piano."[21]

Of course, food constituted an integral part of any reunion. "Then when the business of the day is ended," Folsom stated, "the veterans will march down across the footbridge over Cedar Creek and up the hill to the beautiful home of Captain Felix Corput, where they will be feasted in a manner that will bring up many an anecdote of mule beef and Vicksburg by way of contrast. Mrs. Corput will see that the viands are served and Wes Connor will keep the table in a roar with [the] relation of war experiences, apocryphal and otherwise."[22]

The yarns of their youthful battles, defeats, and victories alternately kept the aged soldiers in stitches or brought tears to their eyes. "Stories both comic and pathetic," a newsman wrote,

> were told recalling incidents of the four-year struggle. One comrade told what Connor had to say when Sergeant Jones read to his detachment the order to hang out a white flag in token of surrender at Vicksburg, on the morning of July 4, 1863. Connor had the towel, made of a meal sack, which served as this white flag, but he don't [*sic*] use the words he used on that occasion any more. Another told about the last time he saw gallant Captain Corput at Salisbury, as he

---

[20] Montgomery M. Folsom, "The Cherokee Artillery," *Atlanta Sunny South*, March 10, 1894, 10; "Valiant Veterans," *Rome Tribune*, December 30, 1891.

[21] "Gray Old Grays," *Rome Tribune*, July 28, 1892.

[22] Montgomery M. Folsom, "The Cherokee Artillery," *Atlanta Sunny South*, March 10, 1894, 10.

> escaped on his famous old horse, "Red Eye." Another of how "Reps" [R. M. Jones] caught the goose, which brought down the house. Major Frank Jones, of Kansas City, who could not be present, told in a letter of Bill Carrell, when hauled up for punishment for killing a hog, putting in the plea that "the hog had tried to bite him, and it was again[st] his principle to let any Tennessee Union swine treat him in any such scandalous way"—and so on.[23]

After the food, music, tales, laughter, and tears, the men departed for home. The *Tribune* author concluded, "Finally the parting hour came and with warm and hearty handshakes the old comrades reluctantly took each his homeward way, resolved that, if alive, he would be on hand at the next reunion...."[24]

Each year the number of veterans diminished until the reunions finally ended. Wesley O. Connor, James Robinson Scott, and Harvell Dempsey Griffin all lived into the 1920s, but the last known survivor of the Cherokee Artillery to "cross over the river and rest in the shade of trees" was John R. Kerr, who died on July 17, 1927. On his deathbed, the old Polk County veteran may well have thought of the way their old battalion commander once described the Cherokee Artillery to another officer during the war:

> Major [J. W.] Johnston, in answer to an inquiry made by the colonel commanding, as to what sort of battery [Van Den] Corput had, said, "Why just the damnedest set of fellows you ever saw; every man in the concern [unit] thinks himself as good as any brigadier general in the army, and he don't mind telling you so if the occasion offers. They are not worth a damn in camp or on the march, and won't do a thing unless they want to, except when you want any fighting done, and then, Colonel, you swear by 'em, for they respond every time you call on 'em."[25]

It seemed a fitting epitaph for a group of ordinary men called upon to perform extraordinarily during America's most defining struggle.

---

[23] Ibid.

[24] "Gray Old Grays," *Rome Tribune*, July 28, 1892.

[25] Ibid.; see appendix, Cherokee Artillery roster.

Acknowledgments

This book simply could not have been written without the support, assistance, and encouragement given to the authors by so many individuals and organizations, particularly those in the Rome, Georgia, area: Margaret Hollingsworth, who spent countless hours patiently transcribing the incalculably valuable diary of her great-great uncle, Wesley Olin Connor; Bob Anderson, who generously lent us his original research and valuable collection of photographs of the Cherokee Artillery; John Carruth, for his unstinting support and enthusiasm, and for sharing his broad knowledge of Civil War–era Rome, Georgia, and Floyd County; and the staffs of the Heritage Room of the Rome/Floyd County Public Library and the Rome Area History Museum for their patient and knowledgeable assistance in locating letters from members of the battery, newspaper articles, artifacts, and other valuable information in their collections.

The authors are also greatly indebted to Dr. John Coski, historian and library director at the Museum of the Confederacy in Richmond, Virginia, for his gracious assistance in searching through and identifying important documents from the Carter Stevenson Papers in the museum's possession; to Dr. C. L. "Chip" Bragg of Thomasville, Georgia, for his willingness to share copies of his research on Marcellus Stovall and the Cherokee Artillery from his book, *Distinction in Every Service*. We also express our gratitude to Terry J. Winschel, former historian at Vicksburg National Battlefield Park, whose willingness to share his knowledge and expertise contributed immeasurably to the Vicksburg chapter, and to Dr. Keith Bohannon, who read the initial draft of the manuscript and whose insightful comments made this a much better book.

Most important of all, we would be greatly remiss if we did not recognize our families for their patient support, love, and encouragement while we pursued this quest to memorialize the brave men of the Cherokee Artillery and their exploits. *Deo Vindice.*

—Zack Waters and Garry Fisher
December 2018

Appendix

Cherokee Artillery Roster

Abrams, J. E. Enlisted February 17, 1862, he was captured at Vicksburg and paroled at Enterprise, AL. Present on the last roll (April 1864), detailed for extra duty as a blacksmith. (Compiled Service Records, hereafter cited as CSRs)

Abrams, James R. Born December 26, 1833, in Lincoln County, NC. He enrolled in the unit on May 18, 1862. Served in western Mississippi, along the Yazoo River and near Morton, MS. Captured at Salisbury, NC, on April 12, 1865, sent to Camp Chase, OH, and was paroled June 13, 1865. He was thirty-one years old and a resident of Floyd County. He received an indigent soldier pension postwar, listing his occupation as laborer. Died June 11, 1904, and buried at Pleasant Hope Cemetery, in Floyd County. (CSRs; Kinney, Shirley F., *Floyd County Confederate Burials*, Rome, Georgia: n.p., 1993, hereafter cited as Kinney)

Albea, J. C. No CSRs. Listed on "The Martyr's Roll," *Rome Weekly Courier*, August 15, 1877, 3 (hereafter cited as "Martyr") by Connor. Wounded June 23, 1863, at Vicksburg, he died July 9, 1863.

Andrews, A. B. Enlisted at Kingston, GA, on February 1, 1864. Only one CSR card in his file. (CSRs)

Anthony, G. A. C. He enlisted February 17, 1862, at Rome and was present on both CSR cards. Listed as killed at Baker's Creek, MS, May 16, 1863. ("Martyr," CSRs)

Anthony, William E. R. He enlisted June 11, 1861, at Camp Brown. Captured at Champion Hill, and exchanged from Fort Delaware, DE, on July 14, 1863. He apparently failed to return to the unit on time and was arrested as a deserter. Was present on the last roll and every previous card. (CSRs; Edward Jordan Lanham, "Battle of Champion Hill: List of Killed" www.battleofchampionhill.org/killed.htm; hereafter cited as Lanham, GCCH)

Attaway, T. D. Listed as a member in Battey's history. No CSRs.

Atwood, S. J. Enlisted February 24, 1862, and was captured and furloughed at Vicksburg. Present on the last roll (detailed as a saddler). (CSRs)

Avery, J. E. F. Died December 24, 1861, at Greeneville, TN, of pneumonia. No CSRS on this soldier, but his demise is mentioned in Connor's diary. (WOC, 12-24-1861)

Bailey, Thomas J. Very little information is available Bailey, who became ill on August 4, 1862. He was sent to his home in Iredell County, NC, where he "died at home in Asheville, NC" on March 15, 1863. ("Martyr," CSRs)

Baird, Josiah. See Josiah Beard.

Baker, John D. Like P. H. Baker, John D. enlisted on March 1, 1862, at Rome and survived the Vicksburg Campaign. Present on the last roll (April 1864). According to his brother's letter, John threatened to "maul" W. S. Gray at Vicksburg. (Baker collection, KMNBP; CSRs)

Baker, Peyton H. Enlisted at Rome on March 1, 1862, and served through the Siege of Vicksburg. Present on last roll, serving in the infirmary (probably as a nurse). Killed at Resaca, May 15, 1864. ("Martyr," CSRs)

Baker, William H. Baker enlisted May 13, 1862, and was surrendered and paroled at Vicksburg. He arrived home (Floyd County) sick and died on August 2, 1863. His wife, Nannie, tried to get the government to pay money due her husband for service, apparently without success. His letters are on file at Kennesaw Mountain NBP. (CSRs)

Barker, C. L. Enlisted February 30, 1864, and was "absent sick" on his only roll card. (CSRs)

Barnett, Benjamin Franklin. Transferred from the 1st Georgia Cavalry on April 1, 1864. Captured at Resaca, May 15, 1864, and sent to Camp Morton, IN. Died on January 20, 1865, of smallpox, at Camp Morton and buried at Greenlawn Cemetery, Indianapolis, IN. According to a family genealogical history, his father was a large landowner who owned sixty slaves. (CSRs)

Barnett, William. Barnett enlisted August 4, 1863, and was present on the last roll. Detailed as "wagon master." Only two cards are in his record. (CSRs)

Bass, LaFayette J. Bass enlisted on March 1, 1862, in Rome. Captured at Vicksburg, MS, on July 4, 1863, but since he was too sick to be furloughed, Bass was sent to Camp Morton, IN. He died December 3, 1863, of pneumonia, and buried in grave no. 557 at Greenlawn Cemetery, Indianapolis, IN; CSRs)

Battey, Dr. Robert. Listed as an orderly sergeant in Battey, *A History of Rome and Floyd County*. No CSRs.

Beard, Josiah. Listed as present on April 1864 roll, having the day before been granted a furlough by Gen. Johnston. Captured by Federals at Dallas, GA, on May 30, 1864, and sent to Rock Island prison in IL. No further record exists regarding the disposition of Josiah Beard. According to a postwar article, listing this soldier as Josiah Baird, he was captured at New Hope Church and died at Rock Island. (*Atlanta Constitution*, August 5, 1895, 3; CSRs)

Bennett, W. Cooper. Bennett enlisted February 21, 1862, at Rome, and served during the Mississippi Campaign along the Yazoo River and at Morton, MS. Connor diary lists W. C. Bennett as being wounded during Atlanta Campaign. Listed as sick on the last roll at Camp Wright near Macon. A report dated October 11, 1864, had him as a CS hospital in Fort Valley, GA. (Connor Diary; CSRs)

Bennett, William Greene (or J.). This soldier served through the Vicksburg Campaign along the Yazoo River and near Morton, MS. Present on the last roll (April 1864). (CSRs)

Billups, J. Early. Billups joined the Cherokee Artillery on May 18, 1862. Captured at Vicksburg and paroled at Enterprise, AL. His last roll was for July 1863, where he was listed as absent sick. (CSRs)

Blassengame, Sidney A. Enlisted June 11, 1861, and fought through the East Tennessee and Vicksburg campaigns, where he was paroled with Pemberton's army. Captured again at Resaca, he was imprisoned at Camp Morton, IN. On February 26, 1865, he was transferred to City Point, VA, for exchange. No further record was found. (CSRs)

Blount, John M. He enrolled in Yeiser's unit on June 11, 1861, at Camp Brown, listing Calhoun, AL, as his place of residence. On April 1, 1863, Maj. Gen. C. L. Stevenson transferred him to the Nitre and Mining Bureau in Knoxville, TN. He was still detailed to the Nitre Bureau on the last roll. (CSRs)

Boling, J. C. He enlisted May 5, 1862, in the 7th Alabama Cavalry and transferred to Corput's Battery by order of Gen. J. E. Johnston. Listed as sick on the last roll (April 1864). Killed May 15, 1864, at Resaca. ("Martyr"; CSRs)

Bowen, George W. Listed as receiving an appointment as 2nd lieutenant on June 11, 1861. No CSRs or other information. (Jones, *Georgia in the War, 1861–1865* (*GITW*), 50)

Bowling, J. W. Enlisted June 11, 1861, at Camp Brown. According to a note in the CSRs, he was left sick at Murfreesboro, TN. He deserted and joined "the Federal army." (CSRs)

Brice, R. P. Enlisted August 15, 1861, at Rome and transferred back to his original unit (possibly the 8th Georgia Infantry) by the War Department in April 1863. (CSRs)

Brice, William W. Enlisted September 12, 1861, at Lynchburg, VA. Served through Vicksburg Campaign and paroled with Pemberton's army. Captured May 15, 1864, at Resaca and sent to Camp Morton, IN, he died March 5, 1865, of pneumonia. Buried in grave no. 1490 at Greenlawn Cemetery at Indianapolis. ("Martyr"; "Crown Hill"; CSRs)

Brisendine, J. J. Enlisted February 20, 1862, and died April 4, 1863, at Vicksburg, MS, of smallpox. Described in records as a twenty-two-year-old farmer, born in NC, and possibly a resident of Cherokee County, AL. Buried in the Vicksburg National Military Park. Described by a comrade as a good soldier and "a pious Christian." ("Martyr"; VNMP; CSRs)

Brisendine, P. H. Enlisted February 25, 1862, at Rome. Captured at Vicksburg and paroled at Enterprise, MS. Present on last roll, and no further record. (CSRs)

Browne, James Courtney (Reverend). Born in Oconee County, GA, on May 10, 1836. Graduated from Mercer University in 1859 and moved to Cave Spring as principal of the Hearn Academy. Enlisted in Cherokee Artillery in June 1, 1861. Severely wounded at Vicksburg (or Jackson, MS) in June 1863, he returned to Cave Spring and while on furlough married Eva Lila Culbertson. Captured at Salisbury, NC, and sent to Camp Chase, OH, where W. O. Connor reports he and Browne refused to take the oath until no Confederate armies were left in action. Returned to Georgia and received ordination as Baptist minister. Served churches in Georgia and South Carolina. (Boykin, *History of the Baptist Denominations in Georgia*, 2:69–70)

Brown, John Thomas. Born January 31, 1846, at Newnan, GA (and lived at Powellville). Enlisted March 2, 1864, in Van Den Corput's Battery at Dalton, GA, and discharged June 1865, at Atlanta, though CSRs show only that he was present on the last roll (April 1864). Married twice (Minerva Farmer in 1865; she died the same year). Married Jennie Sara Toy, February 22, 1871, and they had five boys and three girls. Died April 10, 1914, and buried Jones Chapel Methodist Church Cemetery. (CSRs; http://files.usgwarchives.net/ga/coweta/obits/brownjt.txt)

Cain, Isaac E. Cain enlisted on June 11, 1861, at Camp Brown and fought through East Tennessee and Vicksburg. He stayed with the Cherokee Artillery to the end and was captured at Salisbury, NC. He took the oath of allegiance on June 13, 1865, at Camp Chase, OH, and was listed as a twenty-six-year-old resident of Cherokee County, AL. (CSRs)

Cain, Joseph. This soldier enlisted June 11, 1861, and is listed as a parolee at Vicksburg. Not much additional information is available on Joseph, but he is listed as present on the last roll. (CSRs)

Caldwell, J. D. Very little information is available on Caldwell. He was captured at Vicksburg and received one of the liberal furloughs offered by Gen. Johnston at Dalton. No further data is available. (CSRs)

Camp, LaFayette Emerson. Camp enlisted late, in August 4, 1863, and followed Van Den Corput's unit until the end. Captured at Salisbury, NC, on April 12, 1865, he wound up, like the rest of his comrades, at Camp Chase, OH. He took the oath June 13, 1865, and Union clerks described him as a nineteen-year-old Floyd County resident. (CSRs)

Carnes, Alex. This soldier enlisted on February 22, 1862, at Rome, and, like most of the unit, was captured at Vicksburg. Carnes was listed as present (sick) on the last roll. (CSRs)

Carroll, William J. Carroll enlisted on June 11, 1861, and served to the end. Captured at Vicksburg, he fought at Chattanooga, Atlanta, and the Nashville Campaign. He was captured at Salisbury, NC, on April 12, 1865. Sent to Camp Chase, OH, he took the oath on June 13, 1865. The clerk described him as a twenty-seven-year-old from Floyd County with fair complexion and hair and blue eyes. (CSRs)

Catlett, William A. One of the soldiers who joined the battery in 1864, (April 1864), Catlett hailed from Alabama, and the soldiers nicknamed him "Bud." He was shot through the chest on July 26, 1864, and killed. ("Martyr"; CSRs; WOC)

Champion, Daniel. The records on Daniel are sparse. He enrolled with the unit on September 8, 1862, at Cumberland Gap, TN, and was listed as present, but sick, on the last roster (April 1864). (CSRs)

Champion, James H. Champion enlisted on September 12, 1861, at Lynchburg, VA, and served through the siege of Vicksburg. Captured at Resaca, May 15,

1864, after a large piece of shrapnel hit him in the upper torso, Champion was imprisoned at Camp Douglas, IL. He died January 7, 1865, of gangrene, and is buried at Oak Woods Cemetery, Chicago, IL. (CSRs; Stalling)

Chapman, W. B. This soldier enlisted on February 18, 1862, and served through the Vicksburg Campaign. After being paroled at Enterprise, AL, Chapman returned to duty and the clerk recorded him as "present" on the last roll (April 1864). (CSRs)

Cobourn, Erasmus D. He enlisted April 19, 1862, at Rome and was captured at Vicksburg. He is listed as present on the last roll. Connor diary lists him as being wounded during Atlanta Campaign. (WOC; CSRs)

Connor, Wesley Olin. Born June 18, 1841, in the Anderson District, SC, Connor was author of a valuable diary of the Cherokee Artillery during 1861–1865. He also wrote letters and articles giving valuable insight into the unit's history. He enlisted June 11, 1861, and surrendered with Pemberton's army at Vicksburg. He was captured again at Salisbury, NC, on April 12, 1865, and released on oath from Camp Chase, OH, June 13, 1865. He served as superintendent of Georgia School for the Deaf at Cave Spring for many years. Died February 18, 1920, and buried at Cave Spring Cemetery, Floyd County. (UGA website; CSRs)

Cooper, D. Died at Cumberland Gap, TN, in 1862. No further information. ("Martyr")

Cooper, William J. Cooper enlisted June 12, 1862, at Rome and was then detailed at a bugler. He was part of Pemberton's army surrendered at Vicksburg. During the Atlanta Campaign, he allowed himself to be "captured" at Adairsville on May 18, 1864, and was sent to Rock Island, IL. Two months later he enrolled in the U.S. Navy. (CSRs)

Couey, Isham Houze [J. D., or Isaac H. Coney]. This soldier, or his family, applied for pensions in Georgia and Texas, but confusion over his name in the records caused considerable problems. He was serving in April 12, 1865, when the battery was captured at Salisbury, NC, and Union troops sent him to Camp Chase, OH. He took the oath on June 13, 1865, and the clerk described him as a nineteen-year-old resident of Floyd County, GA. (CSRs)

Couey, Joseph S. [Joseph S. Coney]. Couey enlisted in Yeiser's unit on September 12, 1861, at Lynchburg, VA. Was shown on the last roll as on furlough until May 1864, by order of Gen. J. E. Johnston. (CSRs)

Couey, William C. [William C. Coney, W. Claiborne Coney]. He enlisted on March 1, 1862, at Cave Spring, and served at Vicksburg, Chattanooga, Atlanta, Nashville, and finally fell into Union hands again at Salisbury, NC, on April 12, 1865. He took the oath on June 13, 1865, and was listed as twenty-four years of age and a Floyd County resident. (CSRs)

Cutter, March N. Born April 17, 1816, and died April 22, 1877. No CSR found for Cutter, but he is listed as a member of Van Den Corput's unit in Myrtle Hill Cemetery List.

Davidson, David. Listed on the only record card as a prisoner at Camp Douglas, IL, after being captured at Resaca. (CSRs)

Dean, Henry W. Dean enlisted June 6, 1862, and was captured at the Battle of Champion Hill. He was exchanged July 14, 1863, from Fort Delaware, DE, and was on duty February 1864. There is no further record of his service. (CSRs; Lanham)

Dempsey, A. J. Dempsey enlisted May 19, 1862, and served during the Siege of Vicksburg along the Yazoo River and Morton, MS. He was serving as a teamster for the unit on the last roll. (CSRs)

Dempsey, Caleb M. Dempsey enrolled in the battery on February 12, 1862, at Rome and attained the rank of lieutenant. After being furloughed following Vicksburg, where he received "a gun shot wound in the breast, ball entering in front of breast, breaking the breast bone." After spending considerable time in the Bell Hospital in Rome, he was well enough to rejoin the battery. Captured at Salisbury, NC, on April 12, 1865, and took the oath on June 13, 1865. A Union clerk described him as a twenty-six-year-old resident of Floyd County. W. O. Connor, Felix Corput, and J. C. Marin witnessed his application for a pension. (CSRs; GA pension)

Donahoo [Dunahoe], W. S. Corporal Donahoo enlisted June 11, 1861, and fought in East Tennessee and the Vicksburg Campaign. After being exchanged he was detailed to the Etowah Iron works by order of the War Department. No further records. (CSRs)

Duke, George W. Captured at Resaca, May 15, 1864, and sent to Camp Morton, IN. There he died on June 2, 1864, of inflammation of the lungs, and buried in grave no. 900 at Greenlawn Cemetery in Indianapolis, IN. ("Martyr"; CSRs; "Crown Hill")

Duke, James Lumpkin. Born October 12, 1834 (Walton Co., GA), married Mazary Duke (a cousin), in December 1860. Childhood injury ("thrown from a horse during childhood and dislocated one hip causing a lifetime handicap") gave him a military deferment, but he enlisted in the Cherokee Artillery in 1863. Apparently fought at Chattanooga and Missionary Ridge. On February 1, 1864, he was "honorably discharged from service" due to wounds and "not able [fit] for duty." Active member of UCV Camp #368 (Floyd County, GA) and attended several Cherokee Artillery reunions. Died March 12, 1916, and was buried at Pleasant Valley North Cemetery. (*The Heritage of Floyd County, Georgia, 1833–1999*, 69; CSRs; McKinney)

Duke, W. C. Listed only on Connor roster.

Dunn, James A. Dunn, a resident of Clark County, Arkansas, enlisted in the Cherokee Artillery on October 7, 1863. He was severely wounded at Resaca, May 15, 1864, and shuttled between various CSA hospitals. The Hood hospital in Cuthbert, GA (February 13, 1865) reported Dunn had an ulcer from a gunshot wound, which also broke his fibula. Gangrene developed later, but he survived. Union troops captured him in Central Georgia at war's end, but the youngster refused to take the oath until August 22, 1865. (CSRs)

Eddings, W. E. Eddings enlisted March 12, 1862, at Rome. He was surrendered at Vicksburg with Pemberton's army, and was present on the last roll (April 1864). (CSRs)

Evans, W. E. This soldier enlisted May 4, 1862, at Calhoun, AL. He has only one card in his service records. (CSRs)

Flemister, Robert S. Born in 1832 and died November 21, 1898. No CSR has been found on this soldier, but he was listed as part of "Yeiser's Artillery" in the Myrtle Hill burial list.

Foster, J. F. One of the sadder stories of this list, Foster enlisted January 29, 1863, as a substitute for merchant Bernard Kohn. Killed in a skirmish near Dear (Deer) Creek, MS, the forty-year-old laborer lasted less than three months. His wife, Cornelia, spent months trying (apparently unsuccessfully) to get the money due him for his service. ("Martyr"; CSRs)

Franks (or, Frances), Alexander. Franks enrolled in Yeiser's unit on July 1, 1861, at Nashville, TN. He was captured at Champion Hill, took the oath of allegiance, and enlisted in Battery A, Pennsylvania Light Artillery. (CSRs; Lanham, GCCH)

Fricks, B. F. No record of this soldier found. He signed W. O. Connor's application for a pension, averring that he enlisted on May 1864 and was with the unit at Salisbury, NC, but escaped from the Union troops. (GA pension files)

Fricks (Frix), W. C. This soldier enlisted at Rome on September 1, 1862, and fought in East Tennessee and Vicksburg. After the parole he had difficulty recovering his health, and the last roll (April 1864) listed him as "Sick in the hospital." (CSRs)

Fry (Fray, Frey), Solomon. Fry enlisted on July 1, 1861, at Nashville, TN. Union troops captured him at Champion Hill, and he took the oath, enlisting in Battery A, Pennsylvania Light Artillery. (CSRs; Lanham)

Gaines, William H. This soldier enlisted on April 10, 1864, at Newnan, GA. He was captured at Salisbury, NC, and paroled June 13, 1865. Described as being eighteen years old, he requested transportation to his home in Coweta County, GA. (CSRs)

Gaston, Wiley. Virtually nothing is found in this soldier's records except that he was captured at Salisbury, NC, on April 12, 1865. He took the oath on June 13, 1865, and was described as a twenty-one-year-old resident of Cass (now Bartow) County, Georgia. (CSRs)

Gattis, Charles M. Born April 23, 1845, Charles enlisted March 3, 1862, and served through the East Tennessee and Vicksburg campaigns. Awarded a furlough by Johnston at Dalton, he was scooped up by Yankees on May 23, 1864, at Euharlee Creek. Sent to Rock Island, IL, he refused to take the oath of allegiance and was transferred to Fort Delaware, DE, for exchange on March 2, 1865. Married to Elisa Jennie Hunt on September 29, 1870. He died on October 18, 1911, and was interred at Old Antioch Cemetery, Floyd County. (CSRs; McKinney; GA pension files)

Gattis, C. W. CSA recruiting officers enrolled Gattis on March 3, 1862, at Rome. He was part of Pemberton's army that surrendered at Vicksburg and due to ill health received an appointment to the ordinance department. It did no good. He died March 2, 1864, at Rome (on sick leave), from "sickness contracted during the siege of Vicksburg." ("Martyr"; CSRs)

Gattis, Sidney Hampton. One of the soldiers who enlisted on June 11, 1861, at Camp Brown, serving faithfully to the end of the war. Captured at Vicksburg, he received a furlough by order of Gen. Johnston at Dalton, GA, in early 1864. Returning to Van Den Corput's Battery with several comrades, he was captured at Euharlee Creek, GA, on May 23, 1864. Sent to Rock Island, IL, he endured the bitter winter 1864 and was sent to Fort Delaware, DE, on March 6, 1865, for exchange. Moved to Collins County, Texas, in 1893, and died August 26, 1913. Buried in Van Alstyne Cemetery at Van Alstyne, Texas. His wife applied for a pension in Texas post-war. "Collins Chronicles," Summer 1997/98, 97; CSRs)

Gattis, W. H. Gattis enlisted on April 11, 1864, at Rome and has only one service card. (CSRs)

Gilley, John. One of several Cherokee County, AL, residents who enlisted in Yeiser's unit, Gilley was enrolled June 11, 1861, and saw duty in the Siege of Vicksburg. He served for a while as teamster for a forage wagon, and was captured on April 12, 1865, at Salisbury, NC. He was thirty-three years old in 1865. (CSRs)

Gottis, W. H. See W. H. Gattis.

Graham, H. No record of this soldier found.

Graves, O. H. No record of this soldier found.

Gray, W. S. Gray enlisted August 14, 1862, at Rome, and served through the Vicksburg Campaign, being paroled at Enterprise, AL. Acted as clerk at Vicksburg, and became the butt of cruel jokes. "He has lost friends in our company," according to W. S. Baker letters. Detailed to the infirmary corps on March 25, 1864, (probably as a nurse) and was present on the last roll. Killed in action at Resaca on May 15, 64. ("Martyr"; Baker collection, KMNBP; CSRs)

Gresham, Henry M. [one card as K. Grisham]. Enrolled in the battery August 27, 1863, and was listed as sick in hospital in 12, 1863. Captured at Salisbury, NC, he was a nineteen-year-old Floyd County resident who took the oath June 13, 1865. (CSRs)

Griffin, Harvell Dempsey. Born in Taliaferro County, GA, in 1846. Living with parents in Cave Spring in 1860, and enlisted March 5, 1864, transferring from King's (Polk County) Battery. He was 5' 9", with blue eyes, light hair, and fair complexion. Captured at Salisbury, NC, sent to Camp Chase, OH, and was released June 13, 1865. Married Louisa J. Burns, February 15, 1870 and a second time to Jannine ___ [surname unknown], October 22, 1872. Moved to Tarrant County, TX, in 1895, and applied for a Confederate pension in 1922. He died two years later. Buried in Bourland Cemetery, Tarrant County, TX. (CSRs; "Civil War Veterans of Northeast Texas" [http://www.txfwgs.org/TARRANT_COUNTY/military/civil_war_vets.htm])

Griffin, Thomas. This Thomas Griffin enlisted June 11, 1861, at Camp Brown and fought in East Tennessee and in Mississippi, where he was detailed to the Yazoo River and Morton, MS. Captured at Salisbury, NC, he took the oath of allegiance on June 13, 1865. Union clerks described him as a twenty-five-year-old Floyd County resident with fair complexion, red hair, and brown eyes. (CSRs)

Griffin, Thomas J. Thomas enrolled in Van Den Corput's Battery on March 5, 1864, at Dalton, GA, and was captured April 12, 1865, at Salisbury, NC. Taken to Camp Chase, OH, he took the oath on May 13, 1865. The clerks described Griffin as nineteen years old, with fair complexion, black hair, and brown eyes. He died at the Georgia Confederate Soldier's Home in November 1911. He may have hailed from Coosa County, AL. ("T. J. Griffin," *Atlanta Georgian and News*, November 20, 1911, 5; CSRs)

Hale, Kenton. Hale joined the unit as a bugler on March 1, 1862, but the War Department detailed him to work on the Rome Railroad on September 23, 1863. No further records found. (CSRs)

Hamby, Samuel C. Hamby enlisted July 10, 1862, at Rome and was captured at Vicksburg. Captured again at Resaca on May 15, 1864, he was sent to Camp Morton in Indianapolis, IN. He died there on February 8, 1865, of inflammation of the lungs and was buried at Greenlawn Cemetery, Indianapolis. ("Crown Hill"; CSRs)

Hamil, Wilson L. Sergeant Hamil joined Stovall's battery on June 11, 1861, and served through the Vicksburg Campaign. No further records available. (CSRs)

Hammett, John L. Hammett enlisted on June 11, 1861, and surrendered with the CSA army at Vicksburg. Captured again at Salisbury, NC, after the capitulation of Lee's army, he was sent to Camp Chase, OH. He took the oath on June 13, 1865, and was described as a twenty-one-year-old resident of Fulton County. (CSRs)

Hargis, Wylie. Connor roster; no CSRs located for this soldier.

Harrison, John. Harrison enlisted August 18, 1863, at Rome. His record noted the government owed him a $50.00 signing bounty, but he was listed as sick at Cave Spring on the last roll. Died at home in 1864. ("Martyr"; CSRs)

Hatch, William B. Hatch enlisted in the battery on February 10, 1862, at Rome and fought through the Vicksburg Campaign. The last records show him as on detached service as a teamster. (CSRs)

Hawkins, A. H. No CSRs located on this soldier.

Henderson, J. M. Born on July 4, 1827, Henderson enlisted in the unit on July 23, 1862, at Rome. Captured at Champion Hill, he was sent to Fort Delaware, DE, and exchanged back to the Confederate Army July 3, 1863. Listed as absent at hospital on last roll. Died March 11, 1896, and buried at the Unity Cemetery, Floyd County. (Lanham; Kinney; CSRs)

Henderson, John O. [D.] This soldier enlisted in the Cherokee Artillery on June 27, 1862, at Rome. Was on detached duty along the Yazoo River during the Mississippi siege, but was captured, on April 12, 1865, at Salisbury, NC. Took the oath at Camp Chase (June 13, 1865) and described as thirty-five-year-old Floyd County resident. (CSRs)

Hicks, J. G. See J. G. Hix.

Hills, Jefferson P. Hills was a Paulding County, GA, native who enlisted in Van Den Corput's unit on February 22, 1862. He served through all the battery's major battles, and was captured at Salisbury, NC, on April 12, 1865. Taken to Camp Chase, he took the oath on June 13, 1865. He was twenty-two years of age when released from the military prison. (CSRs)

Hix, A. No records found for this soldier. (CSRs)

Hix, Fontaine T. [Hicks]. Hix joined the unit on June 11, 1861, and fought through the Vicksburg battles. The last roll, dated April 1864, noted Hix was absent, "sick in hospital." Died at Fort Valley, GA, in 1864. ("Martyr"; CSRs)

Hix, J. G. One of the small group of Rebels that enlisted in Yeiser's unit at Lynchburg, VA, on September 12, 1861. Fought during the Siege of Vicksburg, but there are no further records after July 4, 1863. (CSRs)

Hogue [Hoge], William S. Hogue enlisted at Camp Brown on June 11, 1861, and rose to the rank of 2nd lieutenant (dated December 31, 1862). Captured at Vicksburg, he commanded the Cherokee Artillery during the 1864 Tennessee Campaign after Captain Van Den Corput was wounded at Jonesboro, GA. In February 1865, he sent a letter of resignation that was quickly accepted by Maj. Gen. Stevenson. Hogue surrendered May 24, 1865, at Talladega, AL. (CSRs; Jones, *GITW*, 50)

Holland, John S. John enlisted June 11, 1861, at Camp Brown, rising to the rank of orderly sergeant. Captured at Vicksburg, he fought through the Atlanta Campaign until severely wounded on July 22, 1864. Retired to the Invalid Corps in Athens, GA, on September 29, 1864. (CSRs)

Holt, R. A. [H.] Holt enlisted June 11, 1861, and is listed as "absent sick" on most rolls. (CSRs)

Huffman, John H. Huffman enlisted April 1, 1864, at Dalton. Died at Columbia, TN, in November 1864. ("Martyr"; CSRs)

Hume, Isaac Wilson. Born May 3, 1836. Hume enlisted June 11, 1861, and fought through East Tennessee and Vicksburg. While in Mississippi he wrote a letter requesting to be released from the army to build wagons at Macon. The request seems to have been rejected, and Hume attained the rank of sergeant. Captured at Salisbury, NC, on April 12, 1865, and sent to Camp Chase, OH, where he took the oath on June 13, 1865. He died July 11, 1880, and is buried in John Hume Cemetery (Floyd County, GA). (CSRs; Battey, *A History of Rome and Floyd County*, p. 626)

Hunt, Dennis H. Hunt enlisted September 1, 1862, at Cumberland Gap, TN, and served through the Siege of Vicksburg. He deserted to the Federals on July 3, 1864, at Marietta, GA, claiming to be a loyal U.S. citizen who joined the "rebel" army to avoid conscription. Sent to Camp Douglas, IL, he enlisted in the 6th U.S. Volunteers on March 26, 1865. (CSRs)

Hutchings, G. A. See G. A. Hutchins.

Hutchings, Thomas. Hutchings enlisted January 31, 1863. Only a couple of cards are in his file, which note that this soldier was owed a $50.00 signing bonus. May be the "Hutchens" listed as killed at Champion Hill in Connor diary. ("Martyr"; CSRs)

Hutchins, G. A. Enlisted September 12, 1861, at Lynchburg, VA, serving through the East Tennessee and Vicksburg. He attained the rank of corporal and was present on all rolls. (CSRs)

Hydle, W. J. Hydle served through the Vicksburg Campaign, but died February 15, 1864, at Kingston, GA, shot by unit members sent out to arrest him as a deserter. (Connor diary; CSRs; see article in *Memphis Appeal*, February 25, 1864, regarding incident)

Jackson, N. P. Enlisted August 23, 1862, and served through the Vicksburg Campaign as a clerk of the quartermaster corps. The last record shows Jackson received clothing in October 1864 at Augusta, GA. (CSRs)

Johnson [Johnston], Alexander. This soldier enlisted April 9, 1862, and served through the Siege of Vicksburg, and was captured April 12, 1865, at Salisbury, NC. Sent to Camp Chase, OH, he took the oath on June 13, 1865. Described as thirty-seven years old, 6'1" tall, with fair complexion, light hair, and gray eyes. (CSRs)

Johnston [Johnson], Eber Mitchell. Born June 14, 1831, in Franklin County, GA, and enlisted June 11, 1861. Commanded gun crew (during the Vicksburg Campaign) serving along the Yazoo River and at Morton, MS. Sergeant Johnston was captured at Salisbury, NC, and took the oath of allegiance at Camp Chase, OH. He was described as thirty-four years old and a Floyd County resident. Died June 13, 1910 and buried Oakland Cemetery, Floyd County. (CSRs; Kinney)

Johnson [Johnston], R. W. This shadowy figure enlisted on February 18, 1862, at Cave Spring and was captured at Vicksburg. No further record. (CSRs)

Johnson [Johnston], W. This soldier enlisted April 9, 1864, and was present on the last roll (a few days later). (CSRs)

Jones, Benjamin Franklin. Born June 20, 1831, in Gwinnett County, GA. Appointed brigade quartermaster. Postwar, he headed the waterworks system in Kansas City, MO. (*National Cyclopedia of American Biography*, p. 171)

Jones, R. ("Reps") M. Sergeant Jones enlisted June 11, 1861, and served through the fight at Baker's Creek and the Siege of Vicksburg. He commanded a section with a twenty-four-pounder along the Mississippi River. Often detailed as a clerk during 1864, he was placed on certified disability detail. (WOC diary; VNBP records; CSRs)

Kent, Thomas J. Information on Kent is sketchy, but he was nineteen years old when captured at Salisbury, NC. Took the oath on June 13, 1865, and apparently hailed from Floyd County. (CSRs)

Kerr, John R. Kerr, born November 25, 1844, at Yorkville, SC, enlisted when he was sixteen years old (June 11, 1861) and served through the entire war. Part of the army of Vicksburg that Pemberton surrendered, he was captured April 12, 1865, at Salisbury, NC. Sent to Camp Chase, OH, he took the oath June 13, 1865, and was listed as a resident of Floyd County. He died July 18, 1927 (age 83) and was buried in Polk County, GA. (GA pensions; CSRs; Kinney)

King, (Elzaphon) Elzathan, R. King originally organized and commanded the King's Battery Mountaineers (Co. D, 14th Georgia Artillery Battalion) from Polk County. The unit was disbanded in May 8, 1863, when Braxton Bragg assigned virtually the entire unit to Lumsden's Alabama Battery. King served as a private in Van Den Corput's Battery through 1864–1865, and was captured at Salisbury, NC. Imprisoned at Camp Chase, OH, he took the oath on June 13, 1865. Described as thirty-nine years of age, with gray eyes and dark hair and complexion. Died August 10, 1904, and buried at Cave Spring Cemetery, Floyd County. (Kinney; CSRs; C. A. Evans, *Confederate Military History–Georgia*, vol. 6 (Atlanta, Georgia: Confederate Publishing Co, 1899) 199.

King, John T. The Federals captured King twice—at Vicksburg and Salisbury, NC, on April 12, 1865. Sent to Camp Chase, OH, and took the oath on June 13, 1865. Described as twenty-seven years old, with dark hair and complexion and blue eyes, he was a resident of Floyd County. (CSRs)

King, William V. The Paulding County, GA, native joined the unit on June 12, 1862, and was captured at Champion Hill. The records are somewhat confusing, but he apparently was exchanged from Fort Delaware, DE, on July 14, 1863. He then deserted and took the oath of allegiance on October 24, 1864, at Louisville, KY, agreeing to remain north of the Ohio River until the war ended. (CSRs; Lanham)

Kohn, Bernard. Enlisted on June 11, 1861, and discharged January 28, 1863, by furnishing a substitute (J. F. Foster). (CSRs)

Knight, Legit. Knight enlisted March 2, 1862, at Rome, and was part of Pemberton's army that surrendered at Vicksburg. Present on all rolls. (CSRs)

Knight, William M. Knight enlisted on April 4, 1864, at Dalton, GA. Captured December 28, 1864, at Egypt Station, MS. Imprisoned at Alton, Illinois Military Prison, and died February 9, 1865, of smallpox. Buried at Confederate Cemetery Alton. (CSRs; "Crown Hill")

Lamkin, G. W. F. The thirty-five-year-old merchant was a Floyd County native who enlisted September 2, 1862, at Calhoun. Given a Certificate of Disability at Warrenton, MS, due to disease of the lungs (likely tuberculosis). (CSRs)

Lancaster, J. L. Transferred to Van Den Corput's battery in early 1864, from the 7th Alabama Cavalry. One card only on Lancaster, which lists him as "sick" in April 1864. (CSRs)

Laster [Lasiter], Angus M. Born in NC August 14, 1846, and joined the battery on June 16, 1862, at Rome. Captured at Vicksburg. He became separated from his command at Resaca and captured at Euharlee Creek on May 23, 1864. Sent to Rock

Island Prison in IL but transferred for exchange on March 13, 1865. Returned home and married Elizabeth Pope on August 26, 1866, raising six boys and four girls. Occupation listed as farmer. Died July 20, 1925 and buried in the Oakland Cemetery, Floyd County. (CSRs; "The Life of A. M. Lasiter…" (Typescript, Floyd County Library, Special Collections.)

Laster [Lasiter], James C. Enlisted April 11, 1864, at Rome, and captured at Salisbury, NC, April 12, 1865. Transferred to Camp Chase, OH, he took the oath on June 13, 1865. Described as eighteen years of age, standing 5'7", with dark complexion and hair and blue eyes. He was a resident of Floyd County. (CSRs)

Leary [Lary and Larry], Archibald C. Enlisted at Rome on February 17, 1862, and served with the battery at Vicksburg. Captured near Resaca on May 14, 1864, and sent to Rock Island Prison, IL. No further disposition available. (CSRs)

Leary [Lary and Larry], George P. No material is available on time or place of enlistment. The Federals captured Leary at Rome on September 2, 1864. Sent to Camp Douglas, IL, he mustered into U.S. service [5th U.S. Volunteers] on April 14, 1865. (CSRs)

Leazer, Robert N. Leazer enlisted June 14, 1862, at Rome, and was part of Pemberton's army at Vicksburg. Captured again on July 22, 1864, near Atlanta, he was sent to Camp Chase, OH. The Union commandant ordered his release on May 14, 1865. (CSRs)

Lemmon, Jefferson. Born December 24, 1846, in Missouri. Enlisted in 5th Missouri Infantry (CSA). In 1863, transferred to Cherokee Artillery as a hospital steward, where his brother was a surgeon. Attended medical school postwar and was later a physician in Polk County, Missouri (from 1874).

Lesson, Thomas Wells. Enlisted in Van Den Corput's unit on February 14, 1863, at Rome, but apparently resided in Cherokee County, AL. In April 1864, he transferred to the 7th Alabama Cavalry, by order of Gen. J. E. Johnston. Lesson served to the end, surrendering June 3, 1865, at Talladega, AL. (CSRs)

Long, James H. James was part of the unit when it was captured at Vicksburg. He was captured on the retreat from Nashville near Brentwood, TN, and sent to Camp Chase, OH. He was paroled May 2, 1865. (CSRs)

Lott, Lacy [Lacey] H. Lott enlisted in the Cherokee Artillery on June 14, 1862, in Rome. Captured at both Vicksburg and Salisbury, NC, on April 12, 1865. Sent to Camp Chase, OH, he took the oath of allegiance on May 13, 1865. Described as 5'11" tall, with a fair complexion, dark hair and blue eyes, Lott was a thirty-two-year-old resident of Floyd County. (CSRs)

Love, David G. Enlisted February 27, 1862, at Rome, and served at various hospitals in Georgia (Rome and Augusta) and Tennessee (Knoxville) as a nurse. Detailed to quartermaster in Augusta, GA, on October 31, 1864 (last roll). (CSRs)

Lovelady, J. J. Enlisted February 25, 1862, at Rome. Present on all subsequent rolls. (CSRs)

Lovelady, J. M. Lovelady enlisted on September 25, 1863, at Marietta, GA. A month later he deserted to the Federals at Chattanooga, TN. Forwarded to Louisville, KY, he took the oath of allegiance on November 27, 1863, agreeing to stay north of the Ohio River. (CSRs [two cards listed as M. J. Lovelady])

Loyd [and Lloyd], J. J. Loyd served with the unit in East Tennessee and was captured at Vicksburg. He was killed in a firefight at Atlanta on August 17, 1864. ("Martyr"; CSRs [one card as J. G. Loyd]; WOC)

Loyd [Lloyd], William M. Enlisted March 4, 1862, and was killed "by a minie ball" on June 27, 1863, at Vicksburg. Connor noted, "Another good soldier lost to the Confederacy." ("Martyr"; CSRs; WOC)

Lumpkin, John T. John joined the Cherokee Artillery on June 11, 1861, and was killed at Champion Hill on May 16, 1863. ("Martyr"; CSRs; WOC)

Lumpkin, Pleasant J. Enlisted June 11, 1861, achieved the rank of corporal, and was captured at Vicksburg. Present on all rolls, he died in action on August 17, 1864. ("Martyr"; CSRs; WOC)

Madday (or Maddry), William Benton. Born November 28, 1828, and enlisted June 14, 1862, at Rome. Served as the teamster for the battery's forage wagon. Captured at Vicksburg and Salisbury, NC. Took the oath of allegiance June 13, 1865, at Camp Chase, OH. Described as a thirty-seven-year-old with dark complexion and hair and blue eyes. He was a resident of Floyd County and died June 20, 1902 in Louisiana. (CSRs)

Magnus, [J.] Solomon. Enlisted March 1, 1864, at Kingston, GA. KIA at Resaca. Jewish soldier. Had moved to U.S. from Germany in 1849 or 1850 and was described as "a brave soldier for the South." ("Martyr"; Sullivan, "Magnus: A Father's Death and a Son's Redemption"; CSRs)

Marbot, J. L. One CSR card. See Joshua L. Marbut.

Marbut, Joshua L. Enlisted April 9, 1864, at Rome, and captured twenty-one days later at Dallas, GA. Sent to Rock Island Prison, IL, and "discharged" June 6, 1864. (The CSRs show no record that Marbut took the oath or was exchanged. The meaning of "discharged," as used here, remains a mystery.) (CSRs)

Marona, James [or Joseph] L. (also spelled Marina). Born in SC, Marona was a thirty-five-year-old laborer when he enlisted June 18, 1862, at Cave Spring. He died of "congestive chills" in Smith County, MS, on July 20, 1863. Described as having dark complexion and hair and gray eyes. Married to Martha W., who filed a pension claim in Etowah County, AL, after 1910. ("Martyr"; CSRs)

Martin, John C. Enlisted June 27, 1862, at Rome. Surrendered at Vicksburg and paroled at Enterprise, AL. Fought through the Atlanta and Nashville campaigns and again captured at Salisbury, NC, on April 12, 1865. Took the oath at Camp Chase, OH, on June 13, 1865. Became a legend of the unit by leading a foraging group that "appropriated" a citizen's hog at night in January 1865 in MS. At 5'10" and twenty-four years old, he had dark complexion, hair, and eyes and was a resident of Floyd County. (CSRs)

Mason, James. No CSRs on this person.

Mathis, George H. Born on October 18, 1841, and died in mid-1882. He enlisted June 11, 1861, and was present on all rolls. Captured at Vicksburg and paroled at Enterprise, AL. Captured again at Salisbury, NC, on April 12, 1865, Mathis was taken to Camp Chase and signed the oath of allegiance June 13, 1865. Described as twenty-four years old, 5'10½" and a resident of Floyd County. Possibly buried at Mizpah Methodist Church in Floyd County. (Rootsweb; CSRs)

Mathis, Richard Marion (Called Marion). Born May 1, 1842, in Cobb County, GA, and enlisted June 11, 1861. Fought at Vicksburg and paroled July 9, 1863. Captured April 13, 1865, at Salisbury, NC, and sent to Camp Chase, OH. Took the oath June 13, 1865. Described as having dark complexion, black hair, and hazel eyes. Married Frances Annie Elizabeth Williams, February 18, 1866. He was active in the Methodist church. Died in Rome, May 8, 1910, and is buried at Oakland Cemetery in Rome. (CSRs; Kinney)

McCurry, A. C. Enlisted June 11, 1861, from Floyd County. A corporal, McCurry was killed in a firefight near Jackson, MS, on July 13, 1863. ("Martyr"; CSRs. He was the subject of an interesting article, "Unknown Confederate Grave," *Greenville (MS) Times*, November 10, 1900, 2)

McCurry, Eleazor Newton. Born 1843, in Floyd County, GA, and enlisted February 21, 1862, at Rome. Served during the Vicksburg Campaign along the Yazoo River and at Camp Morton. Captured at Salisbury, NC, on April 12, 1865, and sent to Camp Chase. Took the oath on June 13, 1865, and was described as a twenty-two-year-old resident of Floyd County with fair complcxion, dark hair, and blue eyes. He listed his occupation as carpentry and farming on pension form. Died 1912 and buried at Salmon Cemetery, Floyd County, GA. (CSRs; Kinney; GA pension)

McCurry, J. P. No CSRs located for this person.

McKinnore, Thomas. No CSRs located for this person.

McWhorter, Daniel. Died of measles in September 1861 at Lynchburg, VA. ("Martyr"; no CSRs)

McWhorter, Hank. No CSRs located for this person.

McWhorter, Meshack Lowery. Born in 1835, place unknown. Captured at Vicksburg and granted sick leave March 26, 1864. Appointed 2nd lieutenant on April 1, 1862, and 1st lieutenant on December 31, 1862. Lieutenant McWhorter briefly commanded the battery during the Atlanta Campaign. Listed as absent sick on last roll. He died November 14, 1919, and was buried in the Greenwood Cemetery (Polk County, GA). (*Confederates Buried in Polk County, Georgia Cemeteries* (http://files.usgwarchives.net/ga/polk/cemeteries/confederates.txt); CSRs; Jones, *GITW*, 50)

McWhorter, William R. (or P.). Enlisted February 15, 1864, at Kingston, GA. Captured April 12, 1865, at Salisbury, NC, and sent to Camp Chase, OH. Took the oath June 13, 1865. Described as 5'11" with fair complexion, dark hair, and blue eyes. Listed as a resident of Floyd County. (CSRs)

Merritt, R. W. B. Merritt enlisted June 11, 1861, and served as a corporal. Captured at Vicksburg, he was present when the last roll was taken. Transferred to "Gartrell's Georgians" and served with that unit until Nathan Bedford Forrest surrendered at Gainesville, AL, in May 1865. (Towers memoir; Zack Waters Collection, Rome, Georgia; CSRs)

Merritt, William. No CSRs on this person.

Millen, Daniel (or David). Enlisted June 11, 1861, achieving the rank of sergeant. Captured at Vicksburg and again at Salisbury, NC, on April 12, 1865. Taken to Camp Chase, OH, he signed the oath on June 13, 1865. Described as a twenty-five-year-old resident of Floyd County with dark complexion and hair and gray eyes. (CSRs)

Miller, Daniel. One card in CSRs. See Daniel Millen.

Moore, John W. A native of Estill County, KY, Moore enlisted in the Georgia battery on August 15, 1862, at Tazewell, TN. He was captured at Vicksburg and apparently deserted to the Union. He was twenty-three years old and listed as 6'1" with dark hair and eyes. He was held briefly, and released, from the Gratiot Street Prison in St. Louis, MO, in August 1863. (CSRs)

Moore, William Jack. Enlisted March 3, 1862, at Rome. He served as a teamster for the battery's wagons during the Vicksburg Campaign. After being paroled, he returned to the unit. He is listed as sick in the hospital December 20, 1863, the last roll in his CSR. (CSRs)

Morgan, DeWitt C. Morgan enlisted March 4, 1862, and died August 9, 1863, of smallpox at the hospital in Clear Point, SC. He was born in DeKalb County (GA) and was a twenty-five-year-old former medical student when he passed away. Morgan's mother petitioned the Confederate government, apparently without success, several times for money owed to her son for his service. ("Martyr"; CSRs)

Mullen, James Edward. Born in Philadelphia, PA, on October 5, 1836, and died September 22, 1906. No record of service for Mullen, but he is listed as member of the Cherokee Artillery on Myrtle Hill soldiers' list. Buried at Myrtle Hill Cemetery in Rome, GA. (Myrtle Hill Burial list [http://www.interment.net/data/us/ga/floyd/myrtle-hill-cemetery/index.htm])

New, N. C. New enlisted June 11, 1862, at Camp Brown. On February 5, 1862, he requested leave to go home (to Carroll County, GA) as his father had died and there was "no one but women to settle it [the estate]." The request was approved. New was often on sick report and was in the Augusta Hospital on October 8, 1864 (the last report). (CSRs)

Newton, David Oliver. Born August 4, 1837, in Wytheville, VA. Enlisted in Cherokee Artillery on April 15, 1861. Was in all the battles of the unit from East Tennessee through Nashville. On the way to Mississippi (1865) took "a kind of French furlough" and went home to check on his family. Was at Athens, GA, on his way to rejoin the battery, when he learned the war had ended and his comrades had been captured at Salisbury, NC. Lived in Hico, TX, postwar. (Yeary, 566–67. Mamie

Yeary, *Reminiscences of the Boys in Gray: 1861–1865* (Dallas, TX: Smith & Lamar, 1912, 566-67; CSRs)

Newton, Lewis H. Enlisted June 11, 1861, at Camp Brown. Captured at Vicksburg and present on all subsequent rolls. Killed at Resaca, Georgia. Brother of D. O. Newton. ("Martyr"; Yeary, *Boys in Gray*, 567; CSRs)

Newton, William A. Died of camp fever in East Tennessee on May 24, 1862, at Tazewell, TN. Brother of D. O. and L. H. Newton. ("Martyr"; Yeary, *Boys in Gray*, 567)

Palmer, John. No CSRs found. (Connor roster)

Panchen, John Seymore. Born in 1837, and an early volunteer with unit. Accepted the company flag from Savannah Stillwell at Camp Brown, and popular with the soldiers. Rank of sergeant. Transferred as secretary to M. A. Stovall in October 1861. Served thereafter in 3rd Georgia Battalion. One source claims that Panchen was "in command of the Cherokee Artillery" at war's end (possibly those not captured at Salisbury). Banker and active in Atlanta Presbyterian churches postwar. Died January 1, 1919 and buried at Myrtle Hill Cemetery, Rome, GA. (Myrtle Hill Burial List; "Reminiscences of the Third Georgia Battalion," *Sunny South*, March 10, 1894, 10)

Patty, C. W. Enlisted May 2, 1862, in Rome, GA. Listed as "absent sick," on all subsequent rolls. (CSRs)

Patty, J. Enlisted February 23, 1864, at Rome, GA. No further record. (CSRs)

Pennington, Cunningham. Born in 1813 in South Carolina; died August 23, 1885, at Rome, GA. Though never on active service with the unit, he served as a recruiting officer for the Cherokee Artillery and bought the men two guns from the Noble Brothers Foundry when Gov. Brown refused to arm the company. Also sent supplies to the men through the "railroad cars system" while on duty in East Tennessee. (Battey's *History*, 593)

Penny, Henry C. Enlisted February 22, 1862, at Rome, GA. "Henry C. Penny...was killed this morning [May 5, 1863] by sharpshooters" at Vicksburg. ("Martyr"; WOC; CSRs)

Penny, J. M. Enlisted February 22, 1862, at Rome, GA. Detailed as a shoemaker by order of Major Palmer, March 9, 1864. Present on last roll. He filed an Oklahoma pension application, 1915. (CSRs)

Penny, W. C. Captured at Vicksburg, July 4, 1863, and furloughed at Enterprise, AL, July 22, 1863. Last roll shows him sick in hospital April 1864. (CSRs)

Pentecost, M. E. Enlisted August 23, 1862, at Rome. Transferred to the 31st Alabama Infantry Regiment January 24, 1863, by order of Maj. Gen. C. L. Stevenson. (CSRs)

Phillips, William. No CSRs.

Poor, M. M. Enlisted February 7, 1864, at Kingston, GA. Poor had only one CSR record and was listed as present April 1864. (CSRs)

Presley, J. F. No CSRs. (Connor roster)

Presley, William. Presley joined the Cherokee Artillery at Rome on February 21, 1862. Union soldiers arrested him at Rome in May 1864. He voluntarily took the oath on July 11, 1864, and agreed to remain north of the Ohio River. Described in service records as having fair complexion, dark hair, and blue eyes. (CSRs)

Price, Charles P. Enlisted on April 11, 1864, at Rome. Captured at Kingston, Georgia on May 27, 1864, and sent to Rock Island Prison, IL. He died February 10, 1865, of pneumonia and is buried at Rock Island, grave no. 1870. ("Crown Hill"; CSRs)

Price, Joseph R. Enlisted September 5, 1863, at Rome. "Captured" at Marietta, GA, in May 1864, where he claimed to be loyal to the U.S. and had been conscripted into the Rebel service against his will. Sent to Camp Douglas, IL, where he took the oath of allegiance on August 9, 1864, and enlisted in Co. F, 6th U.S. Volunteers. (CSRs)

Ramsey, H. W. One CSR card. See Henry W. Rumsey below.

Ramsey, S. B. One CSR card. See Singleton B. Rumsey.

Ramsey, W. W. One CSR card. See, W. W. Rumsey.

Reese, W. J. Enlisted March 3, 1864, at Newnan, GA. No other records. (CSRs)

Rem, G. R. From Cedartown, GA, and listed as a survivor of the unit in a postwar Rome newspaper.

Richey, William L. Born in South Carolina in 1820. Enlisted February 24, 1862, and was captured at Vicksburg. Attained rank of 2nd Lieutenant and died August 15, 1863, at Mobile, AL. ("Martyr"; CSRs)

Ritter, W. L. One card in CSRs. See William L. Richey above.

Rodgers, Richard W. Enlisted in Van Den Corput's unit February 20, 1862, at Rome. He was captured at Vicksburg and was present for duty at Dalton, GA, in early 1864. No further military records are available. (CSRs)

Rumsey, Henry W. Rumsey was captured at Vicksburg and at Salisbury, NC, on April 12, 1865. Taken to Camp Chase, OH. Took the oath of allegiance on June 13, 1865. He was twenty-five years of age and described as having fair complexion, dark hair, and blue eyes. Residence listed a Cherokee County, AL. (CSRs)

Rumsey, Lemuel B. Born July 12, 1844, in Georgia. Enlisted February 1, 1864, at Kingston, GA, and was captured at Salisbury, NC, on April 12, 1865. Taken to Camp Chase and took the oath in May 1865. Described as having light hair, fair complexion, and blue eyes. He was twenty-two years of age and listed his residence as Cherokee County, AL. Married Nancy Catherine Ursy, and had two children. Lived in Ellis County, Texas, postwar. Died in Colorado Springs, CO, on June 14, 1915, and buried at Bethel United Methodist Church Cemetery in Waxahachie, TX. (CSRs; Obtiuary, Colorado Springs Gazette, 6-16, 1915, 6.)

Rumsey, Singleton B. Born c. 1839 in Georgia. According to Rumsey's pension application (Cherokee County, AL, May 24, 1893), he "was struck on the knee with pieces of bomb shell causing paralysis and is now invalid from said cause." Married. Died in 1904 in Cherokee County, AL. (CSRs; Ursy descendant)

Russell, Andrew R. Captured at Champion Hill and released from Fort Delaware, DE, on July 14, 1863. (Lanham)

Russell, J. H. Listed on Connor roster but no CSRs.

Russell, J. F. Enlisted on June 11, 1861, at Camp Brown. Russell was on detached duty along the Yazoo River and at Morton, MS, during the Siege of Vicksburg. Present on the last roll serving as a teamster and with the ordinance wagon. (CSRs)

Russell, John V. Enlisted September 13, 1862, at Rome, and captured at Vicksburg. Present on last roll, serving as an orderly by order of Gen. J. E. Johnston. (CSRs)

Russell, William. Enlisted in Cherokee Artillery on June 13, 1861, and died at Cumberland Gap, TN, on June 13, 1862. ("Martyr"; WOC)

Russell, William A. A lieutenant (dated December 31, 1862) with the Cherokee Artillery and later acting staff officer for Maj. Gen. C. L. Stevenson. Present on August 27, 1864, but no later record. (CSRs; Jones, *GITW*, 50)

Russell, William Simeon Davis. Enlisted September 13, 1862, at Rome. Served on twenty-four-pounder along the Mississippi River after the fight at Champion Hill. Captured at Vicksburg and paroled. Captured again at Salisbury, NC, on April 12, 1865. Took oath at Camp Chase on June 13, 1865; complexion, hair, and eyes are listed as dark, and residence is recorded as Floyd County, GA. He died in June 1883 at the insane asylum at Milledgeville, GA. (CSRs; GA pension)

Sackwell, James M. See James M. Sockwell.

Sanford, William S. Born in Hall County, GA, in 1837. Had originally enlisted in Co. I, 43rd Georgia Infantry. Sanford enlisted April 17, 1864, at Dalton, GA. Present on all subsequent rolls. Union troops captured Sanford at Salisbury, NC, but he escaped. Paroled April 23, 1865. (CSRs)

Scott, James Robinson. Born July 28, 1844, Scott enlisted July 27, 1863, at Rome, and was in the hospital at Montgomery, AL, 11, 1864. Captured April 16, 1865, at Salisbury, NC, and released May 2, 1865, after taking the oath. He was nineteen years of age when released from Camp Chase. He died March 21, 1925, and is buried in the Cave Spring Cemetery, Floyd County. (CSRs; Kinney)

Scott, John W. Enlisted February 19, 1862, at Rome and on detached service along the Yazoo River at Morton, MS, during the siege of Vicksburg. Died at Selma, AL, on August 15, 1863. ("Martyr"; CSRs)

Scott, Robert P. Scott enlisted June 11, 1861, and on detached service at Morton, MS, when Vicksburg fell. Captured at Salisbury, NC, listing Floyd County as his place of residence. He was thirty-one years of age when he signed the oath of allegiance in May 1865. (CSRs)

Scott, William Linley. Born October 9, 1832, Scott enlisted February 19, 1862, in Rome. During Vicksburg, he was part of the Cherokee Artillery stationed at Morton, MS. Captured at Salisbury, NC, on April 12, 1865, and sent to Camp Chase, OH. He took the oath on May 2, 1865, listing his residence as Floyd County. Described as having fair complexion, dark hair, gray eyes, 5'8" tall, and aged thirty. Died July 27, 1901 and buried at Cave Spring Cemetery, Floyd County. (CSRs; Kinney)

Smith, Thatcher R. Enlisted June 11, 1861. Captured at Resaca, and held at Camp Morton, IN. Transferred to Fort Delaware, DE, for exchange, March 4, 1865. (CSRs)

Sockwell, James M. Enlisted June 11, 1861, and captured at Vicksburg. Listed as complexion fair, hair fair, eyes gray, and 5'8¼" tall. Captured April 12, 1865, at Salisbury, NC, and sent to Camp Chase, OH, and took oath June 26, 1865. A Union clerk recorded his residence as Floyd County, GA. (CSRs)

Stephens, R. M. Enlisted February 20, 1862, at Rome. Captured with the unit at Vicksburg, and present on the last roll. (CSRs)

Stevenson, W. Enlisted September 23, 1863, and present on last roll. Died at Jacksonville, AL, in November 1864. ("Martyr"; CSRs)

Stewart, J. C. W. Enlisted September 15, 1863, and was present on the last roll. (CSRs)

Stillwell, Charles Oliver. Born November 27, 1833, and died June 15, 1895, at his home in Oostanaula, Floyd County, GA. Kinney states he served in Van Den Corput's unit and later "Forrest's Artillery." Postwar farmer and bookkeeper for Howell Cotton Co. A newspaper stated, "No man was so universally beloved, admired, and esteemed as Captain Stillwell." Buried at Myrtle Hill Cemetery, Rome. No record in the CSRs. (Kinney); *Atlanta Constitution*, June 16, 1895, 16)

Stillwell, John E. Appointed as 2nd lieutenant on December 31, 1862. Surrendered with unit at Vicksburg. Commanded Cherokee Artillery at Resaca. Present on the last roll. (CSRs; Carmen papers, LOC; Jones, *GITW*, 50)

Stillwell, Leonidas Baldwin. Enlisted June 11, 1861, at Camp Brown. Surrendered at Vicksburg and rose to the rank of lieutenant. Captured at Resaca on May 15, 1864, and sent to Camp Morton, IN. He died on January 17, 1865, of typhoid-malarial fever and buried at Greenlawn Cemetery, Indianapolis. According to a notice in a Tennessee newspaper, the Stillwell brothers were trying in the 1890s to bring his remains back to Rome for reburial. ("Crown Hill"; CSRs)

Stovall, Marcellus Augustus. Brigadier General, CSA, born at Sparta, GA, September 18, 1818. Served in the "Richmond Blues" in the Second Seminole War, but was expelled from West Point (USMA) for "desertion." Married Sara McKinney in 1842. Moved to Floyd County, GA, in 1846, becoming a wealthy planter. He was elected captain of the Cherokee Artillery in August 1860. In October 1861, Governor Brown appointed him lieutenant-colonel of the 3rd Georgia Battalion of Artillery. Fought in the Kentucky Campaign and at Stones River. Appointed Brigadier General on January 20, 1863, fighting during Atlanta Campaign, winter invasion of

Tennessee and at Bentonville, NC. Wealthy cotton broker in Augusta post-war and "took [an] active interest in redeeming the State from the destruction by negro and carpetbag, and military rule." He died August 4, 1895. (C. L. Bragg, *Distinction in Every Service*)

Sullivan, Arthur T. Born February 15, 1842, in Laurens, SC. Enlisted February 22, 1862, at Rome, and became clerk at division headquarters by order of Maj. Gen. C. L. Stevenson. Present at Durham Station, NC, and surrendered April 26, 1865. Died July 1871 and buried in Myrtle Hill Cemetery in Rome. (McKinney; CSRs)

Summerhill, W. T. No CSRs found on this person. Killed at Resaca on May 15, 1864. (W. O. Connor found Summerhill's canteen at the Resaca battlefield in 1867, noting this soldier joined the unit just before that fight. Connor had apparently never learned this young man's first name.) ("Martyr"; WOC)

Sumter, J. M. No CSRs found on this person.

Thomason, S. Enlisted February 5, 1863, at Calhoun, AL, transferring from the 7th Alabama Cavalry by order of Gen. J. E. Johnston. Present as of April 1864. (CSRs)

Trout, James M. He enlisted February 20, 1862, at Rome, achieving the rank of corporal. Captured at Vicksburg and furloughed from February 1, 1864–May 31, 1864. Captured at Dallas, GA, on May 28, 1864, and sent to Rock Island, IL. He had dark complexion, gray hair, dark eyes, and stood 5'11." He signed the oath of allegiance on November 18, 1864. (CSRs)

Turner, J. F. Turner enlisted March 7, 1864, at Dalton, GA. He was captured April 12, 1865, at Salisbury, NC, taking the oath of allegiance on June 13, 1865. (CSRs)

Van Den Corput, Felix. Born April 10, 1840 (in Brussels, Belgium). Family moved to Floyd County, GA, in 1850, then moved to Cherokee County, AL. Moved back to Floyd County in 1858. Sergeant of Cherokee Artillery (and according to one source "received a commission as Captain in the Quartermaster Department.") The same source stated he served the "entire four years and won the admiration of his comrades in Arms," but CSRs shows he was discharged as "unfit for field service [due to rheumatism] on September 14, 1864. Described as having fair complexion, black hair, brown eyes and stood almost 5'9" in height. Post-war mayor of Macon, GA, for two terms, state senate, chairman of finance committee in state legislature, mayor of Cave Spring, and "led in every enterprise in which...[he] engaged." Died July 7, 1916, and buried at Cave Spring. Apparently dropped "Van Den" from his name postwar. (Harris, *Cave Spring and Van's Valley*, 29–31)

Van Den Corput, G. Captured with the unit at Vicksburg, with no further record of service. (CSRs)

Van Den Corput, Maximillian. Captain of Cherokee Artillery. Born in Brussels, Belgium, in 1825. Moved to the U.S. in the 1850s and was living in Alabama in 1860. Enlisted in the Cherokee Artillery and was promoted to lieutenant (June 11, 1861) and captain (December 31, 1862). Twice commanded Johnson's Artillery

Battalion (including at Resaca). Seriously wounded during the Atlanta Campaign (at Jonesboro) and only rejoined the unit in February 1865. Postwar railroad executive, then architect in Atlanta, GA, with firm of Van Den Corput and Fey. Corresponded with Carmen regarding the Battle of Resaca. Died January 16, 1911, and buried in Atlanta's Oakland Cemetery. Survived by wife, Marie. "Max Corput," https.//en.wikipedia.org/wiki/Maz-Corput.

Wade, Solomon. Captured at Nashville, TN, December 16, 1864, and sent to Camp Chase Prison, OH. Died March 7, 1865, from dysentery and buried at Camp Chase in grave no. 1691. ("Crown Hill"; CSRs)

Wells, S. A. Listed as a member of Corput's Battery in CSRs, but actually a member of Cassell's Kentucky Cavalry Battalion.

Wharton [Whorton], Martin Van Buren. Listed by Connor as serving a twenty-four-pound cannon at Vicksburg, but no CSRs. Killed at Nashville, TN, on December 27, 1864. ("Martyr")

White, J. E. Enlisted February 1, 1862, at Greeneville, TN. Captured at Vicksburg, paroled, and never rejoined the unit. Listed as a deserter. (CSRs)

Whitehead, Joseph J. Born in 1846 in Virginia. He enlisted March 1, 1864, at Ringgold, GA. Served as a teamster and with the ordinance wagon. Present on last roll. (CSRs)

Whitehead, William T. Enlisted June 22, 1862, at Calhoun, Georgia. Described as being 5'5" tall, with light complexion, light hair, and blue eyes. Was listed as a deserter, and was "captured" in Floyd County, 8, 1864. Took the oath and was sent north of the Ohio River. (CSRs)

Wilkerson, Henry C. Enlisted June 11, 1861, at Cobb County, GA (Camp Brown). Slightly wounded and captured at Champion Hill, and exchanged from Fort Delaware, DE, July 14, 1863. Captured at Resaca and died in prison in 1864. Service records also included information on a member of the Georgia Legion, who was severely wounded in Virginia in the Seven Days battles. (Lanham, "Martyr")

Williamson, S. No CSRs.

Wood, Freeman. Enlisted May 8, 1862, at Rome. Was with the group detached to guard the Yazoo River (during Siege of Vicksburg), and served as a teamster and with the ordinance wagons. Present on the last roll. (CSRs)

Woodruff, Edward T. No CSRs listed. Died in Arkansas on April 12, 1903. Pension application 17721, Mrs. F. V. Woodruff 1920. (CSRs)

Woodruff, Moses C. Born April 13, 1836, in NC. Listed as present on all rolls, serving as teamster and with the battery forge. Died April 15, 1893, and buried in the Silver Creek Methodist Cemetery, Floyd County. (Kinney)

Woodruff, W. W. Listed as present on all rolls. (CSRs)

Wright, Moses R. Enlisted November 14, 1863, (sent by Conscript Bureau). Captured by Sherman's men and carried north before he ever reached the company, he died of smallpox. (CSR, GA State Archives)

Yeiser, James Garrard. Born September 7, 1826, at Danville, Kentucky. Attended Centre College (in Kentucky) and fought briefly in the Mexican War. Worked as a druggist in Danville; New Orleans; Savannah; and Rome, Georgia (beginning in 1858). He married Ellen Araminta Marshall in 1853 at New Orleans. Joined Cherokee Artillery in August 1860. Captain in 1861, advanced to major June 11, 1861; commanded the unit in Virginia, North Carolina, and East Tennessee, and had a series of conflicts with Gen. Stovall, the previous commander. In mid-1862, transferred to the Augusta (GA) Powder works and ended the war serving as colonel of state troops in Northeast Georgia. Operated Yeiser Drug Store in post-war Rome, and active in the Masonic order. Yeiser died on March 6, 1895. (http://www.tmason1.com/pafn81.htm; Jones, *GITW*, 50)

Youngblood, William J. Captured at Champion Hill and exchanged from Fort Delaware, DE, on July 14, 1863. Captured again July 5, 1864, at Marietta, GA, and sent to Camp Douglas, IL. Claimed to have been loyal (to Union) and deserted to take the oath. Died September 7, 1864, of smallpox and was buried at Oak Woods Cemetery at Chicago. ("Martyr"; Lanham, CSRs)

Abbreviations

CA	Cherokee Artillery
CCNBP	Chickamauga-Chattanooga National Battlefield Park
CSRs	Compiled Service Records of Confederate Soldiers Who Served in Organizations from the State of Georgia
GDAH	Georgia Department of Archives and History
KMNBP	Kennesaw Mountain National Battlefield Park
LOC	Library of Congress
MAT	*Military Annals of Tennessee*
OR	*War of the Rebellion: A Compilation of the Official Records of the Union and Confederate Armies*
ORN	*U.S. Naval War Records: Official Records of the Union and Confederate Navies*
RC	*Rome (GA) Courier*
SHSP	*Southern Historical Society Papers*
TWC	*Tri-Weekly Courier* (Rome, GA)
WOC	Unpublished diary of Wesley Olin Connor

Bibliography

NEWSPAPERS

Athens *(GA) Southern Watchman*

Atlanta *(GA) Constitution*

Atlanta *(GA) Gate-City Guardian*

Atlanta *(GA) Sunny South*

Atlanta *(GA) Weekly Constitution*

Augusta *(GA) Daily Constitutionalist*

Ballou's Pictorial (Boston, MA)

Gentry (AR) Journal-Advance and Benton County Gazette

Hustler of Rome (GA)

Illustrated New Age (Philadelphia, PA)

Ironton (OH) Register

Louisville (KY) Daily Journal

Macon (GA) Telegraph

Macon (GA) Tri-Weekly Telegraph

Memphis (TN) Daily Appeal

Memphis (TN) Daily Avalanche

National Tribune (Washington, DC)

New Orleans (LA) Times-Picayune

Philadelphia (PA) Press

Richmond (VA) Examiner

Rome (GA) Courier; cited as *RC*.

Rome (GA) News-Tribune

Rome (GA) Tribune

Rome (GA) Tribune Herald

Rome (GA) Tri-Weekly Courier; cited as *TWC*.

Rome (GA) Weekly Courier

Smoky Hill and Republican Union (Junction City, KS)

Southern Confederacy (Atlanta, GA)

Wooster (OH) Republican

PRIMARY SOURCES

Anderson, Bob. Cherokee Artillery papers. Private collection, Rome, GA. Cited as Anderson collection, Rome, GA.

Anderson, Frank. "A Courier at the Battle of Resaca." *Confederate Veteran* 5 (June 1887): 297.

Baker, W. H. Letter collection. Kennesaw Mountain National Battlefield Park, Marietta, GA. Cited as Baker collection, KMNBP.

Beal, R. L. "R. L. Beall Account of Stoneman's Raid." Cornelia Phillips Spencer Papers. Southern Historical Collections, Chapel Hill, NC.

Boynton, H. V. "Second Day's Operation—Battle of Lookout Mountain." Carnes's Tennessee Light Artillery file, Chickamauga-Chattanooga National Military Park, Chickamauga, GA.

Brisendine, J. J., to Miss S. C. Turner. Special Collections. Rome-Floyd County Library, Rome, GA.

Brown, Gov. Joseph E. Letters. Record group 4-2-46, box 148, LOC 1783-05, file 2, Library of Congress, Washington, DC. Cited as Brown letters, LOC.

Brown, Joseph Emerson. File 5-14-1861. Governor, Executive Department, Governor Subject file. Georgia Department of Archives and History, Morrow, GA. Cited as Brown collection, GDAH.

Byers, Samuel. *With Fire and Sword*. New York: Neale, 1911.

Calhoun, William L. *History of the 42nd Regiment, Georgia Volunteers, Confederate States Army*. Atlanta, GA: Sisson Print, 1990.

Candler, Allen Daniel. *The Confederate Records of the State of Georgia*. Volume 1. Atlanta, GA: Chas. P. Byrd, 1909.

Carmen, E. A. Papers. Box 10. Library of Congress, Washington, DC. Cited as Carmen papers, LOC.

Carnes, William W. Letter file. Chickamauga-Chattanooga National Military Park, Chickamauga, GA. Cited as Carnes file, CCNMP.

Cherokee Artillery file. Vicksburg National Battlefield Park, Vicksburg, MS. Cited as CA file, VNBP.

Cherokee Artillery flag—Textile Preservation Associates. Cherokee Artillery flag analysis report. September 20, 1993. In Zack Waters's private collection, Rome, GA.

Cherokee Artillery papers. Private collection of Bob Anderson, Rome, GA. Cited as Anderson collection, Rome, GA.

Clayton, Henry. "Report of Operations of Clayton's Division North of the Tennessee River in the Campaign of the Winter of 1865." *Southern Historical Society Papers* 6 (July–December 1878): 86–95.

Compiled Service Records of Confederate Soldiers Who Served in Organizations from the State of Georgia. Record group 109, roll 10911. National Archives, Washington, DC. Cited as CSRs.

Conner, W. O. "Sixteen Faithful Confederates." *Confederate Veteran* 6 (1898): 505.

Connor–Blakeslee correspondence file. Rome Area History Museum, Rome, GA.

Connor, W. O. Obituary. *Confederate Veteran* 28 (1920): 349.

Connor, Wesley Olin. *Confederate Diary of Wesley Olin Connor of Cave Spring, GA and the Cherokee Artillery*. Transcribed by Margaret Wright Hollingsworth. In author's private collection, Rome, GA. Cited as WOC.

Cox, Jacob D. *Atlanta*. Dayton, OH: Morningside, 1987.

Dabney, T. G. "Gen. A. P. Stewart on Strong Topics." *Confederate Veteran* 17 (1909): 31–32.

"Dedication of Bronze Tablet in Honor of the Botetourt Battery in Vicksburg National Park." *SHSP* 35 (1907): 29–50.

Derry, Joseph T. *Georgia*. Vol. 6 of *Confederate Military History: A Library of Confederate States History*, edited by Gen Clement A. Evans. Atlanta, GA: Confederate Publishing Company, 1899.

Dodd, W. O. "Reminiscences of Hood's Tennessee Campaign." *SHSP* 9 (1881): 518–24.

Dowd, W. F. "Lookout Mountain and Missionary Ridge." *Southern Bivouac* 4 (1885–1886): 397–98.

Dubose, John Witherspoon. *General Joseph Wheeler and the Army of Tennessee*. New York: Neale, 1912.

Gibson, R. L. "Report of Brigadier-General R. L. Gibson of Operations in the Vicinity of Nashville." *SHSP* 4 (July–December 1877): 141–43, 215–23.

Grant, Ulysses S. *Personal Memoirs of Ulysses S. Grant*. New York: DeCapo, 1982.

———. *The Civil War Memoirs of U. S. Grant*. New York: Forge Books, 2002.

Hammond, Paul F. "General Kirby Smith's Campaign in Kentucky." *SHSP* 10 (1882): 249–52.

Head, Thomas A. *Campaigns and Battles of the Sixteenth Tennessee Regiment in the War Between the States*. Nashville, TN: Cumberland Presbyterian Publishing, 1885.

Holland, John C., to Dr. William Forelle. January 20, 1865. MSS #161f. Atlanta History Center: Atlanta, GA.

Humphries, M. W. "Notes on Confederate Artillery Instruction and Service." *Journal of United States Artillery* 2 (1893): 560–88.

Johnston, Joseph E. *Narrative of Military Operations During the War Between of the States*. Bloomington: Indiana State University Press, 1959.

Jones, J. H. "The Rank and File at Vicksburg." *Publications of the Mississippi Historical Society* 7 (1903): 17–32.

Kilpatrick, Robert Lang. "The Fifth Ohio Infantry at Resaca." In vol. 4 of *Sketches of War History, 1861–1865, Papers Prepared for the Ohio Commandery of the Military Order of the Loyal Legion of the United States, 1890–1896*, edited by W. H. Chamberlin, 246–54. Cincinnati: Robert Clarke & Co., 1896.

Lee, Stephen D. "The Campaigns of Generals Grant and Sherman against Vicksburg in December 1862 and January 1st and 2nd, 1863, Known as the Chickasaw Bayou Campaign." *Publications of the Mississippi Historical Society* 4 (1901): 15–36.

Lee, S. D. "Lieutenant-General S. D. Lee's Report of the Tennessee Campaign Beginning September 29, 1864." *SHSP* 3 (January–June 1877): 64–71.

Lindsley, J. B. *Military Annals of Tennessee*. Wilmington, NC: Broadfoot, 1995.

"Major John William Johnston." *Confederate Veteran* 19 (1911): 116–17.

Manigault, A. M. *A Carolinian Goes to War: The Civil War Narrative of Arthur Middleton Manigault, Brigadier General, Confederate States of America*. Edited by R. Lockwood Tower. Columbia: University of South Carolina Press, 1983.

Mason, Frank H. "General Stoneman's Last Campaign." In vol. 3 of *Sketches of War History, 1861–1865, Papers Prepared for the Ohio Commandery of the Military Order of the Loyal Legion of the United States, 1888–1890*, edited by Robert Hunter, 23–29. Cincinnati: Robert Clarke & Co., 1890.

Mathes, James Harvey. *The Old Guard in Gray: Researches in the Annals of the Confederate Historical Association*. Memphis, TN: Press of the SC Tool & Co., 1887.

McMurray, W. J. *History of the Twentieth Tennessee Regiment, Volunteer Infantry, Confederate States of America.* Nashville, TN: Publication Committee of the United Confederate Veterans, 1904.

McNeilly, James H. "Retreat from Tennessee." *Confederate Veteran* 26 (1918): 305.

Morgan, George W. "Assault on Chickasaw Bluff." In vol. 3 of *Battles and Leaders of the Civil War*, edited by Robert Underwood Johnson and Clarence Clough Buel, 462–71. New York: The Century Co., 1887–1888.

———. "Cumberland Gap." In vol. 3 of *Battles and Leaders of the Civil War*, edited by Robert Underwood Johnson and Clarence Clough Buel, 62–69. New York: The Century Co., 1887–1888.

Phillips, Wm., to "Dear Gov." No date. LOC 1-1-5, box 47, LOC 335-10. Library of Congress, Washington, DC.

Porter, David Dixon. *Incidents and Anecdotes of the Civil War.* New York: Appleton, 1885.

———. *The Naval History of the Civil War.* New York: Appleton, 1886.

Quad, M. *Field, Fort, and Fleet.* Detroit, MI: Detroit Free Press, 1885.

Ritter, W. L. "An Incident of the Deer Creek Expedition of 1863." *SHSP* 9 (1881): 280–81.

———. "Sketch of the Third Battery of Maryland Artillery." *SHSP* 5 (1877): 37–44; 7 (1879): 247–49; 10 (1882): 328–32, 392–402, 464–71; 11 (1883): 113–18, 186–93, 432–42; 12 (1884): 170–72.

Roman, Alfred. *The Military Operations of General Beauregard in the War between the States, 1861–1865.* Volume 2. New York: Harpers Brothers, 1883.

Sherman, William T. *Home Letters of General Sherman.* New York: Scribner & Sons, 1909.

Smartt, J. P. "Walthall on the Battle of Lookout." *Confederate Veteran* 2 (1898): 562–64.

Southern Historical Association. "John J. Seay." In vol. 1 of *Memoirs of Georgia*, 679–80. Atlanta, GA: The Southern Historical Association, 1895.

Stevenson, Carter L. "Report of Major-General Carter L. Stevenson of the Tennessee Campaign." *SHSP* 3 (January–June 1877): 161.

Stovall, M. A. Scrapbooks. 4 vols. Georgia Historical Society, Savannah, GA.

Strong, Robert Hale. *A Yankee Private's Civil War*. Chicago, IL: Regency, 1961.

Travis, Benjamin F. *The Story of the Twenty-fifth Michigan*. Kalamazoo, MI: Kalamazoo Publishing, 1897.

Trowbridge, Brig. Gen. Luther S. "The Stoneman Raid of 1865." *Journal of the United States Cavalry Association* 4 (1891): 195–96.

U.S. Census Records for Georgia, 1860. Georgia Department of Archives and History, Morrow, GA.

U.S. Census Records for Mississippi, 1860. Library of Congress, Washington, DC.

U.S. War Department. *U.S. Naval War Records: Official Records of the Union and Confederate Navies*. 30 vols. Washington, DC: Government Printing Office, 1894–1927. Cited as *ORN*.

U.S. War Department. *War of the Rebellion: A Compilation of the Official Records of the Union and Confederate Armies*. 127 vols. Washington, DC: Government Printing Office, 1880–1901. Cited as *OR*.

Watkins, Sam R. *Co. Aytch: A Sideshow of the Big Show*. Wilmington, NC: Broadfoot, 1990.

Wilder, Theodore. *History of Co. C, Seventh Regiment Ohio Volunteer Infantry*. Oberlin, OH: J. B. T. Marsh, 1866.

SECONDARY SOURCES

Allardice, Bruce S. *More Generals in Gray*. Baton Rouge: Louisiana State University Press, 1995.

Anderson, Bob. "James Garrard Yeiser." Terry Mason's Family History Site. Accessed August 19, 2019, http://www.tmason1.com/pafn83.htm.

Arnold, John R. *Grant Wins the War: Decision at Vicksburg*. New York: John Wiley, 1997.

Atkins, Jonathan M. *Parties, Politics, and Sectional Conflict in Tennessee, 1832–1861*. Knoxville: University of Tennessee Press, 1997.

Aycock, Roger. *All Roads to Rome*. Roswell, GA: W. H. Wolfe, 1982.

Ballard, Michael B. *The Civil War in Mississippi: Major Campaigns and Battles*. Jackson: University of Mississippi Press, 2011.

———. *Pemberton: The General Who Lost Vicksburg*. Jackson: University of Mississippi Press, 1999.

Bastain, David F. *Grant's Canal: The Union Attempt to Bypass Vicksburg*. Shippensburg, PA: White Mane, 1995.

Battey, George MacGruder, Jr. *A History of Rome and Floyd County.* Atlanta: Cherokee Publishing, 1979.

Baumgartner, Richard A., and Larry M. Strayer. *Kennesaw Mountain, June 1864: Bitter Stand Off at the Gibraltar of Georgia.* Huntington, WV: Blue Acorn Press, 1998.

Bearss, Edwin Coles. *Grant Strikes a Fatal Blow.* Vol. 2 of *The Campaign for Vicksburg.* Dayton, OH: Morningside, 1986.

———. "The Vicksburg Campaign: Grant Marches West: The Battles of Champion Hill and Big Black Bridge." *Blue & Gray* 18/, 2001): 6–24, 44–52.

Black, Robert C. III. *The Railroads of the Confederacy.* Chapel Hill: University of North Carolina Press, 1988.

Black, Robert W. *Cavalry Raids of the Civil War.* Mechanicsburg, PA: Stackpole Books, 2004.

Bohannon, Keith S. "He exhibited the highest soldierly qualities: General Edward C. Walthall's Confederate Service," 2016. Unpublished manuscript, Zack C. Wathers collection, Rome, GA.

Boozer, Harriett Farris. *Long, Long Ago, 1776–1976: A Genealogical Record of the Farris, Wells, Keltner, Wynne, Russell, Roberts families in America.* Sandy Springs, GA: n.p., 1976.

Boykin, Samuel. *History of the Baptist Denominations in Georgia.* 2 vols. Reprint, Paris, AR: Baptist Standard Bearer, 2001.

Bradley, Mark L. *Last Stand in the Carolinas: The Battle of Bentonville.* Campbell, CA: Savas Woodbury, 1996.

———. *This Astounding Close: The Road to Bennett Place.* Chapel Hill: University of North Carolina Press, 2000.

Bragg, C. L. *Distinction in Every Service: General Marcellus A. Stovall.* Shippensburg, PA: White Mane, 2002.

"Brig. Gen. Seth Barton, Vicksburg Report." Battle of Champion Hill (James and Rebecca Drake). Accessed August 19, 2019, http://www.battleofchampionhill.org/barton.htm.

Brown, Kent Masterton. "The Long Road Back to Kentucky." American Battlefield Trust. Accessed http://www.civilwar.org/battlefields/perryville/perryville-history-articles/kentuckymasterson.html.

Buttovich, Brad. *Battle of Allatoona: Civil War Skirmish in Bartow County, Georgia.* Mt. Pleasant, SC: Arcadia, 2014.

Castel, Albert. *Decision in the West: The Atlanta Campaign of 1864.* Lawrence: University of Kansas Press, 1992.

———. "'…The Heavens and Earth Had Suddenly Come Together': The Battle of Peachtree Creek." In *The Campaign for Atlanta & The March to the Sea*, volumes 1 and 2, edited by Thomas P. Savas and David A. Woodbury, 23–47. Campbell, CA: Savas Woodbury, 1994.

Chastain, Brian. "When Yankees Fought Yankees: Galvanized Troops in Battle during the War Between the States." The Breckinridge Greys. Accessed March 17, 2017, http://breckinridgegreys.org/galvanized1.html.

Cheairs Nathaniel Hughes, Jr. *General William J. Hardee: Old Reliable*. Baton Rouge: Louisiana State University Press, 1992.

Coffman, Richard M., and Kurt D. Graham. *To Honor These Men: A History of the Phillips Georgia Legion Infantry Battalion*. Macon: Mercer University Press, 2007.

"Collins /county Confederate Pension Applications" files. usgarchives.net/tx/collins/military/civilwar/collinscsa.txt.

Connelly, Thomas L. *The Army of the Heartland: The Army of Tennessee, 1861–1862*. Baton Rouge: Louisiana State University Press, 1967.

———. *Autumn of Glory: The Army of Tennessee, 1862–1865*. Baton Rouge: Louisiana State University Press, 1971.

Cozzens, Peter. *The Shipwreck of Their Hopes: The Battles for Chattanooga*. Urbana: University of Illinois Press, 1994.

———. *This Horrible Sound: The Battle of Chickamauga*. Champlain: University of Illinois Press, 1996.

Cunliffe, Marcus. *Soldiers and Civilians: Martial Spirit in America, 1775–1865*. New York: Little Brown, 1968.

Daniel, Larry J. *Cannoneers in Gray: The Field Artillery of the Army of Tennessee, 1861–1865*. Tuscaloosa: University of Alabama Press, 1984.

———. *Soldiering in the Army of Tennessee: A Portrait of Life in a Confederate Army*. Chapel Hill: University of North Carolina Press, 1991.

Davis, Robert S. "Cannon Makers of the Confederacy: The Noble Foundry and its Tools." *Tools & Technology* 7 (1998): 1–4.

Davis, Stephen. "The Battles of Atlanta: Events from July 10 to September 2, 1864." *Blue & Gray* 6/6 (August 1989): 8–39, 45–53.

———. "The Great Snowball Battle." *Civil War Times Illustrated* 15 (June 1976): 32–35.

Davis, William C. "Cumberland Gap, 1862." *Civil War Times Illustrated* 10 (1971): 25–29.

DeBerry, J. H. "Kirby Smith's Bluegrass Invasion." *America's Civil War* 10/1 (March 1997): 54–60, 88–89.

Drennan, Lt. William. "Lt. William Drennan, Ordinance Officer of Featherston's Brigade, Letters to His Wife, Georgia Torrey Drennan, *Siege of Vicksburg Journal*." Transcribed and edited by Dan Edwards. Battle of Champion Hill (James and Rebecca Drake). Accessed June 24, 2017, http://www.battleofchampionhill.org/drennan/htm.

Durham, Walter T. "Tennessee Heritage." Tennessee Secretary of State Website. Accessed August 19, 2019, https://sos.tn.gov/products/tsla/tennessee-heritage-walter-durham.

Escott, Paul D. "Georgia." In *The Confederate Governors,* edited by W. Buck Yearns, 69–82. Athens: University of Georgia Press, 1985.

Evans, C. A. *Confederate Military History–Georgia,* vol. 6, Atlanta: Confederate Publishing Co.. 1899.

Evans, David. *Sherman's Horsemen: Union Cavalry Operations in the Atlanta Campaign.* Bloomington: Indiana University Press, 1999.

Faust, Patricia L., ed. *Historical Times Illustrated Encyclopedia of the Civil War*. New York: Harper & Row, 1986.

"Felton, William Harrell." Biographical Directory of the United States Congress 1774–Present. Accessed November 18, 2016, http://bioguide.congress.gov/scripts/biodisplay.pl?index=F000070.

Fisher, Garry D. Compiled Service Roster of Cherokee Artillery. Private collection. Personal roster prepared by William O. Connor—unpublished.

"Folsom, Montgomery Morgan." Find a Grave. Accessed January 18, 2016, https://www.findagrave.com/memorial/45599528/montgomery-morgan-folsom.

Gassman, Wade Bannister. "A History of Rome and Floyd County, Georgia in the Civil War." Master's thesis, Emory University, 1963.

"Georgia Artillery Units." Accessed June 3, 2017, http://freepages.military.rootsweb.ancestry.com/~pudig/GAGuns.htm.

"Georgia Pension Records." https//vault.georgiaarchives.org/digital/collection/testapps.

Glatthaar, Joseph T. *General Lee's Army: From Victory to Collapse*. New York, Free Press, 2008.

Groce, W. Todd. *Mountain Rebels: East Tennessee Confederates, 1860–1870.* Knoxville: University of Tennessee Press, 2007.

Harris, James Coffee. *Cave Spring and Van's Valley*. Cave Spring, GA: n.p., 1927.

Hartley, Chris J. *Stoneman's Raid 1865*. Winston-Salem, NC: John F. Blair, 2010.

Hatfield, Edward A. "The Freedman's Bureau." New Georgia Encyclopedia: History and Archaeology: Civil War & Reconstruction, 1861–1877. September 24, 2015. Accessed November 18, 2016, https://www.georgiaencyclopedia.org/articles/history-archaeology/freedmens-bureau.

Hattaway, Herman. *General Stephen D. Lee*. Jackson: University of Mississippi Press, 1976.

Henry, Robert Selph. *"First With the Most": Forrest*. New York: Mallard Press, 1968.

"Heritage of Floyd County, Georgia, 1833–1999" (N.C., County Heritage, 1999).

Hess, Earl J. *Banners to the Breeze: The Kentucky Campaign, Corinth and Stones River*. Lincoln: University of Nebraska Press, 2010.

———. *Braxton Bragg: The Most Hated Man in the Confederacy*. Chapel Hill: University of North Carolina Press, 2016.

———. *Kennesaw Mountain: Sherman, Johnston, and the Atlanta Campaign*. Chapel Hill: University of North Carolina Press, 2013.

Hewitt, Lawrence L. "Carter Littlepage Stevenson." In vol. 6 of *The Confederate General*, edited by William C. Davis, vol. 6, pp. 8–9. Washington, DC: National Historical Society 1991.

Hood, Stephen M. *John Bell Hood: The Rise, Fall, and Resurrection of a Confederate General*. Eldorado, CA: Savas Beatie, 2013.

Horn, Stanley F. *The Army of Tennessee*. Wilmington, NC: Broadfoot, 1987.

Joiner, Gary D. *Mr. Lincoln's Brown Water Navy: The Mississippi Squadron*. Lanham, MD: Rowman & Littlefield, 2007.

———. *Through the Howling Wilderness: The 1864 Red River Campaign and Union Failure in the West*. Knoxville: University of Tennessee Press, 2014.

Jones, Chas. Edward. *Georgia in the War 1861–1865*. Atlanta: Foote and Davies, 1909.

Kelly, Dennis. "The Battle of Kennesaw Mountain—Actions from June 10 to July 19, 1864." *Blue & Gray* 6/5 (June 1989): 8–30, 46–58.

Kinsland, William S. "A Band of Brothers: The Men and Legend of the 52nd Georgia Regiment." *North Georgia Journal* 2 (Summer 1985): 9–29 (part 1); 2 (Fall 1985): 18–39 (part 2).

Kinney, Shirley F. *Floyd County Confederate Burials. A Compilation Prepared for the United Daughters of the Confederacy* (Rome, Georgia: n.p., 1993).

Kiper, Richard L. *Major General John Alexander McClernand: Politician in Uniform.* Kent: Kent State University Press, 1999.

Kirk, Michael. "States Which Seceded." Ohio State University Department of History: Ehistory. https://ehistory.osu.edu/articles/states-which-seceded.

Krick, Robert K. *Lee's Colonels: A Biographical Register of the Field Officers of the Army of Northern Virginia.* Wilmington, NC: Broadfoot, 2009.

Lanham, Edward Jordan. "Crown Hill," freepages.rootsweb.com/~indiana42nd/historyconfederateBurials—Hill_Rev/v.pdf.

Lanham, Edward Jordan. "Georgia Casualties at Champion's Hill (Baker's Creek)." Accessed August 24, 2019, http://battleofchampionhill.org/georgia1.pdf.

Lepa, Jack H. *The Civil War in Tennessee, 1862–1863.* Jefferson, NC: McFarland & Co., 2007.

"Letter from Alfred Cumming to Stephen D. Lee." Battle of Champion Hill (James and Rebecca Drake). Accessed June 24, 2017, http://battleofchampionhill.org/history/cummings.htm.]

Lindsley, John B. *Military Annals of Tennessee. Confederate.* 1886. Wilmington, NC: Broadfoot, 1995.

Long, E. B. *The Civil War Day by Day: An Almanac, 1861–1865.* Boston, MA: DaCapo, 1985.

Longacre, Edward G. *Cavalry of the Heartland: The Mounted Forces of the Army of Tennessee.* Lincoln, NE: Bison Books, 1999.

Mahon, John K. *The American Militia: Decade of Decision, 1789–1800.* Gainesville: University of Florida Press, 1960.

McDonald, Archie. "Seth Maxwell Barton." In vol. 1 of *The Confederate General,* edited by William C. Davis, 66–69. Washington, DC: National Historical Society 1991.

McDonough, James Lee, and Thomas L. Connelly. *Five Tragic Hours: The Battle of Franklin.* Knoxville: University of Tennessee Press, 1983.

McMurry, Richard M. "The Affair at the Kolb Farm." *Civil War Times Illustrated* 7 (December 1968): 20–27.

———. *Atlanta 1864: Last Chance for the Confederacy.* Lincoln, NE: University of Nebraska Press, 2000.

———. "The Atlanta Campaign: Rocky Face Ridge to the Dallas Line—The Battles of May 1864." *Blue & Gray* 6/1989): 10–23, 46–62.

———. "Confederate Morale in the Atlanta Campaign of 1864." *Georgia Historical Quarterly* 54/2 (Summer 1970): 226–43.

———. "A Policy So Disastrous: Joseph E. Johnston's Atlanta Campaign." In *The Campaign for Atlanta & The March to the Sea*, volumes 1 and 2, edited by Thomas P. Savas and David A. Woodbury, 223–48. Campbell, CA: Savas Woodbury, 1994.

"Missouri, Biographies." www.mygenealolgyhound.com/missouri-biographies/mo-polk-county-biographies/jefferson-lemon-genealogy-polcounty-missouri-,orrisville-mo.html#

"Memoirs of the Civil War: W. L. Truman." Cedarcroft Farm (Bill and Sandra Wayne). Accessed June 24, 2017, http://www.cedarcroft.com/cw/memoir/. The original (CA6257) is housed at the State Historical Society, Columbia, Missouri.

Miles, Jim. *Fields of Glory: A History and Tour Guide of the Atlanta Campaign.* Nashville, TN: Rutledge Hill Press, 2000.

Mull, Steve. "Answering the Call." *Northwest Georgia History & Genealogical Quarterly* 18 (1986): 1–12.

Murphree, Ridgeway Boyd. "Rebel Sovereigns: The Civil War Leadership of Governors John Milton of Florida and Joseph Brown of Georgia, 1861–1865." Ph.D. dissertation, Florida State University, 2006.

Niven, Alexander C. "Joseph E. Brown: Confederate Obstructionist." *Georgia Historical Quarterly* 42/3 (September 1958): 233–57.

Noe, Kenneth W. *Reluctant Rebels: The Confederates Who Joined the Army After 1861.* Chapel Hill: University of North Carolina Press, 2010.

Northern, William J., et al., eds. "Felix Van Den Corput." In vol. 6 of *Men of Mark in Georgia: A Complete and Elaborate History of the State....* Atlanta: A. B. Caldwell, 1912.

Nulty, William H. *Confederate Florida: The Road to Olustee.* Tuscaloosa: University of Alabama Press, 2014.

Parks, W. A. Rev. "The Siege and Fall of Vicksburg." Barton and Stovall History/Heritage Assoc. Accessed June 24, 2017. http://generalbartonandstovall.com/html/52ndGeorgia.html

Perkins, Marletta. "Battle of Tazewell." 14th Kentucky Volunteer Infantry Website. Accessed August 19, 2019, http://joepayne.org/battle/main.htm.

Perry, James M. *Touched with Fire: Five Generals and the Civil War Battles that Made Them*. New York: Public Affairs, 2003.

Reynolds, Hughes. *The Coosa Valley from DeSoto to Hydro-electric Power*. Cynthiana, KY: Hobson Books, 1944.

Roper, Daniel M. "I Know the Place." *Georgia Backroads* 15/1 (Spring 2016): 4–6.

Savas, Thomas P., and David A. Woodbury, eds. *The Campaign for Atlanta & The March to the Sea*. Vols. 1 and 2. Campbell, CA: Savas Woodbury, 1994.

Scaife, William R. *The Campaign for Atlanta*. Atlanta, GA: Scaife, 1985.

———. *Hood's Campaign for Tennessee*. Atlanta, GA: Scaife, 1986.

———. "Sherman's March to the Sea." *Blue & Gray* 7/ 1989): 11–32, 38–42.

———. "Waltz between the Rivers: An Overview of the Campaign from the Oostanaula to the Etowah." In *The Campaign for Atlanta & The March to the Sea*, volumes 1 and 2, edited by Thomas P. Savas and David A. Woodbury, 269–95. Campbell, CA: Savas Woodbury, 1994.

Scaife, William R., and William Harris Bragg. *Joe Brown's Pets*. Atlanta, GA: Civil War Publications, 1992.

Secrist, Phillip. "Resaca: For Sherman a Moment of Truth." *Atlanta Historical Society Journal* 22/2 (Spring 1978): 8–41.

Seymour, Digby Gordon. *Divided Loyalties: Fort Sanders and the Civil War in East Tennessee*. Knoxville: University of Tennessee Press, 1963.

Smedlund, William S. *Camp Fires of Georgia Troops, 1861–1865*. Lithonia, GA: Kennesaw Mountain Press, 1994.

Smith, Derek. *In the Lion's Mouth*. Mechanicsburg, PA: Stackpole, 2011.

Smith, Timothy B. *Champion Hill: Decisive Battle for Vicksburg*. El Dorado Hills, CA: Savas Beatie, 2004.

Snellgrove, Benjamin. "Marcellus Augustus Stovall." In vol. 6 of *The Confederate General*, edited by William C. Davis, 12–13. Washington, DC: National Historical Society, 1991.

Stephens, Larry D. *Bound for Glory: A History of the 30th Alabama Infantry, CSA*. Ann Arbor, MI: Sheridan, 2005.

Stevenson, Maj. Gen. Carter L. Report. Battle of Champion Hill (James and Rebecca Drake). http://battleofchampionhill.org/stevenson.htm

Street, James, Jr. *The Struggle for Tennessee*. Alexandria, VA: Time-Life, 1985.

Strode, Hudson. *Jefferson Davis: Confederate President*. New York: Harcourt Brace, 1959.

Sullivan, Jack. "Magnus: A Father's Death and a Son's Redemption." Those Pre-Pro Whiskey Men! (Blog). Accessed May 14, 2017, www.pre-prowhiskeymen.blogspot.2014/09/magnus-fathers-death-and-sons-redemption.html.

Sword, Wiley. "The Battle above the Clouds: The Fight for Lookout Mountain 1863." *Blue & Gray* 18/ 2000): 6–20, 43–56.

———. *Embrace an Angry Wind*. New York: Harper Collins, 1992.

———. "John Bell Hood's Desperate Hour at Nashville." *Blue & Gray* 11/ 1993): 13–23, 38–50.

———. *Mountains Touched with Fire: Chattanooga Besieged, 1863*. New York, St. Martin's, 1950.

Thomas, Dean S. *Cannons: Introduction to Civil War Artillery*. Gettysburg, PA: Thomas Publications, 1985.

Tucker, Spencer C., ed. *The Civil War Naval Encyclopedia*. Santa Barbara, CA: ABC-CLIO, 2011.

Walker, Scott. *Hell's Broke Loose in Georgia: Survival in a Civil War Regiment*. Athens: University of Georgia Press, 2007.

Warner, Ezra J. *Generals in Blue: Lives of Union Commanders*. Baton Rouge: Louisiana State University Press, 1999.

Waters, Zack C. "Gartrell's Georgians: Nathan Bedford Forrest's Teenaged Warrior." *Georgia Backroads* 8/1 (Spring 2009): 10–15.

———. "The Wildest Disorder Reigned: Night Attack on Santa Rosa Island." *North & South* 13/2 (June 2011): 46–53.

Weaver, Jeffrey C. *54th Virginia Infantry*. Lynchburg, VA: H. E. Howard, 1993.

Winschel, Terrence J. *Vicksburg: Fall of the Confederate Gibraltar*. Abilene, TX: McWhiney Foundation Press, 1999.

Woodworth, Steven E. *Jefferson Davis and His Generals: The Failure of Confederate Command in the West*. Lawrence: University of Kansas Press, 1990.

———. *Nothing but Victory: The Army of the Tennessee*. New York: Knopf, 2005.

———. "A Reassessment of Confederate Command Options During the Winter of 1863–1864." In *The Campaign for Atlanta & The March to the Sea*, volumes 1 and 2, edited by Thomas P. Savas and David A. Woodbury, 1–22. Campbell, CA: Savas Woodbury, 1994.

———. *Six Armies in Tennessee: The Chickamauga and Chattanooga Campaigns.* Lincoln, NE: Bison Books, 1999.

Yearly, Mamie. *Reminiscences of the Boys in Gray: 1861–1865*. Dallas, Texas: Smith and Lamar, 1912.

Index